CALIFORNIA ESTATE ADMINISTRATION

Paralegal Titles from Delmar Publishers

Legal Writing, 2nd Ed., Steve Barber, 1997
Administration of Wills, Trusts, and Estates, 2nd Ed., Gordon W. Brown, 1997
Basics of Legal Document Preparation, Robert R. Cummins, 1997
Constitutional Law: Cases and Commentary, Daniel E. Hall, 1997
Criminal Procedure and the Constitution, Daniel E. Hall, 1997
Survey of Criminal Law, 2nd Ed., Daniel E. Hall, 1997
California Estate Administration, Zella Mack, 1997
Torts and Personal Injury Law, 2nd Ed., Cathy J. Okrent, William R. Buckley, 1997
California Criminal Law and Procedure, William D. Raymond Jr., Daniel E. Hall, 1997
The Law of Corporations, Partnerships, and Sole Proprietorships, 2nd Ed.,
    Angela Schneeman, 1997
Texas Legal Research, 2nd Ed., Pamela R. Tepper, Peggy N. Kerley, 1997

Legal Research, Steve Barber, Mark A. McCormick, 1996
Wills, Estates, and Trusts, Jay H. Gingrich, 1996
Criminal Law and Procedure, 2nd Ed., Daniel E. Hall, 1996
Introduction to Environmental Law, Harold Hickock, 1996
Civil Litigation, 2nd Ed., Peggy N. Kerley, Joanne Banker Hames, Paul A. Sukys, 1996
Client Accounting for the Law Firm, Elaine M. Langston, 1996
Law Office Management, 2nd Ed., Jonathan Lynton, Terri Mick Lyndall,
    Donna Masinter, 1996
Foundations of Law: Cases, Commentary, and Ethics, 2nd Ed., Ransford C. Pyle, 1996
Administrative Law and Procedure, Elizabeth C. Richardson, 1996
Legal Research and Writing, David J. Smith, 1996

Legal Research and Writing, Carol M. Bast, 1995
Federal Taxation, Susan G. Covins, 1995
Everything You Need to Know About Being a Legal Assistant, Chere B. Estrin, 1995
Paralegals in New York Law, Eric M. Gansberg, 1995
Ballentine's Legal Dictionary and Thesaurus, Jonathan S. Lynton, 1995
Legal Terminology with Flashcards, Cathy J. Okrent, 1995
Wills, Trusts, and Estate Administration for Paralegals, Mark A. Stewart, 1995
The Law of Contracts and the Uniform Commercial Code, Pamela R. Tepper, 1995
Life Outside the Law Firm: Non-Traditional Careers for Paralegals, Karen Treffinger, 1995

An Introduction to Paralegal Studies, David G. Cooper, Michael J. Gibson, 1994
Administrative Law, Daniel E. Hall, 1994
Ballentine's Law Dictionary: Legal Assistant Edition, Jack G. Handler, 1994
The Law of Real Property, Michael P. Kearns, 1994
Ballentine's Thesaurus for Legal Research and Writing, Jonathan S. Lynton, 1994
Legal Ethics and Professional Responsibility, Jonathan S. Lynton, Terri Mick Lyndall, 1994
Criminal Law for Paralegals, Daniel J. Markey, Jr., Mary Queen Donnelly, 1994
Family Law, Ransford C. Pyle, 1994
Paralegals in American Law: Introduction to Paralegalism, Angela Schneeman, 1994
Intellectual Property, Richard Stim, 1994

CALIFORNIA ESTATE ADMINISTRATION

Zella Mack

DELMAR

THOMSON LEARNING

Africa • Australia • Canada • Denmark • Japan • Mexico • New Zealand • Philippines
Puerto Rico • Singapore • Spain • United Kingdom • United States

Cover Design: Douglas J. Hyldelund

Delmar Staff

Acquisitions Editor: Christopher Anzalone
Editorial Assistant: Judy A. Roberts
Developmental Editor: Jeffrey D. Litton

Project Editor: Eugenia L.Orlandi
Production Coordinator: Linda J. Helfrich
Art & Design Coordinator: Douglas J. Hyldelund

Printed in the United States of America
7 8 9 10 XXX

For more information, contact Delmar, 3 Columbia Circle, PO Box 15015, Albany, NY 12212-0515; or find us on the World Wide Web at http://www.delmar.com

International Division List

Asia
Thomson Learning
60 Albert Street, #15-01
Albert Complex
Singapore 189969
Tel: 65 336 6411
Fax: 65 336 7411

Australia/New Zealand:
Nelson/Thomson Learning
102 Dodds Street
South Melbourne, Victoria 3205
Australia
Tel: 61 39 685 4111
Fax: 61 39 685 4199

Latin America:
Thomson Learning
Seneca, 53
Colonia Polanco
11560 Mexico D.F. Mexico
Tel: 525-281-2906
Fax: 525-281-2656

Japan:
Thomson Learning
Palaceside Building 5F
1-1-1 Hitotsubashi, Chiyoda-ku
Tokyo 100 0003 Japan
Tel: 813 5218 6544
Fax: 813 5218 6551

UK/Europe/Middle East
Thomson Learning
Berkshire House
168-173 High Holborn
London
WC1V 7AA United Kingdom
Tel: 44 171 497 1422
Fax: 44 171 497 1426

Canada:
Nelson/Thomson Learning
1120 Birchmount Road
Scarborough, Ontario
Canada M1K 5G4
Tel: 416-752-9100
Fax: 416-752-8102

Library of Congress Cataloging-in-Publication Data
Mack, Zella.
    California estate administration / Zella Mack.
        p. cm.
    Includes bibliographical references and index.
    ISBN 0-8273-7305-8
    1. Executors and administrations—California. 2. Probate law and practice—California.
    3. Legal assistants—California—Handbooks, manuals, etc. I. Title.
KFC210.Z9M33   1997
346.79405'2—dc20   95-49736
[347.940652]   CIP

CONTENTS

≡ CHAPTER 4   Inventory and Appraisement   56

≡ CHAPTER 5   Accounting and Closing the Estate   71

PREFACE

This text is an introduction to the study of probate for those who are considering or planning to enter the probate field. The desirable qualities for the probate paralegal are discussed. For example, the chapter on the representative of the estate (the administrator or executor of the estate) gives an idea of the duties of the paralegal in probate, as well as of the representative. This discussion should help those who are making a decision about whether to enter the probate field.

This book is also intended to be a textbook for paralegal colleges teaching estate administration and, for this reason, assumes no prior knowledge of probate procedure on the part of the reader.

First and foremost, however, the book is written for the probate paralegal, for those legal assistants who are either working within a law office or working as freelance probate paralegals employed by attorneys or working under the supervision of attorneys who are responsible for the paralegal's work product. The book covers as many phases of probate work as is feasible, including taxation, in order to be helpful in the more difficult or advanced work of those more experienced in probate work, and in order to serve as a ready reference book.

Legal secretaries who are either occasionally involved in a probate proceeding or who work for a practitioner solely engaged in probate practice will also find the book to be a valuable reference.

Further, this book should be an asset to attorneys who have not yet done probate work. Some attorneys seem reluctant to undertake probate work as part of their general practice because they are unfamiliar with the field. Probate, however, is a field well suited for the services of a paralegal, which can mean reduced costs to the client. At the same time, the probate field can be profitable for the attorney. It is one the general practitioner should not overlook. Although there are traps for the unwary in probate, as in any other field, knowledge of the field will help lessen the likelihood of claims of malpractice.

The vocabulary used in the probate field is explained in a Running Glossary (definitions are inserted at the bottom of the pages on which the words appear) and in the Glossary at the end of the book. The beginner who is familiar with these words will be at an advantage when commencing a probate course or using this book for self-study prior to employment in the field. The words, of course, become more meaningful after study and working in the field. The Glossary is also important for the beginning paralegal in terms of spelling. A misspelled word will jump from the page to the trained eye and earmark the user as a novice. The terms followed by a dagger (†) were taken from Lynton, *Ballentine's Legal Dictionary and Thesaurus* (Lawyers Cooperative Publishing, 1995).

The probate client and the general public are often critical of the time required to process an estate and may blame the lawyer. Knowledge of the statute requirements will give the layperson a better idea of the time requirements and what is involved in processing an estate. The writer hopes that any reading of this book by a layperson will make that person more aware of the need to consult an attorney for estate planning, as the book should alert lay readers to problems that arise from the lack of such planning. Also explained herein are options available to survivors of a decedent, as well as the duties of those who are appointed the legal representatives of an estate. The need for consultation with the family lawyer on probate issues is stressed.

The attention of lay readers is also directed to *How to Live—and Die—with California Probate (Wills, Trusts, and Estate Planning in Layman's Language)*, (Second Edition), written by Leland Alan Stark, Editor, in association with the Beverly Hills Bar Association, and published by the Gulf Publishing Company, Book Division, Houston, Texas.

The subjects of estate planning, trust administration, revocable and irrevocable trusts, and probate ethics and practice are covered in a general way in this text in order to give the student some familiarity with trusts and their role in estate planning, which is critical to effective estate management and administration. The legal assistant needs some knowledge of the terminology of these subjects, and of the purposes they serve, to better comprehend what the attorney is working to achieve for the client.

Zella Mack

ABOUT THE AUTHOR

Zella Mack is the author of *California Paralegal's Guide* (Fourth Edition). She has written a paralegal column called "Paralegal Practices" for the Sacramento legal newspaper, *The Daily Recorder*. Ms. Mack is a Certified Legal Assistant (NALA). In 1982, she became a CLA Specialist in Probate and Estate Planning.

Ms. Mack has worked in many types of law offices, ranging from partnerships to corporate law firms, including some of the most prestigious law firms in the country such as Pillsbury, Madison & Sutro in San Francisco, and Ropes, Gray in Boston. Her work has been in general practice that included probate and insurance cases. She has also been a Judicial Secretary in the Court of Appeals in California, where her duties included reviewing the facts in a number of probate cases on appeal.

Ms. Mack, who has a Bachelor of Arts degree from the University of California at Berkeley, has served as a conservator of a California estate for six years and as a Special Administrator for three years. In the process of updating her book, *California Paralegal's Guide* (Fourth Edition), and in writing this book, she has attended a number of probate seminars. She has also taught a fundamentals of legal assisting course and legal secretarial training courses under the auspices of the Sacramento County Bar Association and the Sacramento Legal Secretaries Association.

Associations of which Ms. Mack is a member include the National Federation of Paralegal Associations, the National Association of Legal Assistants, the Sacramento Association of Legal Assistants, the California Writers Club, and the Sacramento Legal Secretaries Association.

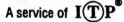

CHAPTER 1

THE PARALEGAL IN PROBATE

§ 1.1 Introduction

The **administration of an estate** means basically to collect together the assets of a person who has died, pay off his or her creditors, and then distribute the remaining assets to the persons who are entitled to them under a will. If the decedent left no will, assets are distributed under the intestate law of the state. The administration of estates has traditionally been a field in which the nonlawyer can be of great help to the attorney.

Probate includes not only the administration of estates but also conservatorships and guardianships. Estate planning and taxation of estates is a growing part of probate.

As with other legal fields, the probate field has grown in complexity. In California, probate procedure has changed rapidly, as attempts have been made to make probate law more uniform and to cover all contingencies. In recent years, **paralegals (legal assistants)** have entered this field. Unlike their predecessors, who usually had to learn the work on the job, they have had probate and other paralegal courses in college, a decided advantage. This training has increased the paralegal's value. Learning on the job may be a good way to learn, but it is never an efficient way to learn.

SIDEBAR The terms **paralegal** and **legal assistant** are used interchangeably in this book. **Paralegal** seems to be the more generic word. In the future, as the profession becomes more defined, a new vocabulary may evolve.

A number of paralegals, after working in the field, have chosen to become independent freelancers in the probate field. In the probate field, as in other fields of law, all work must be done under the general supervision of an attorney. A legal assistant is permitted to perform any task that is properly delegated and supervised by an attorney as long as the attorney is ultimately responsible to the client and assumes complete professional responsibility for the work product. The same restriction, that

■■■■■■ TERMS ■■■■■■

administration of estate† The management of a decedent's estate by an administrator or executor so that all the decedent's assets are collected, all debts, administration expenses, and taxes are paid, and all remaining assets are distributed to the persons entitled to receive them.

probate† The judicial act whereby a will is adjudicated to be valid; to prove a will to be valid in probate court.

paralegal (legal assistant)† A person who, although not at attorney, performs many of the functions of an attorney under an attorney's supervision.

of working under the supervision of an attorney, applies to independent paralegals as well as to those who are employed in law firms. Some probate independents have met with notable success.

In at least a few of the larger firms where there is a heavy workload of probate, the lead paralegals have the title "Probate Administrator." This title is also appropriate in smaller firms where the principal law practice is in probate. It is a proper title in any law office where the paralegal is handling primarily probate work.

Qualities of the Probate Paralegal

The probate paralegal is ordinarily one who likes to take the initiative, to work "independently." A good probate paralegal also has the desire to help people. Often the probate paralegal is involved with persons recently bereaved, and the paralegal needs understanding, tact, and sympathy, as well as patience.

In work habits, the paralegal should be accurate and good at detail and organization. The paralegal does not have to be an accountant, but it helps to be "good at figures." The more accurate the records, the easier it will be to do an estate accounting, when everything must balance. A knowledge of bookkeeping is helpful in a firm that is involved in probate with an ongoing business. A good memory also helps, as in any other field.

Some legal assistants like probate and would not want to do any other kind of legal work. Others seem to have no affinity for probate and are, shall we say, less than enthusiastic. In other words, paralegals seem to either like it a lot or not like it at all.

A big attraction of the probate field remains, in the opinion of this author, in the work itself.

Duties of the Paralegal in Probate

Probate practice requires a great deal of detailed paper work that is very time-consuming. To participate in the administration of estates, the paralegal must become proficient in record-keeping, preparation of inventories and appraisements, valuation of assets, accountings, various petitions, real estate sales, summary administration of estates, distribution and closing of estates, forms to transfer stock and motor vehicles, and applications for social security benefits and life insurance proceeds.

Probate work also involves the preparation of federal and state inheritance (in older cases) and income tax returns, both fiduciary and individual. The greater the expertise of the paralegal in taxation, the more invaluable the services to the firm. In larger firms, the tax work may be reviewed by, and the paralegal may need to consult, lawyers who are also tax experts.

The following lists of typical tasks performed by paralegals in estates and trusts and in tax and financial planning are paraphrased from the Legal Assistant Catalog of The Institute for Paralegal Training:

- Estates and trusts

  - Conducting initial interviews
  - Researching and preparing estate plans
  - Preparing probate petitions and inventories of assets
  - Preparing federal estate tax returns and state inheritance tax returns
  - Preparing federal and state income tax returns, both individual and fiduciary
  - Maintaining checkbooks, journals, and ledgers
  - Preparing court accountings
  - Assisting with postmortem tax planning
  - Transferring and registering securities

- Tax and financial planning

  - Researching and preparing personal financial plans
  - Conducting client interviews to obtain financial information
  - Preparing inventories of assets
  - Preparing federal estate and gift tax returns
  - Preparing federal and state corporate, partnership, and individual income tax returns
  - Preparing federal and state fiduciary income tax returns
  - Evaluating the tax implications of real estate syndications, tax shelters, and business plans
  - Comparing tax and financial aspects of various employee benefit plans
  - Utilizing computers to prepare tax returns and for financial planning purposes
  - Evaluating financial statements
  - Organizing and maintaining client files

See also the "Function of Paralegals" chart and the "Chart for Procedural Steps in Probate" in this author's book *California Paralegal's Guide* (Fourth Edition), Chapter 2.

§ 1.2   The Initial Interview

Ordinarily the attorney will be the first person to meet with the client, at which time the client will retain the attorney. The attorney may introduce the legal assistant at the first interview and explain to the client the function of the legal assistant.

An interview with a client in a probate proceeding is conducted in much the same way as an interview with any other client, but one additional consideration may be involved. The client, usually the person who will be the representative of the estate, that is, the executor or administrator, is often a close family member of the decedent, frequently the spouse, and very recently bereaved. The legal assistant should be kind and sensitive to the client's feelings, since a number of fairly personal questions must be asked. Often the surviving spouse is being asked to concentrate on and deal with monetary considerations at a time when such matters are furthest from his or her immediate concerns.

The client should be interviewed by the legal assistant in a comfortable setting in a private office where the legal assistant will be subject to a minimum of interruptions. The legal assistant can save time in the interview by working from a fact sheet, which can be typed or prepared on a word processor and duplicated. Figure 1–1 contains a suggested fact sheet. Each office will wish to make variations in this or other suggested forms.

§ 1.3   First Things to Be Done

Some things must be taken care of almost immediately after the death of the **decedent.** Funeral arrangements must be made, and ordinarily a family member makes these arrangements. The decedent may have made a pre-need plan with a mortuary for detailed arrangements and payment, but if not, the personal representative will have to make payment.

The legal assistant can be helpful in the following ways:

1. Order the needed copies of the **death certificate**, if this has not been done. A copy may be needed for each bank account and for each stock

---

TERMS

decedent†   A legal term for a person who has died.

death certificate†   The official proof of death issued by an appropriate public officer.

FIGURE 1–1
A suggested fact
sheet for the initial
client interview

FACT SHEET

Name and address of Client: _____

Phone nos.: Home: _____ Office: _____

Relationship to Decedent: _____

Name of Decedent: _____

Last address of Decedent: _____

Date of death: _____

Social Security no.: _____

(Obtain 4 certified copies of the death certificate.)

Did Decedent leave a will? Yes _____ No _____

Specific bequests [indicate whether adult or minor (under age 18)]:

_____

_____

_____

Does the will refer to the Independent Administration of Estates Act?

  Yes _____ No _____

Names and addresses (and Social Security nos.) of all heirs at law (indicate
  blood relationship) of Decedent. Include ages of minors.

_____

_____

_____

_____

_____

Names and addresses of parents if living:

_____

_____

Names of any children who predeceased Decedent:

_____

_____

Names and addresses of any surviving issue of predeceased children:

_____

_____

Name and address of Decedent's accountant:

_____

Name of insurance broker (if any):

_____

FIGURE 1–1
(continued)

Was Decedent receiving Medi-Cal benefits? Yes _____   No _____
   (If so, see Probate Code sections 215 and 1215 requiring notice of death.)

Was Decedent receiving a retirement pension, or does Decedent have retirement benefits? Yes _____   No _____
   If so, from whom?

   _____

ASSETS OF ESTATE

Estimated total value of estate: $ _____

(Property and detailed descriptions may be obtained later; at this time it is sufficient
to determine whether property is valued at more than $60,000.) For complete
data, obtain the following information:

Real Property
Address: _____
Parcel no.:_____
Title in name(s) of: _____
Estimated value: $ _____

Address: _____
Parcel no.:_____
Title in name(s) of: _____
Estimated value: $ _____

Personal Property
Cash on hand: $ _____
Estimated value:
   Furniture, furnishings, and personal effects: $ _____
   Paintings: $ _____
   Antiques: $ _____
   Jewelry: $ _____
   Furs: $ _____
   Other: $ _____
      Total $ _____

Bank Accounts
Name and address of bank, account number, type of account, how title held, and
balance at date of death.
   Total $ _____
   1. _____
      _____

FIGURE 1–1
(continued)

2. _____
_____

3. _____
_____

Stocks
Name of company, number of shares, type, and how stock held.
1. _____
2. _____
3. _____

Automobiles
Year, make and model, how title held.
1. _____
2. _____
3. _____

Municipal Bonds (if any)
    Full description including CUSIP number, date of maturity, date of purchase
and cost if known, rate of interest, and dates dividends payable.
1. _____
2. _____
3. _____

Life Insurance
Name of owner and amount, name of beneficiary, and name of company.
1. _____
2. _____
3. _____

Annual Income
Real property income (rents, etc.): $ _____
Income from personal property, i.e.,
    interest, dividends, bonds, etc.: $ _____
        Total Estimated Annual Income: $ _____

Is family allowance needed?   Yes _____   No _____
If yes, how much estimated: $ _____

If safe deposit box, name and address of bank:

_____

transferred. The mortuary usually inquires about certificates needed at the time the funeral arrangements are made. Advise the mortuary to file a creditor's claim in the estate if necessary. Provide the mortuary with a claim form if one is needed.

2. Ascertain the amount of burial charges and whether the mortuary has been paid. Probate Code section 8400(b) permits an executor to pay the funeral charges before he or she qualifies as the executor.

3. If the personal representative is not a relative, he or she should talk to members of the family and determine which of them are the natural heirs of the decedent. The **natural heirs** are the persons who, under the law, would take the decedent's property in the absence of a will. If there is a will, the names of the beneficiaries will appear in it once it is located. The personal representative will need the addresses of all natural heirs or beneficiaries.

4. At the same time, the personal representative should inquire about the needs for income of any family members, such as the spouse or children. A petition for family allowance may have to be made, and if so, a decision has to be made regarding the amount to be requested.

5. Unless the residence of the deceased is occupied, for instance, by a surviving spouse, the representative will need to secure the house from entry by unauthorized persons and make appropriate arrangements for any valuables remaining in the home. An unoccupied house is a target for burglary and vandalism.

6. If the decedent's residence is left unoccupied, arrangements will have to be made with the post office or any new resident about the decedent's mail. Utility and telephone companies, gardeners, insurance companies that insure the home, and so on, must be notified. Accounts in the decedent's name should be canceled and arrangements for payment made, especially where utilities or telephone will be needed by another occupant.

7. Credit cards and memberships in clubs should be discontinued immediately.

8. Locate any **will** of the decedent and any **codicils**, instructions, or notes concerning the will or the intent of the decedent regarding his

---

TERMS

natural heirs† Heirs of the body.

will† An instrument by which a person (the testator) makes a disposition of his or her property, to take effect after his or her death.

codicil† An addition or supplement to a will, which adds to or modifies the will without replacing or revoking it.

or her estate. If there is a will but it is not going to be offered for probate, file it with the county clerk for safekeeping.

9. Contact the banks and savings and loan companies and determine their individual requirements. Furnish them with a certified copy of the death certificate.

10. Contact each bank where decedent maintained a savings account. Have the account updated and interest entered as of the date of death. (The value of the estate is its fair market value at date of death.)

11. Check for cash in the possession of the decedent at the time of death. A person usually has some cash, no matter how small, on his or her person. This item should not be overlooked.

12. If the decedent was the owner of rentals, determine the amount of any rents on hand that were collected before the death of the decedent but had not been deposited. These should be listed and entered as "cash on hand" in the inventory.

13. Make a note of any rents due and uncollected on the date of death.

14. Ascertain outstanding debts of the decedent, such as those from department stores, major credit cards, promissory notes, and loans, as of the date of death.

15. Determine any benefits to which the decedent may have been entitled, such as a death benefit under Social Security or Veterans Administration, a retirement plan, or a company pension plan.

16. Income tax returns, federal and California, for the three years prior to death should be located. Estimate the current year's taxes due, and gather information needed for current and subsequent tax returns.

17. The representative should look for any gift tax returns and review them.

18. Any securities, jewelry, or other small items of substantial value should be placed in a safe-deposit box in the name of the estate.

19. Any property that the decedent rented and for which a current charge is being incurred, such as an automobile or an apartment, should be returned or discontinued. It may be economical, however, to continue to rent an apartment until disposition can be made of possessions.

20. Determine whether the decedent had any insurance policies. Coverage, particularly of real property, may not have been kept updated and may be inadequate. The representative should check the adequacy of coverage and increase it if necessary.

21. Strictly speaking, there is no duty to notify creditors to file claims (other than the publication of notice to creditors). This writer, how-

ever, believes that courtesy requires that known creditors be advised that they will need to file a claim if their bills are to be paid.

Some law offices prepare a letter or booklet outlining the duties and responsibilities of the personal representative that provides details about what is expected of the person in that role.

§ 1.4 Locating Assets

If the representative was very close to the decedent, all assets may be known. Many times, however, assets are not all self-evident, and they are sometimes found in hard-to-imagine places.

Hiding Places

Many people have a few hiding places in the house where they keep cash, better jewelry, passbooks, or whatever. Since they are meant to be hiding places, they may be very unlikely places indeed. Drawers, locked or unlocked, may hold valuable papers and belongings. Valuables also have been found under mattresses, in refrigerators, in boxes in closets, and in any other place you can imagine.

Do Not Go Alone

Ordinarily a search will be made by the personal representative, perhaps assisted by members of the family. Sometimes if a person lived alone, and there are no surviving relatives, the legal assistant will be the one to make a search. He or she should not go alone, since if a specific item or cash were missing or claimed to be missing, the legal assistant would be in a position to be suspected or accused of taking the item or cash.

Search for Key Papers

A search of papers, including accounting books and bill receipts, may reveal the location of safe-deposit boxes and passbooks for bank and savings and loan accounts. Deposit receipts or statements may reveal money market accounts, for which passbooks ordinarily are not issued. Monthly statements from a brokerage bond may have been issued and accumulated among decedent's papers. If so, the name of the account executive usually appears on the statements, and he or she should be contacted for information about securities or other holdings. Inquire about the broker's document requirements and furnish him or her with a certified copy of the death certificate.

Check for any insurance policies that may be due and for any coverage that is inadequate and should be changed, especially on a home that is now unoccupied and to which danger of damage is increased. Check also for evidence of life insurance policies.

Superseded passbooks may present clues to funds, as may canceled checks and any accounting books. The decedent's broker, insurance agent, and banker may be able to provide additional information.

Old Stock Certificates

Old stock certificates may be found, perhaps in a trunk or attic, and therefore presumed worthless, or next to it. The majority are worthless, but not all. To determine whether they have any value, check first with the stockbroker to learn if the stock is being traded. The stockbroker or his or her firm may be willing to research it. The company may have merged with another company, in which case a letter can be written to the transfer agent whose name appears on the face of the certificate.

Inquiry also can be made of the financial exchanges at their public information offices, which keep records of all stocks traded. These are (1) the New York Stock Exchange, Public Information Office, (2) the American Stock Exchange, Ruling & Inquiries Department, and (3) the National Association of Securities Dealers, Public Information Department, Washington, D.C.

If you wish to look further, the business office of the local library should have reference guides on obsolete securities. For a small fee, a private investigator such as Standard & Poor's Central Inquiry Department may be hired. It is possible that even if the stock is worthless, the certificate may have value as an antique to a collector. R. M. Smythe & Co. reportedly appraises the value of such items as antiques and traces obsolete securities.

§ 1.5 Other Matters Needing Attention

Need for Family Allowance

The attorney will ask the representative about any immediate need for money on the part of family members such as the surviving spouse and children. Then he or she will determine whether a petition for a family allowance will be needed and, if so, the amount required.

Ongoing Business

The decedent may have had employees whose salaries need to be paid. Either someone will continue the business or other arrangements will be made, but in either event, the legal assistant should be alert that there may be pressing necessities in this area.

Out-of-State Property

Inquiry should be made about whether the decedent owned any interest in out-of-state property and whether an ancillary proceeding will be needed.

Letter to Personal Representative

A form stating the duties of the personal representative has been prepared by the Judicial Council and appears in Chapter 2. Letters cannot be issued until the representative acknowledges receipt of a copy of this statement.

§ 1.6 The Computer in Probate

The computer in the law office has various uses in the probate field, as in other fields. Freelancing probate paralegals have used computers to great advantage. Yet, the use of computers has not been maximized. Not all law offices have even introduced them, but more firms are adding them all the time.

As the use of computers has become more widespread in probate, companies have developed software especially for the probate field.

CHAPTER 2

THE PERSONAL REPRESENTATIVE

§ 2.1 The Personal Representative—Generally

An **administrator** or an **executor** is the **personal representative** of an estate and as such is an officer of the court and acts in a trust, or **fiduciary,** capacity. The personal representative signs an oath (contained in the letters testamentary, or the letters of administration) that he or she will faithfully perform his or her duties.

If there is more than one executor or administrator, they are "coexecutors" or "coadministrators" and sign all pleadings and perform their duties jointly. Both of them should have a conference with the attorney for the estate as soon as possible.

Administrator CTA

If the decedent left a will but did not name an executor therein, or the named executor does not desire to act or is incapacitated, the personal representative is called an "administrator with the will annexed" [sometimes written **administrator CTA (cum testamento annexo),** though this term is less commonly used now].

TERMS

administrator† A person who is appointed by the court to manage the estate of a person either who died without a will or whose will failed to name an executor or named an executor who declined or was ineligible to serve.

executor† A person designated by a testator to carry out the directions and requests in the testator's will and to dispose of his or her property according to the provisions of his or her will.

personal representative† Ordinarily, the executor or administrator of a decedent's estate, although the term may also include others such as guardians, conservators, and trustees.

fiduciary† A person who is entrusted with handling money or property for another person, for example, an executor, a trustee, or a guardian.

administrator CTA (cum testamento annexo)† The court-appointed administrator of the estate of a decedent whose will failed to name an executor or whose named executor cannot or refuses to serve.

Special Administrator

A **special administrator** may be appointed if the circumstances of the estate require the immediate appointment of a personal representative, as where there is a delay in granting **letters testamentary,** where an executor or administrator dies or is suspended or removed, or where there is a will contest pending (Prob. Code § 8540).

A special administrator may be appointed for a specified term or on such terms as the court directs. The court may appoint a special administrator to perform a particular act, in which event request for approval of the act may be included in the petition for appointment, and approval may be made at the same time as the appointment. The letters for a particular act shall include a notation of that act. Such a special administrator has no duty to take any other action to protect the estate.

The appointment of a special administrator may be made at any time without notice or on such notice to interested persons as the court deems reasonable.

Ordinarily the court will give preference to the person named as executor or entitled to appointment as the personal representative under Probate Code section 8461 *et seq*. But if no executor is named in the will, or if the sole executor or all the executors named in the will have waived the right to appointment or are for any reason unwilling or unable to act, and no one comes forth, the court may appoint the public administrator.

Letters are issued after the special administrator gives a **bond** as required by Probate Code section 8480 (except in the case of a public administrator) and takes the oath in the letters.

If the will or all the **beneficiaries** waive a bond, the court shall direct that no bond be given. The court, however, on petition of an interested person or on its own motion, may for good cause shown require a bond (Prob. Code § 8481).

The special administrator has all the powers listed in Probate Code section 8544. In addition, the special administrator may be granted the

---

TERMS

special administrator† An administrator who administers some aspect of the estate of a decedent, as opposed to a general administrator, who administers the whole of the estate.

letters testamentary† A document issued by the probate court appointing the executor of the estate of a decedent who died leaving a will.

bond† An obligation to pay a sum of money upon the happening of a stated event.

beneficiary† A person who has inherited or is entitled to inherit under a will, a person for whom property is held in trust, or a person who is entitled to the proceeds of a life insurance policy when the insured dies.

same powers, duties, and obligations of a general personal representative where proper under Probate Code section 8545, in which event the letters shall so state.

The powers of a special administrator cease if a general personal representative is appointed, as provided in Probate Code section 8546.

The commissions and allowances of the special administrator and the fees of the attorney for the special administrator are fixed by the court.

§ 2.2 Duties of the Personal Representative

At the outset of the estate proceeding, the attorney should delineate the duties of the personal representative. Strictly speaking, it is the duty of the personal representative to do much of the administrative work. Not all personal representatives, however, have a business background. They may not be experienced in keeping records. Leaving the administrative work to such a personal representative can result in unnecessary delay in straightening out the records and balancing the account. In some cases, if everything is left to the personal representative, it simply may not get done. Then the attorney is faced with explaining to the beneficiaries and devisees why time is passing and the work is remaining undone. For this reason, some attorneys have their office do all the work.

The personal representative's duties, generally speaking, are to collect the **assets** of the estate and to conserve the estate for the **heirs, devisees,** or **legatees.** In performing these duties, the representative will need to obtain a complete inventory and appraisement of the estate, publish notice to creditors, pay all the just debts of the decedent, file all required tax returns and pay all taxes due, prepare for filing with the court a complete and final accounting together with a petition for distribution, and distribute the estate to the persons entitled thereto under the will and the law. These are the basic duties involved in all formal probate proceedings.

TERMS

asset† Anything of value owned by a person or an organization. Assets include not only all real property and personal property, but intangible property such as bills, notes, stock, and accounts receivable.

heirs† Persons who are entitled to inherit real or personal property of a decedent who dies intestate; persons receiving property by descent.

devisee† The beneficiary of a devise.

legatee† A person who receives personal property as a beneficiary under a will, although the word is often loosely used to mean a person who receives a testamentary gift of either personal property or real property.

Although these duties, strictly speaking, are the duties of the personal representative, as a matter of practice, most of them frequently devolve upon the legal assistant. The legal assistant performs them with the assistance of the executor or administrator, who may be the only one who possesses the needed information, and under the general supervision of an attorney. The attorney should determine what assistance will have to be given the personal representative to obtain the needed information.

In the past, some law firms issued a letter to personal representatives advising them of their duties and what would be expected of them. Now the Judicial Council has prepared a form specifying the duties and liabilities of the personal representative (Figure 2–1). Before letters are issued, the personal representative (other than a trust company) must acknowledge receipt of a copy of this form (or of a statement of duties and liabilities of the office). An acknowledgment form, which is part of the Judicial Council's form, is filed with the court.

There always should be a clear-cut delineation of the duties to be performed by the personal representative and the attorney's office. Close contact between the attorney's office and the representative should be maintained to ensure that everything is done, and done on time. This is simply good practice.

§ 2.3 Powers of the Personal Representative

Without prior court authorization, the personal representative may deposit any money belonging to the estate with one or more banks or savings and loan associations within the state (Prob. Code § 9652). The personal representative also may deposit money in an insured account in a financial institution (Prob. Code § 9700). Money deposited without an order of the court may be withdrawn without an order of the court (Prob. Code § 9700). Investments in direct obligations of the United States or the State of California, maturing not later than one year, also may be made without prior authorization (Prob. Code § 9730).

The personal representative may deposit personal property with a trust company for safekeeping and, unless the court orders otherwise, may withdraw it (Prob. Code § 9701). On petition of the executor or administrator and upon good cause, the court may authorize the executor or administrator to invest money held for the benefit of the estate in units of a common trust fund described in Financial Code section 1564. The common trust fund shall have as its objective investment primarily in short-term, fixed-income obligations (Prob. Code § 9730).

When the claims have been paid or otherwise secured but the estate is not in a condition to be closed, surplus monies may be invested in any

TO COURT CLERK: This form is CONFIDENTIA... local rule requires the Acknowledgment of Receipt to have a Social Security or driver's license number.

ATTORNEY OR PARTY WITHOUT ATTORNEY *(Name and Address)*:	TELEPHONE NO..	FOR COURT USE ONLY
ATTORNEY FOR *(Name)*:		

SUPERIOR COURT OF CALIFORNIA, COUNTY OF
STREET ADDRESS: SACRAMENTO SUPERIOR COURT
MAILING ADDRESS: 720 9th ST.
CITY AND ZIP CODE: SACRAMENTO, CA 95814
BRANCH NAME:

ESTATE OF (NAME):

DECEDENT

DUTIES AND LIABILITIES OF PERSONAL REPRESENTATIVE and Acknowledgment of Receipt	CASE NUMBER:

DUTIES AND LIABILITIES OF PERSONAL REPRESENTATIVE

When you have been appointed by the court as personal representative of an estate, you become an officer of the court and assume certain duties and obligations. An attorney is best qualified to advise you about these matters. You should clearly understand the following:

1. MANAGING THE ESTATE'S ASSETS

a. Prudent investments
You must manage the estate assets with the care of a prudent person dealing with someone else's property. This means you must be cautious and you may not make any speculative investments.

b. Keep estate assets separate
You must keep the money and property in this estate separate from anyone else's, including your own. When you open a bank account for the estate, the account name must indicate that it is an estate account and not your personal account. Never deposit estate funds in your personal account or otherwise commingle them with anyone else's property. Securities in the estate must also be held in a name that shows they are estate property and not your personal property.

c. Interest-bearing accounts and other investments
Except for checking accounts intended for ordinary administration expenses, estate accounts must earn interest. You may deposit estate funds in insured accounts in financial institutions, but you should consult with an attorney before making other investments.

d. Other restrictions
There are many other restrictions on your authority to deal with estate property. You should not spend any of the estate's money unless you have received permission from the court or have been advised to do so by an attorney. You may reimburse yourself for official court costs paid by you to the county clerk and for the premium on your bond. Without prior order of the court, you may not pay fees to yourself or to your attorney, if you have one. If you do not obtain the court's permission when it is required, you may be removed as personal representative or you may be required to reimburse the estate from your own personal funds, or both. You should consult with an attorney concerning the legal requirements affecting sales, leases, mortgages, and investments of estate property.

2. INVENTORY OF ESTATE PROPERTY

a. Locate the estate's property
You must attempt to locate and take possession of all the decedent's property to be administered in the estate.

b. Determine the value of the property
You must arrange to have a court-appointed referee determine the value of the property unless the appointment is waived by the court. (You, rather than the referee, must determine the value of certain "cash items." An attorney can advise you about how to do this.)

c. File an inventory and appraisal
Within four months after your appointment as personal representative, you must file with the court an inventory and appraisal of all the assets in the estate.

(Continued on reverse)

Form Adopted by the Judicial Council of California DE-147 [New July 1, 1989]	DUTIES AND LIABILITIES OF PERSONAL REPRESENTATIVE (Probate)	Probate Code, § 8404

FIGURE 2–1 Duties and Liabilities of Personal Representative form

ESTATE OF (NAME):	CASE NUMBER:
DECEDENT	

d. File a change of ownership

At the time you file the inventory and appraisal, you must also file a change of ownership statement with the county recorder or assessor in each county where the decedent owned real property at the time of death, as provided in section 480 of the California Revenue and Taxation Code.

3. NOTICE TO CREDITORS

You must mail a notice of administration to each known creditor of the decedent within four months after your appointment as personal representative. If the decedent received Medi-Cal assistance you must notify the State Director of Health Services within 90 days after appointment.

4. INSURANCE

You should determine that there is appropriate and adequate insurance covering the assets and risks of the estate. Maintain the insurance in force during the entire period of the administration.

5. RECORD KEEPING

a. Keep accounts

You must keep complete and accurate records of each financial transaction affecting the estate. You will have to prepare an account of all money and property you have received, what you have spent, and the date of each transaction. You must describe in detail what you have left after the payment of expenses.

b. Court review

Your account will be reviewed by the court. Save your receipts because the court may ask to review them. If you do not file your accounts as required, the court will order you to do so. You may be removed as personal representative if you fail to comply.

6. CONSULTING AN ATTORNEY

If you have an attorney, you should cooperate with the attorney at all times. You and your attorney are responsible for completing the estate administration as promptly as possible. When in doubt, contact your attorney.

> **NOTICE: This statement of duties and liabilities is a summary and is not a complete statement of the law. Your conduct as a personal representative is governed by the law itself and not by this summary.**

ACKNOWLEDGMENT OF RECEIPT

1. I have petitioned the court to be appointed as a personal representative of the estate of *(specify)*:

2. I acknowledge that I have received a copy of this statement of the duties and liabilities of the office of personal representative.

Date:

....
(TYPE OR PRINT NAME)

▶ _____
(SIGNATURE OF PETITIONER)

*Social Security No.: _____ *Driver's License No.: _____

Date:

....
(TYPE OR PRINT NAME)

▶ _____
(SIGNATURE OF PETITIONER)

*Social Security No.: _____ *Driver's License No.: _____

Date:

....
(TYPE OR PRINT NAME)

▶ _____
(SIGNATURE OF PETITIONER)

*Social Security No.: _____ *Driver's License No.: _____

*Supply these numbers only if required to do so by local court rule. The law requires the court to keep this information CONFIDENTIAL. (Probate Code, § 8404(a).)

DE-147 (New July 1, 1989) **DUTIES AND LIABILITIES OF PERSONAL REPRESENTATIVE** Page two
(Probate)

FIGURE 2–1 *(continued)*

manner provided by the will, after hearing and notice as prescribed by Probate Code section 1220. The personal representative may not speculate with estate assets (Prob. Code § 9732).

The management and operation of a business may be continued for six months, but only six months, without obtaining permission of the court. To continue a business more than six months, a petition must be filed, a hearing given pursuant to Probate Code section 1220, and an order obtained authorizing the continuation (Prob. Code § 9760).

Probate Code section 9941 permits the personal representative to lease real property without authorization of the court where the rental does not exceed $5,000 a month and the term does not exceed one year. If the lease is from month to month, the personal representative may lease the property regardless of the amount of rental charged.

§ 2.4 Public Employees Retirement System (PERS)

Many decedents are employees of the state government (or federal or city governments), and it is the personal representative's duty to determine if the decedent is entitled to any further benefits and to collect them. Following are the steps to be taken when a Public Employees Retirement System (PERS) annuitant dies.

The first thing to do is to notify PERS, by phone or mail. Following are the address and phone number at the time of this writing:

P.O. Box 1953
Sacramento, CA 95809
Attention: Section 490
Phone: (916) 445-5030

The following information will be needed by PERS:

1. Date of death.
2. Decedent's name, Social Security number, and PERS retirement number.
3. Name and address of surviving spouse or other next of kin, or of the person who will be handling the estate.
4. Name and address of the person providing notice of death if other than the personal representative.

The documents required by PERS are:

1. Certified copy of death certificate.

2. A copy of any newspaper clipping reporting the death.

3. If any death benefits are payable to the estate, letters testamentary from the executor or letters of administration from the administrator.

4. Marriage or birth certificate of the deceased.

The forms to be completed and returned to PERS are:

1. Survivor Information Questionnaire/Claimant Statement.

2. Health and Dental Insurance Enrollment Forms. (Coverage for entitled beneficiaries or survivors under approved health and dental insurance plans is automatically continued, but confirmation of the enrollment will be sent after this form is submitted.)

If the personal representative finds or comes into possession of a state warrant issued to the decedent after the date of the decedent's death, it should be promptly returned to PERS. If the personal representative finds that someone else has mailed such a warrant for deposit, the personal representative will have to issue a check for the amount and send it to PERS. Any unpaid accrued allowance will be paid to the eligible beneficiary.

§ 2.5 Special Notices

If a request for special notice (Figure 2–2) has been served upon the personal representative or the attorney pursuant to Probate Code section 1250, the personal representative must give special notice to that person of the filing of the petitions, accounts, and reports mentioned in Probate Code section 1250. The notice must be given at least fifteen days before the hearing. Proof of mailing of the notice should be filed with the court (Prob. Code §§ 1252, 1260). (See Figure 2–2.) A similar request for special notice of the filing of the inventory and appraisement or other paper may be made under Probate Code section 1250, in which event the personal representative must give notice no later than fifteen days after the filing of the inventory and appraisement or other paper. Proof of mailing should be filed with the court before the hearing.

ATTORNEY OR PARTY WITHOUT ATTORNEY *(Name and Address)*:	TELEPHONE NO.:	*FOR COURT USE ONLY*

ATTORNEY FOR *(Name)*:

SUPERIOR COURT OF CALIFORNIA, COUNTY OF
STREET ADDRESS: SACRAMENTO SUPERIOR COURT
MAILING ADDRESS: 720 9th ST
CITY AND ZIP CODE: SACRAMENTO, CA 95814
BRANCH NAME:

ESTATE OF (NAME):

DECEDENT

REQUEST FOR SPECIAL NOTICE

CASE NUMBER:

To the personal representative:

1. I am a person interested in the estate of *(name)*:

2. I REQUEST SPECIAL NOTICE of *(complete only a or b)*
   a. ☐ the following matters *(specify)*:

   b. ☐ the following matters *(check applicable boxes)*:
      (1) ☐ **all the matters** listed in Probate Code section 1250(c)   *(Do not check boxes (2)–(8).)*
      (2) ☐ inventories and appraisals of property, including supplements
      (3) ☐ accountings by the personal representative
      (4) ☐ reports of the status of administration
      (5) ☐ objections to an appraisal
      (6) ☐ petitions for the sale of property
      (7) ☐ Spousal Property Petition (Probate Code, § 13650)
      (8) ☐ other petitions: ☐ all petitions ☐ the following petitions *(specify)*:

3. SEND THE NOTICES TO
   a. ☐ me at the following address *(specify)*:

   b. ☐ my attorney at the following address *(specify)*:

Date:

▶

....
(TYPE OR PRINT NAME)

(SIGNATURE)

☐ Attorney for person requesting special notice *(client's name)*:

(Continued on reverse)

Form Approved by the
Judicial Council of California
DE-154 [Rev. July 1, 1989]

REQUEST FOR SPECIAL NOTICE
(Probate)

Probate Code, § 1250

FIGURE 2–2   Request for Special Notice form

ESTATE OF (NAME):	CASE NUMBER:
DECEDENT	

> **NOTE:** A formal proof of service or a written admission of service must accompany this Request for Special Notice when it is filed with the court.
>
> You must have your request served on either the personal representative or the attorney for the personal representative or obtain a signed Admission of Service *(see below)*.

PROOF OF ☐ MAILING ☐ PERSONAL DELIVERY   TO PERSONAL REPRESENTATIVE

1. I am not a party to this proceeding. At the time of mailing or delivery I was at least 18 years of age.
2. My residence or business address is *(specify)*:

3. I mailed or delivered a copy of this Request for Special Notice to the
   ☐ personal representative
   ☐ attorney for the personal representative

   as follows *(check either a or b)*:

   a. ☐ **First-class mail.** I deposited a copy of the request with the United States Postal Service, in a sealed envelope with postage fully prepaid. I used first-class mail. I am a resident of or employed in the county where the mailing occurred. The envelope was addressed and mailed as follows:
      (1) Name of person served:
      (2) Address on envelope:

      (3) Date of mailing:
      (4) Place of mailing *(city and state)*:

   b. ☐ **Personal delivery.** I personally delivered a copy of the request as follows:
      (1) Name of personal representative or attorney served:
      (2) Address where delivered:

      (3) Date delivered:
      (4) Time delivered:

   I declare under penalty of perjury under the laws of the State of California that the foregoing is true and correct.
   Date:

   ....   ▶ _____
   (TYPE OR PRINT NAME)   (SIGNATURE OF DECLARANT)

ADMISSION OF SERVICE

1. I am the ☐ personal representative ☐ attorney for the personal representative.

2. I ACKNOWLEDGE that I was served a copy of the foregoing Request for Special Notice.

Date:

....   ▶ _____
(TYPE OR PRINT NAME)   (SIGNATURE)

DE-154 [Rev. July 1, 1989]   **REQUEST FOR SPECIAL NOTICE**   Page two
                                                    (Probate)

FIGURE 2–2   *(continued)*

CHAPTER 3

FORMAL PROBATE PROCEEDINGS— TESTATE ESTATES

This chapter and subsequent chapters deal with "full" or "formal" probate. Until recently, virtually all estates had to be probated. Legislation in recent years has provided several alternatives to formal probate. These methods are discussed in Chapter 11.

§ 3.1 Probate Code

In 1990, California enacted Probate Code Chapter 769 and the former California Probate Code was repealed in its entirety. The new code continues the sections of the previous code without changing section numbers, but it omits "obsolete material and make[s] numerous technical, clarifying, conforming and minor substantive revisions in the existing provisions." The "significant revisions" are set out in the California Law Revision Commission's Recommendations. The new Probate Code became operative July 1, 1991, and has since been amended.

The notice provisions in the new code do not apply where the notice was delivered, mailed, posted, or first published before July 1, 1991.

The California Law Revision Commission (4000 Middlefield Road, Suite D-2, Palo Alto, CA 94303–4739) made available its Recommendations Proposing New Probate Code in December of 1989 and its Revised and Supplemental Comments to the New Probate Code in September of 1990. There is a charge for these publications, but they are helpful in working with the various sections of the code, as their comments deal not only with the changes but also with the background of the sections.

§ 3.2 "Formal" Probate

An estate proceeding is commenced by the filing of a petition for probate of will in a **testate** proceeding, or the filing of a petition for letters of administration in an **intestate** proceeding (where there is no will). When the petition for probate of will is granted, the will is "admitted to probate" by the court and certified as being the genuine last will and

---

TERMS

testate† Pertaining to a person, or to the property of a person, who dies leaving a valid will.

intestate† Pertaining to a person, or to the property of a person, who dies without leaving a valid will.

testament of the decedent. The same printed form is used in both testate and intestate proceedings, but the appropriate boxes must be checked.

No statute limits the time within which an application to probate a will must be made. An executor named in a will, however, may be held to have renounced his or her right to act if he or she does not petition for letters testamentary within thirty days after the date of death (Prob. Code § 324).

Ordinarily the executor named in the will is the petitioning party. Frequently a second executor is named in the will to act if the executor declines to act or has died. In the event there is no such person, any devisee or legatee named in the will or any other person interested in the estate (including a creditor) may petition the court to have the will probated. The facts will be stated in the petition.

Access to Safe-Deposit Boxes

Before a will can be probated, it must be located. Frequently the will is in a safe-deposit box in a bank or savings and loan association. Without the will, letters cannot be issued, since the will usually names an executor.

Former Revenue and Taxation Code section 14344, repealed in 1980, prohibited removal from the safe-deposit box of anything but a will or burial instructions without the consent of the California Controller. Most financial institutions continued to permit a member of the decedent's family to access a safe-deposit box to remove a will and any instructions for disposition of remains if the person had a key and produced a death certificate. Sometimes, however, a financial institution would not want to permit access to the safe-deposit box until *after* letters were issued. To eliminate the problem, in 1991, Probate Code section 331 was added.

This section provides that a person who has a key to a safe-deposit box may, before issuance of letters and without waiting forty days after death, and after providing "reasonable proof" of his or her identity, obtain access to the safe-deposit box solely for the purposes specified in that section. Reasonable proof is provided if the requirements of Probate Code section 13104 are met. The person must present proof of the decedent's death such as a certified copy of the decedent's death certificate or a written statement of death from the coroner, treating physician, or hospital or institution where the decedent died.

The safe-deposit box must be opened under the supervision of an officer or employee of the financial institution and an inventory of its contents made. All wills and trust instruments removed from the safe-deposit box must be photocopied and placed in the safe-deposit box until the personal representative of the estate or other legally authorized person removes the contents. The person may remove instructions for the disposition of the decedent's remains as well as the will, but no other contents may be removed by the person given access under Probate Code section 331. The financial institution may charge for the photocopying and must keep a record of the identity of the person allowed access to the box.

Under Probate Code section 330, the decedent's personal property, including the keys to the residence, may be delivered to the decedent's surviving spouse, relative, or the person acting as conservator or guardian of the estate at the time of death. The property may not be delivered if the person delivering it knows or has reason to believe there is a dispute over the right to possession of the property. Reasonable proof of the status and identity of the person to whom the property is delivered can be ascertained from any document described in Probate Code section 13104, subdivision (d), and the person delivering property under this section is not liable for loss or damage to the property caused by the person to whom the property is delivered.

Formal Probate—Advantages

One advantage of formal probate is to ensure that the survivors will be free and clear of any further liability. In a formal probate, a creditor must file a **creditor's claim** within a specified period or he or she cannot claim payment. Once notice to creditors is published as specified and notice of administration has been given as required, creditors cannot make enforceable claims.

In proceedings other than formal probate, claims do not have to be accepted. If a creditor presents a claim to a relative of the deceased or another person the creditor considers responsible, that person may return the claim with a note stating, for example, "Your creditor's claim is returned herewith, because there is no probate proceeding to process this claim." (This does not mean that the debt is not valid or that it cannot be collected.)

Any taxes due must be paid. The Internal Revenue Service is assured of being paid any taxes due, since assets must be inventoried and tax returns filed as required.

In formal probate, the provisions of the **testator's** will are carried out. If there is no will, the property goes to the decedent's heirs at law if it can be determined who they are and where they are located. Distribution to the heirs at law, of course, may not be what the decedent would have desired.

TERMS

creditor's claim   A document that creditors are required to file in an estate before they may be paid from the assets of the estate.

testator†   A person who dies leaving a valid will.

The title to properties will be cleared and distribution of properties made to persons entitled thereto. The final order of distribution guarantees legal ownership. This avoids problems with title insurance companies when real property is involved or with stock transfer agents where stock has been distributed.

Another advantage of a formal probate proceeding may be income tax savings. While the estate is open, income taxes are paid on the income of the estate proceeding, that is, the estate is a separate taxpaying entity. As soon as the assets are delivered to the beneficiaries, the beneficiaries pay income tax on any income generated by the assets, whether real property, cash, or other. The income tax payable by the estate may not be as high as a beneficiary's tax. A beneficiary who is already in a higher tax bracket could be pushed into an even higher bracket by the additional income-producing assets. Formal probate may or may not offer income tax advantages to the beneficiaries of the property. If it does, the income tax savings can be considerable. In any event, this is an important consideration in the handling of the probate, although the assets, of course, must be distributed at the appropriate time.

In a probate proceeding, a professional fiduciary can be appointed, which may be so advantageous as to offset the cost of probate. If an estate involves both an ongoing business and a farm, for example, responsibilities will not have to be divided as they would be if, for example, an executor was in charge of the farm and a surviving spouse was handling the business.

Some properties that do not have to be probated are still subject to tax. Such properties include **joint tenancy** property, **Totten trusts**, **trust** accounts naming a beneficiary, **pensions**, **annuities**, insurance with a named beneficiary, and **inter vivos trusts**.

TERMS

joint tenancy†   An estate in land or in personal property held by two or more persons jointly, with equal rights to share in its enjoyment.

Totten trust†   A trust created by a bank deposit which a person makes with his money in his own name as trustee for another person.

trust†   A fiduciary relationship involving a trustee who holds trust property for the benefit or use of a beneficiary.

pension†   A retirement benefit in the form of a periodic payment, usually monthly, made to a retired employee from a fund created by the employer's contributions, or by the joint contributions of the employer and employee, over the period the employee worked for the employer.

annuity†   A yearly payment of a fixed sum of money for life or for a stated number of years.

inter vivos trust†   A trust that is effective during the lifetime of the creator of the trust; a living trust.

Formal Probate—Disadvantages

A disadvantage of formal probate is the probate fees, which are established by California statute for attorneys and executors. Both attorneys and executors receive the same amount of ordinary fees as provided by the statute. Extraordinary fees, for both attorneys and executors, are for the court to determine and depend upon the amount and value of the work performed for the estate.

If an election is made to probate when probate is not needed, it should be borne in mind that the executor's commissions and attorney fees will be incurred. Both halves of community property should not be included in an estate.

Where a **testamentary trust** (that is, a trust in a will) makes specific bequests to persons other than the issue of the decedent, formal probate is necessary.

Probate takes time, depending upon the complexity of the estate. If sales of **real property** are required, more time is needed. Under the best of circumstances, it takes time to get the executor appointed, execute a bond, if any, gather the assets, inventory the assets, get them appraised, give notice to creditors, do an accounting, and prepare any necessary petitions.

Further, the assets of the estate are not available to the family for some time, and the family's plans may be delayed. On the other hand, a family allowance may be obtainable if a probate proceeding is on file.

§ 3.3   Filing of Will

The original will is filed with the court at the time of filing the petition for probate of will (within thirty days of the date of death, if feasible).

The legal assistant should have several photocopies made of the will before the filing. The number of copies needed will vary. Usually the heirs want a copy of the will and may request a copy. At least one copy is required for the office file. A minimum of four copies is suggested. Additional copies may be made if needed.

If a will cannot be personally delivered to the county clerk, it should be mailed by registered mail, return receipt requested, together with a

---

TERMS

testamentary trust†   A trust created by will.

real property†   Land, including things located on it or attached to it directly or indirectly; real estate.

letter of transmittal with endorsement for receipt on a copy of the letter for return, along with a stamped, self-addressed envelope.

Petition for Probate of Will

At a minimum, an original and two copies of the petition are prepared. Probate Code section 326 provides that a petition for probate of will must contain the following:

1. the jurisdictional facts;
2. whether the person named as executor of the will consents to act as executor;
3. the street number, street, city, and county of the decedent's residence at the time of his or her death;
4. the names, ages, residences, and relation to the decedent of heirs, devisees and legatees of the decedent;
5. the character and estimated value of the property of the estate; and
6. the name of the person for whom the letters are **prayed.**

The printed forms will cover all of the above requirements of the code.

If a petitioner, objector, or respondent is absent from the county or for some other reason is unable to sign or verify the document, the person's attorney may, if the petitioner, objector, or respondent is not a fiduciary, sign or verify the petition, objection, or response (Prob. Code § 1023). A copy of the will is attached to the original petition and also to each copy of the petition. When the original petition is filed with the county clerk, a filing fee (the amount of which varies from county to county and is subject to change) is required.

The legal assistant should obtain and study the probate policy memoranda for the particular county in which the petition is to be filed. In most cases, this is the county in which the law office is located. Attorneys occasionally probate estates in other counties, however, and the policy memoranda for that county should be reviewed. A particular county may have devised forms for use in that county.

The Judicial Council has published a form that can be used for a petition for probate of will or for letters of administration (Figure 3–1).

TERMS

prayer†   Portion of a bill in equity or a petition that asks for equitable relief and specifies the relief sought.

ATTORNEY OR PARTY WITHOUT ATTORNEY *(Name and Address)*

ARTHUR ANDREW
Attorney at Law   (916) 447-0923
123 Sandor Place
Sacramento, California 95814

TELEPHONE NO

FOR COURT USE ONLY

ATTORNEY FOR *(Name)*   Petitioner

SUPERIOR COURT OF CALIFORNIA, COUNTY OF

STREET ADDRESS   720 - 9th Street

MAILING ADDRESS

CITY AND ZIP CODE   Sacramento, California 95814

BRANCH NAME

ESTATE OF (NAME):

KENNETH BELL, also known as KENNETH K. BELL

DECEDENT

PETITION FOR

(For deaths after
December 31, 1984)

[X]	Probate of Will and for Letters Testamentary
[ ]	Probate of Will and for, Letters of Administration with Will Annexed
[ ]	Letters of Administration
[ ]	Letters of Special Administration
[ ]	Authorization to Administer Under the Independent Administration of Estates Act [ ] with limited authority

CASE NUMBER   92457

HEARING DATE

DEPT.   TIME

1. Publication will be in *(specify name of newspaper)*: The Daily Recorder
   a. [X] Publication requested.
   b. [ ] Publication to be arranged.

> *Arthur Andrew*
> (Signature of attorney or party without attorney)

2. Petitioner *(name of each)*: CLARICE BELL
   requests
   a. [X] decedent's will and codicils, if any, be admitted to probate.
   b. [X] *(name)*: CLARICE BELL
   be appointed (1) [X] executor   (3) [ ] administrator
            (2) [ ] administrator with will annexed   (4) [ ] special administrator
   and Letters issue upon qualification.
   c. [X] that [X] full [ ] limited authority be granted to administer under the Independent Administration of Estates Act.
   d. [X] bond not be required for the reasons stated in item 3d.
      [ ] $ bond be fixed. It will be furnished by an admitted surety insurer or as otherwise provided by law. *(Specify reasons in Attachment 2d if the amount is different from the maximum required by Probate Code, § 8482.)*
      [ ] $ in deposits in a blocked account be allowed. Receipts will be filed. *(Specify institution and location)*:

3. a. Decedent died on *(date)*: Jan. 7, 19   at *(place)*: Sacramento, California
      [X] a resident of the county named above.
      [ ] a nonresident of California and left an estate in the county named above located at *(specify location permitting publication in the newspaper named in item 1)*:
   b. Street address, city, and county of decedent's residence at time of death:
      145 Perry Avenue, Sacramento, County of Sacramento
   c. Character and estimated value of the property of the estate
      (1) Personal property .... $ 313,000
      (2) Annual gross income from
         (i) [X] real property .... $ 11,000
         (iii) [X] personal property ...... $ 24,000
                Total ...... $
      (3) Real property: $ *(If full authority under the Independent Administration of Estates Act is requested, state the fair market value of the real property less encumbrances.)*
   d. [X] Will waives bond. [ ] Special administrator is the named executor and the will waives bond.
      [ ] All beneficiaries are adults and have waived bond, and the will does not require a bond. *(Affix waiver as Attachment 3d.)*
      [ ] All heirs at law are adults and have waived bond. *(Affix waiver as Attachment 3d.)*
      [ ] Sole personal representative is a corporate fiduciary.

(Continued on reverse)

Form Approved by the
Judicial Council of California
DE 111 [Rev July 1 1989]

PETITION FOR PROBATE

Probate Code, §§ 8002, 10450

FIGURE 3–1   Petition for Probate form

ESTATE OF (NAME):	CASE NUMBER:
KENNETH BELL, also known as KENNETH K. BELL DECEDENT	92457

3. e. ☐ Decedent died intestate.
   ☒ Copy of decedent's will dated: Nov. 15,1982 ☐ codicils dated: *are affixed as Attachment 3e.*
      ☒ The will and all codicils are self-proving *(Probate Code, § 8220).*

   f. **Appointment of personal representative** *(check all applicable boxes)*

   > *Attach a typed copy of a holographic will and a translation of a foreign language will.*

   (1) Appointment of executor or administrator with will annexed
      ☒ Proposed executor is named as executor in the will and consents to act.
      ☐ No executor is named in the will.
      ☐ Proposed personal representative is a nominee of a person entitled to Letters. *(Affix nomination as Attachment 3f(1).)*
      ☐ Other named executors will not act because of ☐ death ☐ declination ☐ other reasons *(specify in Attachment 3f(1)).*

   (2) Appointment of administrator
      ☐ Petitioner is a person entitled to Letters. *(If necessary, explain priority in Attachment 3f(2).)*
      ☐ Petitioner is a nominee of a person entitled to Letters. *(Affix nomination as Attachment 3f(2).)*
      ☐ Petitioner is related to the decedent as *(specify):*

   (3) ☐ Appointment of special administrator requested. *(Specify grounds and requested powers in Attachment 3f(3).)*

   g. Proposed personal representative is a ☒ resident of California ☐ nonresident of California *(affix statement of permanent address as Attachment 3g)* ☒ resident of the United States ☐ nonresident of the United States.

4. ☒ Decedent's will does not preclude administration of this estate under the Independent Administration of Estates Act.

5. a. The decedent is survived by
   (1) ☒ spouse ☐ no spouse as follows: ☐ divorced or never married ☐ spouse deceased
   (2) ☒ child as follows: ☒ natural or adopted ☐ natural adopted by a third party ☐ step ☐ foster
      ☐ no child
   (3) ☐ issue of a predeceased child ☐ no issue of a predeceased child

   b. Petitioner ☐ has no actual knowledge of facts ☒ has actual knowledge of facts reasonably giving rise to a parent-child relationship under Probate Code section 6408(b).

   c. ☒ All surviving children and issue of predeceased children have been listed in item 8.

6. *(Complete if decedent was survived by (1) a spouse but no issue (only a or b apply); or (2) no spouse or issue. Check the first box that applies):*
   a. ☐ The decedent is survived by a parent or parents who are listed in item 8.
   b. ☐ The decedent is survived by issue of deceased parents, all of whom are listed in item 8.
   c. ☐ The decedent is survived by a grandparent or grandparents who are listed in item 8.
   d. ☐ The decedent is survived by issue of grandparents, all of whom are listed in item 8.
   e. ☐ The decedent is survived by issue of a predeceased spouse, all of whom are listed in item 8.
   f. ☐ The decedent is survived by next of kin, all of whom are listed in item 8.
   g. ☐ The decedent is survived by parents of a predeceased spouse or issue of those parents, if both are predeceased, all of whom are listed in item 8.

7. *(Complete only if no spouse or issue survived the decedent)* Decedent ☐ had no predeceased spouse ☐ had a predeceased spouse who (1) ☐ died not more than 15 years before decedent owning an interest in real property that passed to decedent,
   (2) ☐ died not more than five years before decedent owning personal property valued at $10,000 or more that passed to decedent,
   (3) ☐ neither (1) nor (2) apply. *(If you checked (1) or (2), check only the first box that applies):*
   a. ☐ The decedent is survived by issue of a predeceased spouse, all of whom are listed in item 8.
   b. ☐ The decedent is survived by a parent or parents of the predeceased spouse who are listed in item 8.
   c. ☐ The decedent is survived by issue of a parent of the predeceased spouse, all of whom are listed in item 8.
   d. ☐ The decedent is survived by next of kin of the decedent, all of whom are listed in item 8.
   e. ☐ The decedent is survived by next of kin of the predeceased spouse, all of whom are listed in item 8.

8. **Listed in Attachment 8** are the names, relationships, ages, and addresses of all persons named in decedent's will and codicils, whether living or deceased, and all persons checked in items 5, 6, and 7, so far as known to or reasonably ascertainable by petitioner, including stepchild and foster child heirs and devisees to whom notice is to be given under Probate Code section 1207.

9. ☒ Number of pages attached: 1

Date: February 10, 19__

▶ _____
(SIGNATURE OF PETITIONER*)

▶ *Clarice Bell*
(SIGNATURE OF PETITIONER*)

I declare under penalty of perjury under the laws of the State of California that the foregoing is true and correct.
Date: February 10, 19__
......Clarice Bell......
(TYPE OR PRINT NAME)

▶ *Clarice Bell*
(SIGNATURE OF PETITIONER*)

* All petitioners must sign the petition. Only one need sign the declaration.

DE 111 (Rev July 1 1989)   **PETITION FOR PROBATE**   Page two

FIGURE 3–1   *(continued)*

Notice of Petition to Administer Estate

The notice provisions in the new code do not apply where notice was delivered, mailed, posted, or first published before July 1, 1991. Consult former code sections applicable as of the date of the notice. The annotated codes may contain enough information in the history of the section.

An original and three copies of the petition are prepared for delivery to the clerk for issuance at the time of filing. The clerk will set the hearing on a date not less than fifteen days nor more than thirty days from the date of filing the petition. In some counties, a date may be preselected and filled in on the form before presentation to the clerk.

At the request of the petitioner made at time of filing the petition, the hearing shall be set for a day not less than thirty nor more than forty-five days after the petition is filed and the petitioner serves and publishes notice of the hearing [Prob. Code § 8003(a), (b)].

Publication

The notice must be published in a newspaper of general circulation in the city where the decedent resided at the time of death or where the decedent's property is located if the court has jurisdiction over the estate pursuant to Probate Code section 7052. If there is no city newspaper, or the decedent did not reside in a city, or the property is not located in a city, then notice shall be published in a newspaper of general circulation in the county in which the decedent resided or the property is located. If there is no county newspaper, notice shall be published in a newspaper of general circulation in California nearest to the county seat of the county in which the decedent resided or the property is located, and which is circulated in the area of the county in which the decedent resided or the property is located (Prob. Code §§ 8003, 8121).

City means a charter city as defined in Government Code section 34101 or a general law city as defined in Government Code section 34102.

The first publication of the notice shall be at least fifteen days before the hearing. Publication of the notice in a newspaper that is published once a week or more often, in three publications with at least five days intervening between the first and last publication dates and not counting those dates, will be sufficient (Prob. Code § 8121).

§ 3.4 Responsibilities of the Paralegal

The legal assistant should deliver one conformed copy of the notice to the newspaper for publication and arrange to obtain from the newspaper sufficient printed copies of the notice to mail to all heirs, devisees, and legatees.

At least fifteen days prior to the hearing, a notice of the hearing (the notice of death form may be used) must be either personally served or mailed, postage prepaid, to each heir, devisee and legatee, and nonpetitioning executor at their respective places of residence or mailing addresses, if known. If addresses are not known, the notice should be mailed to the county seat of the county where the proceedings are pending. This notice shall advise the person receiving the notice of the right to request special notice pursuant to Probate Code section 1250.

If the estate involves or may involve a testamentary trust for charitable purposes (other than a **charitable trust** with resident designated trustee, or a devise for charitable purposes without an identified devisee), notice of the hearing and a copy of the petition and will must be personally served or served by mail on the Attorney General in Sacramento. A declaration or affidavit of mailing the notice is filed (included as part of the form) (Prob. Code § 8111).

A form is available for the notice of petition to administer the estate (Figure 3–2). This Judicial Council form would be used in San Francisco and Los Angeles counties. Sacramento County uses a different form. A proof of service form is part of the Judicial Council form.

Notice to Decedent's Heirs

Relatives who are not "blood" relatives of the decedent are not heirs of the decedent under the law. For example, a spouse's relatives are not blood relatives, nor are sisters-in-law or brothers-in-law.

Probate Code section 10 directs that a fifteen-day notice be given to each heir of the testator, each devisee and legatee named in the will, and each person named as executor who is not petitioning. Probate Code section 44 defines *heirs* to mean the persons, including the surviving spouse, who are entitled to the property of a decedent under the statutes of intestate succession. The legal assistant should determine from the representative the blood relationship of each person whose name is given as a relative in the initial interview.

TERMS

charitable trust†   A trust established for a charitable purpose.

ATTORNEY OR PARTY WITHOUT ATTORNEY *(Name and Address)*:

ARTHUR ANDREW
Attorney at Law
123 Sandor Place
Sacramento, California 95814

TELEPHONE NO.: (916) 447-0923

FOR COURT USE ONLY

ATTORNEY FOR *(Name)*: Petitioner

SUPERIOR COURT OF CALIFORNIA, COUNTY OF

STREET ADDRESS: 720 - 9th Street
MAILING ADDRESS:
CITY AND ZIP CODE: Sacramento, California 95814
BRANCH NAME:

ESTATE OF (NAME):

KENNETH BELL, also known as KENNETH K. BELL DECEDENT

NOTICE OF PETITION TO ADMINISTER ESTATE
OF *(name)*:

CASE NUMBER: 92457

1. To all heirs, beneficiaries, creditors, contingent creditors, and persons who may otherwise be interested in the will or estate, or both, of *(specify all names by which decedent was known)*:

   KENNETH BELL, also known as KENNETH K. BELL
   CLARICE BELL

2. A PETITION has been filed by *(name of petitioner)*:
   in the Superior Court of California, County of *(specify)*: Sacramento

3. THE PETITION requests that *(name)*: Clarice Bell
   be appointed as personal representative to administer the estate of the decedent.

4. [X] THE PETITION requests the decedent's WILL and codicils, if any, be admitted to probate. The will and any codicils are available for examination in the file kept by the court.

5. [X] THE PETITION requests authority to administer the estate under the Independent Administration of Estates Act. (This authority will allow the personal representative to take many actions without obtaining court approval. Before taking certain very important actions, however, the personal representative will be required to give notice to interested persons unless they have waived notice or consented to the proposed action.) The independent administration authority will be granted unless an interested person files an objection to the petition and shows good cause why the court should not grant the authority.

6. [ ] A PETITION for determination of or confirmation of property passing to or belonging to a surviving spouse under California Probate Code section 13650 IS JOINED with the petition to administer the estate.

7. A HEARING on the petition will be held

   on *(date)*: Mar. 15, 19—   at *(time)*: 9:00 A.M. in Dept.: 17   Room:

   located at *(address of court)*: 720 - 9th Street, Sacramento, California 95814

8. IF YOU OBJECT to the granting of the petition, you should appear at the hearing and state your objections or file written objections with the court before the hearing. Your appearance may be in person or by your attorney.

9. IF YOU ARE A CREDITOR or a contingent creditor of the deceased, you must file your claim with the court and mail a copy to the personal representative appointed by the court within four months from the date of first issuance of letters as provided in section 9100 of the California Probate Code. The time for filing claims will not expire before four months from the hearing date noticed above.

10. YOU MAY EXAMINE the file kept by the court. If you are a person interested in the estate, you may file with the court a formal Request for Special Notice of the filing of an inventory and appraisal of estate assets or of any petition or account as provided in section 1250 of the California Probate Code. A Request for Special Notice form is available from the court clerk.

11. [ ] Petitioner [X] Attorney for petitioner *(name)*: Arthur Andrew

    (address): 123 Sandor Place
    Sacramento, CA 95814

    ▶ *Arthur Andrew*

    (SIGNATURE OF [ ] PETITIONER [X] ATTORNEY FOR PETITIONER)

12. This notice was mailed on *(date)*: February 24, 19   ,at *(place)*: Sacramento   California.
    (Continued on reverse)

NOTE: If this notice is published, print the caption, beginning with the words NOTICE OF PETITION, and do not print the information from the form above the caption. The caption and decedent's name must be printed in at least 8-point type and the text in at least 7-point type. Print the case number as part of the caption. Print items preceded by a box only if the box is checked. Do not print the *italicized* instructions in parentheses, the paragraph numbers, the mailing information, or the material on the reverse.

Form Approved by the
Judicial Council of California
DE 121 (Rev. July 1, 1989)

NOTICE OF PETITION TO ADMINISTER ESTATE
(Probate)

Probate Code § 8100

FIGURE 3–2   Notice of Petition to Administer Estate form

ESTATE OF (NAME):	CASE NUMBER:
KENNETH BELL, also known as KENNETH K. BELL DECEDENT	92457

PROOF OF SERVICE BY MAIL

1. I am over the age of 18 and not a party to this cause. I am a resident of or employed in the county where the mailing occurred.

2. My residence or business address is *(specify)*: 123 Sandor Place, Sacramento, California 95814.

3. I served the foregoing **Notice of Petition** to Administer Estate on each person named below by enclosing a copy in an envelope addressed as shown below AND

   a. [X] depositing the sealed envelope with the United States Postal Service with the postage fully prepaid.

   b. [ ] placing the envelope for collection and mailing on the date and at the place shown in item 4 following our ordinary business practices. I am readily familiar with this business' practice for collecting and processing correspondence for mailing. On the same day that correspondence is placed for collection and mailing, it is deposited in the ordinary course of business with the United States Postal Service in a sealed envelope with postage fully prepaid.

4. a. Date of deposit: February 24, 19   b. Place of deposit *(city and state)*: Sacramento, California

5. [X] I served with the Notice of Petition to Administer Estate a copy of the petition and other documents referred to in the notice.

I declare under penalty of perjury under the laws of the State of California that the foregoing is true and correct.

Date: February 24, 19

..........Marie McFall..................
    (TYPE OR PRINT NAME)

▶ *Marie McFall*
    (SIGNATURE OF DECLARANT)

NAME AND ADDRESS OF EACH PERSON TO WHOM NOTICE WAS MAILED

Kerry Bell
145 Perry Avenue
Sacramento, California 95817

Morton Bell
789 Walter Avenue
Sacramento, California 95820

DE-121 [Rev. July 1, 1989]   **NOTICE OF PETITION TO ADMINISTER ESTATE**   Page two
                                                  (Probate)

FIGURE 3–2 *(continued)*

A statute may direct that notice be given to relatives of the decedent of the first degree, second degree, and so on. The degrees of relationship to the decedent are as follows:

- *First degree*: children and parents

- *Second degree*: brothers, sisters, grandchildren, and grandparents

- *Third degree*: nephews, nieces, aunts, and uncles

- *Fourth degree*: grandnephews, grandnieces, and first cousins

- *Fifth degree*: first cousins once removed

- *Sixth degree*: first cousins twice removed

For the purpose of determining intestate succession, notice should be given when the relationship of parent and child exists between a person and the person's foster parent or stepparent if both of the following requirements are satisfied: "(a) The relationship began during the person's minority and continued throughout the joint lifetimes of the person and the person's foster parent or stepparent and (b) It is established by clear and convincing evidence that the foster parent or stepparent would have adopted the person but for a legal barrier" (Prob. Code § 6454).

Probate Code section 26 reads: "Child' means any individual entitled to take as a child under this code by intestate succession from the parent whose relationship is involved." Probate Code section 1207, however, provides that notice need not be given to a person who may be an heir because of a possible parent-child relationship between a stepchild and a stepparent or between a foster child and a foster parent unless the person required to give notice has actual knowledge of facts that would reasonably lead them to believe that under Probate Code section 6454, the parent-child relationship exists between the stepchild and stepparent or the foster child and foster parent.

The Uniform Probate Code requires that persons who may have an interest in a deceased person's property must be notified (80 AM. JUR. 2D *Wills* § 932). The California Probate Code, however, contains no such provision. The Supreme Court of Georgia, in *McKnight v. Boggs,* 253 Ga. 537, 322 S.E.2d 283 (1984) concluded that persons who could possibly inherit under a different will must be notified. In the *McKnight* case, a prior will had been filed for probate in the same county and the court held that due process had been violated in that it failed to require that notice be given to "propounders and beneficiaries of another purported will of the decedent which [had] been filed previously for probate within the same county."

Before the Hearing

The legal assistant has additional responsibilities before the hearing is held. Briefly, they include:

1. Check that the newspaper has filed its Affidavit of Publication of Notice of Probate of Will.
2. Arrange for proof of will.
3. Prepare an Order for Probate (original and five copies) (Figure 3–3).
4. Prepare an Order Appointing Probate Referee (original and one copy) (Figure 3–4).
5. Prepare the Letters Testamentary or Letters of Administration (original and five copies minimum) (Figure 3–5). One certified copy will be needed for each bank account, safe-deposit box, issuer of securities, and so on.
6. Prepare a Proof of **Subscribing Witness** (Figure 3–6). Affix a photocopy of the will to this form.
7. Notify the representative of the date of the hearing.

The forms listed in numbers 3 through 6 (Figures 3–3 through 3–6) will be needed for the hearings.

Arranging for Proof of Will

In an uncontested proceeding, the will may be admitted to probate on the testimony of one of the subscribing witnesses only, if the evidence shows that the will was executed in all particulars as required by law. Arrangements should be made for the witness or witnesses to appear in court and testify.

Evidence may be received by an affidavit of the witness to which a photographic copy of the will is attached (Proof of Subscribing Witness form) or by an affidavit in the original will that includes or incorporates the attestation clause (Prob. Code § 8220). The latter is called a **self-proving will.**

If no witness is available (within the meaning of Evidence Code section 240), the court may permit proof of the will by proof of the testator's

TERMS

subscribing witness A person who either sees a document signed or hears the signer acknowledge his or her signature, and who signs his or her name to the document to attest to the validity of the document.

self-proving will A will that includes an affidavit and incorporates an attestation clause as part of the will.

ATTORNEY OR PARTY WITHOUT ATTORNEY *(Name and Address)*: TELEPHONE NO.:

ARTHUR ANDREW (916) 447-0923
Attorney at Law
123 Sandor Place
Sacramento, CA 95814
ATTORNEY FOR *(Name)*: Executor

FOR COURT USE ONLY

SUPERIOR COURT OF CALIFORNIA, COUNTY OF SACRAMENTO
STREET ADDRESS: 720 - 9th St.
MAILING ADDRESS:
CITY AND ZIP CODE: Sacramento, CA 95814
BRANCH NAME:

ESTATE OF (NAME):

KENNETH BELL, also known as KENNETH K. BELL
DECEDENT

ORDER FOR PROBATE

ORDER
APPOINTING
- [x] Executor
- [ ] Administrator with Will Annexed
- [ ] Administrator [ ] Special Administrator
- [x] Order Authorizing Independent Administration of Estate
  - [x] with full authority [ ] with limited authority

CASE NUMBER:

92457

1. Date of hearing: Mar. 15, 19 Time: 9:00 a.m Dept/Rm: 17 Judge:

THE COURT FINDS

2. a. All notices required by law have been given.
   b. Decedent died on *(date)*: January 7, 19
      (1) [x] a resident of the California county named above
      (2) [ ] a nonresident of California and left an estate in the county named above
   c. Decedent died
      (1) [ ] intestate
      (2) [x] testate and decedent's will dated: November 15, 1982
          and each codicil dated:
          was admitted to probate by Minute Order on *(date)*: March 15, 19

THE COURT ORDERS

3. *(Name)*: CLARICE BELL
   is appointed personal representative:
   a. [x] Executor of the decedent's will
   b. [ ] Administrator with will annexed
   c. [ ] Administrator
   d. [ ] Special Administrator
      (1) [ ] with general powers
      (2) [ ] with special powers as specified in Attachment 3d
      (3) [ ] without notice of hearing

   and letters shall issue on qualification.

4. a. [x] Full authority is granted to administer the estate under the Independent Administration of Estates Act.
   b. [ ] Limited authority is granted to administer the estate under the Independent Administration of Estates Act (there is no authority, without court supervision, to (1) sell or exchange real property or (2) grant an option to purchase real property or (3) borrow money with the loan secured by an encumbrance upon real property).

5. a. [x] Bond is not required.
   b. [ ] Bond is fixed at: $ to be furnished by an authorized surety company or as otherwise provided by law.
   c. [ ] Deposits of: $ are ordered to be placed in a blocked account at *(specify institution and location)*:
      and receipts shall be filed. No withdrawals shall be made without a court order.

6. [x] *(Name)*: JANE DOE is appointed probate referee.

Date: March 15, 19

7. [0] Number of pages attached:

Raymond McKenna
JUDGE OF THE SUPERIOR COURT

[ ] Signature follows last attachment.

Form Approved by the
Judicial Council of California
DE 140 (Rev. July 1, 1988)

ORDER FOR PROBATE

Probate Code, § 329

FIGURE 3–3 Order for Probate form

ARTHUR ANDREW
123 Sandor Place
Sacramento. CA 95814
(916) 447-0923

Attorney   for Petitioner _____

SUPERIOR COURT OF THE STATE OF CALIFORNIA
FOR THE COUNTY OF SACRAMENTO

Estate of

    KENNETH BELL, also known as
    KENNETH K. BELL,

                              Deceased.

No.   Dept.

ORDER APPOINTING PROBATE REFEREE

ORDER APPOINTING PROBATE REFEREE:

IT IS HEREBY ORDERED, that   JANE DOE,
a duly appointed, qualified and acting   Probate Referee   in and for the County above named, and

a disinterested person   , competent and capable to act,   she   is hereby appointed   referee of

the estate of   Kenneth Bell, aka Kenneth X. Bell   , deceased.

Date .. March 15, 19... ....

Raymond Mc Kenna
Judge of the Superior Court

Local Probate Form P-20
Revised 12-1-87

FIGURE 3–4   Order Appointing Probate Referee

ATTORNEY OR PARTY WITHOUT ATTORNEY *(Name and Address)*:	TELEPHONE NO.:	FOR COURT USE ONLY
ARTHUR ANDREW Attorney at Law 123 Sandor Place Sacramento, CA 95814	(916) 447-0923	

ATTORNEY FOR *(Name)*: Executor

SUPERIOR COURT OF CALIFORNIA, COUNTY OF

STREET ADDRESS: 720 - 9th Street

MAILING ADDRESS:

CITY AND ZIP CODE: Sacramento, CA 95814

BRANCH NAME:

ESTATE OF (NAME):

KENNETH BELL, also known as KENNETH K. BELL

DECEDENT

LETTERS

[x] TESTAMENTARY   [ ] OF ADMINISTRATION

[ ] OF ADMINISTRATION WITH WILL ANNEXED   [ ] SPECIAL ADMINISTRATION

CASE NUMBER: 92457

LETTERS

1. [x] The last will of the decedent named above having been proved, the court appoints *(name)*:

    CLARICE BELL

    a. [x] Executor
    b. [ ] Administrator with will annexed

2. [ ] The court appoints *(name)*:

    a. [ ] Administrator of the decedent's estate
    b. [ ] Special administrator of decedent's estate
        (1) [ ] with the special powers specified in the Order for Probate
        (2) [ ] with the powers of a general administrator

3. [x] The personal representative is authorized to administer the estate under the Independent Administration of Estates Act [x] with full authority [ ] with limited authority (no authority, without court supervision, to (1) sell or exchange real property or (2) grant an option to purchase real property or (3) borrow money with the loan secured by an encumbrance upon real property).

WITNESS, clerk of the court, with seal of the court affixed.

Date: March 15, 19

Clerk, by _R. Sims_ , Deputy

(SEAL)

AFFIRMATION

1. [ ] PUBLIC ADMINISTRATOR: No affirmation required (Prob. Code, § 1140(b)).

2. [x] INDIVIDUAL: I solemnly affirm that I will perform the duties of personal representative according to law.

3. [ ] INSTITUTIONAL FIDUCIARY *(name)*:

    I solemnly affirm that the institution will perform the duties of personal representative according to law. I make this affirmation for myself as an individual and on behalf of the institution as an officer. *(Name and title)*:

4. Executed on *(date)*: February 10, 19___

    at *(place)*: Sacramento, , California.

    Clarice Bell
    (SIGNATURE)

CERTIFICATION

I certify that this document is a correct copy of the original on file in my office and the letters issued the personal representative appointed above have not been revoked, annulled, or set aside, and are still in full force and effect.

(SEAL)

Date: Feb. 10, 19

Clerk, by _R. Sims_
(DEPUTY)

Form Approved by the
Judicial Council of California
DE 150 (Rev. July 1, 1988)

LETTERS
(Probate)

Probate Code, §§ 463, 465, 501, 502, 540
Code of Civil Procedure, § 2015.6

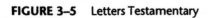

FIGURE 3–5   Letters Testamentary

ATTORNEY OR PARTY WITHOUT ATTORNEY (Name and Address):   TELEPHONE NO.:

— ARTHUR ANDREW   (916) 447-0932
Attorney at Law
123 Sandor Place
Sacramento, CA 95814
ATTORNEY FOR (Name): Executor

SUPERIOR COURT OF CALIFORNIA, COUNTY OF   SACRAMENTO
STREET ADDRESS: 720 - 9th Street
MAILING ADDRESS:
CITY AND ZIP CODE: Sacramento, California 95814
BRANCH NAME:

ESTATE OF (NAME):

KENNETH BELL, also known as KENNETH K. BELL
DECEDENT

FOR COURT USE ONLY

PROOF OF SUBSCRIBING WITNESS
(For decedents dying after December 31, 1984)

CASE NUMBER:
92457

1. I am one of the attesting witnesses to the instrument of which attachment 1 is a photographic copy. I have examined attachment 1 and my signature is on it.

   a. [x] The name of the decedent was signed in the presence of the attesting witnesses present at the same time by
      [x] the decedent personally.
      [ ] another person in the decedent's presence and by the decedent's direction.

   b. [ ] The decedent acknowledged in the presence of the attesting witnesses present at the same time that the decedent's name was signed by
      [ ] the decedent personally.
      [ ] another person in the decedent's presence and by the decedent's direction.

   c. [x] The decedent acknowledged in the presence of the attesting witnesses present at the same time that the instrument signed was decedent's
      [x] will.
      [ ] codicil.

2. When I signed the instrument, I understood that it was decedent's [x] will [ ] codicil.

3. I have no knowledge of any facts indicating that the instrument, or any part of it, was procured by duress, menace, fraud, or undue influence.

I declare under penalty of perjury under the laws of the State of California that the foregoing is true and correct.

Date: February 20, 19

Dallas Throckmorton
(TYPE OR PRINT NAME)

▶ *Dallas Throckmorton*
(SIGNATURE OF WITNESS)

456 Vera St., Sacramento, CA 95816
(ADDRESS)

ATTORNEY'S CERTIFICATION

(Check local court rules for requirements for certifying copies of wills and codicils)

I am an active member of The State Bar of California. I declare under penalty of perjury under the laws of the State of California that attachment 1 is a photographic copy of every page of the [x] will [ ] codicil heretofore presented for probate.

Date: February 20, 19

Arthur Andrew
(TYPE OR PRINT NAME)

▶ *Arthur Andrew*
(SIGNATURE OF ATTORNEY)

Form Approved by the
Judicial Council of California
DE-131 (New January 1, 1985)

PROOF OF SUBSCRIBING WITNESS
(Probate)

FIGURE 3–6   Proof of Subscribing Witness

handwriting and that of any one of the subscribing witnesses or by receipt in evidence either of a "writing in the will bearing the signatures of all subscribing witnesses" or an "affidavit of a person with personal knowledge of the circumstances of the execution" of the will (Prob. Code § 8221).

If none of the subscribing witnesses reside in the county but the deposition of one of them can be taken elsewhere, the court may direct a deposition to be taken. The court may authorize a photographic copy of the will to be made and presented to the witness, and the same questions are asked as if the original will were present (Prob. Code § 8220).

§ 3.5 The Bond

Unless the will requires a bond, if a verified petition for letters testamentary or administration alleges that all beneficiaries have waived in writing the filing of a bond, and written waivers are attached to the petition, the court shall direct that no bond be filed [Prob. Code § 8481(a)].

Probate Code section 8481(b), however, provides that the court, upon its own motion or upon petition of any person interested in the estate, may for good cause require a bond, either before or after letters issue. Special administrators (other than public administrators), unless the will requires a bond, must furnish such a bond if the court so directs (Prob. Code §§ 8542, 8480).

Amount of Bond (Prob. Code § 8482)

If a **surety company** is involved, the approximate value of the property in the estate, the probable annual gross income of the estate, and, if independent administration is granted as to real property, the estimated net proceeds of the real property authorized to be sold under Probate Code section 10400 *et seq.* must be determined in order for the court to fix the amount of the surety bond required. If personal sureties are involved, the bond will be twice the amount required of a surety company. The petitioner signs the application for bond, and arrangements are made with the insurance company for issuance of the bond.

If a bond is given by an admitted surety insurer, the court may establish a fixed minimum amount based on the minimum premium required by

---

TERMS

surety company†   A company engaged in the business of acting as a surety, i.e., one who promises to pay the debt or to satisfy the obligation of another.

the insurer [Prob. Code § 8482(b)]. An additional bond shall be required before confirming the sale of real property [Prob. Code § 8482(c)].

When the representative deposits money or securities in an insured account in a California financial institution, the money may be withdrawn without order of court (Prob. Code § 9700). Money and securities so deposited, including earnings, may be excluded when computing the amount of the bond, or if the amount of the bond is already given or fixed, it may be reduced to a reasonable amount (Prob. Code § 8483).

§ 3.6   Creditors

The procedures discussed in this section apply equally to estate proceedings for an estate of a decedent with or without a will, that is, testate or intestate.

Probate Code sections 9000 through 9304 apply to all proceedings filed on or after July 1, 1988. Proceedings filed before that date are governed by the old law then in effect.

The statutory notice of administration to creditors must be given within four months after the time letters are first issued, except where the personal representative does not learn of the creditor until less than thirty days before the four-month period expires. The personal representative must give notice within thirty days after he or she first has knowledge of the creditor (Prob. Code § 9051).

Notice of administration to the creditors is given as provided in Probate Code section 1215 in addition to publication under Probate Code section 8120 (Prob. Code § 9050; *see*, Prob. Code § 9054). A notice of administration to creditors must be sent to any known creditor. The Judicial Council has a form for this notice (Figure 3–7).

A creditor is "known" if the personal representative is aware that the creditor has demanded payment from the decedent or the estate, as defined in Probate Code section 9050. The personal representative may elect to treat the demand as a claim filed and established by paying the claim before thirty days after the four-month period if the debt is justly due and paid in good faith, the amount is the true amount owing, and the estate is solvent (Prob. Code § 9154). No notice of administration to such a creditor is required (Prob. Code § 9054).

The representative should take reasonable steps to ascertain who the creditors are, and the attorney should notify the client of his or her duty to give statutory notice to creditors as prescribed. This is true even though Probate Code section 9053 states that neither the personal representative nor the attorney for the personal representative is required to make a search for unknown creditors.

NOTICE OF ADMINISTRATION *
OF THE ESTATE OF

_____

(NAME)
DECEDENT

NOTICE TO CREDITORS

1. *(Name)*:
   (Address):

   is the **personal representative** of the **ESTATE OF** *(name)*:   who is deceased.

2. The personal representative **HAS BEGUN ADMINISTRATION** of the decedent's estate in the

   a. **SUPERIOR COURT OF CALIFORNIA, COUNTY OF**
      STREET ADDRESS:
      MAILING ADDRESS:
      CITY AND ZIP CODE:
      BRANCH NAME:

   b. **Case Number** *(specify)*:

3. You must **FILE YOUR CLAIM** with the court clerk (address in item 2a) AND mail or deliver a copy to the personal representative before the later of the following dates as provided in section 9100 of the California Probate Code:

   a. **four months after** *(date)*: [_____], the date letters (authority to act for the estate) were first issued to the personal representative, **OR**

   b. **thirty days after** *(date)*: [_____], the date this notice was mailed or personally delivered to you.

> You may obtain a **CREDITOR'S CLAIM FORM** from any superior court clerk. *(Judicial Council form No. DE-172, Creditor's Claim.)* **A letter is not sufficient.**
> If you use the mail to file your claim with the court, for your protection you should send your claim by certified mail, with return receipt requested. If you mail a copy of your claim to the personal representative, you should also use certified mail.

(Proof of Service on reverse)

* Use this form in estates begun on or after July 1, 1988.

Form Approved by the
Judicial Council of California
DE-157 [New July 1, 1988]

NOTICE OF ADMINISTRATION TO CREDITORS
(Probate)

Probate Code, §§ 9050, 9052

FIGURE 3–7   Notice of Administration to Creditors

[Optional]

PROOF OF SERVICE BY MAIL

1. I am over the age of 18 and not a party to this cause. I am a resident of or employed in the county where the mailing occurred.
2. My residence or business address is *(specify)*:

3. I served the foregoing **Notice of Administration to Creditors** on each person named below by enclosing a copy in an envelope addressed as shown below AND
   a. ☐ **depositing** the sealed envelope with the United States Postal Service with the postage fully prepaid.
   b. ☐ **placing** the envelope for collection and mailing on the date and at the place shown in item 4 following our ordinary business practices. I am readily familiar with this business' practice for collecting and processing correspondence for mailing. On the same day that correspondence is placed for collection and mailing, it is deposited in the ordinary course of business with the United States Postal Service in a sealed envelope with postage fully prepaid.

4. a. Date of deposit: b. Place of deposit *(city and state)*:

   I declare under penalty of perjury under the laws of the State of California that the foregoing is true and correct.

Date:

. . . .   ▶   _____
(TYPE OR PRINT NAME)   (SIGNATURE OF DECLARANT)

NAME AND ADDRESS OF EACH PERSON TO WHOM NOTICE WAS MAILED

DE-157 [New July 1, 1988]   **NOTICE OF ADMINISTRATION TO CREDITORS**   Page two
                                    (Probate)

FIGURE 3–7 *(continued)*

The United States Supreme Court, in *Tulsa v. Pope,* 485 U.S. 478, 491 (1988), stated that "if appellant's identity as creditor was known or 'reasonably ascertainable,' then the Due Process Clause requires that appellant be given '[n]otice by mail or other means as certain to ensure actual notice.'" *Mennonite Board of Missions v. Adams,* 462 U.S. 791, 800 (1983). Probate Code section 9392 implements the rule in the *Tulsa* case, giving creditors, who had no knowledge of estate administration before an order was made for distribution, a remedy against distributees to the extent payment cannot be obtained from the estate. There is a one-year statute of limitations (Code Civ. Proc. § 353). Subdivision (c) of section 9392, however, provides that nothing in the section affects the rights of a purchaser or encumbrancer of property in good faith and for value from a person who is personally liable under the section. It does not require rescission of a distribution already made.

Upon petition by a creditor and notice of hearing pursuant to Probate Code section 1220, the court may allow a claim to be filed after the expiration of the time for filing if the creditor establishes:

1. that neither the creditor nor his or her attorney had actual knowledge of the administration of the estate more than fifteen days before the expiration of the time prescribed by section 9100 and that the creditor's petition was filed within thirty days after either the creditor or his or her attorney had actual knowledge of the administration, whichever occurred first;

2. that neither the creditor nor his or her attorney had knowledge of the existence of the claim more than fifteen days before the expiration of the time provided in section 9100 and that the creditor's petition was filed within thirty days after either the creditor or his or her attorney had knowledge of the existence of the claim, whichever occurred first [Prob. Code § 9103(a)].

It is probably a good idea to include in the account a statement that the personal representative has made every effort to locate and give notice to all reasonably ascertainable creditors along with a description of these efforts. Some courts may require such a statement. Local rules should be checked.

If the personal representative or the attorney for the personal representative gives notice, or fails to give notice, to a creditor in **good faith,**

TERMS

good faith†   The absence of improper motive or of a negligent disregard of the rights of others; the honest and reasonable belief that one's conduct is proper.

the personal representative or the attorney is not liable for giving notice or failing to give notice (Prob. Code § 9053). If the personal representative and the attorney have acted in good faith and the assets of the estate have not been distributed, an after-discovered creditor may still be paid without personal liability on the part of either the personal representative or the attorney. If, however, the creditor establishes that **bad faith** caused him or her to file late and meets the requirement of Probate Code section 9053(b)(2) and (3), the creditor's remedy is not against the estate but against the personal representative or the attorney who acted in bad faith.

A creditor's claim must be supported by an affidavit, and the personal representative may require vouchers of proof (Prob. Code § 9151). Figure 3–8 is the creditor's claim form that has been approved by the Judicial Council.

If the personal representative allows the claim, it is then presented to the judge for approval. If the judge approves the claim, it should be filed within thirty days. Allowance or approval of a claim tolls the statute of limitations as to the part allowed or approved.

If the personal representative rejects the claim, he or she should serve an allowance or rejection of creditor's claim (Figure 3–9), and it is advisable to send this form by certified or registered mail, return receipt requested. Statutes of limitation run on creditors' claims on file from the time of service of the notice of rejection.

If the personal representative or the court or judge, thirty days after the claim is filed, has refused or neglected to act on the claim, the creditor has the option on the thirtieth day of deeming the refusal or neglect as equivalent to a notice of rejection (Prob. Code § 9256).

If the claim is due at the time notice of rejection is given, there is a three-month statute of limitation for filing an action on the claim. If the claim is not due at the time of giving notice of rejection, the statute of limitation is three months after the claim becomes due [Prob. Code § 9353(a)(2); *see also* Prob. Code § 9353(b)].

When an action is pending against the decedent at the time of his or her death, the plaintiff files a claim with the clerk or presents it to the personal representative or administrator within the prescribed period. See Probate Code section 9370 for other requirements relating to such claims.

TERMS

bad faith† A devious or deceitful intent, motivated by self-interest, ill will, or a concealed purpose.

FIGURE 3–8 Creditor's Claim form

ESTATE OF (NAME):	CASE NUMBER:
DECEDENT	

PROOF OF ☐ MAILING ☐ PERSONAL DELIVERY TO CREDITOR

1. At the time of mailing or personal delivery I was at least 18 years of age and not a party to this proceeding.

2. My residence or business address is *(specify)*:

3. I mailed or personally delivered a copy of the **Allowance or Rejection of Creditor's Claim** as follows *(complete either a or b)*:

   a. ☐ **Mail.** I am a resident of or employed in the county where the mailing occurred.
      (1) I enclosed a copy in an envelope AND
         (i) ☐ **deposited** the sealed envelope with the United States Postal Service with the postage fully prepaid.
         (ii) ☐ **placed** the envelope for collection and mailing on the date and at the place shown in items below following our ordinary business practices. I am readily familiar with this business' practice for collecting and processing correspondence for mailing. On the same day that correspondence is placed for collection and mailing, it is deposited in the ordinary course of business with the United States Postal Service in a sealed envelope with postage fully prepaid.
      (2) The envelope was addressed and mailed first-class as follows:
         (i) Name of creditor served:
         (ii) Address on envelope:

         (iii) Date of mailing:
         (iv) Place of mailing *(city and state)*:

   b. ☐ **Personal delivery.** I personally delivered a copy to the creditor as follows:
      (1) Name of creditor served:
      (2) Address where delivered:

      (3) Date delivered:
      (4) Time delivered:

I declare under penalty of perjury under the laws of the State of California that the foregoing is true and correct.

Date:

....
(TYPE OR PRINT NAME OF DECLARANT)

▶ _____
(SIGNATURE OF DECLARANT)

DE-174 [New July 1, 1988] **ALLOWANCE OR REJECTION OF CREDITOR'S CLAIM** Page two
(Probate)

FIGURE 3–8 *(continued)*

ATTORNEY OR CREDITOR WITHOUT ATTORNEY (Name and Address):   TELEPHONE NO.:

EVERLAND FUNERAL CORP.   448-2533
789 Flower St.
Sacramento, CA 95814

FOR COURT USE ONLY

ATTORNEY FOR (Name):

SUPERIOR COURT OF CALIFORNIA, COUNTY OF   SACRAMENTO
STREET ADDRESS: 720 - 9th St.
MAILING ADDRESS:
CITY AND ZIP CODE: Sacramento, CA 95814
BRANCH NAME:

ESTATE OF (NAME):

KENNETH BELL, aka KENNETH K. BELL
DECEDENT

CREDITOR'S CLAIM*
(for estate administration proceedings filed after June 30, 1988)

CASE NUMBER:
92457

You must file this claim with the court clerk at the court address above before the LATER of (a) four months after the date letters (authority to act for the estate) were first issued to the personal representative, or (b) thirty days after the date Notice of Administration was given to the creditor, if notice was given as provided in Probate Code section 9051. Mail or deliver a copy of this claim to the personal representative. A proof of service is on the reverse.

1. Total amount of the claim: $ 1,496.72
2. Claimant (name):
   a. ☐ an individual.
   b. ☒ an individual or entity doing business under the fictitious name of (specify): Everland Funeral Corp.

   c. ☐ a partnership. The person signing has authority to sign on behalf of the partnership.
   d. ☐ a corporation. The person signing has authority to sign on behalf of the corporation.
   e. ☐ other (specify):
3. Address of claimant (specify):
   Everland Funeral Corp., 789 Flower St., Sacramento, CA 95814

4. Claimant is ☒ the creditor ☐ a person acting on behalf of creditor (state reason):

5. ☐ Claimant is ☐ the personal representative ☐ the attorney for the personal representative.
   (Claims against the estate by the personal representative and the attorney for the personal representative must be filed within the claim period allowed in Probate Code section 9100. See the notice box above.)
6. I am authorized to make this claim which is just and due or may become due. All payments on or offsets to the claim have been credited. Facts supporting the claim are ☒ on reverse ☐ attached.

I declare under penalty of perjury under the laws of the State of California that this creditor's claim is true and correct.
Date: March 20, 19—

.George. Moore..........................   ► ~~~George~~~
(TYPE OR PRINT NAME AND TITLE)   (SIGNATURE OF CLAIMANT)

INSTRUCTIONS TO CLAIMANT

A. On the reverse, itemize the claim and show the date the service was rendered or the debt incurred. Describe the item or service in detail, and indicate the amount claimed for each item. Do not include debts incurred after the date of death, except funeral claims.
B. If the claim is not due or contingent, or the amount is not yet ascertainable, state the facts supporting the claim.
C. If the claim is secured by a note or other written instrument, the original or a copy must be attached (state why original is unavailable). If secured by mortgage, deed of trust, or other lien on property that is of record, it is sufficient to describe the security and refer to the date or volume and page, and county where recorded. (See Probate Code section 9152.)
D. Mail or take this original claim to the court clerk's office for filing. If mailed, use certified mail, with return receipt requested.
E. Mail or deliver a copy to the personal representative. Complete the Proof of Mailing or Personal Delivery on the reverse.
F. The personal representative will notify you when your claim is allowed or rejected.

(Continued on reverse)

* See instructions before completing. Use Creditor's Claim form No. DE-170 for estates filed before July 1, 1988.

Form Approved by the
Judicial Council of California
DE-172 (New July 1, 1988)

CREDITOR'S CLAIM
(Probate)

Probate Code, §§ 9000 et seq., 9153

FIGURE 3–9   Allowance or Rejection of Creditor's Claim form

ESTATE OF (NAME): KENNETH BELL, aka KENNETH K. BELL DECEDENT	CASE NUMBER: 92457

FACTS SUPPORTING THE CREDITOR'S CLAIM

☐ See attachment *(if space is insufficient)*

Date of Item	Item and Supporting Facts	Amount Claimed
1/8/89	Basic mortuary service Funeral service charge Honarium (clergy) Certified copies of death certificate Casket (including tax)	$ 340.00 50.00 70.00 24.00 1,012,72
	TOTAL:	1,496.72
	TOTAL	$ 1,496.72

PROOF OF ☒ **MAILING** ☐ **PERSONAL DELIVERY** **TO PERSONAL REPRESENTATIVE**

(Be sure to mail or take the original to the court clerk's office for filing)

1. I am the creditor or a person acting on behalf of the creditor. At the time of mailing or delivery I was at least 18 years of age.
2. My residence or business address is *(specify)*:

Zerlina Oliver, 789 Flower St. Sacramento, CA 95814

3. I mailed or delivered a copy of this Creditor's Claim to the personal representative as follows *(check either a or b below)*:

a. ☒ First-class mail. I deposited a copy of the claim with the United States Postal Service, in a sealed envelope with postage fully prepaid. I used first-class mail. I am a resident of or employed in the county where the mailing occurred. The envelope was addressed and mailed as follows:

(1) Name of personal representative served: Clarice Bell
(2) Address on envelope: c/o Arthur Andrew, Esq., 123 Sandor Place, Sacramento, CA 95814
(3) Date of mailing: March 22, 19—
(4) Place of mailing *(city and state)*: Sacramento, California

b. ☐ Personal delivery. I personally delivered a copy of the claim to the personal representative as follows:

(1) Name of personal representative served:
(2) Address where delivered:

(3) Date delivered:
(4) Time delivered:

I declare under penalty of perjury under the laws of the State of California that the foregoing is true and correct.

Date: March 22, 19 .

...George Moore.......................
(TYPE OR PRINT NAME OF CLAIMANT)

► *Zerlina Oliver*
(SIGNATURE OF CLAIMANT)

DE-172 [New July 1, 1988]

CREDITOR'S CLAIM
(Probate)

Page two

FIGURE 3–9 *(continued)*

Payment of Debts

Certain debts of the decedent have priority for payment over other debts. If an estate does not have sufficient assets to pay all the debts, the debts are paid off in the order of priority, to the extent of funds available, and the remaining debts are not paid (Prob. Code § 11420). If all the debts for which priority is established are paid and there are some assets remaining but not enough to pay all the creditors, the rest of the creditors are paid on a **pro rata** basis.

After payment of required federal and state taxes, the order for priority for payment is established in Probate Code sections 11420 and 11421 as follows:

1. Expenses of administration constitute preferred charges. *In re Jameson's Estate,* 93 Cal. App. 2d 35 (1949). Expenses of administration refers primarily to the costs and expenses of the probate proceeding itself, that is, filing fees, costs of publication, and so on that have arisen from the necessity of probating the estate. *In re Allen's Estate,* 42 Cal. App. 2d 346, 350 (1941) stated:

   "Expenses of administration", within the meaning of the statutes giving preference thereto, now section 950 of the Probate Code, have always been understood as referring primarily to the costs and expenses of the probate proceedings themselves, and which have arisen because of the necessity of probating the estate. Certain obligations are imposed by law upon the administrator, because of which he has been allowed to claim a preference for money he has necessarily expended in preserving the property of the estate, including taxes, assessments, insurance, repairs, cost of necessary assistance, and many other such things. (*Ludwig v. Superior Court,* 217 Cal. 499 [19 Pac. (2d) 984]; *Estate of Smith, supra.*) Such a preference, as an expense of administration, has not been allowed to outsiders who furnished such things without being under an obligation so to do.

2. Funeral expenses are a debt of the estate, not of the decedent. *In re Cornitius's Estate,* 154 Cal. App. 2d 422, 427–428 (1957). The funeral and last illness expenses are proper charges against the decedent's estate. *In re Ockerlander's Estate,* 195 Cal. App. 2d 185, 188 (1961).

3. Expenses of last illness.

─────────────── TERMS ───────────────

pro rata† Means "in proportion to"; proportionately according to the share, interest, or liability of each person.

4. Family allowance.
5. Wage claims.
6. Obligations secured by mortgage, deed of trust, or other **lien**, including but not limited to a judgment lien, in the order of their priority, so far as they may be paid out of the proceeds of the property subject to lien. If proceeds are insufficient, the remaining obligation is classed with general debts.
7. General debts, including judgments not secured by a lien and all other debts not included in a prior class.

Probate Code section 11005 provides that if debts are paid without verified claims allowed and approved, where justly due and paid for in good faith in a solvent estate, the court shall allow the sums so paid. The representative should proceed with caution when paying debts for which claims have not been presented and approved, since he or she could be personally liable for debts paid with estate money. A representative who advances his or her own money is at risk, and the reason for the disbursement should be carefully scrutinized. The courts have held that representatives who advance money to preserve estate property are entitled to be reimbursed from estate assets before ordinary debts and obligations are paid. *In re Smith's Estate*, 16 Cal. App. 2d 239 (1936).

In *Quigley v. Nash,* 1 Cal. 2d 502, 506–507 (1934), the court held that items allowed as general debts against an estate which covered expenditures necessary for the preservation of the property of the estate and which, if made by an administrator regularly appointed to settle the estate, would have been proper charges of administration to be paid in the course of administration without the necessity of any formal claim and before payment of any general or preferred claim, should have been allowed as preferred charges against the estate.

TERMS

lien† A claim or charge on, or right against, personal property, or an encumbrance on real property, for the payment of a debt.

CHAPTER 4

INVENTORY AND APPRAISEMENT

The inventory and appraisement is a very important document in the estate proceeding. Care and attention should be given to it. It is the basic document to which the court looks to determine the value of the estate when it fixes a bond or grants a family allowance. The legal assistant also looks to this document when determining any gain or loss for assets sold.

SIDEBAR

In the estates of decedents dying before June 8, 1981, when the California inheritance tax was repealed, the listing of assets makes it possible for the probate referee to determine the value of the estate and fix any inheritance tax due.

The inventory and appraisement also serves to inform all interested persons of the assets of the estate. Such persons include the heirs, persons taking under the will, beneficiaries under a trust, creditors, and the state controller.

§ 4.1 Time for Filing

Timely filing of the **inventory** is the representative's duty, and the representative should be advised of the requirement and possible consequences. Although the filing of the inventory is the personal representative's duty, in practice the legal assistant probably will be the one to prepare it. The legal assistant should have the date for filing the inventory calendared and make certain that the inventory is actually filed.

The inventory and appraisement form must be prepared and filed with the county clerk within four months after letters are issued to the personal representative, or within such further time as the court may allow [Prob. Code § 8800(b)]. The personal representative may file partial inventories and **appraisals** as appropriate under the circumstances of the case, but all shall be filed before the expiration of the four-month period unless the court allows that further time is reasonable under the circumstances of the particular case [Prob. Code § 8800(b)].

Upon petition, the court may waive appraisal by a referee under Probate Code section 8903. If the market value of certain assets of the estate

---

TERMS

inventory† An itemized list or schedule of assets, property or other articles, sometimes with notations of their value.

appraisal† Valuation; a determination of the worth or value of something.

cannot be readily determined, an appraisal by a probate referee may be required by the court. A hearing on the petition may not be sooner than fifteen days after the petition is filed. Local rules should always be checked also, as some counties such as Los Angeles County, do not permit waiver except under extraordinary circumstances.

Each inventory and appraisement or supplemental inventory and appraisement shall be mailed to anyone requesting special notice under Probate Code section 1250 no later than fifteen days after the inventory and appraisement is filed with the court (Prob. Code § 1252). Since the probate referee needs time to make appraisals within the time limit, the legal assistant should commence the preparation of the inventory at an early date after the appointment of the representative. The referee should be told of any hearing date as soon as it is set.

Under Probate Code section 8804, the personal representative may be held liable for any injury to the estate or any person interested in the estate arising directly from failure to file within the time prescribed. Letters may be revoked by the court.

§ 4.2 Preparation of Inventory

The inventory is prepared from a complete list of assets and financial obligations that is ordinarily furnished by the client, the representative. A separate sheet may be used to list each category, so that if the estate is large enough to require the filing of a federal estate tax (Form 706), the appropriate sheets may be used for both the 706 and the inventory and appraisement. There is no hard-and-fast rule for the listing of categories, but each category and item should be numbered and described in detail.

The inventory and appraisement is prepared and submitted to the referee, complete except for the value of the items the referee must appraise. (*See* Prob. Code § 8901; § 4.3, this chapter.) The legal assistant must be careful not to include for the referee's appraisal any items that may be appraised by the representative, particularly since the fee of the referee is based on the value of the property he or she appraises. The values listed are the values as of the date of death. (Income from real property, bank interest, and dividends accruing after the date of death is *income* to the estate and will be included in the income tax returns.)

The printed inventory and appraisement contains a statement of the attorney regarding bond. Some counties, such as Alameda and Los Angeles counties, require that the inventory contain this statement even if a bond has been waived. The legal assistant should check the local rules.

Complete legal descriptions of real property are required in the document. The legal assistant may have to ask the client for further documentation such as deeds or other legal documents. These documents should be handled and stored with extreme care, since often they are originals.

Separate Property

What is separate property? All property that is not community (or quasi-community) property can be said to be separate property. Generally speaking, **separate property** is property that a person acquires before marriage; during marriage by gift, devise, or bequeath; or after marriage has been terminated by legal separation. Such property is subject to the exclusive control of the spouse who owns it.

Separate property is subject to probate unless it is personal property that can be handled under a summary proceeding, if the value of the assets does not exceed the value prescribed for summary proceedings.

Until 1975, the husband had control of **community property.** Under current law, both husband and wife have management and control of community property. The presumption now is that property standing in the name of the wife alone is community property, and the burden falls on the wife to prove that it is her separate property. Previously, the burden was on the husband.

When it is necessary to trace a certain property because a person, for tax or heirship reasons, wishes to establish the property, the legal assistant can be particularly valuable in searching for written evidence or proof of the intent of the first owner. The question of whether property is community or separate property, however, is a legal concept, the determination of which should be made by the attorney.

Often separate property of the husband and wife becomes so commingled during a marriage that it is impossible to determine which is which. The surviving spouse may no longer be certain of whether the property is separate or community property. Special problems arise when the value of separate property has been enhanced by community services or funds—for example, where the parties use community funds to make improvements on a parcel of real property that is separate property, or where the husband is a general contractor or handyman and remodels a house owned by his wife as separate property. If the properties have become so mixed that they cannot be distinguished, the presumption is that they are community property.

In complex situations in which the parties cannot agree, the party claiming separate property has the **burden of proof.** Considerable expertise may be required to determine whether property is separate or community property. The client should be asked at the outset about the source of all property. The intent of the owner of the property is important, but "[i]t is not necessary to show that the [parties] understood or intended that property traceable to separate property should remain separate." *In re Marriage of Lucas,* 27 Cal. 3d 808, 815 (1980).

Regarding taxes, whether property is separate or community property may not be as important now as it was previously in view of the elimination of California inheritance tax and the changes in federal estate tax laws. The total tax situation of the estate and estate planning, however, may make it important. The surviving spouse will not want to pay any tax on property that is actually his or her separate property but now appears to be part of the community property of the decedent and surviving spouse.

Questions of separate versus community property also arise in dissolutions. The Tax Reform Act of 1984 provides that no gain or loss will be recognized on transfers between spouses or former spouses if transfer was incident to divorce (except for nonresident alien transferees). Transfers made within one year after the divorce are conclusively presumed to be incident to divorce. A transfer is also incident to a divorce if it is "related to the cessation of marriage" [IRC § 1041(c)]. The new rules apply to transfers made after July 18, 1984, unless the transfer was pursuant to an instrument in effect on or before that date and both spouses elect to have the new rules apply.

Gift tax consequences arose under former law, both California and federal, when converting separate property to community property. Certain transfers of real property into joint tenancy did not constitute a gift unless the donors had elected to treat the transfer as a gift. (See former Rev. & Tax. Code §§ 15310, 15104.5; Rev. Rul. 77-359, 1977-2, Cum. Bull. 24; former IRC § 2515.) Now a limited power of appointment over the property must be given to the donor's spouse to constitute a gift (Rev. & Tax Code § 2523).

TERMS

burden of proof†   The duty of establishing the truth of a matter; the duty of proving a fact that is in dispute.

Listing Property

Separate and community property should be segregated in the inventory and appraisement. The list of community property may be preceded by language such as "Decedent's Community Property One-Half Interest in the Following," or each item of community property may be preceded with "an undivided one-half interest in [description of asset]." The listed value would be one-half the total value of that item of community property. The legal assistant should determine whether the attorney has a preference about the manner in which property is listed.

Joint tenancy property is not subject to probate but may be listed in the inventory, in a separate attachment with a heading designating it as joint tenancy property, for appraisal only. This provides an "official" basis for the value of the property at the date of death in the event of a later sale.

Occasionally, although it appears the property is held in joint tenancy, the husband and wife may have had an agreement that the joint tenancy property was community property. The will may confirm the spouse's share of community property to the spouse. Such property should be listed as community property.

Bank account listings should show the date on which interest was last posted or give the "balance at date of death" and state underneath, "Unpaid interest accrued to death" with the amounts. Listing money market accounts, which are now prevalent and for which passbooks often are not issued, may involve getting the numbers of the account and contacting the bank for interest amounts. The decedent's possessions usually include statements from banks indicating numbers of accounts and balances, since monthly statements are issued by most banks and savings and loan associations.

Community Property

If an election is made by the surviving spouse to submit both halves of the community property to probate, there may be a problem with substantiating the statutory fee on the survivor's half. This problem may be solved by an agreement among the parties and attorneys.

Corrected or Amended Inventory

If a mistake is made in the inventory, as in the listing of an asset, a corrected inventory should be filed. The same form may be used by inserting the word *corrected* before the title. Only the correction need be stated. List the item correctly, adding "This is in lieu of" with the incorrect listing.

Supplemental Inventory

If any property is discovered after the inventory is filed, a supplemental inventory must be filed. The property must be appraised within four months after its discovery, or within such further time as the court determines to be reasonable (Prob. Code § 8801). (Local rules should be consulted for this requirement if the newly discovered assets are of nominal value.) The procedure for a supplemental inventory is the same as that for the first inventory, except the box before the word *supplemental* is checked in the title of the form. On the supplemental inventory and appraisement, only the new asset should be listed.

§ 4.3 Valuation of Assets by Personal Representative or Administrator and Probate Referee

Upon appointment of the probate referee by the court, the original and one copy of the inventory and appraisement should be given to the referee. Probate Code section 8901 provides that certain assets of the estate for which the fair market value is readily ascertainable, such as cash items, are to be appraised by the personal representative. Other items for which the fair market value is not readily ascertainable are appraised by the probate referee (Prob. Code § 8902). If cash is the only asset of the estate, an appraisal need not be filed. The inventory will suffice.

The lists below are compiled in part from Probate Code section 8901 and in part from the *Probate Referees' Procedure Guide*, 1994 Revision, available from the Daily Journal Corporation. *The Probate Referees' Procedure Guide* contains other information of interest and value as well as examples of how to list various items.

Personal Representative Appraisal

Attachment 1 lists the property appraised by the personal representative:

- Money and other cash items (such as a check, draft, money order, or similar instrument issued on or before date of decedent's death that can be immediately converted to cash);

- Checks issued after date of decedent's death for wages earned before death;

- Refund checks (including tax and utility refunds and Medicare, medical insurance, and other health care reimbursements and payments);

- Accounts (as defined in Probate Code section 21) in financial institutions (including checking, savings, certificate of deposit, share, multiple capital certificate, and so on);

- Cash deposits and money market funds or accounts, whether in a financial institution or otherwise (including a brokerage cash account);

- Proceeds of life and accident insurance policies and retirement plans and annuities payable on death in lump-sum amounts, even if not paid in a lump sum;

- United States coin and currency in circulation and worth no more than face value;

- Cash dividends declared and payable to shareholder as of a date before the date at which assets are appraised; and

- Social Security and veterans' lump-sum death benefits payable to the estate;

All property not shown in Attachment 1 is to be appraised by the referee.

Referee Appraisal

The items to be appraised by the referee are listed on Attachment 2:

- Cash dividends declared but payable to the shareholder after the date on which assets are to be appraised;

- Bond coupons that mature after the date on which appraisal is to be made;

- Promissory notes and loans, secured and unsecured;

- Accounts receivable;

- Contractual rights to receive money;

- Bonds, stocks, and securities of all types, listed or unlisted (including Treasury notes, bills, and bonds, whether or not they qualify for payment of federal estate taxes);

- Any item not in United States dollars;

- Payments from escrow not closed before the date on which assets are to be appraised;

- Coin collections;

- Cash, cash items, and any other assets that would be appraised by the representative except for the fact that the item is an asset of a partnership, joint venture, trust, or other entity or is an asset of another decedent's estate;

- Right to receive distribution of any assets, including cash, from another estate or trust, judgments, or ongoing litigation;

- Amounts on deposit represented by United States Treasury certificates of indebtedness;

- Amounts on deposit represented by certificates of beneficial interest;

- Insurance proceeds not payable in a lump sum; and

- Insurance annuities.

Completion of Valuation

After the valuation has been completed, if the bond determined at the outset is insufficient, it is the attorney's duty to see that the bond is increased. The legal assistant should be alert to this possibility.

The values fixed by the referee may well be accepted by the Internal Revenue Service as the values for federal estate tax purposes, although the IRS is not bound by the referee's values. This is yet another, and important, reason for giving attention to the inventory and appraisement. It is in this area that the attorney can render invaluable services to the client.

A referee will normally welcome any information the attorney's office can provide by way of background or suggested values where appropriate. The attorney may have a justifiable value in mind. Many attorneys discuss the valuations with the referee. Information on comparable sales in the area may be obtained and offered. An offer already received for the property would be of interest to the referee. The legal assistant can obtain helpful information for the attorney, but because of the importance of the tax consequences, the legal assistant may be well advised not to discuss these matters with the referee directly, at least not in the absence of explicit and express instructions from his or her attorney-employer to do so.

Probate Code section 10309 requires that real property be sold for at least at ninety percent of the appraised value. If the property is to be sold and the appraisal is too high, an adequate bid may not be obtainable, requiring a reappraisal. Now that the California inheritance tax has been eliminated, on the other hand, higher values, for depreciation purposes, on specific bequests of real property that is income property are desirable. If the property is to be sold, however, the stepped-up basis is of primary consideration. These are substantial monetary considerations that the attorney will have in mind.

Valuation of assets other than real property, such as limited partnerships, ongoing businesses, and promissory notes, present special problems in assessing value with which the attorney will be involved and make the final decision. Limited partnerships not publicly traded may take more time to evaluate. If a promissory note is listed, consider whether it is a secure note, apt to be paid, and generating income. A note valued at less than face value, that is, discounted, may not be an acceptable valuation for the Internal Revenue Service. If commercial property must be valued by the referee, income figures for the property will be needed. If there is an automobile, find out its mileage and general condition. Stocks are run through a computer to determine their value. Accrued dividends, that is, dividends that are earned as of the date of death, should appear in the inventory and appraisement. The referee should be given as much information about these items as possible.

Do not fill in amounts of any items the referee is supposed to appraise, or at least use pencil, and do not fill in the total on the first page. Provide the referee with any information you have that would support higher or lower values than those that would be expected.

§ 4.4   Notice of Filing Inventory and Appraisement

The original and a copy of the inventory and appraisement should be filed with the county clerk within four months after issuance of letters to a personal representative (Prob. Code § 8800). At the same time the inventory and appraisement is filed, the personal representative is required to file a certification either that the requirements of section 480 of the Revenue and Taxation Code are not applicable because the decedent did not own any California real property at the time of death or that a change of ownership statement was filed with the county recorder or assessor of each county in California in which the decedent owned property at the time of death [Prob. Code § 8800(d)].

On the filing of an inventory and appraisal (or supplemental inventory and appraisal), a copy should be mailed to each person who has requested special notice pursuant to Probate Code section 1252 (Prob. Code § 8803). Proof of mailing shall be filed with the court.

§ 4.5 Fees of Probate Referee

The probate referee will return the original inventory and appraisement to the attorney, along with a statement of fees for services. As a practical matter, it may be better for the legal assistant to ask the personal representative for a check and then personally forward it to the referee.

The referee's fees are computed as follows (Prob. Code § 8961): one-tenth of one percent of total value of assets appraised (but not less than $75 or more than $10,000 for each estate), plus actual and necessary expenses. The referee is required to file with the inventory a verified account of his or her disbursements.

Upon application of the probate referee, the court may allow a fee in excess of the $10,000 maximum if it determines that the reasonable value of the referee's services exceeds $10,000 (Prob. Code § 8963). Notice of hearing on such an application is given to all persons who have requested special notice, to each known heir and devisee whose interests in the estate are affected, and to the State of California if any portion of the estate escheats to it and its interest in the estate is affected, as provided in Probate Code section 1220 (Prob. Code § 8963).

The percentage fee is based upon only the items appraised by the referee. The value of the items appraised by the personal representative pursuant to Probate Code section 8901 or by an independent expert pursuant to section 8904 are not included in computation of the fee (Prob. Code § 8961). If more than one probate referee appraises or participates in appraisal of property in the estate, each receives the share of the commission agreed upon by them or, absent an agreement, what the court allows, but in no case shall the total commission exceed the maximum allowable for a single referee (Prob. Code § 8964).

The Judicial Council issues a form for inventory and appraisement (see Figure 4–1). On the sample form, the appraisals have been completed. At the time the legal assistant gives the form to the probate referee, the amount for item 2 (total appraisal by referee) will be blank, as will the declaration at the bottom of the page. Attachment 1, containing the items here appraised by the personal representative, will be completed as shown. Attachment 2 will leave the amounts of the appraised values blank to be completed by the referee.

ATTORNEY OR PARTY WITHOUT ATTORNEY *(Name and Address)*:   TELEPHONE NO.:   FOR COURT USE ONLY

ARTHUR ANDREW   (916) 447-0923
Attorney at Law
123 Sandor Place
Sacramento, California 95814

ATTORNEY FOR *(Name)*:

SUPERIOR COURT OF CALIFORNIA, COUNTY OF
STREET ADDRESS: 720 - 9th Street
MAILING ADDRESS:
CITY AND ZIP CODE: Sacramento, California 95814
BRANCH NAME:

ESTATE OF (NAME):
KENNETH BELL, also known as KENNETH K. BELL
[X] DECEDENT   [ ] CONSERVATEE   [ ] MINOR

INVENTORY AND APPRAISEMENT

[ ] Complete   [X] Final
[ ] Partial No.:   [ ] Supplemental
[ ] Reappraisal for Sale

CASE NUMBER:
92457

Date of Death of Decedent or of Appointment of Guardian or Conservator:

APPRAISALS

1. Total appraisal by representative (attachment 1) .... $ 184,301.00
2. Total appraisal by referee (attachment 2) .... $
   TOTAL: $

DECLARATION OF REPRESENTATIVE

3. Attachments 1 and 2 together with all prior inventories filed contain a true statement of
   [X] all [ ] a portion of the estate that has come to my knowledge or possession, including particularly all money and all just claims the estate has against me. I have truly, honestly, and impartially appraised to the best of my ability each item set forth in attachment 1.
4. [ ] No probate referee is required [ ] by order of the court dated *(specify)*:

I declare under penalty of perjury under the laws of the State of California that the foregoing is true and correct.
Date: April 15, 19—

..... Clarice Bell .....   ▶ *Clarice Bell*
(TYPE OR PRINT NAME) (Include title if corporate officer)   (SIGNATURE OF PERSONAL REPRESENTATIVE)

STATEMENT REGARDING BOND
(Complete if required by local court rule)

5. [X] Bond is waived.
6. [ ] Sole personal representative is a corporate fiduciary.
7. [ ] Bond filed in the amount of: $ [ ] Sufficient [ ] Insufficient
8. [ ] Receipts for: $ have been filed with the court for deposits in a blocked account
   at *(specify institution and location)*:

Date: April 15, 19   ▶ *Arthur Andrew*
                                      (SIGNATURE OF ATTORNEY OR PARTY WITHOUT ATTORNEY)

DECLARATION OF PROBATE REFEREE

9. I have truly, honestly, and impartially appraised to the best of my ability each item set forth in attachment 2.
10. A true account of my commission and expenses actually and necessarily incurred pursuant to my appointment is
    Statutory commission: $
    Expenses *(specify)*: $
    TOTAL: $

I declare under penalty of perjury under the laws of the State of California that the foregoing is true and correct.
Date:

                                      ▶
..... Milton Schwinn .....
(TYPE OR PRINT NAME)   (SIGNATURE OF REFEREE)

(Instructions on reverse)

Form Approved by the
Judicial Council of California
DE-160, GC-040 (Rev. January 1, 1985)

INVENTORY AND APPRAISEMENT
(Probate)

Prob C 600-611,
2610-2616

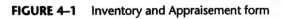

FIGURE 4–1   Inventory and Appraisement form

ESTATE OF:
KENNETH BELL, also known as
KENNETH K. BELL, Deceased.

CASE NUMBER
92457

ATTACHMENT NO: 1

(IN DECEDENTS' ESTATES, ATTACHMENTS MUST CONFORM TO PROBATE CODE 601
REGARDING COMMUNITY AND SEPARATE PROPERTY)

PAGE . 1 . OF . 2 . TOTAL PAGES
(ADD PAGES AS REQUIRED)

DECEDENT'S COMMUNITY PROPERTY ONE-HALF INTEREST IN THE FOLLOWING:

Item No.	Description		Appraised value
1.	Cash found in possession of decedent	1/2	$ 258.25
2.	Cash in Cash Management Account #2345 at Pacific Savings Bank, Main Street, Sacramento, California	1/2	90,000.00
3.	Savings account No. 2-022705-8, Atlantic Savings & Loan Association, Main Street, Sacramento, California	1/2	85,000.00
4.	2-1/2 Year T-Note Certificate #061-00581-4, 12%, Better Future Savings and Loan Association, 700 L Street, Sacramento, California	1/2	9,042.75
	TOTAL ATTACHMENT ONE:		$184,301.00

Form Approved by the
Judicial Council of California
Effective January 1, 1976

INVENTORY AND APPRAISEMENT (ATTACHMENT)

Prob C 481.
800-805, 784.
1550, 1901

FIGURE 4-1 *(continued)*

ESTATE OF.

CASE NUMBER
92457

ATTACHMENT NO:

(IN DECEDENTS' ESTATES. ATTACHMENTS MUST CONFORM TO PROBATE CODE 601
REGARDING COMMUNITY AND SEPARATE PROPERTY)

PAGE **2** OF **2** TOTAL PAGES
(ADD PAGES AS REQUIRED)

DECEDENT'S SEPARATE PROPERTY:

Item No.	Description		Appraised value
1.	One yellow gold diamond ring		$ 9,000.00
2.	Single family dwelling located at 9020 Boykin Way, Sacramento, described as the West 59.00 feet of the East 590.00 feet of Lot 1248, as shown on the "Plat of Elvira," recorded in the office of the County Recorder, January 23, 1909, in Book 8 of Maps, Map No. 41		
	Assessor's Parcel No. 006-174-0200		150,000.00

DECEDENT'S COMMUNITY PROPERTY ONE-HALF INTEREST
IN THE FOLLOWING:

3.	Two original oil paintings by Matt Bonnett	1/2	3,000.00
4.	1985 Mercedes 450 SL Engine No. LSO58C807	1/2	22,000.00
5.	1984 Lincoln Continental, Engine No. 7538042	1/2	10,000.00
6.	Household furniture, furnishings and personal effects located at 145 Perry Avenue, Sacramento, California	1/2	1,750.00
7.	5,000 shares AT&T 5% preferred stock (CUSIP No. 030177)	1/2	72,000.00
	Accrued but unpaid dividends	1/2	6,000.00
8.	1,000 shares Pacific Gas and Electric Co. common stock, par $10 each ((CUSIP 694308)	1/2	5,000.00
	Accrued but unpaid dividends	1/2	900.00
9.	Personal resience located at 145 Perry Avenue, Sacramento, County of Sacramento, California, more particularly described as follows:		
	Lot 9 on that map entitled "Plat of Deodora Ridge," as recorded in Book 6 of Maps at Page 8, Official Records of Sacramento County, California		
	Assessor's Parcel No. 006-290-0200	1/2	145,000.00

TOTAL ATTACHMENT 2: $424,650.00

Form Approved by the
Judicial Council of California
Effective January 1, 1976

INVENTORY AND APPRAISEMENT (ATTACHMENT)

Prob C 481.
600-605, 784.
1550, 1901

FIGURE 4-1 *(continued)*

§ 4.6 Objections to Inventory and Appraisement

Under Probate Code section 8906, any interested person may file a written objection to the appraisement with the court. This can be done at any time prior to the hearing on the petition for final decree of distribution. The clerk fixes a date for hearing on the objection that is not less than fifteen days after it is filed.

The objecting person must give notice of the hearing, together with a copy of the objection, to the persons and in the manner provided by Probate Code section 1220. The notice must be accompanied by a copy of the objection. If the probate referee made the appraisement, a copy of the objection also must be mailed to him or her at least fifteen days before the time set for the hearing. The person objecting has the burden of proof.

Probate Code section 11000 also makes provision for any person interested in an accounting filed in an estate to contest the same, including the value of assets shown on the inventory and appraisement.

CHAPTER 5

ACCOUNTING AND CLOSING THE ESTATE

One of the major complaints of the lay public is that it takes too long to probate an estate. Typically, heirs and beneficiaries eagerly await the distribution. Certain procedural steps require a minimum of time to lapse. More time might be required where there is an ongoing business, sales to be made, or other problems. An estate can be very complicated. Large estates are apt to require more work and time. But too often the delays are not unavoidable. An estate should be closed as soon as it is ready. The legal assistant can help to prevent delays.

§ 5.1 When to Close the Estate

A section in the Probate Code (first enacted as section 1025.5 in 1976 and now section 12200), applicable only to estates of persons dying on or after January 1, 1977, provides that a personal representative shall either petition for an order for final distribution of the estate or make a report of status of administration no later than one year after the date of issuance of letters in an estate for which a federal estate tax return is not required, or no later than eighteen months if a federal estate tax return is required. When such a report is filed, the court may either require the filing of the petition for final distribution or permit administration to continue upon specified terms and conditions, including an account under Probate Code section 10950.

Section 12200 of the Probate Code provides that if a personal representative does not petition for final distribution or make a report when required, the court may, on petition of any interested person or on its own motion, cite the personal representative to appear before the court and show the condition of the estate and the reasons why the estate cannot be distributed and closed. On hearing the citation, the court may order the administration of the estate to continue or order the personal representative to file a petition for final distribution. Legal assistants and attorneys should be mindful of this section and prevent its application to the estates they are handling.

Continuation of an estate to pay a family allowance is not in the best interests of the estate or interested persons except under the conditions specified in section 12203.

The determination of whether the estate is in proper condition to be closed requires a complete review of the file. The legal assistant or probate administrator should have developed and maintained some kind of customized checklist of the various documents and procedures required in the estate. The first step would be to review this checklist.

§ 5.2 Preliminary Distribution

A preliminary distribution of an estate may be made even though the estate is not in a condition to be finally closed and distributed. Probate Code sections 11620 *et seq*. permit a preliminary distribution of an estate, after notice and hearing, when two months have elapsed after the first issuance of letters to a general personal representative.

Preliminary distribution may be made with or without bond, as the court determines. If the court orders distribution before four months have elapsed after letters are first issued, the court must require a bond. After four months have elapsed, the court may require a bond. The bond required is given by the distributee, filed with the court, and conditioned on payment of the distributee's proper share of the debts of the estate, not exceeding the amount distributed.

No more than an aggregate of fifty percent of the net value of the estate, as defined, may be distributed under Probate Code section 11623(b), although this section is not the exclusive means by which the representative may make preliminary distribution.

In a proceeding under the Independent Administration of Estates Act, notwithstanding Probate Code section 1220(f), the court may not dispense with notice unless the time for filing creditors' claims has expired. No loss to creditors or injury to the estate or any interested party can occur as a result of a preliminary distribution. There should be no question about the sufficiency of funds to pay all creditors. Ordinarily a preliminary distribution is not attempted if the estate is heavily indebted.

Before any kind of distribution is made, the will should be read very carefully to make certain there is no survivorship limitation of thirty days or more. No distribution should be made if the survivorship period has not expired.

Distribution may be a practical solution, but the risk of criticism is always present if some dispute arises about the items in question. Any contest of the will, however, would have been filed before the hearing on the petition for probate.

The inventory and appraisement must be on file. The financial condition of the estate usually can be summarized to show the court the condition of the estate without a formal accounting. If a bank is the fiduciary, an interim account is more apt to be filed.

If the estate is going to be liable for a federal estate tax, the tax should either have been paid or the petition should make it evident that there is plenty of cash available to pay the tax.

Frequently preliminary distribution is made to a decedent's surviving spouse or children upon their request. Sometimes property distributed is property that was specifically bequeathed so there is no question about who will ultimately receive it. Distribution of the residual of the estate is not ordinarily requested, and a court is not likely to permit such distribution. Such a distribution has income tax consequences because the distributee rather than the estate then has to pay the income tax on the money distributed.

When a preliminary distribution is made, a receipt from any distributee should be obtained. The recipient acknowledges having received the property, but with no claim of title. This is sometimes called a **bailee's receipt**. The written receipt is necessary for proof of delivery.

One reason for preliminary distribution may be security. Art objects, antiques, paintings, and so on may have substantial intrinsic value and should be removed from the house for security reasons.

The tax situation of the estate and of persons to whom preliminary distribution is to be made should be reviewed before distribution is made. There may be tactical advantages in using a preliminary distribution. An elderly person may prefer to have the money earlier. In some instances, a distribution may avoid controversy or litigation against the estate, which would be costly. For instance, if distribution can be made to a beneficiary who is not happy, then he or she is not in a position to ask the court to cite the personal representative under Probate Code section 12202 to appear and show cause why the estate cannot be distributed or closed, thereby avoiding the necessity of filing a status report pursuant to section 12200. On the other hand, if the client is a beneficiary rather than the personal representative, a petition under 12202 provides a weapon against the estate.

In considering a preliminary distribution, Internal Revenue Code section 2032(a) is of importance. If property is distributed within six months after the death of the decedent, that property must be valued as of the date of distribution. Property not distributed, sold, exchanged, or otherwise disposed of within six months after death shall be valued as of a date six months after the decedent's death. It may not be desirable to have the remainder of the estate fixed at a value as of the alternate valuation date (that is, six months after death). If the representative has performed some discretionary acts, an early review by the court will decide any issue regarding those acts.

TERMS

---

bailee's receipt† An acknowledgment in writing from the person to whom money or property is entrusted that such money or property has been received.

§ 5.3   Tax Aspects of Distribution

The tax effects of distribution are of primary importance. The estate is a separate tax entity and subject to income tax rates that may be at a lower level than those of the distributees. If a partial distribution is made, the income tax liability of the estate is reduced. Information about the income tax brackets of the distributees should be obtained to the extent feasible during the fact-gathering stage. An explanation of the monetary significance of this information should suffice to overcome any reluctance on their part. The tax aspects of distribution can be extremely complicated and require utmost care and consideration. Effort must be made to please all the beneficiaries, even though it may not be possible. If the client is the personal representative, it is important to see that he or she fulfills the duties of the fiduciary to protect himself or herself from any claim.

The choosing of an accounting period should be carefully considered from a tax standpoint.

§ 5.4   Final Accounting and Petition for Distribution

Under Probate Code section 10950, the court, on its own motion or on petition of an interested person, may order an account at any time. The court shall order an account on the petition of an interested person made more than one year after the last account was filed or, if no account was previously filed, more than one year after issuance of letters to the personal representative. The court order shall specify the time within which the personal representative must file an account.

Probate Code section 11001 makes provision for any person interested in an accounting filed in an estate to contest the same, including the value of assets shown on the inventory and appraisement. A creditor who has not been paid may petition for an account under section 10954(c)(2). If an item appears in the inventory, it must be accounted for in the final account either by showing the cash from its sale, or any gain or loss from the sale, or as an item to be distributed.

Ordinarily, if an estate is not expected to be kept open for an extended period of time, the representative will wait and file the final account and petition for distribution when the estate is ready to be closed. This is more economical for the estate. Such a wait may be inadvisable, however, if the administration is to be protracted and beneficiaries or others involved in the estate are critical of the representative. In such cases, an interim account may have to be filed.

Probate Code section 10951 says that the personal representative shall file a final account and petition for order of final distribution when the estate is in a condition to be closed. Failure to take the appropriate steps to prepare an estate for closing, or to close the estate when it is ready, is a major cause of client dissatisfaction, not to mention the dissatisfaction of the heirs who await distribution.

In the event an estate is not quite ready to close within a year of the date of issuance of letters, the court is not likely to expect an accounting to be filed and then, say a couple months later, another accounting and petition for final distribution. If the estate is ready for distribution at the end of a year, a first and final account and report of the representative along with the petition for distribution can be prepared at the same time, in one document.

The petition should have a full title that covers all relief sought in the petition. The Los Angeles Probate Policy Memorandum (and the City and County of San Francisco) requires that the caption of petitions be all-inclusive as to the relief sought in the petition so the matter may be properly calendared and posted and filing fees, if any, may be determined. If any part of the estate is to be distributed to a trust, the caption must so indicate. The calendar department is not required to read the body of the petition or the prayer to determine the adequacy of the posting.

The Sacramento County Probate Policy Manual requires that papers presented for filing conform to the California Rules of Court section 201. Figure 5–1 is a sample caption. See Appendix A for a sample of a complete Final Account.

Waiver of Accounting

An account is not required when all persons entitled to distribution of the estate meet certain conditions specified in Probate Code section 10954, as where the person has executed and filed a written waiver of account or a written acknowledgment that the person's interest has been satisfied or adequate provision has been made for satisfaction in full of the person's interest. This provision does not apply to a **residuary devisee** or

---

TERMS

residuary devisee†   The beneficiary of a devise by a testator of the remainder of his or her real property.

```
ARTHUR ANDREW
Attorney at Law
123 Sandor Place
Sacramento, CA 95814
Telephone:  (916)

Attorney for Executor




                    SUPERIOR COURT OF CALIFORNIA

                       COUNTY OF SACRAMENTO




Estate of KENNETH BELL,    )   No. 92457        Dept. No. 17
also known as              )
KENNETH K. BELL,           )   FIRST AND FINAL ACCOUNT AND
                           )   PETITION FOR STATUTORY EXECUTOR'S
          Deceased.        )   COMMISSION AND ATTORNEY'S STATU-
                           )   TORY AND EXTRAORDINARY FEES, FOR
                           )   APPROVAL OF PRELIMINARY DISTRIBU-
                           )   TION, AND FOR FINAL DISTRIBUTION
                           )
                           )
_____)
```

FIGURE 5–1 Caption of final account

a devisee whose interest in the estate is subject to **abatement**, payment of expenses, or accrual of interest or income. Other provisions are found in the same section for a person entitled to distribution who is a minor, conservatee, trustee, incapacitated, unborn, whose identity or address is unknown, or who is in a designated class of persons unascertained or not

TERMS

abatement† The process of determining the distribution of the assets left by a deceased in his or her will when the assets are insufficient to satisfy all the bequests made in the will.

in being, where a **guardian ad litem** has been appointed to represent that person.

Sometimes the executor is the only beneficiary of the entire estate, in which event an accounting is apt to be waived. Where the accounting is waived, the personal representative must file a report at the time the final account otherwise would have been required, showing the amount of fees or commission paid or payable to the personal representative and to the attorneys, and setting forth the basis for determining that amount [Prob. Code § 10954(c)(1)].

The Account

The legal assistant should check the local rules to determine the form required for the account. The Sacramento County Probate Rules section 15.60 requires that every account contain receipts, gains on sales, disbursements, losses on sales, other credits, and a detailed list of property on hand. The schedule of receipts and disbursements shall show the nature or purpose of each item and the date thereof, the identity of the payor or payee, and the amount received or disbursed. Interaccount transfers or capital changes should not be reflected as receipts or disbursements. Each account is also to contain a recapitulation or summary in substantially the form in Figure 5–2.

San Francisco and Los Angeles counties use virtually the same form for the summary of account.

There are two basic types of accounts. One is called a categorized account and the other a chronological account (with some variations). In the **categorized account**, the receipts are grouped together into categories, such as rental receipts, stock dividends, and interest, and the disbursements are likewise grouped into categories such as mortgage payments, nursing bills, doctor bills, and so on. The summary of account makes a general breakdown necessary. In a larger estate, the categorization method is apt to be the preferred one. The **chronological account**, on the other hand, is perhaps more common, easier to maintain, and makes the estate more understandable. The chronological account contains a list of each receipt with the amount, the date, and the source and a list of disburse-

---

TERMS

guardian ad litem† A person appointed by the court to represent and protect the interests of a minor or an incompetent person during litigation.

categorized account An account in which receipts are grouped together by category, not chronology.

chronological account An account that lists receipts in the order in which payments are made, not by category.

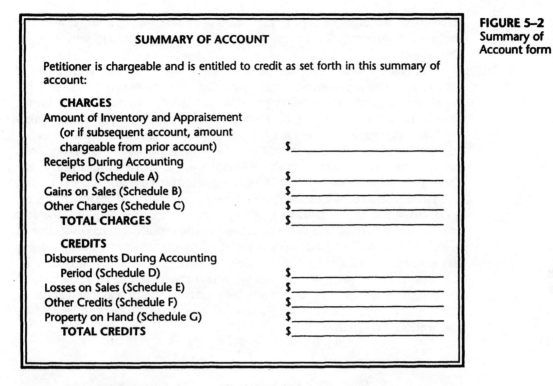

SUMMARY OF ACCOUNT

Petitioner is chargeable and is entitled to credit as set forth in this summary of account:

CHARGES

Amount of Inventory and Appraisement
(or if subsequent account, amount
chargeable from prior account) $_____

Receipts During Accounting
Period (Schedule A) $_____

Gains on Sales (Schedule B) $_____

Other Charges (Schedule C) $_____

  TOTAL CHARGES $_____

CREDITS

Disbursements During Accounting
Period (Schedule D) $_____

Losses on Sales (Schedule E) $_____

Other Credits (Schedule F) $_____

Property on Hand (Schedule G) $_____

  TOTAL CREDITS $_____

FIGURE 5–2
Summary of
Account form

ments that shows each payee and the date payment was made. The account can be a combination of the two forms. Types of receipts can be grouped together under categories such as rents, interest on savings, and miscellaneous, and disbursements under headings such as creditors' claims, debts of decedent paid, miscellaneous administrative expenses, expenses of maintaining the home, expenses of sale of the home, expenses of sale paid out of escrow, mortgages and liens, and expenses of the apartment house.

The chronological account is in all probability easier to prepare. Errors creep in more readily when the list has to be taken apart and put together again, and the errors may be difficult to find. But the categorized account readily shows the amount spent for a particular type of expense if that is of particular interest or concern. For example, if a parcel of property is bequeathed to a specific heir or beneficiary and the expenses incurred in connection with that property are to be subtracted to determine the net to the recipient, this is more readily done by the categorized account. The categorized account should include the date of each payment, the amount paid, and the name of the payee, the same as the chronological account.

Monthly rents from the same person may be grouped together. Shares of stock received as dividends or because of a stock split are not included as income. Receipts of a principal should be shown separately, and not

as income. Receipts of a principal should be shown separately, and not included as income. Sales receipts are recorded as principal, with gain or loss reported.

The type of account chosen may depend upon the preference of the attorney or the representative or upon the type of records kept. In both types of accounts, the credits and charges must balance, which is not always easy to do. If the representative keeps the books and makes mistakes, the legal assistant may spend an undue amount of time balancing the account. Occasionally a representative mingles his or her own funds with estate funds. For these reasons, in most cases it is preferable that the legal assistant rather than the representative maintain the books.

The account tells the court about the financial transactions that have occurred since the inception of the estate proceeding or since the last account if more than one account is filed in the estate. The account should reveal all that has occurred in the estate—any transfers from an account, any conversion of assets. The account also contains a petition for settlement of the account, for fees, and for authority to distribute the estate to the beneficiaries. In the event of an interim account, such as a first account current and report, any partial payment of commissions and fees to be made should be included.

§ 5.5 Accounts—Contents

There is no model form that can be copied and changed to produce the account, but form books are useful for determining the appropriate language. Each account is different. The following checklist provides a sample of some of the types of paragraphs that might be needed in an account:

- Intestacy, where there is no will;

- Distribution to nonresidents;

- Conditions subsequent;

- **Uniform Gifts to Minors Act;**

- Disclaimer of interest;

TERMS

Uniform Gifts to Minors Act†   A uniform law that allows gifts of money and securities to be made the subject of a transfer to a custodian for the benefit of a minor.

- Income received during administration from property not specifically devised or bequeathed;

- Partial allowance of statutory compensation;

- Preliminary distribution;

- For estates of decedents dying before June 9, 1982, California inheritance taxes;

- No creditors' claims were filed;

- No federal estate tax return was filed;

- Total tax liability;

- Prorated estate tax; and

- Reserve for taxes.

The paragraph for the last entry, for instance, might read something like: "The executor is hereby authorized and directed to retain a fund of Sixteen Thousand Dollars ($16,000) to secure the payment of possible federal estate taxes and expenses relevant thereto until all matters relating to the determination and payment of said taxes and expenses have been completed."

Check a California forms book to determine which of these paragraphs and others needed.

Exhibit A—Account

This consists of the summary of account that appears in the first part of the account. The totals are taken from the schedules that follow.

Schedule A—Receipts

This is a listing of all receipts received by the executor since the date of the decedent's death, for example, receipts for rent, interest on savings, health insurance claims, Social Security, and refunds. The inventory should be checked against the schedule of receipts.

The interest accruing up to the date of death should have been determined at that time, so the interest received and listed here is only the interest that has accrued since the date of death. A problem can arise here, however, if the executor did not determine the interest that was payable at the date of death. By the time an executor is appointed, there has been a lapse of time, and the amount of interest accrued by the time of appointment is higher than that at the date of death. Passbooks should be taken to the banks or savings and loan associations for updating at the time of the accounting.

Principal collected must be differentiated from interest collected or a duplication will occur and the account will not balance. Any item listed in the inventory necessarily remains an item of principal.

Schedule B—Gain on Sale

A gain or loss arises when the appraised value in the inventory differs from the sale price. If a home is appraised at $96,000, for example, that is the value shown in the inventory. If the house is sold for $122,500, a gain of $26,500 is shown in Schedule B. If the house is sold for $80,000, a loss of $16,000 is shown. A gain or loss is added to or subtracted from the value of the estate and changes the amount on which the statutory fees are based. For instance, in the event of a gain, there are expenses of sale that are deductible for income tax purposes. On the sale of a home, there are not apt to be deductions for depreciation, unless part of the home was used as an office or at some time the home was rented, but on an apartment house or commercial property sale, depreciation taken affects the net gain or loss.

Schedule C—Disbursements

The disbursements consist of all sums paid out by the representative, including creditors' claims approved by the representative and the court debts of the decedent, miscellaneous administrative expenses, expenses incurred in connection with a residence of the decedent, expenses of sales, mortgages paid off, real property taxes, and any other such sums.

Debts owed to the United States or the State of California are to be given preference under both federal and state laws. Probate Code section 11420 lists the order of priority in which the remaining debts of the decedent shall be paid as follows:

1. Expenses of administration.
2. Funeral expenses.
3. Expenses of last illness.
4. Family allowance.
5. Wage claims.
6. Obligations secured by a mortgage or deeds of trust and other liens, in the order of their priority, so far as they may be paid out of the proceeds of the encumbered property. If the proceeds are insufficient, the unsatisfied part of the debt shall be classed with the general demands against the estate.
7. General debts, including judgments that are not liens and all other debts not included in a prior class.

The personal representative first must retain enough money to pay the expenses of administration, then he or she must pay the funeral expenses, the expenses of the last illness, any family allowance, and wage claims. At that point, the personal representative need not pay any other debt or legacy until ordered to do so by the court (Prob. Code § 11422).

The funeral expenses and expenses of last illness are deemed to be debts payable out of the estate of the deceased spouse rather than being charged to the community share of a surviving spouse, without regard to the financial circumstances of the surviving spouse and the liability of the surviving spouse or any other person (Prob. Code § 11446). If the expenses of the last illness are taken on the 706, only one-half may be taken, but if an election is made to take them on the income tax return and the return is a joint return of the decedent and the surviving spouse, all of them may be taken. (See Rev. Rul. 78–242, IRB 1978–25.)

Schedule D—Property on Hand

Schedule D consists of property on hand at the date of preparation of the account. The legal assistant should verify all the items, and the items should be listed in the same order in which they appear in the inventory and appraisement.

Schedule E—Property Distributed

This lists any property that has been distributed out of the estate such as furniture, furnishings, automobiles, clothing, furs, and jewelry. In this schedule, the items are listed individually in the order in which they appear in the inventory and appraisement, and using the same valuations.

Other Schedules

The legal assistant should check the local probate rules of the county in which the estate is pending for any other schedules that may be required.

Other Credits

This schedule is necessary when property listed in the inventory is no longer in the estate and is not accounted for by a sale or otherwise. **Homestead property** may have been distributed to a surviving spouse, or

---

TERMS

homestead property† Real property that is free and clear of the claims of creditors, provided the owner occupies the property as his or her home; the place of residence of the family.

there may have been a property loss by fire or flood not covered by insurance. The estate may have been sued for, and lost, a parcel of property that was in the inventory.

Other Expenses

Travel and other expenses made for the preservation of the estate are allowable. Travel expenses for carrying on business are allowed after a personal representative or special administrator is appointed.

Expenses of the personal representative reasonably necessary to administer the estate, such as repairs to property, accountant's services beyond ordinary business, and sometimes office expenses, are allowable.

Any debt of a personal representative to the decedent must be accounted for, whether paid or unpaid.

Schedule—Creditors' Claims

The representative should file a creditor's claim if he or she paid the expenses of the last illness and the funeral, "especially if he [or she] is not the sole distributee and others may object to payment without approval."

The representative may wish to list unverified claims presented (for example, bills or statements) as a separate category.

Some attorneys think that if the account is prepared by a professional fiduciary, such as a bank experienced in this type of accounting, there is no need to check the account. Since banks ordinarily are not expected to make mistakes, reliance on the accuracy of the accounting may prove safe. It is more prudent, however, to fully review the account and the accuracy of the figures. The schedules should add up, and the account should be in balance. The manner in which the account is computed and presented also should be considered. If there is an error of any kind, it is better for everyone if it is discovered before presentation to the court, while there is still an opportunity to correct it. The experienced legal assistant can be of great assistance in checking the account.

§ 5.6   Compensation

Four months after issuance of letters, a personal representative or an attorney who has rendered services to an executor or administrator may petition the court for an allowance upon fees. Notice of such a petition must be served fifteen days before the hearing pursuant to Probate Code section 1220.

Ordinary Fees

In most cases, both the executor's or administrator's fee and the attorney's fee are requested in the final account and petition for distribution. The executor's or administrator's compensation is currently computed the same as the attorney's fee, pursuant to Probate Code section 10800, as follows. Of the amount of the estate accounted for:

First	$15,000	4%
Next	$85,000	3%
Next	$900,000	2%
Next	$9,000,000	1%
Next	$15,000,000	1/2%
Above	$25,000,000	Reasonable amount to be determined by the court

The estate accounted for includes the total amount of inventory, plus gains over appraisal value on sales, plus receipts, less losses on sales, and without regard to encumbrances or other obligations on property and whether or not a sale has taken place. For example, if a piece of real property is inventoried at a value of $400,000, the fee is figured on its value of $400,000 without subtracting the amount of any mortgage on the property. If a sale of the property were made, the mortgage would have been paid off. For instance, if the mortgage was for $200,000 and, without regard to other charges, the property netted $200,000, the fee would be computed on the $400,000 value. (This fee may be justifiable. A mortgage can mean more time and work.)

The above schedule is not applicable if the personal representative's compensation is provided for in the will or if he or she renounces compensation. The compensation provided by the will shall be the full and only compensation for the services of the attorney unless the attorney petitions the court to be relieved from the provisions of the will. The court may order an amount greater than that provided by the will. Any agreement for higher compensation entered into between the personal representative and the attorney, however, is void (Prob. Code § 10831).

The court is to apportion the amount paid to the attorneys for the personal representative according to the services rendered by each attorney or as otherwise agreed to by the attorneys.

Sacramento County (Probate Policy Manual section 706) recommends a schedule in substantially the form shown in Figure 5–3.

FIGURE 5–3
Schedule of Fees
and
Commissions

AMOUNT OF ESTATE ACCOUNTED FOR AND COMPUTATION OF STATUTORY FEES AND COMMISSIONS		
Amount of Estate Accounted for		
Inventory and Appraisement	$	
Receipts During Accounting Period (Schedule A)	$	
Gains on Sales (Schedule B)	$	
TOTAL	$	
Losses on Sales (Schedule D)	$	
TOTAL	$	
Computation of Statutory Fees and Commissions		
Four percent (4%) on $15,000	$	600.00
Three percent (3%) on $85,000	$	2,550.00
Two percent (2%) on $900,000	$	18,000.00
One percent (1%) on excess	$	
TOTAL	$	

This is known as the **statutory fee,** or **ordinary fee.**

The legal assistant should bear in mind that the court has discretion, in Sacramento County at least, to reduce the fees of both the attorney and the executor or administrator if the estate is not closed within the prescribed time and the delay in filing was caused by factors within the control of the representative or the attorney or the delay was not in the best interests of the estate and persons interested in the estate. Protection of the attorney in this regard may be afforded by letters to the executor or administrator outlining what has to be done and fixing dates for completion of the various steps. If the client is slow to respond, the legal assistant can follow up with the client.

Checklists of services for which ordinary fees may be allowed and for which they have been denied follow. The lists are taken from a paper entitled "Attorneys Fees in Probate—A Working Paper," prepared by

TERMS

statutory fees The fees that are allowed to be paid to the personal representative and attorney by virtue of a statute.

ordinary fees The fees that are allowed to be paid to the personal representative and attorney for services that are customary or usual in the administration of an estate.

Honorable Billy G. Mills, former Supervising Judge, Central Probate, Los Angeles County Superior Court.

Ordinary Fees May Be Allowed

- Necessary, beneficial, and uncomplicated matters;
- All matters of probate;
- Incidental expenses, *i.e.,* local telephone calls, postage, auto mileage, stenographic services, and stationery;
- Payment of taxes;
- Necessary repairs;
- Petition and disbursement of authorized family allowance;
- Locating and assembling estate assets;
- Resisting appeals by distributees;
- Collecting rents, claims, and interest;
- Leasing property;
- Accounting and making payments necessary to complete administration;
- Managing adversarial suit of estate;
- Contracting attorney in distant state;
- Necessary litigation regarding estate;
- Settlement services;
- Necessary travel expenses;
- Maintaining action to set aside deed;
- Reducing estate to possession of representative;
- Preserving common fund;
- Construction of a will;
- Postdistribution activities;
- Contract by sole beneficiary;
- Defending codicils;
- Defending testamentary instrument;
- Services producing no unusual benefit to estate; and
- Services performed by bank as administrator.

Ordinary Fees Not Allowed

- Procuring letters of administration;
- Poor investments contrary to directions;
- Protecting interests of representative or single beneficiary versus estate;
- Unsuccessful appeal of order appointing representative;
- Administrator contesting probate;
- Prosecution of negligent representative:
- Litigation of adverse claims of heirs;
- Services that should have been done by representative;
- Appeal of unrelated matters;
- Study of stock market;
- Litigation strictly between claimants;
- Recovery for overpayment;
- Services under agreement not to charge; and
- Charge for deposition not on record or appeal.

Extraordinary Services

The fees for extraordinary services, unlike the statutory, or ordinary, fees, are at the discretion of the court. Former Probate Code section 902 provided that **extraordinary fees** might be awarded by the court for services such as contested or litigated claims against the estate; the successful defense of a will that is contested either before or after the will is admitted to probate; the preparation of estate, inheritance, income, sales, or other tax returns and the adjustment, litigation, or payment of any of such taxes; litigation in regard to the property of the estate; and other litigation or special services necessary for the executor or administrator to prosecute, defend, or perform. Probate Code section 902 was repealed, however, and replaced by sections 10800 through 10801. The list of examples in Probate Code section 902 is not included in section 10801,

---

TERMS

---

extraordinary fees The fees that are allowed to be paid to the personal representative and attorney for services that are not of the regular, usual, or customary kind in the administration of an estate.

but the omission was not intended to change the law (Substitute Comment 10801, Cal. Law Rev. Comm'n, Revised and Supplemental Comments to the New Probate Code).

Under the new sections, the following services of the personal representative, in the discretion of the court, may be considered for extraordinary fees: sales or mortgages of real or personal property; carrying on the decedent's business; court proceedings to determine the testator's intention concerning undisclosed beneficiaries; defense of the personal representative's account (answering interrogatories; attending depositions; conferring with attorneys to prepare for depositions, interrogatories, and trial; attending trial); and securing a loan to pay debts of the estate. Cases are cited in support of this list in the California Law Revisions Commission's recommendation proposing the new probate code, published December 1989.

The personal representative cannot serve as the estate attorney and receive dual compensation unless expressly authorized by the decedent's will (Prob. Code § 10804).

Extraordinary services include services by a paralegal performed under the direction and supervision of an attorney. The petition or application should provide the hours spent and the services performed by the paralegal (Prob. Code § 10810). In Los Angeles County (and possibly others), the paralegal's qualifications must be set forth in a declaration attached to the petition.

The court in *In re Estate of Walker,* 221 Cal. App. 2d 792, 795 (1963), stated that if the court decides the statutory fees sufficiently compensate for statutory and extraordinary services, no extraordinary fees will be allowed:

> In making an allowance for such services, or in disallowing a claim therefor, the court may take into consideration all matters relating to the administration of the particular estate, such as the value of the estate, the kind and character of the assets, the effort involved in the care and preservation of estate property, and such other facts as bear upon the labor and effort of the executor, administrator and attorney in the routine administration of the estate. Finally, the amount of the ordinary fees to which such persons are entitled under the provisions of sections 901 and 910 may be considered, and if, under all the facts and circumstances bearing upon the administration of the estate, the sum allowed by law as ordinary compensation appears to be adequate, just and reasonable compensation for all services rendered, even though some extraordinary services may have in fact been performed, the probate court may, in the exercise of the discretion conferred upon it by the statute, disallow all claims for extraordinary compensation.

The representative-client should be asked whether they wish to request extraordinary fees and be informed in detail about the services for which these fees may be granted. Out of the goodness of his or her heart, the representative may wish to leave more in the estate for the heirs or beneficiaries. If the representative is also an heir or beneficiary, he or she should consult with the attorney about the tax effects on the estate and on his or her own income tax situation. Consideration will have to be given to the time of distribution and to whether the representative will take a specific bequest of money or property or a share or all the residue.

If the closing appears unduly delayed, a court may not look as favorably on the granting of extraordinary fees.

Checklists of services for which extraordinary fees may be allowed and for which they have been denied follow. The lists are taken from a paper entitled "Attorneys Fees in Probate—A Working Paper," prepared by Honorable Billy G. Mills, former Supervising Judge, Central Probate, Los Angeles County Superior Court.

Extraordinary Fees May Be Allowed

- Extraordinary legal services;

- Uncommon, remarkable, or rare services;

- Services from which all devisees must benefit;

- Services in aid of a duty owed by the executor;

- Litigation benefitting estate;

- Services of an attorney who acts for an absconding, deceased, or incompetent executor;

- Sales or mortgages of real or personal property;

- Contested claims against the estate or property;

- Preparation of tax returns;

- Litigation relating to estate property;

- Carrying on the decedent's business;

- Securing a loan to pay estate debts;

- Appeal from ruling adverse to estate;

- Preparing and filing demurrer and answer;

- Legal advice in connection with administration in other states;

- Managing property (*e.g.*, summer resort or apartment house);

- Sales of bonds, stocks, and notes;

- Unlawful detainer action;

- Order for interpretation or construction of a complicated will;
- Defense of an eminent domain suit;
- Successful defense of the personal representative;
- Heirship proceeding;
- Preserving common fund;
- Defending executor's account;
- Distribution of assets;
- Extraordinary efforts to locate assets;
- Filing fees, clerk fees, and travel expenses for the benefit of the estate;
- Exceptions filed without reasonable causes and good faith; and
- Services as attorney instead of as representative.

Extraordinary Fees Not Allowed

- Representative resisting claims individually;
- Services out of proportion to value thereof;
- Casual examination was sufficient;
- Prior to initiation of probate proceedings;
- Adverse to estate interests;
- Unnecessary litigation;
- Depositions not in record or on appeal;
- Special proceeding initiated by individual personally;
- Where heirs, legatees, and devisees are not joined; and
- An account is set forth herein.

§ 5.7 Notice of Hearing on Account

At least fifteen days before any hearing on an account, the executor or administrator must give notice of hearing on the account to each known heir and devisee whose interest in the estate is affected by the account and petition and to the Attorney General if any portion of the estate escheats to it and its interest is affected by the account and petition.

Notice also must be given to the personal representative and to all persons who have given notice of appearance, either in person or by attorney. If notice is given by attorney, the notice is mailed to the attorney.

Subject to Probate Code section 1212, the notice shall be given to the person's place of business or place of residence, if known, unless the court dispenses with notice. If the address is unknown, notice shall be given as the court may require as provided in Code of Civil Procedure section 413.30 (Prob. Code § 1212).

Notice shall be given fifteen days before the hearing to anyone requesting special notice pursuant to Probate Code section 1250. Notice shall be given by mail to the person named in the request at the address set forth in the request. A copy of the petition, report, account, or other paper shall be enclosed (Prob. Code § 1252).

Proof of giving notice shall be made at or before the hearing. If the court is satisfied that notice has been regularly given or that the party entitled to notice has waived it, the court shall so find in its order. When the order becomes final, it is conclusive on all persons (Prob. Code § 1200.5). (See notice of hearing form in Figure 5–4.)

Hearing on Final Account

The vouchers are filed at the time of the hearing, if required (Prob. Code § 925).

Reasons Account Might Not Be Settled

Reasons for delay in settling accounts are set out in the California Continuing Education of the Bar's (CEB's) *California Decedent Estate Administration*, volume 2, section 19.16. The legal assistant may want to check this list for any deficiencies when preparing the account.

Reserve for Taxes

Any federal estate tax must be assessed either within three years after the date the return is filed or within three years after the date the estate tax is due, whichever is later. In the meantime, the estate remains liable. This assessment period can be reduced to eighteen months under certain circumstances by making a request for prompt assessment.

ATTORNEY OR PARTY WITHOUT ATTORNEY *(Name and Address)*:	TELEPHONE NO.:	FOR COURT USE ONLY

ATTORNEY FOR *(Name)*:

SUPERIOR COURT OF CALIFORNIA, COUNTY OF

STREET ADDRESS:

MAILING ADDRESS: SACRAMENTO SUPERIOR COURT

CITY AND ZIP CODE: 720 9th ST.

BRANCH NAME: SACRAMENTO, CA 95814

ESTATE OF (NAME):

DECEDENT

NOTICE OF HEARING (Probate)	CASE NUMBER:

> This notice is required by law. This notice does not require you to appear in court, but you may attend the hearing if you wish.

1. NOTICE is given that *(name)*:

   (representative capacity, if any):

   has filed *(specify)*:*

2. You may refer to the filed documents for further particulars. *(All of the case documents filed with the court are available for examination in the case file kept by the court clerk.)*

3. A HEARING on the matter will be held as follows:

   Date: Time: Dept.:   Room:

   Address of court ☐ shown above ☐ is:

. . . .   ☐ Attorney or party _____

              (TYPE OR PRINT NAME)   (SIGNATURE)

Date: ☐ Clerk, by _____ , Deputy

4. This notice was mailed on *(date)*:   at *(place)*:

(Continued on reverse)

* Do not use this form to give notice of hearing of the petition for administration *(see Probate Code, § 8100)*.

Form Approved by the
Judicial Council of California
DE-120 [Rev. July 1, 1989]   **NOTICE OF HEARING**
(Probate)   Probate Code, §§ 1211, 1215, 1216, 1230

FIGURE 5–4   Notice of Hearing form

ESTATE OF (NAME):

DECEDENT

CASE NUMBER:

CLERK'S CERTIFICATE OF ☐ POSTING ☐ MAILING

I certify that I am not a party to this cause and that a copy of the foregoing **Notice of Hearing (Probate)**

1. ☐ was posted at *(address)*:

   on *(date)*:

2. ☐ was served on each person named below. Each notice was enclosed in an envelope with postage fully prepaid. Each envelope was addressed to a person whose name and address is given below, sealed, and deposited with the United States Postal Service at *(place)*:   California,
   on *(date)*:

   Date: Clerk, by _____ , Deputy

PROOF OF SERVICE BY MAIL

1. I am over the age of 18 and not a party to this cause. I am a resident of or employed in the county where the mailing occurred.
2. My residence or business address is *(specify)*:

3. I served the foregoing **Notice of Hearing (Probate)** on each person named below by enclosing a copy in an envelope addressed as shown below AND
   a. ☐ depositing the sealed envelope with the United States Postal Service with the postage fully prepaid.
   b. ☐ placing the envelope for collection and mailing on the date and at the place shown in item 4 following our ordinary business practices. I am readily familiar with this business' practice for collecting and processing correspondence for mailing. On the same day that correspondence is placed for collection and mailing, it is deposited in the ordinary course of business with the United States Postal Service in a sealed envelope with postage fully prepaid.

4. a. Date mailed: b. Place mailed *(city, state)*:

5. ☐ I served with the *Notice of Hearing (Probate)* a copy of the petition or other document referred to in the notice.

   I declare under penalty of perjury under the laws of the State of California that the foregoing is true and correct.

Date:

....   ▶ _____
(TYPE OR PRINT NAME)   (SIGNATURE OF DECLARANT)

NAME AND ADDRESS OF EACH PERSON TO WHOM NOTICE WAS MAILED

DE-120 (Rev. July 1, 1988)

NOTICE OF HEARING
(Probate)

Page two

Probate Code, §§ 1201, 1204

FIGURE 5–4   *(continued)*

The executor or administrator may apply for a release from personal liability, and the IRS must make a determination of the tax within nine months after the request or the filing of the return, whichever is later. The executor is entitled to a receipt or other writing showing the release from personal liability for any deficiency in tax later found to be due and is entitled to a receipt or writing showing such discharge (IRC § 2204).

If a federal estate tax has been paid in the estate but has not been audited, the petition will contain a request for a reserve fund to pay any possible federal estate taxes that may later be determined to be owing upon audit. Once the cash is distributed out of the estate to various heirs and beneficiaries, if taxes are found to be owing, the representative who is responsible for payment can be in a bad spot if he or she must look to the beneficiaries for a return of sufficient cash to pay the taxes. Some beneficiaries may have spent the cash, and others may have it tied up and be reluctant to return it. Litigation, which may or may not prove successful, can be costly, and interest accrues on the amount owing in the meantime.

Some attorneys draft a letter agreement among the beneficiaries authorizing the executor to hold the fund as their agent, perhaps giving them the income. If this is done, 1099s will have to be furnished to each of the beneficiaries, as the interest is taxable to them.

The existing estate account may be utilized for the reserve fund. In a very large estate or where the reserve is expected to be held for a long term, the funds may be placed in a Treasury certificate or account.

A paragraph will be placed in the order providing for such a fund.

§ 5.8   Order Settling First and Final Account

Before the hearing on the final account and petition, an order settling the first and final account and report of executor allowing extraordinary compensation and of final distribution under the will is prepared (an original and at least three copies). The title should correspond to the caption of the account, report, and petition. If the attorney or executor is not requesting extraordinary fees, the words *extraordinary compensation* will not be part of the title. *Judgment* or *decree* may be substituted for *order*.

At the time of making distribution, a statement of any receipts and disbursements since the rendition of the final account must be reported and filed. Any settlement of such items, together with an estimate of the expenses of closing the estate, must be made by the court and included in the order or decree, or the court may order notice to be given of the settlement of such supplementary account (Prob. Code § 1020.5). (For a sample form of the order, see Figure 5–5.)

Although the attorney's and executor's fees are statutory and therefore capable of being computed, it is good practice to wait to pay them until they have been approved by the court.

The original order will be signed by the judge and filed in the proceeding. The representative should be furnished a copy, and one office copy will be needed. Additional copies may be needed as well.

Generally speaking, all matters requested by the petitioner in the prayer should be covered in the order. For example, if the account alleges that no requests for special notice have been filed in the within proceeding, the order should find that "No requests for special notice have been filed in the within proceeding." If the prayer requests that the account be set for hearing and that notice be given as required by law, the order should find that "Notice of the hearing on the aforesaid account, report, and petition has been duly and regularly given as required by law."

§ 5.9 Hearing on Final Account

The vouchers may be filed at the time of the hearing, and they must be filed if so ordered by the court or if a person interested in the estate files a written request for them with the clerk and serves a copy on the executor or administrator or attorney at least five days prior to the time for hearing (Prob. Code § 925). The vouchers retained by the executor or administrator or on file with the clerk of the court must be retained for one year after the decree of distribution becomes final. The executor or administrator or the clerk of the court may then destroy the vouchers unless within the one-year period a person interested in the estate has filed a written request that they be retained, in which event the vouchers may not be destroyed until after three years from the time the decree of distribution becomes final. A decree of distribution becomes final thirty days after signature. (Prob. Code § 925). As a matter of good practice, vouchers should be retained for at least three years.

After the order is signed by the judge, the estate is ready for distribution to the heirs and distributees. The executor or administrator is authorized to employ or retain tax counsel, tax auditors, accountants, or other tax experts for the performance of any action that such persons may lawfully perform in the computation, reporting, or making of tax returns, or in negotiations or litigation that is necessary for the final determination and payment of taxes, and to pay such persons from funds of the estate (Prob. Code § 902).

ARTHUR ANDREW
Attorney at Law
123 Sandor Place
Sacramento, CA 95814
Telephone: (916) 447-0923

Attorney for Executor

SUPERIOR COURT OF CALIFORNIA,

COUNTY OF SACRAMENTO

Estate of KENNETH BELL,   )   No. 92457
also known as   )
KENNETH K. BELL,   )   ORDER SETTLING FIRST AND FINAL
)   ACCOUNT, ALLOWING STATUTORY
    Deceased.   )   EXECUTOR'S COMMISSION, ATTORNEY'S
)   STATUTORY AND EXTRAORDINARY FEES,
)   APPROVING PRELIMINARY DISTRIBU-
)   TION, AND DECREE OF FINAL DIS-
)   TRIBUTION
)

The First and Final Account and Petition for Statutory
Executor's Commission and Attorney's Statutory and Extraordinary
Fees, for Approval of Preliminary Distribution, and for Final
Distribution having come on regularly for hearing on December 20,
19 __, in Department 17 of the above-entitled Court, the Honorable
Raymond McKenna, Judge presiding, and no one appearing to object
or except to the account and petition for the granting of relief
therein requested, the Court having heard and considered the
evidence, hereby finds and concludes as follows:

1. Notice of the hearing on the aforesaid account and
petition has been duly and regularly given as required by
law.

1

FIGURE 5–5 Form of order

2. No request for special notice has been filed in the within proceedings.

3. Notice to creditors has been duly given as required by law and the time for filing claims has expired.

4. All federal and California estate taxes due have been paid.

5. All of the allegations in said account and petition are true and correct.

6. The executor of the estate of the decedent has in her possession belonging to the estate a balance of the appraised value of $606,707.57, of which $359,947.82 is in cash.

Good cause appearing therefor, the Court hereby settles said account, approves said preliminary distribution, and grants said petition as follows:

IT IS HEREBY ORDERED AND DECREED that:

1. The First and Final Account and Petition for Statutory Executor's Commission and Attorney's Statutory and Extraordinary Fees, for Approval of Preliminary Distribution, and Petition for Final Distribution is hereby settled, allowed and approved as filed and all acts and transactions relating to the matters in said account and petition as set forth therein are ratified, confirmed and approved.

2. The advance distribution to Morton Bell, decedent's brother, of the yellow gold diamond ring, having an appraised value of Nine Thousand Dollars ($9,000.00), and to decedent's son, Kerry Bell, of the 1985 Mercedes 450 SL automobile, engine LS057C807, having an appraised value of

2

FIGURE 5–5 *(continued)*

Twenty-two Thousand Dollars ($22,000.00), is hereby approved.

3.   The payment of debts of the decedent pursuant to Probate Code section 929 in the amount of Six Hundred Seventy-six and 81/100ths Dollars ($676.81) is hereby approved.

4.   The executor is hereby authorized and directed to pay Fourteen Thousand One Hundred Ninety-nine and 26/100ths Dollars ($14,199.26) to herself as executor as her statutory commission for her ordinary services to the estate.

5.   The executor is hereby authorized and directed to pay Fourteen Thousand One Hundred Ninety-nine and 26/100ths Dollars ($14,199.26) to her attorney as his statutory commission for his ordinary services to the executor and the estate.

6.   The executor is hereby authorized and directed to pay Four Thousand Dollars ($4,000.00) to Arthur Andrew as extraordinary attorney's fees for extraordinary services to the executor and to the estate.

7.   The executor is hereby authorized and directed to distribute the residue of the estate pursuant to the terms of the decedent's will.

DATED: December 20, 19__.

Raymond McKenna

Judge of the Superior Courts

3

FIGURE 5–5   *(continued)*

Objections to Account

Under Probate Code section 927, any person interested in an estate may appear and file written exceptions to an account and contest the same, including the valuation of assets. In *In re Estate of Kovacs*, 227 Cal. App. 2d 308, 301 (1964), the court stated:

> The code does not define the phrase . . . or enumerate the kinds of persons who fall within that category. The fact that the Legislature has seen fit to use a term of such generality suggests an intention that the right to a hearing be afforded liberally and not limited to a few easily identified classes such as creditors and heirs.

If a court finds, however, that exceptions to an accounting filed after January 1, 1982, were filed without reasonable cause and good faith, the court is authorized to order that the fees of the executor or administrator and of his or her attorney, and any costs for defending the accounting, be charged against the person or persons who filed the written exceptions.

§ 5.10 Transferring Assets After Decree of Distribution

At the time of distribution, the representative should advise the distributees of the tax basis for the property they receive. If any real property is to be transferred to a distributee, a certified copy of the decree of distribution must be recorded in the county in which the real property is located. The same is true if an order has been made setting apart a homestead (Prob. Code § 1222). The distributee of real property should advise the tax collector of the county in which the property is located to mail the tax bills to his or her address.

The legal assistant can discuss with the recipient of real property whether a new fire insurance policy is to be taken out or whether the current policy will be endorsed to show the change in ownership. The estate should have no further liability in connection with the property or for premiums, and a refund may be due the estate, but the new owner should be protected against potential loss.

Items of personal property ordinarily have no ownership record. Only actual delivery is required.

FIGURE 5–6
Receipt on
Distribution
form

> [Title of Court and Cause]
>
> No.
>
> RECEIPT ON DISTRIBUTION
>
> The undersigned, _____, acknowledges receipt from the executor [or administrator] of the estate of _____ of cash in the amount of _____ Dollars and No Cents ($) pursuant to the Decree of Final Distribution in the above-entitled estate dated _____, _____.
>
> Dated _____, _____
>
> _____

The Receipt

A receipt must be obtained from each heir or beneficiary for filing in court. (A form of such a receipt is shown in Figure 5–6.)

After Distribution

After the receipts are obtained from the distributees, the executor or administrator signs the printed form of the declaration for final discharge (in some counties this form is combined with a final discharge form). An original and at least three copies should be prepared. A copy of the printed form of the declaration for final discharge used in Sacramento County is provided as a sample (see Figure 5–7).

In Los Angeles County the printed form of the final discharge and order is entitled "Affidavit or Declaration for Final Discharge and Order" and "Order of Final Discharge." In the City and County of San Francisco, the document is entitled "Declaration for Final Discharge" and "Order of Final Discharge."

This signed document is presented to the judge, who signs the order of final discharge. A copy is mailed to the bonding company to have the bond released. Courtesy and good practice call for furnishing a copy to the estate's representative for his or her records.

Cash reconciliation is required by the Alameda Probate and Adoption Policy Manual section 1603.

Name, Address and Telephone No. of Attorney(s)

ARTHUR ANDREW
Attorney at Law
123 Sandor Place
Sacramento, CA 95814
(916) 447-0923

Space Below for Use of Court Clerk Only

Attorney   for Petitioner _____

SUPERIOR COURT OF THE STATE OF CALIFORNIA
FOR THE COUNTY OF SACRAMENTO

Estate of

KENNETH BELL, aka KENNETH K. BELL,

No. 123457   Dept. 17

DECLARATION FOR
FINAL DISCHARGE

Deceased.

I am the __Executor__ of the __will__ of the above-
    (executor, etc.)   (will/estate)

named decedent; I have paid all sums of money due from me as __Executor__
                                                              (executor, etc.)

_____ , and have delivered up, under the judgment of distribution herein, all the property of the estate

to the parties entitled, and receipts of the respective distributees are on file. I have performed all the acts lawfully required of me

as __Executor.__
        (executor, etc.)

I declare under penalty of perjury that the foregoing is true and correct.

Executed on __January 17__ , 19__ , at Sacramento, California.

                                        Clarice Bell
                                        (Signature of representative)

FINAL DISCHARGE

It appears to the Court, and the Court finds that the facts stated in the foregoing Declaration for Final Discharge are true.

IT IS ORDERED that __CLARICE BELL__ is discharged
                        (name of representative)

as __Executor__ and that __she is__ and _____ executrix
        (executor, etc.)   (he/she)   (he/she)

are discharged and released from all liability to be incurred hereafter.

Dated _____ .

                            Merton Myron
                            JUDGE OF THE SUPERIOR COURT

FIGURE 5–7   Final discharge and order

§ 5.11 Supplemental Account

A supplemental account of any receipts and disbursements made after the final account must be reported and filed at the time of making distribution, together with an estimate of the expenses of closing the estate, and included in the court order or decree. Otherwise, the court may order notice to be given of the supplemental account the same as with other accounts (Prob. Code § 1020.5).

§ 5.12 Closing the File

Closing the office file, as distinguished from a formal closing of the estate, is another matter. Some practitioners wait three to four years so that the file will not have to be reopened if an income tax return of the estate is audited. The IRS may audit returns three years after the returns are filed. There is no statute of limitations on auditing a return if fraud is suspected.

CHAPTER 6

SALES OF REAL AND PERSONAL PROPERTY

Sales of real or personal property may not be involved in an estate, but such sales are probably more commonplace, and perhaps more involved, than a number of other procedures with which the legal assistant will need to become familiar, such as a petition for an order to sell securities (Prob. Code § 10200); a petition for an order to borrow money and mortgage property (Prob. Code § 9800); a petition for an order to lease property (Prob. Code § 9942); and a petition for a preliminary distribution (Prob. Code § 11620 *et seq.*)—to name only a few. This text deals mainly with the basic pleadings used in probating an uncontested estate. This chapter covers only the most salient points regarding sales.

There are many form books available. For discussion of particular points of law, the legal assistant is directed to Marshall and Garb, *California Probate Procedure* (5th ed., vol. 1, ch. 14, Sales).

SIDEBAR

---

§ 6.1 Sales of Real Property

If the will directs certain property to be sold or gives authority to sell property, the personal representative may sell real or **personal property**. If there is no such direction in the will, the representative nevertheless has the power to sell real or personal property to pay debts, devises, family allowance, and expenses of administration or taxes. The representative also may sell real and personal property where the sale is to the advantage of the estate and in the best interests of the interested persons (Prob. Code § 10000).

The will may give specific directions for sale. For example, the will may direct that a particular property be sold or specify the mode of selling. If so, these directions must be closely followed and the sale reported to the court for confirmation (Prob. Code § 10002).

The court may determine that the personal representative be relieved of the duty to comply with the directions under the will, in which case the court will make an order and specify the mode and terms and conditions of selling, the particular property to be sold, or both (Prob. Code § 10002).

TERMS

personal property† All property other than real property, including stock, bonds, or a mortgage.

When the sale of real or personal property is considered, the legal assistant should first check the will of the decedent to see if it enumerates any special powers to be given to the executor or administrator regarding sales. For instance, the will may contain a provision similar to the following:

> My Executor shall have power to sell, exchange, encumber and lease property of my estate at public or private sales, with or without notice, without court order or confirmation, and on such terms and conditions, including credit, as my Executor in his discretion deems advisable.

If the will contains such authorizing language, notice of the sale will not be required, and it will not be necessary to show the court that the sale is necessary or advantageous for the estate (Prob. Code § 10303). Even if the will contains such language, however, the sale must be reported to the court for confirmation (Prob. Code § 10308) except as provided by Probate Code section 10503, in a case in which the personal representative is exercising authority under the Independent Administration of Estates Act. In such a case, no notice of the sale is required, though the personal representative may decide to give notice.

Discretionary Sale

Estate property may be sold to pay debts, legacies, family allowance, or expenses. There is no priority between real and personal property. Subject to Probate Code sections 21400 through 21406 and 10001 through 10002, the personal representative may use discretion regarding which property is to be sold first; whether to sell the entire interest or lesser interest of the estate; and whether to sell property through a public auction or a private sale (Prob. Code § 10003). Whether property is sold through public or private sale, the administrator must seek the best result for the estate (Prob. Code § 10250).

Generally speaking, administrators with the will annexed have the same authority over estates as executors named in the will, but if a power or authority of the executor is discretionary and not conferred by law, it is not deemed to be conferred upon an administrator with the will annexed. If the power of sale of the executor is discretionary, therefore, it is not conferred upon the administrator with the will annexed, and such an administrator must comply with the requirements for notice and authorization (Prob. Code § 8442).

Probate Code section 10305 provides that any sale by public auction be made in the county in which the real property lies. If the property lies in two or more counties, it may be sold in either county. The sale must be made between the hours of 9 A.M. and 9 P.M. and must be made on the day named in the notice of sale unless the sale is postponed. The majority of sales of estate real property are private, however, so that is the type of sale we shall discuss here.

Necessity for Sale

A sale can be necessary for a number of reasons. The most obvious reason is the need for cash to pay debts and taxes or to carry out a provision of the will. Tax consequences for the estate and the devisees are a consideration in deciding to sell. If the sale is necessary, expenses of sale may be deducted on the federal estate tax form.

If the proceeds of real or personal property are to be divided among several heirs, amount and shares are best established in the estate proceeding. Outside the estate proceeding, heirs may never be able to agree on a sale price or on terms of sale if they are not close and generally in agreement. Sometimes sales within an estate proceeding lessen disputes among the heirs. The court will consider dissension among the heirs in determining the necessity of sale.

Written objections to confirmation of a sale may be made by anyone interested in the estate, and a hearing will be held on the objections. Witnesses may be called to testify (Prob. Code § 10261).

If a piece of real property is specifically bequeathed and the estate has sufficient cash to meet its obligations, the property need not be sold in the estate, and probably cannot be, unless there is some reason to do so. The devisee may wish to have a freer hand in selling the property than he or she would have in a sale in an estate proceeding.

An executor or administrator is authorized to grant an option to purchase real property by Probate Code section 584.3.

Preparing for Sale

A property should be exposed to the highest number of possible buyers in order to obtain the maximum bid. Prospective buyers must be made aware that a property is for sale or they will not make a bid. At the hearing on the return of sale, the court is likely to inquire about the exposure made.

The legal assistant can prepare a sales brochure on the property, emphasizing its desirable features, and mail the brochure to real estate brokers in the area. To avoid questions or disputes later, this circular should make it clear that (a) any sale made is subject to confirmation by the court, and (b) any real estate commission paid to a broker will be only that which the court allows on confirmation of sale. Brokers will request keys to inspect the property and the legal assistant can make arrangements for loaning them keys and for their return. Brokers should be cautioned about locking the premises unless other arrangements can be made, such as leaving the key with a responsible party nearby. A lock box may need to be installed on the property. The property also can be advertised in newspapers, and an open house can be held.

The legal assistant can expect phone calls from brokers and others requesting information about the property and should make an effort to obtain any pertinent information from the appropriate parties. If an apartment house is for sale, inquiries from buyers can be expected about gross rents, expenses such as taxes and utilities, condition of property, assumability of loan, and the like.

Brokers may prefer to have an exclusive listing, that is, the exclusive right to sell the property for a specified period of time, and such a right may be granted by the representative in writing up to ninety days upon obtaining prior permission of the court (Prob. Code § 10150).

The title company that is to close the **escrow** can advise the legal assistant about the documents they will need in order to close the sale.

§ 6.2 Payment of Legatees and Devisees

Probate Code section 750 directs that the provisions of the testator's will designating the estate to be appropriated for debts, expenses of administration, and family allowance be followed as far as the estate is sufficient. If it is insufficient, the portion not disposed of by the will is next appropriated. If that portion is not sufficient, property given to residuary legatees and devisees and all other property devised and bequeathed is liable in proportion to value or amount. Specific devises and legacies are exempt, however, if they appear to the court to be necessary to carry into effect the intention of the testator and there is sufficient cash or other estate assets to allow the exemption.

When property given by will to other than the residuary legatees must necessarily be sold for payment of debts, expenses, or family allowance, the other devisees and legatees will have to contribute according to their interests as determined by the court at the time of distribution (Prob. Code § 753). To illustrate, say the decedent made three specific bequests of $20,000 each and gave a house and lot to a fourth person. The estate needs

---

TERMS

escrow† A written instrument, money, or other property deposited by the grantor with a third party (the escrow holder) until the performance of a condition or the happening of a certain event, upon the occurrence of which the property is to be delivered to the grantee.

$5,000 more in cash to pay necessary expenses. The house and lot are sold, and the net is $50,000. Does the fourth person receive the $50,000 less the $5,000 expenses? No, that would be unfair. The other three devisees must pay a proportionate share of the expenses, as determined by the court, out of their devises (Prob. Code § 753). The real property need not and could not be sold, however, if the fourth person were in a position and willing to pay the $5,000 of expenses.

§ 6.3 Notice of Sale of Real Property at Private Sale

If the will gives authority for sale of property or directs its sale, no notice is required (Prob. Code § 10303). The personal representative, however, may give notice if he or she wishes to do so. If the property is being sold under the Independent Administration of Estates Act, no notice need be given unless local rules so require.

Otherwise, if the value of the property exceeds $5,000, a notice of the intention to sell real property at a private sale must be published pursuant to Government Code section 6063a. If the value is under $5,000, the representative may, in lieu of publication, post the notice of sale at the courthouse pursuant to Probate Code section 10301. If property is being sold for not more than $5,000, posting is sufficient. Except as provided by section 10302 (for shortening of time), posting must be completed at least fifteen days before a private sale or before the day of the auction in the case of sale at a public auction (Prob. Code § 10301).

The contents of the notice of sale are found in Probate Code section 10304. The description in the notice should be the same as that in the inventory. The same description also should be used in the report of sale and petition for order confirming the sale of real property. If the property is being sold **as is**, the notice should so state. When property is sold as is, no warranty is made by the seller about its condition.

The terms of sale in the notice fix the terms of the sale itself. The return and petition, therefore, must conform. The legal assistant should refer to the notice at the time of drafting the return.

TERMS

as is†   A sale without an express or implied warranty in which the buyer takes a chance in making the purchase.

In Los Angeles County, if the notice specifies cash and the sale returned is upon a credit, higher offers made on either cash or credit shall be considered only if the representative, in person or through his or her attorney, informs the court prior to confirmation that the offer is acceptable. If the offer returned is for cash and a higher offer is made on credit, the representative must similarly indicate its acceptability before the confirmation (Los Angeles County Probate Rules, Rule 10.98).

Sacramento County Probate Policy Manual section 606 provides that the notice of sale of real property should normally call for "cash or such credit terms and conditions as the personal representative and the court may approve." If the property is not being sold for cash, the notice should contain language similar to the following: "Terms of sale cash in lawful money of the United States on confirmation of sale, or part cash and balance evidenced by note secured by Mortgage or Trust Deed on the property so sold."

The notice of intention to sell real property at a private sale must be published at least three times during a ten-day period in a newspaper published at least weekly in the county where the property is located, and there must be at least five days (not counting the dates of publication) between the first and last publication date, and the first publication must be at least fifteen days before the date of sale (Prob. Code §§ 10300, 10301, 10303; Gov. Code § 6063a). The court may shorten the time to five days (Prob. Code § 10308). A form for the notice of intention to sell real property at a private sale is shown in Figure 6–1.

Note that the notice specifies the bid must be either cash or part cash and balance evidenced by note secured by mortgage or trust deed. Credit terms must be specified.

The sale may take place not later than one year after the day stated in the notice as the day on or after which the sale will be made (Prob. Code § 10306).

Service of Notice of Hearing on Report of Sale and Petition for Order Confirming Sale of Real Property

Probate Code section 10308 requires notice of hearing on the petition for confirmation as provided in Probate Code section 1220 and posting as required by section 1230. Notice must be given fifteen days before hearing to the personal representative and all persons who have given notice of appearance in the estate proceeding in person or by attorney. If appearance was by attorney, notice must be given to the attorney and to anyone who has requested special notice of sale under Probate Code section 1250.

Notice shall be personally delivered (Prob. Code § 1216) or delivered by first-class mail (includes certified, registered, and express mail) or by

FIGURE 6–1
Notice of
Intention to
Sell form

[caption of case]

NOTICE OF INTENTION TO SELL
REAL PROPERTY AT PRIVATE SALE

Notice is hereby given that the undersigned will sell at private sale, to the highest and best bidder, subject to confirmation of said Superior Court, on or after the 25th day of June, 1995, at the office of Arthur Andrew, 123 Sandor Place, Sacramento, California 95814, all the right, title and interest of said deceased at the time of death and all the right, title and interest that the estate has acquired by operation of law or otherwise than or in addition to that of said deceased, at the time of death, in and to all the certain real property situated in the County of Sacramento, State of California, particularly described as follows:

Single family dwelling located at 9020 Boykin Way, Sacramento, described as the West 59.00 feet of the East 590.00 feet of Lot 1248, as shown on the "plat of Elvira" recorded in the office of the County Recorder, January 23, 1909, in Book 8 of Maps, Map No. 41. Assessor's Parcel No. 006–175–0200.

Terms of sale cash in lawful money of the United States on confirmation of sale, or part cash and balance evidenced by note secured by Mortgage or Trust Deed on the property so sold. Ten percent of amount bid to be deposited with bid.

Bid or bids to be in writing and will be received at the aforesaid office at any time after the first publication hereof and before date of sale.

Dated this 25th day of June, 1995.

_____

Executor of the Estate of said Decedent

Arthur Andrew
123 Sandor Place
Sacramento, CA 95814

airmail if the person's address is outside the United States (Prob. Code § 1215).

Proof of giving the notice must be made at or before the hearing. If the court is satisfied that notice has been regularly given or that the party entitled to notice has waived it, the court shall so find in its order, which is conclusive on all persons when the order becomes final (Prob. Code § 1260).

For a form for the notice of hearing, see Figure 6–2.

Receiving Bids

The notice (Figure 6–2) should specify the place for prospective purchasers to submit their bids. This can be, and often is, the attorney's office.

ATTORNEY OR PARTY WITHOUT ATTORNEY *(Name and Address)*:

TELEPHONE NO.

FOR COURT USE ONLY

ARTHUR ANDREW
Attorney at Law
123 Sandor Place
Sacramento, CA 95814

447-0923

ATTORNEY FOR *(Name)*: Clarice Bell

SUPERIOR COURT OF CALIFORNIA, COUNTY OF

STREET ADDRESS: 720 - 9th St.

MAILING ADDRESS:

CITY AND ZIP CODE: Sacramento, CA 95814

BRANCH NAME:

ESTATE OF *(NAME)*:

KENNETH BELL, also known as KENNETH K. BELL

DECEDENT

NOTICE OF HEARING
(Probate)

CASE NUMBER:

92457

> This notice is required by law. This notice does not require you to appear in court, but you may attend the hearing if you wish.

1. NOTICE is given that *(name)*: CLARICE BELL

   (representative capacity, if any): Executor

   has filed *(specify)*:* Report of Sale and Petition for Order Confirming Sale of Real Property

2. You may refer to the filed documents for further particulars. *(All of the case documents filed with the court are available for examination in the case file kept by the court clerk.)*

3. A HEARING on the matter will be held as follows:

   Date: July 31, 19. Time: 9:15 a.m. Dept.: 17 Room:
   Address of court [x] shown above [ ] is: 720 - 9th St., Sacramento, California 95814

CLARICE BELL ....
(TYPE OR PRINT NAME)

[X] Attorney or party *Clarice Bell*
(SIGNATURE)

Date: July 1, 19.

[ ] Clerk, by _R. Sims_ . Deputy

4. This notice was mailed on *(date)*: July 2, 19. at *(place)*: Sacramento, California.

(Continued on reverse)

* Do not use this form to give notice of hearing of the petition for administration *(see Probate Code, § 8100)*.

Form Approved by the
Judicial Council of California
DE 120 (Rev. July 1 1989

NOTICE OF HEARING
(Probate)

Probate Code §§ 1211 1215 1216 1230

FIGURE 6-2 Notice of Hearing

ESTATE OF (NAME):	CASE NUMBER:
KENNETH BELL, also known as KENNETH K. BELL DECEDENT	92457

CLERK'S CERTIFICATE OF ☐ POSTING ☐ MAILING

I certify that I am not a party to this cause and that a copy of the foregoing Notice of Hearing (Probate)

1. ☐ was posted at (address):

   on (date):

2. ☐ was served on each person named below. Each notice was enclosed in an envelope with postage fully prepaid. Each envelope was addressed to a person whose name and address is given below, sealed, and deposited with the United States Postal Service at (place): . California,

   on (date):

Date: Clerk, by _____ Deputy

PROOF OF SERVICE BY MAIL

1. I am over the age of 18 and not a party to this cause. I am a resident of or employed in the county where the mailing occurred.
2. My residence or business address is (specify): 123 Sandor Place, Sacramento, California 95814

3. I served the foregoing Notice of Hearing (Probate) on each person named below by enclosing a copy in an envelope addressed as shown below AND
   a. ☒ depositing the sealed envelope with the United States Postal Service with the postage fully prepaid.
   b. ☐ placing the envelope for collection and mailing on the date and at the place shown in item 4 following our ordinary business practices. I am readily familiar with this business' practice for collecting and processing correspondence for mailing. On the same day that correspondence is placed for collection and mailing, it is deposited in the ordinary course of business with the United States Postal Service in a sealed envelope with postage fully prepaid.

4. a. Date of deposit: July 2, 19   b. Place of deposit (city and state): Sacramento, California

5. ☒ I served with the Notice of Hearing (Probate) a copy of the petition or other document referred to in the notice.

   I declare under penalty of perjury under the laws of the State of California that the foregoing is true and correct.

Date:

.............Marian Morange.............   ▶ *Marian Morange*
(TYPE OR PRINT NAME)   (SIGNATURE OF DECLARANT)

NAME AND ADDRESS OF EACH PERSON TO WHOM NOTICE WAS MAILED

Kerry Bell
145 Perry Avenue
Sacramento. California 95817

Morton Bell
789 Walter Avenue
Sacramento, California 95820

DE-120 (Rev. July 1, 1988)   **NOTICE OF HEARING**   Page two
                                 (Probate)   Probate Code, §§ 1201, 1204

FIGURE 6–2   *(continued)*

The form of the bid should conform to the notice. The bid should contain the title of the estate proceeding and the court number and be entitled "Bid for Purchase of Real Property." The text of the bid might read:

To Clarice Bell, executor of the will of the above-named decedent:

The undersigned hereby offers the sum of $120,000 in cash [or terms of credit] for purchase of the real property belonging to the estate of the decedent, commonly known and referred to as 145 Perry Avenue, Sacramento, California, and more particularly described as follows: Lot 9 on that map entitled "Plat of Deodora Ridge," as recorded in Book 6 of Maps at Page 8, Official Records of Sacramento County, California; Assessor's Parcel No. 006-290-0200.

If the legal description of the property is very long, it can be attached separately as an Exhibit A.

The bid offered must be at least ninety percent of the appraised value of the property. The referee must have appraised the property's value within one year of the date of sale or the court will not approve the sale and a reappraisal will be ordered. The legal assistant who is alert to this possibility can have a reappraisal made before the court so orders. The reappraisal may be made by letter. The court also may order a reappraisal if the appraisal is too low or too high. In the latter event, an offer of ninety percent of the appraised value may not be obtainable, and therefore, a reappraisal may be necessary to sell the property.

The legal assistant may tell potential bidders the appraised value of the property and the amount of real property taxes, and may arrange appointments to look at the property, but ordinarily should not divulge the amount of any bid to other potential bidders.

§ 6.4 Real and Personal Property Sold as a Unit

Real and personal property may be sold as a unit and with one bid when it seems desirable for the estate. For example, when selling an apartment house that contains furniture, stoves, refrigerators, drapes, and the like, the only practical way to sell it is as one unit. Ordinarily an apartment house is appraised by the referee as a unit, but the bid on the property must be for at least ninety percent of the total appraised value whether the property has been appraised as a unit or separately. The notice requirements are the same as for any other sale.

Bids must be in writing and should conform to the terms of the notice. They need not be sealed. Local rules determine the amount of deposit that must accompany bids, usually ten percent of the offer. The deposit should be in either cash or certified or cashier's check, not a personal check. This deposit should not be held by the broker or deposited in escrow. The representative of the estate can hold it, but depositing it in the attorney's trust account in the name of the bidder is better practice. This makes for an easier and faster return should the bidder default or the sale not be confirmed.

§ 6.5   Report of Sale

After a satisfactory bid has been received and a higher bid does not seem likely, the bid is accepted, subject to court approval. The bidder should be notified that the bid is accepted, and a report of sale and petition for order confirming the sale of real property is made to the court. Other bidders on the property should be notified of the date of the hearing in case they wish to appear and make an overbid in court. The report and petition must be made within thirty days after the sale (Prob. Code § 10308), and the petition must be verified.

The Judicial Council has prepared a printed form for the report of sale and petition for order confirming the sale of real property, the use of which is optional. For that form, together with the form for the order confirming the sale of real property, see Figures 6–3 and 6–4.

Use of a checklist by the legal assistant when working on sales may avoid some of the common mistakes that can cause problems with the petition for confirmation of sale. Notice of hearing on the petition is given pursuant to Probate Code section 1220 and posted as provided in Probate Code section 1230. The clerk posts notice of the hearing at the courthouse of the county where the proceedings are pending at least fifteen days before the hearing. Notices are also sent by the petitioner or the person filing the report, at least fifteen days before the hearing, to the personal representative and to all persons who have given notice of appearance in the estate proceeding in person or by an attorney. If the person appeared by an attorney, the notice shall be mailed to the attorney (unless the section requiring notice specifies the persons required to be given notice). If the will gives the property to a specific person, notice also should be sent to that devisee (unless, in Los Angeles County, consent of the devisee or legatee if filed).

Notice is given by personal service or by mail addressed to them at the address in the request for special notice, if any, otherwise at their offices or places of residence, if known, and if not known, to the county seat of the county in which proceedings are pending (Prob. Code § 1220).

ATTORNEY OR PARTY WITHOUT ATTORNEY *(Name and Address)*:
ARTHUR ANDREW
Attorney at Law
123 Sandor Place
Sacramento, CA 95814

TELEPHONE NO.: 447-0923

FOR COURT USE ONLY

ATTORNEY FOR *(Name)*: Clarice Bell

SUPERIOR COURT OF CALIFORNIA, COUNTY OF
STREET ADDRESS: 720 - 9th St.
MAILING ADDRESS:
CITY AND ZIP CODE: Sacramento, CA 95814
BRANCH NAME:

ESTATE OF (NAME):
KENNETH BELL, also known as KENNETH K. BELL
[X] DECEDENT   [ ] CONSERVATEE   [ ] MINOR

CASE NUMBER: 92457

**REPORT OF SALE AND PETITION FOR ORDER CONFIRMING
SALE OF REAL PROPERTY**
[ ] And Sale of Other Property Sold as a Unit

HEARING DATE: July 31, 19__
DEPT.: 17   TIME: 9:15 a.m.

1. **Petitioner** *(name of each)*: Clarice Bell

   is the [X] executor   [ ] special administrator   [ ] purchaser *(30 days have passed
   [ ] administrator with will annexed   [ ] conservator   since the sale—attach declaration)*
   [ ] administrator   [ ] guardian
   of the estate and requests a court order for

   a. confirmation of sale of the estate's interest in the real property described in Attachment 2e.
   b. [ ] confirmation of sale of the estate's interest in other property sold as a unit as described in Attachment 2c.
   c. [ ] approval of commission of: % in the amount of: $ *(see local court rules)*.
   d. additional bond [ ] is fixed at: $ [X] is not required.

2. **Description of property sold**
   a. Interest sold
      [X] 100%   [ ] Undivided   %
   b. [X] Improved
      [ ] Unimproved
   c. [ ] Real property sold as a unit with other property *(describe in Attachment 2c)*.
   d. Street address and location:
      9020 Boykin Way, Sacramento, California 95823

   e. Legal description is affixed as Attachment 2e *(attach)*.

3. **Appraisal**
   a. Date of death of decedent or appointment of conservator or guardian: January 7, 19
   b. Appraised value at above date: $ 150,000.00
   c. Reappraised value within one year prior to the hearing: $ [ ] Amount includes value of other property sold
      as a unit.   *(If more than one year has elapsed from date 3a to the date of the hearing, reappraisal is necessary.)*
   d. Appraisal or reappraisal
      [ ] has been filed   [ ] will be filed

4. **Manner and terms of sale**
   a. Name of purchaser and manner of vesting title *(specify)*:

   b. [ ] Purchaser is [ ] the personal representative [ ] the attorney for the personal representative.
   c. Sale was [X] private [ ] public   on *(date)*:
   d. Amount bid: $ 170,000.00   Deposit: $ 40,000.00
   e. Payment
      [X] Cash   [ ] Credit *(see Attachment 4e)*
   f. [ ] Other terms of sale *(see Attachment 4f)*
   g. [ ] Mode of sale specified in will [ ] petitioner requests relief from complying for the reasons stated in Attachment 4g.
   h. [ ] Terms comply with Probate Code, § 2542 *(guardianships and conservatorships only)*

                              (Continued on reverse)

Form Approved by the
Judicial Council of California
DE-260, GC-060 [Rev. July 1, 1988]

**REPORT OF SALE AND PETITION FOR ORDER CONFIRMING
SALE OF REAL PROPERTY**
(Probate)

Probate Code. §§ 2540, 10308

FIGURE 6–3   Report of Sale and Petition for Order Confirming Sale of Real Property

ESTATE OF (NAME): KENNETH BELL, also known as KENNETH K. BELL	CASE NUMBER: 92457

5. Commission
- a. ☐ Sale without broker
- b. ☐ A written ☐ exclusive ☐ nonexclusive   contract for commission was entered into with *(name)*:
- c. ☒ Purchaser was procured by *(name)*:
  a licensed real estate broker who is not buying for his or her account.
- d. ☐ Commission is to be divided as follows:

6. Bond
- a. Amount before sale: $ ☒ none
- b. Additional amount needed: $ ☒ none
- c. ☐ Proceeds are to be deposited in a blocked account. Receipts will be filed. *(Specify institution and location)*:

7. Notice of sale
- a. ☒ Published ☐ posted as permitted by Probate Code, § 10301 ($5,000 or less)
- b. ☒ Will authorizes sale of the property
- c. ☐ Will directs sale of the property

8. Notice of hearing
- a. Specific devisee
  - (1) ☐ None
  - (2) ☐ Consent to be filed
  - (3) ☒ Written notice will be given
- b. Special notice
  - (1) ☒ None requested
  - (2) ☐ Has been or will be waived
  - (3) ☐ Required written notice will be given
- c. Personal representative
  - (1) ☒ Petitioner (none required)
  - (2) ☐ Consent to be filed
  - (3) ☐ Written notice will be given

9. Reason for sale *(need not complete if 7b or 7c checked)*
- a. ☐ Necessary to pay
  - (1) ☐ debts
  - (2) ☐ devises
  - (3) ☐ family allowance
  - (4) ☐ expenses of administration
  - (5) ☐ taxes
- b. ☒ The sale is to the advantage of the estate and in the best interest of the interested persons.

10. Overbid required amount of first overbid: $

11. Petitioner's efforts to obtain the highest and best price reasonably attainable for the property were as follows *(specify activities taken to expose the property to the market, e.g., multiple listings, advertising, open houses, etc.)*:

A summary of data regarding the property and its availability for sale was sent to the brokers in the area, it was listed in a leaflet for brokers and more than thirty inquiries regarding it sale were received from different realtors and prospective buyers. This resulted in receipt of four bids exceeding the appraisal price, the within sale being the highest bid received.

12. ☐ Number of pages attached:

▶ _____   ▶ *Clarice Bell*
(SIGNATURE OF PETITIONER*)   (SIGNATURE OF PETITIONER*)

I declare under penalty of perjury under the laws of the State of California that the foregoing is true and correct.
Date:

......Clarice Bell......   ▶ *Clarice Bell*
(TYPE OR PRINT NAME)   (SIGNATURE OF PETITIONER*)

* All petitioners must sign the petition. Only one need sign the declaration.

DE-260, GC-060 [Rev. July 1, 1988]

REPORT OF SALE AND PETITION FOR ORDER CONFIRMING SALE OF REAL PROPERTY
(Probate)

Page two

FIGURE 6–3   *(continued)*

ATTORNEY OR PARTY WITHOUT ATTORNEY *(Name and Address)*:

TELEPHONE NO.: 447-0923

[X] RECORDING requested by and return to:
ARTHUR ANDREW
Attorney at Law
123 Sandor Place
Sacramento, CA 95814

ATTORNEY FOR *(Name)*: Clarice Bell

SUPERIOR COURT OF CALIFORNIA, COUNTY OF

STREET ADDRESS: 720 - 9th St.

MAILING ADDRESS:

CITY AND ZIP CODE: Sacramento, CA 95814

BRANCH NAME:

ESTATE OF (NAME):
KENNETH BELL, also known as KENNETH K. BELL
[X] DECEDENT [ ] CONSERVATEE [ ] MINOR

ORDER CONFIRMING SALE OF REAL PROPERTY
[ ] And Confirming Sale of Other Property as a Unit

FOR COURT USE ONLY

CASE NUMBER: 92457

1. Hearing date: Jul. 31, 19   Time: 9:15 am   Dept: 17   Rm:

THE COURT FINDS

2. All notices required by law were given and, if required, proof of notice of sale was made.
3. a. [ ] Sale was authorized or directed by the will
   b. [X] Good reason existed for the sale
   of the property commonly described as *(street address or location)*:
   9020 Boykin Way, Sacramento, California
4. The sale was legally made and fairly conducted.
5. The confirmed sale price is not disproportionate to the value of the property.
6. [X] Private sale: The amount bid is 90% or more of the appraised value of the property as appraised within one year of the date of the hearing.
7. An offer exceeding the amount bid by the statutory percentages
   [ ] cannot be obtained [X] was obtained in open court. The offer complies with all applicable law.
8. The personal representative has made reasonable efforts to obtain the highest and best price reasonably attainable for the property.

THE COURT ORDERS

9. The sale of the real property legally described [X] on reverse [ ] in Attachment 9
   [ ] and other property sold as a unit described [ ] on reverse [ ] in Attachment 9a
   is confirmed to *(name)*:
   MARTHA RAYNOR
   (manner of vesting title): Martha Raynor, a single person,

   for the sale price of: $ 170,000.00   on the following terms *(use attachment or reverse if necessary)*:

10. The personal representative *(name)*: Clarice Bell
    is directed to execute and deliver a conveyance of the estate's interest in the property described in item 9
    [ ] and other property described in item 9   upon receipt of the consideration for the sale.
11. a. [X] No additional bond is required.
    b. [ ] Personal representative shall give an additional bond for: $, surety, or otherwise, as provided by law.
    c. [ ] Net sale proceeds shall be deposited by escrow holder in a blocked account to be withdrawn only on court order. Receipts shall be filed. *(Specify institution and location)*:

12. a. [ ] No commission is payable.
    b. [X] A commission from the proceeds of the sale is approved in the amount of: $ 6,000.00
       to be paid as follows: Cash

Date: July 31, 19

Raymond McKenna
JUDGE OF THE SUPERIOR COURT   [ ] Signature follows last attachment.

13. [ ] Number of pages attached: 14. [X] Legal description on reverse.

Form Approved by the
Judicial Council of California
DE-265, GC-065 (Rev. July 1, 1988)

ORDER CONFIRMING SALE OF REAL PROPERTY
(Probate)

Probate Code, §§ 2543, 10313

FIGURE 6–4   Order Confirming Sale of Real Property

ESTATE OF (NAME):	CASE NUMBER:
— KENNETH BELL, also known as KENNETH K. BELL	92457

15. [x] Legal description of the [x] real property [ ] personal property   in item **9** *(describe)*:

Single family dwelling located at 9020 Boykin Way, City of Sacramento, County of Sacramento, California, described as the West 59.00 feet of the East 590.00 feet of Lot 1248, as shown on the "Plat of Elvira," recorded in the office of the County Recorder, January 23, 1909, in Book 8 of Maps, Map No. 41
    Assessor's Parcel No. 006-175-0200

CLERK'S CERTIFICATE

[SEAL]

I certify that the foregoing Order Confirming Sale of Real Property, including any attached description of real or personal property, is a true and correct copy of the original on file in my office.

Date: July 31, 19   CLERK, by _____ , Deputy

DE-266, GC-065 (Rev. July 1, 1988)   **ORDER CONFIRMING SALE OF REAL PROPERTY**   Page two
                                                     (Probate)

FIGURE 6–4   *(continued)*

Proof of the giving of notice is required to be made at the hearing. The court finds in its order that notice has been regularly given, and when the order becomes final it is conclusive upon all persons.

§ 6.6 Court Hearing

All persons who have made bids on the property or even indicated interest in the property should be informed of the time and place of the hearing on confirmation so they may attend the hearing and protect their interests if increased bids are made. Any bidder on the property may decide to go higher to get the property. Obtaining the highest price available from a qualified buyer is in the best interests of the estate. An attorney would be remiss in his or her duties if prospective bidders were not notified, and such failure could have serious consequences. The legal assistant should be sure that this is done and may also obtain a form of overbid for the attorney to take to court.

Any increased bid made in court must be in writing and be accompanied by a ten-percent deposit. The first overbid must exceed the original highest bid by at least ten percent on the first $10,000 of the sale price and five percent on the balance of the amount of the original bid in excess of $10,000. For example, the first overbid on a $100,000 high bid would have to be in the amount of $105,500. Further overbids can be in any amount, unless the court requires bids in higher multiples. The person who overbids might be expected to produce a down payment of ten percent of the offer as evidence of a good faith offer and a qualified buyer.

The attorney and the estate's representative should be present in court at the hearing. If the attorney cannot be present, the representative has to advise the court of his or her approval. In Los Angeles and San Francisco counties (and perhaps other counties), the court will not proceed if bidding is involved unless the attorney is present or the representative requests that the sale proceed without the presence of the attorney. The legal assistant should check local rules.

If the sale returned is for credit and a higher offer is for cash or on credit, whether on the same or different credit terms, the court may not consider the higher offer unless the personal representative informs the court, in person or by counsel, prior to confirmation of sale, that the offer is acceptable. The estate may need the cash urgently or there may be other reasons (Prob. Code § 10311).

§ 6.7   Brokers' Fees

A broker is entitled to a fee for a sale. In a number of areas, a six-percent fee is allowed. In Los Angeles County, local rules provide that upon confirmation of a sale of real property, the court will not allow a broker's commission in excess of five percent (except when the sale is for less than $500) unless justified by exceptional circumstances (Los Angeles County Probate Rules, Rule 10.93). In Sacramento County, the court will not approve a broker's fee in excess of six percent on improved property. For sale of unimproved property, the court allows ten percent on the first $20,000, eight percent on the next $30,000, and five percent on an amount over $50,000. Commissions are computed on gross selling price less points and costs of structural pest control inspection and repairs, if any.

If the bid returned for confirmation is made by a person not represented by an agent or broker and the successful bidder is represented by an agent or broker, the compensation of the successful agent or broker shall not exceed one-half of the difference between the amount of the original bid and the amount of the successful bid [Prob. Code § 10162(a)]. The compensation of a broker who holds an exclusive listing is not limited by this section. If no broker holds an exclusive listing but the bid returned for confirmation was obtained by an agent or broker and the court confirms the bid or an increased bid made at the hearing, the court allows the broker who obtains the sale the fair compensation determined on the full amount of the sale (Prob. Code §§ 10161, 10162.3). Probate Code section 10165 provides for compensation where the sale is made on an increased bid through a broker.

Where an agent has an exclusive right to sell, the court allows him or her compensation based on the full amount of the sale if either (a) the bid returned for confirmation is made by a person not represented by an agent or broker and the court confirms the sale on that bid, or (b) the bid returned to the court is made by a person represented by an agent or broker and the court confirms the sale to that purchaser on an increased bid made at the hearing (Prob. Code § 10162.5). If an agent or broker has an exclusive listing and the bid returned for confirmation was procured by an agent or broker and the court confirms the sale, the compensation is determined on the full amount of the sale but is divided between the agent or broker with the exclusive contract and the other agent or broker as they have agreed on, or if they do not make an agreement, is divided equally (Prob. Code § 10162.7).

If the bid returned to the court for confirmation is made by a person not represented by an agent or broker and the court confirms the sale on an increased bid of a purchaser not secured by a broker, the compensation is based on the amount of the original bid (Prob. Code § 10162.5).

If the broker, directly or indirectly, is the purchaser or has any interest in the purchaser, the estate is not liable to the broker (Prob. Code § 10160.5).

Other provisions for compensation of brokers are found in Probate Code sections 11063 through 11067.

§ 6.8 The Escrow

After the hearing is held and the court approves a sale of the property, an escrow should be opened, though not legally required. The sale is turned over to the escrow holder, a neutral third party, for completion. The escrow holder may be a title insurance company, a bank, a savings and loan association, or an independent escrow company. Ordinarily the escrow is handled by a title insurance company. When the escrow is opened, a number is issued. The legal assistant should use this number for reference in all communications, oral or written, with the escrow holder.

The buyer and seller prepare their own instructions to the escrow holder. If there is a conflict in the instructions, the escrow holder has the duty to resolve it or to call it to the attention of the buyer and seller so they can do so.

A termite inspection of the property may be requested by the buyer, typically before an offer or bid is made. If any recommendations are made as a result of the inspection, the seller is usually expected to carry them out at his or her own expense, although the buyer and seller may agree to another arrangement such as splitting the expense. Instructions should be furnished to the escrow holder in accordance with their agreement. Most counties permit sales of property as is, in which event no termite inspection is required.

Various fees are payable from the escrow, such as a fee for issuing the title policy, documentary stamps for transferring the property, recordation fees, reconveyance fees, escrow fees, and so on. Who is to pay these charges ordinarily is settled in the offer or bid, since such charges, like an increase or decrease in the sale price, help to fix the net price to the seller. The custom varies from county to county regarding who pays what, but the seller and buyer can make any kind of agreement they wish regarding payment. Instructions should be given to the escrow holder if any change is made.

A preliminary title report should always be requested and a title search made to make sure the sellers are the legal owners and that no one else can claim any right to title to the property involved. A title insurance policy also must be ordered.

There are two types of title policies, reportedly sold in all states except Iowa: the California Land Title Association (CLTA) policy, the standard policy that is sometimes called the owner's policy, and the American Land Title Association (ALTA) policy, sometimes called the lender's policy.

The **lender's policy** insures the mortgage lender against losses from title risks, but it does not insure the owner's equity. It is more costly and apt to be requested only where banks or savings and loan associations are the lenders, especially if they are out of state and unable to inspect the property personally. The ALTA policy covers any off-record matters such as a creek running through the living room.

The **owner's policy** shows anything of record in the county in which the real property is located—any judgments recorded, taxes owing, deeds of trust, or liens—and insures that everything is as shown in the preliminary title report. It protects the property owner from losing his or her equity from an uninsured title risk. The CLTA policy covers contingencies such as the seller's signature on the deed being forged, a forged signature on a will, or the seller being a person who is mentally incompetent and has a guardian. The insurers defend against title claims such as recording errors, marital and community property rights and agreements, unpaid tax liens, illegal acts by trustees, defective foreclosures, and other claims. As a practical matter, the title companies ordinarily do a thorough search of title to minimize their risk.

If the property is mortgaged, the amount owing must be determined and paid. The escrow holder will usually demand that the mortgage holder furnish the balance owing on the mortgage, since the unpaid balance on the mortgage is ordinarily paid out of escrow. The mortgagor may require the seller to make any subsequent payments by certified or cashier's check so they will not have to wait until personal checks clear before stating the amount owing.

Rents, taxes, premiums on insurance, interest, and other expenses of the property are usually prorated as of recordation of deed. In sales of residential properties, such as an apartment house, security deposits, advance rents, or future lease credits ordinarily are credited to the pur-

---

████ TERMS ████

lender's policy   A title insurance policy that insures the mortgage lender against losses from title risks and unrecorded matters but does not insure the owner's equity.

owner's policy   A title insurance policy that protects the property owner from loss of equity from title risks and any recorded matters.

chaser, but other agreements can be made. Any such agreements should be included in the offer.

The offer to buy is a valid and binding contract between the parties. Once signed, the offer cannot legally be withdrawn by the purchaser, and the seller may not change his or her mind. In nonprobate sales, the offer may be made subject to certain conditions, including physical inspection of the property, ability to obtain a specified loan on certain terms, and pest control clearance.

Arrangements for insurance must be made. The purchaser may want to obtain insurance from the seller's insurance company, in which case a new policy will have to be issued, or at least a binder to cover the property as soon as the new deed is recorded. The seller will want to cancel his or her insurance as of the time he or she is no longer the legal owner.

§ 6.9   Summary of Procedure for Selling Real Property at Private Sale

The following summarizes the various steps discussed in the preceding sections:

- Expose the property to be sold to the market. Consider employment of broker by written contract and whether an exclusive listing is to be given;

- Publish Notice of Intention to Sell Real Property at Private Sale;

- Facilitate the inspection of the property by prospective purchasers;

- Receive bids;

- Serve and file Report of Sale and Petition for Order Confirming Sale of Real Property;

- Give notice of the hearing on the report of sale;

- File the declaration of mailing on the notice of hearing;

- Advise the highest bidders and other prospective purchasers of the date of the hearing on the petition;

- Advise the representative of the hearing date;

- Prepare Order Confirming Sale of Real Property;

- Attend the hearing and make the sale;

- Open escrow;

- Check bond and increase it if not covered to the extent of sale price;

- Prepare administrator's or executor's deed and any escrow instructions; and

- Approve proposed distribution of escrow proceeds and deeds.

§ 6.10 Sales of Personal Property

The representative may sell personal property pursuant to Probate Code section 10254 *et seq.* Personal property can be said to be any property that is not real property. Notice must be posted at the courthouse or published fifteen days before the date of a private sale or the day of a public auction sale pursuant to the Government Code section 6063a. If published, notice must be published three times during a ten-day period in a newspaper published at least weekly in the county in which the probate proceeding is pending, with at least five days between the first and last publication dates (excluding the publication dates). The representative may both post the notice and publish it (Prob. Code § 10250). If shown to be in the best interests of the estate, the notice period may be shortened by the court to five days. If publication time is shortened, publication shall be pursuant to Government Code section 6061 (Prob. Code § 10251).

The notice must contain the time and place of the sale and a brief description of the property. The notice shall state whether the sale is private or by public auction. If it is a private sale, the notice must provide information about where bids and offers will be received and must state the day on or after which the sale will be made. If the sale is a public auction, the time and place of the sale and a brief description of the personal property to be sold must be provided in the notice (Prob. Code § 10253).

The representative of the estate may sell, without the need for court confirmation or approval, and at public auction or private sale, personal property of a decedent that (a) is perishable, (b) will depreciate in value if not disposed of promptly, (c) will incur loss or expense by being kept, or (d) is necessary to provide the family allowance pending receipt of other sufficient funds [Prob. Code § 10259(a)]. The title to such personal property will pass on sale without confirmation by court, but the personal representative is responsible for the actual value of the property unless the sale is reported to and approved by the court (Prob. Code § 10259).

No clear-cut rules exist about what property may be classified as depreciating property. If storage payments are being made for goods such as cars and furnishings, it would seem reasonable for the court to approve their sale. Likewise, furnishings and valuables in a vacant house are subject to vandalism and theft, and obtaining insurance on property inside a vacant house, as well as on the house itself, can present a problem.

A representative acting under the Independent Administration of Estates Act may sell or exchange certain personal property without court supervision, but a notice of the proposed action must be served in certain circumstances (Prob. Code §§ 10530, 10580 *et seq.*; see generally §§ 10500–10600). No notice is required if the will directs or authorizes the sale of the property (Prob. Code § 10252).

Sales of Securities

Stocks and other securities may be surrendered or sold upon obtaining an order of the court for sale. Subsequent court confirmation is not required.

A petition is prepared and filed with the clerk, who sets the petition for hearing and gives notice as required by Probate Code section 1220 and posting as required by section 1230. The court or judge may order notice to be given for a shorter period or dispensed with altogether [(Prob. Code § 10200(d)].

No notice need be given if the minimum selling price is fixed by the court or the securities are to be sold on an established stock or bond exchange or are securities designated as a national market system security, and so on, sold through a registered broker-dealer. (See also Prob. Code §§ 10200–10207.)

CHAPTER 7

FEDERAL AND STATE INCOME TAX AND CALIFORNIA PICKUP TAX

§ 7.1 Income Taxes

The legal assistant should take notice of the date of death, since that date determines the **alternate valuation date** (if an alternate valuation date is chosen), which indicates the time left before the decedent's final income tax return must be filed. (See Chapter 9, Federal Estate Taxation.) A choice of calendar year or fiscal year for filing future tax returns for the estate must be made.

Estates with taxable years ending two or more years after the date of death must pay estimated tax in the same manner as living individuals. Quarterly estimated tax payments are due April 15, June 15, September 15, and January 15. Estates are required to make estimated tax payments only after taxable years ending two or more years after the decedent's death [IRC § 6154(1)]. California conforms to this federal law.

The legal assistant should also check to see whether the decedent filed returns for earlier years.

There are three tax returns to consider. A larger estate will use a 706 federal estate tax return, and there are also the decedent's final income tax return and one or more fiduciary income tax returns.

Time for Filing Decedent's Final Income Tax Return

The decedent's taxable year for income taxes ends on the date of death. Usually a return must be filed, but it may be that no return is required if the decedent's estate does not meet the gross income test (at the time of this writing, $600). A check should be made in the amount current at the time of filing [IRC § 642(b)]. The personal representative files decedent's final income tax return.

Gross income levels at which federal tax returns (1041s) had to be filed in 1995, even if no tax was owed, were as follows. Levels are divided under categories describing the decedent:

- Single (including divorced and legally separated)
  Under 65 $6,250
  65 or older $7,200

TERMS

alternate valuation date†   The date an estate administrator can choose as an alternative to the date of death for the valuation of a decedent's estate for federal estate tax purposes, which is six months after the date of death or the date the property is disposed of, whichever comes first.

- Head of household
Under 65	$8,050
65 or older	$9,000

- Married and living with spouse at end of 1994 (or on date of death), filing joint return
Both spouses under 65	$11,250
65 or older, one spouse	$12,000
65 or older, both spouses	$12,750

- Married, separate returns
Any age	$2,450

- Married, not living with spouse at end of 1994 (or on date spouse died)
Any age	$2,450

- Widowed before 1994 and not remarried in 1994
  Single
Under 65	$6,250
65 or older	$7,200

  Head of household
Under 65	$8,050
65 or older	$9,000

- Qualifying widow(er) with dependent child
Under 65	$8,800
65 or older	$9,550

Other categories exist for which different gross income requirements apply, and gross income requirements can differ from year to year.

The final tax return of the decedent is due on the same date on which it would have been due if the decedent were still alive. If the decedent had been paying income taxes on a calendar-year basis, the final return is due by April 15 of the year following the year of the decedent's death.

Joint Returns

Either the personal representative or the surviving spouse may file a joint return. The surviving spouse may file if the decedent did not make a return for the taxable year for which the joint return is to be made and if no personal representative has been appointed before the time of making the joint return or before the last day for filing the return of the surviving spouse, including any extensions of time for filing.

The decedent and the surviving spouse must have the same taxable year. A joint return may not be filed by the surviving spouse if he or she changes the accounting period to a fiscal year after the decedent's death and only a fractional part of the year remains in that fiscal year.

If the personal representative files a separate return for the decedent and the surviving spouse files a joint return, the joint return is disaffirmed if the disaffirmance is made within one year after the last day for filing the return of the surviving spouse. The surviving spouse's return is then treated as separate, and a new return will not be required from the surviving spouse. Tax will be computed on the basis of the joint return after deducting the items includible in the decedent's return.

The surviving spouse is not entitled to file a joint return for the year of the decedent's death if he or she remarries before the close of that taxable year. The surviving spouse should be made aware of the tax consequences of remarriage in case he or she would choose to postpone remarriage. A joint return may be filed with the new spouse under certain conditions and may prove more advantageous, depending on the incomes involved.

§ 7.2 California Estate Tax

The California inheritance tax and gift taxes were repealed as of June 8, 1982. California, however, still imposes two "death taxes": the estate tax and a generation-skipping transfer tax. Both are **pickup taxes**, meaning the tax otherwise would be paid to the federal government.

A federal generation-skipping transfer tax was added by the Tax Reform Act of 1986, retroactively repealing Chapter 13 of the Internal Revenue Code of 1954. (Generation-skipping taxes are further discussed in Chapter 13. The California generation-skipping tax return is due at the same time as the federal tax. It is intended to obtain for California the benefit of the credit allowed against the federal generation-skipping transfer tax.

The pickup tax applies in all estates where a federal estate tax is payable. California imposes an estate tax equal to the portion, if any, of the maximum amount of the credit for state death taxes allowable under federal estate tax law attributable to property located in the State of California. In no event shall the estate tax imposed result in a total death tax liability to the State of California and the United States in excess of the death tax liability to the United States that would result if this section (Rev. & Tax Code § 13301) were not in effect. (See generally Rev. & Tax. Code §§ 13302–14302.)

TERMS

pickup tax A tax that would be paid to one branch of government but is picked up by another branch.

The California estate tax return to be used is Form ET-1. This form is due at the same time as the federal estate tax form (Form 706) (nine months from date of death unless an extension is granted). The legal assistant will need information from Form 706 (questions 1 and 2b) to compute the tax. The ET-1 is filed with the Controller's office in Sacramento. The tax is payable to the State Treasurer through the Controller. The form is reproduced in Figure 7–1.

For California residents who are **transferors**, the tax applies to all real or personal property except real property located outside California and tangible personal property permanently outside California. For nonresident transferors, the tax applies only to real property in California and tangible personal property permanently in California. The tax also may apply to intangible personal property of nonresident transferors if the transferors reside outside the United States and have a situs in California. (See Rev. & Tax. Code §§ 13303, 13641, 13851; see also IRC § 2518.)

Procedure Where Death Occurred Before June 8, 1982

Where death occurred before June 8, 1982, the following must be furnished to the Division of Tax Administration:

- Two copies of the petition for probate or, if an estate is not being probated, for the fact of death;

- If inventory is being prepared, an original and two copies of the inventory; otherwise, an extra copy of the petition or schedule if a copy of appraised values is desired;

- Original and one copy of the inheritance tax declaration (Form IT-22);

- Original and one copy of the marital property declaration (Form IT-3) where applicable;

- If nonresidence is claimed, an original and one copy of the residence declaration (Form IT-2);

- Two copies of any other schedule, declaration of contribution, and exhibits attached and made a part of the above documents by reference;

- One copy of the order appointing a probate referee (in some counties); and

TERMS

transferor†   A person who places property in the hands of another; passing property from the ownership or possession of one person to the ownership or possession of another, whether by the act of the parties or by operation of law.

This form is to be used only for estates of decedents who died after June 8, 1982.
Return is due and tax is payable nine months after date of death.

STATE OF CALIFORNIA

ESTATE TAX RETURN

DO NOT USE THIS SPACE

MAIL RETURN TO:
State Controller
Division of Tax Administration
P.O. Box 247
Sacramento, California 95802

Decedent's Name (First, middle, last)

Date of Death

County of Probate (enter "N/A" if no probate proceeding)

Probate Case No.

Social Security No.

Domicile at Date of Death (City, County, State or Country) (If claimed decedent was not domiciled in California, attach Form IT-2)

Name of personal representative or person filing return

Address

Telephone No.

Name of Attorney

Address

Telephone No.

A COPY OF THE FEDERAL ESTATE TAX RETURN, FORM 706, <u>MUST</u> BE FILED WITH THIS RETURN

An extension to file the Federal Estate Tax Return has _____ has not _____ been granted until (date) _____.
A true copy of the extension must be attached to qualify for a like California extension.

COMPUTATION OF TAX:

1. Total state death tax credit allowable for Federal estate tax purposes (IRS Form 706, pg. 1, line 13) $ _____

2. Proration of Federal estate tax state death tax credit: (complete only if there is property located in states other than California)
   a. Gross value for Federal estate tax purposes of property located in California (identify on attached Federal estate tax return) $ _____
   b. Gross value of decedent's estate for Federal estate tax purposes (IRS Form 706, pg. 1, line 1) $ _____
   c. Percent of estate of Federal estate tax purposes located in California (line 2(a) divided by line 2(b))   _____ %

3. Tax payable to California (line 1 multiplied by line 2(c) or amount from line 1 if no entries on line 2) $ _____

4. Late filing penalty (5% of line 3 for each month or portion thereof maximum penalty 25%) $ _____

5. Interest at 12% per annum on amount on line 3 from due date of return to date of payment $ _____

6. Total tax, penalty and interest due (total of lines 3, 4 and 5) $ _____

REMITTANCES SHOULD BE MADE PAYABLE TO STATE TREASURER

I DECLARE UNDER PENALTY OF PERJURY THAT THIS RETURN, INCLUDING ANY ATTACHMENTS, HAS BEEN EXAMINED BY ME AND TO THE BEST OF MY KNOWLEDGE AND BELIEF IS TRUE, CORRECT AND COMPLETE. IF PREPARED BY A PERSON OTHER THAN THE DECLARANT, HIS OR HER DECLARATION IS BASED ON ALL INFORMATION OF WHICH HE OR SHE HAS ANY KNOWLEDGE.

Signature of person filing return

Date

Address

Signature of person preparing this return

Date

Address

ET-1 (Org. 1/83)

FIGURE 7–1 California Estate Tax Return form

INSTRUCTIONS FOR CALIFORNIA ESTATE TAX RETURN

GENERAL INFORMATION:

- This return must be filed for the estate of every decedent with property in California whose date of death is on or after June 9, 1982, if Federal Estate Tax Return (IRS Form 706) is required to be filed.

- This return must be filed by the personal representative of the estate. "Personal representative" means the personal representative of the decedent or, if there is no personal representative appointed, qualified and acting within California, any person who is in actual or constructive possession of any property included in the gross estate of the decedent.

- **DUE DATE**—The return is due and any tax liability is payable on or before nine (9) months from the date of death.

- A copy of the Federal Estate Tax Return and any approved extensions must be filed with this return.

- If an amended Federal Estate Tax Return is filed, an amended California Estate Tax Return must immediately be filed together with a copy of the amended Federal Estate Tax Return and payment of any additional tax plus interest, if any.

- Written notice of final determination of the Federal Estate Tax must be given within 60 days of the determination together with payment of any additional tax plus interest, if any.

SPECIFIC INSTRUCTIONS:

- Line 2(a)—"Property located in California" of a California resident includes real property located in California; tangible personal property having an actual situs in California; and all intangible personal property, wherever the notes, bonds, stock certificates or other evidence, if any, of the ownership of the intangible personal property may be physically located or wherever the banks or other debtors of the decedent may be located or domiciled.

- "Property located in California" of a non-resident of California who is a resident of the United States includes real property located in California and tangible personal property having an actual situs in California.

- "Property located in California" of a non-resident of the United States includes real property located in California, tangible personal property having a situs in California; and all intangible personal property in California including all stock of a corporation organized under the laws of California or which has its principal place of business or does a major part of its business in California or of a federal corporation or national bank which has its principal place of business or does the major part of its business in California, excluding, however, savings accounts in savings and loan associations operating under the authority of the Division of Savings and Loan or the Federal Home Loan Bank board and bank deposits, unless those deposits are held and used in connection with a business conducted or operated, in whole or in part, in California.

- Line 4—A like extension to file will be granted if the Internal Revenue Service has granted an extension to file the federal estate tax return.

- Line 5—An extension of time to file does not relieve the payment of interest.

- Line 6—If a payment is insufficient to cover the total amount due, it will be applied first against penalties due, then interest and then to the payment of tax.

FIGURE 7–1   *(continued)*

- Two copies of the will, if any, even if it is not being used or probated.

After the Division of Tax Administration has determined whether any tax is due, the legal assistant should have the petition set for hearing. Any inheritance tax does not have to be paid before a decree is obtained.

A certified copy of the death decree establishing death and the certificate of release of lien, if any, also should be recorded.

§ 7.3 Other Forms

Since the repeal of the inheritance tax, no forms for consent to transfer or for release of lien are required for an estate where the decedent died on or after 12:01 A.M., June 9, 1982. Other tax documents previously required (IT-22s, IT-3s, and supporting affidavits) also do not need to be submitted in an estate where the decedent died after this date.

The California Probate Referees Association has developed a form called "Appraisal Report of California Probate Referee." The person requesting the appointment of a referee lists on this form descriptions of property to be appraised, such as real property, stocks, bonds, notes, and personal property. Valuations can be as of the date of death, the six-month alternative valuation date permitted for federal estate tax purposes, or another designated date.

Referees make appraisals in probate matters to confirm real property sales and to determine the share allocated to pretermitted heirs, liability for debts, the amount of bond, and the amount of attorneys' and personal representative's fees and commissions. Appraisals of referees are used in other areas as well, such as the administration of guardianships and conservatorships, the determination of fair market value, and in efficiency judgment proceedings. [See Nicora, "Changes in California Probate Administration and the Role of California Probate Referees," *CEB Estate Planning & California Probate Reporter* (Feb. 1983).]

CHAPTER 8

FEDERAL ESTATE TAXATION

All estates are subject to an estate tax levied by the federal government. In practice, this tax is levied on a relatively small number of estates, since only the larger estates are required to file a return and pay a tax. This tax is levied on the total amount of the estate and is payable out of the assets of the estate, not from the share of any particular beneficiary. The relationship of the beneficiaries has no effect on the amount of the tax (unlike the repealed California state inheritance tax).

The legal assistant who is going to be proficient in the probate field should become familiar with all the requirements relating to tax returns and learn how to properly complete the estate tax returns. The attorney should discuss with the legal assistant any specific instructions and any special problems concerning a given estate and should review the Form 708 before it is signed. In some law firms, attorneys choose to have this phase of administration handled by an accountant.

Completion of the tax return involves considerable knowledge of federal estate tax laws. The representative of the estate is confronted with many decisions during the administration period that can result in substantial tax savings or losses to the estate and its beneficiaries. The tax identities of the decedent while living and of beneficiaries are critical to sound decisions. The personal representative may require considerable advice and guidance to perform the requisite duties properly.

§ 8.1   Form SS-4—Application for Employer Identification Number

Form SS-4 should be filed with the IRS in order to obtain a tax identification number for the estate. The number issued by the IRS should be included on all the tax returns of the estate. A fiscal year date will be requested on the form. If no decision has been made about what fiscal year would be best, write "pending" on the form. A determination can be made when the first return is filed. Calendar year reporting is usually easier in terms of bookkeeping, but the tax savings possible by choosing a fiscal year may outweigh the extra time and work required. (See Figure 8–1.)

Form **SS-4**
(Rev. December 1993)
Department of the Treasury
Internal Revenue Service

Application for Employer Identification Number

(For use by employers, corporations, partnerships, trusts, estates, churches, government agencies, certain individuals, and others. See instructions.)

EIN

OMB No. 1545-0003
Expires 12-31-96

Please type or print clearly.

1 Name of applicant (Legal name) (See instructions.)
Estate of Kenneth Bell, aka Kenneth K. Bell, Deceased

2 Trade name of business, if different from name in line 1

3 Executor, trustee, "care of" name
Clarice Bell

4a Mailing address (street address) (room, apt., or suite no.)
121 Sandor Place

5a Business address, if different from address in lines 4a and 4b

4b City, state, and ZIP code
Sacramento, CA 95814

5b City, state, and ZIP code

6 County and state where principal business is located

7 Name of principal officer, general partner, grantor, owner, or trustor—SSN required (See instructions.) ▶

8a Type of entity (Check only one box.) (See instructions.)
☐ Sole Proprietor (SSN) _____
☐ REMIC   ☐ Personal service corp.
☐ State/local government   ☐ National guard
☐ Other nonprofit organization (specify) _____
☐ Other (specify) ▶ _____

☒ Estate (SSN of decedent) 563 226723
☐ Plan administrator-SSN _____
☐ Other corporation (specify) _____
☐ Federal government/military   ☐ Church or church controlled organization

☐ Trust
☐ Partnership
☐ Farmers' cooperative

(enter GEN if applicable) _____

8b If a corporation, name the state or foreign country (if applicable) where incorporated ▶
State
Foreign country

9 Reason for applying (Check only one box.)
☐ Started new business (specify) ▶ _____
☐ Hired employees
☐ Created a pension plan (specify type) ▶ _____
☐ Banking purpose (specify) ▶ _____
☐ Changed type of organization (specify) ▶ _____
☐ Purchased going business
☐ Created a trust (specify) ▶ _____
☐ Other (specify) ▶

10 Date business started or acquired (Mo., day, year) (See instructions.)

11 Enter closing month of accounting year. (See instructions.)

12 First date wages or annuities were paid or will be paid (Mo., day, year). **Note:** If applicant is a withholding agent, enter date income will first be paid to nonresident alien. (Mo., day, year) . . . . ▶   N/A

13 Enter highest number of employees expected in the next 12 months. **Note:** If the applicant does not expect to have any employees during the period, enter "0." . . . . ▶

	Nonagricultural	Agricultural	Household
	0	0	0

14 Principal activity (See instructions.) ▶ Administration of probate estate

15 Is the principal business activity manufacturing? . . . . ☐ Yes ☒ No
If "Yes," principal product and raw material used ▶

16 To whom are most of the products or services sold? Please check the appropriate box.   ☐ Business (wholesale)
☐ Public (retail)   ☐ Other (specify) ▶   ☒ N/A

17a Has the applicant ever applied for an identification number for this or any other business? . . . . ☐ Yes ☒ No
Note: If "Yes," please complete lines 17b and 17c.

17b If you checked the "Yes" box in line 17a, give applicant's legal name and trade name, if different than name shown on prior application.

Legal name ▶   Trade name ▶

17c Enter approximate date, city, and state where the application was filed and the previous employer identification number if known.

Approximate date when filed (Mo., day, year) | City and state where filed   Previous EIN

Under penalties of perjury, I declare that I have examined this application and to the best of my knowledge and belief it is true, correct, and complete | Business telephone number (include area code)

Name and title (Please type or print clearly.) ▶

Signature ▶   Date ▶

Note: Do not write below this line.   For official use only.

Please leave blank ▶	Geo.	Ind.	Class	Size	Reason for applying

For Paperwork Reduction Act Notice, see attached instructions.   Cat. No. 16055N   Form **SS-4** (Rev. 12-93)

FIGURE 8–1   Application for Employer Identification Number

Form SS-4 (Rev. 12-93)   Page **2**

General Instructions

(Section references are to the Internal Revenue Code unless otherwise noted.)

Purpose

Use Form SS-4 to apply for an employer identification number (EIN). An EIN is a nine-digit number (for example, 12-3456789) assigned to sole proprietors, corporations, partnerships, estates, trusts, and other entities for filing and reporting purposes. The information you provide on this form will establish your filing and reporting requirements.

Who Must File

You must file this form if you have not obtained an EIN before and

● You pay wages to one or more employees.

● You are required to have an EIN to use on any return, statement, or other document, even if you are not an employer.

● You are a withholding agent required to withhold taxes on income, other than wages, paid to a nonresident alien (individual, corporation, partnership, etc.). A withholding agent may be an agent, broker, fiduciary, manager, tenant, or spouse, and is required to file **Form 1042**, Annual Withholding Tax Return for U.S. Source Income of Foreign Persons.

● You file **Schedule C**, Profit or Loss From Business, or **Schedule F**, Profit or Loss From Farming, of **Form 1040**, U.S. Individual Income Tax Return, and have a Keogh plan or are required to file excise, employment, or alcohol, tobacco, or firearms returns.

The following must use EINs even if they do not have any employees:

● Trusts, except the following:

1. Certain grantor-owned revocable trusts (see the Instructions for Form 1040).

2. Individual Retirement Arrangement (IRA) trusts, unless the trust has to file **Form 990-T**, Exempt Organization Business Income Tax Return (See the Instructions for Form 990-T.)

● Estates

● Partnerships

● REMICS (real estate mortgage investment conduits) (See the instructions for **Form 1066**, U.S. Real Estate Mortgage Investment Conduit Income Tax Return.)

● Corporations

● Nonprofit organizations (churches, clubs, etc.)

● Farmers' cooperatives

● Plan administrators (A plan administrator is the person or group of persons specified as the administrator by the instrument under which the plan is operated.)

Note: *Household employers are not required to file Form SS-4 to get an EIN. An EIN may be assigned to you without filing Form SS-4 if your only employees are household employees (domestic workers) in your private home. To have an EIN assigned to you, write "NONE" in the space for the EIN on **Form 942**, Employer's Quarterly Tax Return for Household Employees, when you file it.*

When To Apply for A New EIN

New Business.—If you become the new owner of an existing business, **DO NOT** use the EIN of the former owner. If you already have an EIN, use that number. If you do not have an EIN, apply for one on this form. If you become the "owner" of a corporation by acquiring its stock, use the corporation's EIN.

Changes in Organization or Ownership.—If you already have an EIN, you may need to get a new one if either the organization or ownership of your business changes. If you incorporate a sole proprietorship or form a partnership, you must get a new EIN. However, **DO NOT** apply for a new EIN if you change only the name of your business.

File Only One Form SS-4.—File only one Form SS-4, regardless of the number of businesses operated or trade names under which a business operates. However, each corporation in an affiliated group must file a separate application.

EIN Applied For, But Not Received.—If you do not have an EIN by the time a return is due, write "Applied for" and the date you applied in the space shown for the number. **DO NOT** show your social security number as an EIN on returns.

If you do not have an EIN by the time a tax deposit is due, send your payment to the Internal Revenue service center for your filing area. (See **Where To Apply** below.) Make your check or money order payable to Internal Revenue Service and show your name (as shown on Form SS-4), address, kind of tax, period covered, and date you applied for an EIN.

For more information about EINs, see **Pub. 583**, Taxpayers Starting a Business and **Pub. 1635**, EINs Made Easy.

How To Apply

You can apply for an EIN either by mail or by telephone. You can get an EIN immediately by calling the Tele-TIN phone number for the service center for your state, or you can send the completed Form SS-4 directly to the service center to receive your EIN in the mail.

Application by Tele-TIN.—Under the Tele-TIN program, you can receive your EIN over the telephone and use it

immediately to file a return or make a payment. To receive an EIN by phone, complete Form SS-4, then call the Tele-TIN phone number listed for your state under **Where To Apply**. The person making the call must be authorized to sign the form (see **Signature block** on page 3).

An IRS representative will use the information from the Form SS-4 to establish your account and assign you an EIN. Write the number you are given on the upper right-hand corner of the form, sign and date it.

You should mail or FAX the signed SS-4 within 24 hours to the Tele-TIN Unit at the service center address for your state. The IRS representative will give you the FAX number. The FAX numbers are also listed in Pub. 1635.

Taxpayer representatives can receive their client's EIN by phone if they first send a facsimile (FAX) of a completed **Form 2848**, Power of Attorney and Declaration of Representative, or **Form 8821**, Tax Information Authorization, to the Tele-TIN unit. The Form 2848 or Form 8821 will be used solely to release the EIN to the representative authorized on the form.

Application by Mail.—Complete Form SS-4 at least 4 to 5 weeks before you will need an EIN. Sign and date the application and mail it to the service center address for your state. You will receive your EIN in the mail in approximately 4 weeks.

Where To Apply

The Tele-TIN phone numbers listed below will involve a long-distance charge to callers outside of the local calling area, and should be used only to apply for an EIN. THE NUMBERS MAY CHANGE WITHOUT NOTICE. Use 1-800-829-1040 to verify a number or to ask about an application by mail or other Federal tax matters.

If your principal business, office or agency, or legal residence in the case of an individual, is located in:	Call the Tele-TIN phone number shown or file with the Internal Revenue Service center at:
Florida, Georgia, South Carolina	Attn: Entity Control Atlanta, GA 39901 (404) 455-2360
New Jersey, New York City and counties of Nassau, Rockland, Suffolk, and Westchester	Attn: Entity Control Holtsville, NY 00501 (516) 447-4955
New York (all other counties), Connecticut, Maine, Massachusetts, New Hampshire, Rhode Island, Vermont	Attn: Entity Control Andover, MA 05501 (508) 474-9717
Illinois, Iowa, Minnesota, Missouri, Wisconsin	Attn: Entity Control Stop 57A 2306 E. Bannister Rd. Kansas City, MO 64131 (816) 926-5999
Delaware, District of Columbia, Maryland, Pennsylvania, Virginia	Attn: Entity Control Philadelphia, PA 19255 (215) 574-2400

FIGURE 8–1 *(continued)*

Form SS-4 (Rev. 12-93)

Indiana, Kentucky, Michigan, Ohio, West Virginia	Attn: Entity Control Cincinnati, OH 45999 (606) 292-5467
Kansas, New Mexico, Oklahoma, Texas	Attn: Entity Control Austin, TX 73301 (512) 462-7843
Alaska, Arizona, California (counties of Alpine, Amador, Butte, Calaveras, Colusa, Contra Costa, Del Norte, El Dorado, Glenn, Humboldt, Lake, Lassen, Marin, Mendocino, Modoc, Napa, Nevada, Placer, Plumas, Sacramento, San Joaquin, Shasta, Sierra, Siskiyou, Solano, Sonoma, Sutter, Tehama, Trinity, Yolo, and Yuba), Colorado, Idaho, Montana, Nebraska, Nevada, North Dakota, Oregon, South Dakota, Utah, Washington, Wyoming	Attn: Entity Control Mail Stop 6271-T P.O. Box 9950 Ogden, UT 84409 (801) 620-7645
California (all other counties), Hawaii	Attn: Entity Control Fresno, CA 93888 (209) 452-4010
Alabama, Arkansas, Louisiana, Mississippi, North Carolina, Tennessee	Attn: Entity Control Memphis, TN 37501 (901) 365-5970

If you have no legal residence, principal place of business, or principal office or agency in any state, file your form with the Internal Revenue Service Center, Philadelphia, PA 19255 or call (215) 574-2400.

Specific Instructions

The instructions that follow are for those items that are not self-explanatory. Enter N/A (nonapplicable) on the lines that do not apply.

Line 1.—Enter the legal name of the entity applying for the EIN exactly as it appears on the social security card, charter, or other applicable legal document.

Individuals.—Enter the first name, middle initial, and last name.

Trusts.—Enter the name of the trust.

Estate of a decedent.—Enter the name of the estate.

Partnerships.—Enter the legal name of the partnership as it appears in the partnership agreement.

Corporations.—Enter the corporate name as set forth in the corporation charter or other legal document creating it.

Plan administrators.—Enter the name of the plan administrator. A plan administrator who already has an EIN should use that number.

Line 2.—Enter the trade name of the business if different from the legal name. The trade name is the "doing business as" name.

Note: *Use the full legal name on line 1 on all tax returns filed for the entity. However, if you enter a trade name on line 2 and choose to use the trade name instead of the legal name, enter the trade name on all returns you file. To prevent processing delays and errors, **always** use either the legal name only or the trade name only on all tax returns.*

Line 3.—Trusts enter the name of the trustee. Estates enter the name of the executor, administrator, or other fiduciary. If the entity applying has a designated person to receive tax information, enter that person's name as the "care of" person. Print or type the first name, middle initial, and last name.

Line 7.—Enter the first name, middle initial, last name, and social security number (SSN) of a principal officer if the business is a corporation; of a general partner if a partnership; and of a grantor owner, or trustor if a trust.

Line 8a.—Check the box that best describes the type of entity applying for the EIN. If not specifically mentioned, check the "other" box and enter the type of entity. Do not enter N/A.

Sole proprietor.—Check this box if you file Schedule C or F (Form 1040) and have a Keogh plan, or are required to file excise, employment, or alcohol, tobacco, or firearms returns. Enter your SSN (social security number) in the space provided.

Plan administrator.—If the plan administrator is an individual, enter the plan administrator's SSN in the space provided.

Withholding agent.—If you are a withholding agent required to file Form 1042, check the "other" box and enter "withholding agent."

REMICs.—Check this box if the entity has elected to be treated as a real estate mortgage investment conduit (REMIC). See the Instructions for Form 1066 for more information.

Personal service corporations.—Check this box if the entity is a personal service corporation. An entity is a personal service corporation for a tax year only if:

● The principal activity of the entity during the testing period (prior tax year) for the tax year is the performance of personal services substantially by employee-owners.

● The employee-owners own 10 percent of the fair market value of the outstanding stock in the entity on the last day of the testing period.

Personal services include performance of services in such fields as health, law, accounting, consulting, etc. For more information about personal service corporations, see the instructions for **Form 1120**, U.S. Corporation Income Tax Return, and **Pub. 542,** Tax Information on Corporations.

Other corporations.—This box is for any corporation other than a personal service corporation. If you check this box, enter the type of corporation (such as insurance company) in the space provided.

Other nonprofit organizations.—Check this box if the nonprofit organization is

other than a church or church-controlled organization and specify the type of nonprofit organization (for example, an educational organization.)

If the organization also seeks tax-exempt status, you must file either **Package 1023** or **Package 1024,** Application for Recognition of Exemption. Get **Pub. 557,** Tax-Exempt Status for Your Organization, for more information.

Group exemption number (GEN).—If the organization is covered by a group exemption letter, enter the four-digit GEN. (Do not confuse the GEN with the nine-digit EIN.) If you do not know the GEN, contact the parent organization. Get Pub. 557 for more information about group exemption numbers.

Line 9.—Check only **one** box. Do not enter N/A.

Started new business.—Check this box if you are starting a new business that requires an EIN. If you check this box, enter the type of business being started. **DO NOT** apply if you already have an EIN and are only adding another place of business.

Changed type of organization.—Check this box if the business is changing its type of organization, for example, if the business was a sole proprietorship and has been incorporated or has become a partnership. If you check this box, specify in the space provided the type of change made, for example, "from sole proprietorship to partnership."

Purchased going business.—Check this box if you purchased an existing business. DO NOT use the former owner's EIN. Use your own EIN if you already have one.

Hired employees.—Check this box if the existing business is requesting an EIN because it has hired or is hiring employees and is therefore required to file employment tax returns. **DO NOT** apply if you already have an EIN and are only hiring employees. If you are hiring household employees, see **Note** under **Who Must File** on page 2.

Created a trust.—Check this box if you created a trust, and enter the type of trust created.

Note: *DO NOT file this form if you are the individual-grantor/owner of a revocable trust. You must use your SSN for the trust. See the instructions for Form 1040.*

Created a pension plan.—Check this box if you have created a pension plan and need this number for reporting purposes. Also, enter the type of plan created.

Banking purpose.—Check this box if you are requesting an EIN for banking purposes only and enter the banking purpose (for example, a bowling league for depositing dues, an investment club for dividend and interest reporting, etc.).

FIGURE 8–1 *(continued)*

Other (specify).—Check this box if you are requesting an EIN for any reason other than those for which there are checkboxes, and enter the reason.

Line 10.—If you are starting a new business, enter the starting date of the business. If the business you acquired is already operating, enter the date you acquired the business. Trusts should enter the date the trust was legally created. Estates should enter the date of death of the decedent whose name appears on line 1 or the date when the estate was legally funded.

Line 11.—Enter the last month of your accounting year or tax year. An accounting or tax year is usually 12 consecutive months, either a calendar year or a fiscal year (including a period of 52 or 53 weeks). A calendar year is 12 consecutive months ending on December 31. A fiscal year is either 12 consecutive months ending on the last day of any month other than December or a 52-53 week year. For more information on accounting periods, see **Pub. 538,** Accounting Periods and Methods.

Individuals.—Your tax year generally will be a calendar year.

Partnerships.—Partnerships generally must adopt the tax year of either (1) the majority partners; (2) the principal partners; (3) the tax year that results in the least aggregate (total) deferral of income; or (4) some other tax year. (See the Instructions for **Form 1065,** U.S. Partnership Return of Income, for more information.)

REMICs.—Remics must have a calendar year as their tax year.

Personal service corporations.—A personal service corporation generally must adopt a calendar year unless:

● It can establish a business purpose for having a different tax year, or

● It elects under section 444 to have a tax year other than a calendar year.

Trusts.—Generally, a trust must adopt a calendar year except for the following:

● Tax-exempt trusts,

● Charitable trusts, and

● Grantor-owned trusts.

Line 12.—If the business has or will have employees, enter the date on which the business began or will begin to pay wages. If the business does not plan to have employees, enter N/A.

Withholding agent.—Enter the date you began or will begin to pay income to a nonresident alien. This also applies to individuals who are required to file Form 1042 to report alimony paid to a nonresident alien.

Line 14.—Generally, enter the exact type of business being operated (for example, advertising agency, farm, food or beverage establishment, labor union, real estate agency, steam laundry, rental of coin-operated vending machine, investment club, etc.). Also state if the business will involve the sale or distribution of alcoholic beverages.

Governmental.—Enter the type of organization (state, county, school district, or municipality, etc.).

Nonprofit organization (other than governmental).—Enter whether organized for religious, educational, or humane purposes, and the principal activity (for example, religious organization—hospital, charitable).

Mining and quarrying.—Specify the process and the principal product (for example, mining bituminous coal, contract drilling for oil, quarrying dimension stone, etc.).

Contract construction.—Specify whether general contracting or special trade contracting. Also, show the type of work normally performed (for example, general contractor for residential buildings, electrical subcontractor, etc.).

Food or beverage establishments.—Specify the type of establishment and state whether you employ workers who receive tips (for example, lounge—yes).

Trade.—Specify the type of sales and the principal line of goods sold (for example, wholesale dairy products, manufacturer's representative for mining machinery, retail hardware, etc.).

Manufacturing.—Specify the type of establishment operated (for example, sawmill, vegetable cannery, etc.).

Signature block.—The application must be signed by: (1) the individual, if the applicant is an individual, (2) the president, vice president, or other principal officer, if the applicant is a corporation, (3) a responsible and duly authorized member or officer having knowledge of its affairs, if the applicant is a partnership or other unincorporated organization, or (4) the fiduciary, if the applicant is a trust or estate.

Some Useful Publications

You may get the following publications for additional information on the subjects covered on this form. To get these and other free forms and publications, call 1-800-TAX-FORM (1-800-829-3676).

Pub. 1635, EINs Made Easy

Pub. 538, Accounting Periods and Methods

Pub. 541, Tax Information on Partnerships

Pub. 542, Tax Information on Corporations

Pub. 557, Tax-Exempt Status for Your Organization

Pub. 583, Taxpayers Starting A Business

Pub. 937, Employment Taxes and Information Returns

Package 1023, Application for Recognition of Exemption

Package 1024, Application for Recognition of Exemption Under Section 501(a) or for Determination Under Section 120

Paperwork Reduction Act Notice

We ask for the information on this form to carry out the Internal Revenue laws of the United States. You are required to give us the information. We need it to ensure that you are complying with these laws and to allow us to figure and collect the right amount of tax.

The time needed to complete and file this form will vary depending on individual circumstances. The estimated average time is:

Recordkeeping . . . . . . 7 min.

Learning about the law or the form . . . . . . 18 min.

Preparing the form . . . . . 44 min.

Copying, assembling, and sending the form to the IRS . 20 min.

If you have comments concerning the accuracy of these time estimates or suggestions for making this form more simple, we would be happy to hear from you. You can write to both the **Internal Revenue Service,** Attention: Reports Clearance Officer, PC:FP, Washington, DC 20224; and the **Office of Management and Budget,** Paperwork Reduction Project (1545-0003), Washington, DC 20503. **DO NOT** send this form to either of these offices. Instead, see **Where To Apply** on page 2.

Printed on recycled paper

U.S. Government Printing Office: 1994 — 387-095/00295

FIGURE 8–1 *(continued)*

§ 8.2   Form 706 for Small Estates

Simplified Format for Small Estates

The short format for use where the total gross is $500,000 or less is no longer available, since these estates are not required to file an estate tax return. If the decedent died in 1986 or later and the total gross estate is $600,000 or less, no return needs to be filed.

Who Must File a 706 [United States Estate (and Generation-Skipping Transfer) Tax Return]

Determination of whether a federal estate tax return must be filed is made by adding (1) the amount of the gross estate valued as of the date of death; (2) adjusted taxable gifts under IRC section 2001(b) made by the decedent after December 31, 1976; and (3) the total specific exemption allowed under IRC section 2521 (as in effect before repeal by the Tax Reform Act of 1976) with respect to gifts made by the decedent after September 8, 1976. Unless the total figure exceeds the exemption equivalent listed below for the particular year, no return (Form 706) need be filed:

1977	$120,000
1978	134,000
1979	147,000
1980	161,000
1981	175,000
1982	225,000
1983	275,000
1984	325,000
1985	400,000
1986	500,000
1987 and subsequent years	600,000

The gross estate figure is determined by computing the value of the following:

- Certain transfers made during the decedent's life without an adequate and full consideration in money or money's worth;

- Annuities;

- Joint estates with right of survivorship;

- Tenancies by the entirety;

- Life insurance proceeds (even though payable to beneficiaries other than the estate);

- Property over which the decedent possessed a general power of appointment;

- Dower or courtesy (or statutory estate) of the surviving spouse; and

- Community property to the extent of the decedent's interest as defined by applicable law.

["Instructions for Form 706 (Revised August 1993)," published by the Internal Revenue Service.] Also available from the IRS are the following: "Federal Estate and Gift Taxes" (Publication 448); "Tax Information for Survivors, Executors and Administrators" (Publication 559); and "Interrelated Computations for Estate and Gift Taxes" (Publication 904).

SIDEBAR   The legal assistant should study the Internal Revenue Service publications, and the Internal Revenue Code and Regulations should be available for reference. These publications are revised periodically and are available from the Internal Revenue Service free of charge. These resources also can be found in most law libraries. Usually the law office will subscribe to one or more tax services as well, such as those published by Commerce Clearing House and Research Institute of America.

Specific Instructions

The instruction booklet for Form 706 contains a number of specific instructions, and much of the information below is based on this booklet (as revised in July 1990).

The first three pages of Form 706 and all required schedules must be filed. Schedules A through I must be filed, as appropriate, to support the entries in lines 1 through 9 of the recapitulation. If "O" is entered for any item of the tax recapitulation on page 1, only Schedule F needs to be filed. If a credit for foreign death taxes is claimed, Schedule P is required, and form 706CE (Certificate of Payment of Foreign Death Tax) should be attached to support any credit claimed.

Which 706 Form to Use

New law results in new forms and booklets, so the legal assistant should check with the IRS for the latest revisions of these publications. Following are the revisions of Form 706 that are to be used according to the decedent's date of death:

- October 1991 revision for decedents who died after October 8, 1990, and before January 1, 1993;

- July 1990 revision for decedents who died after December 31, 1989, and before October 9, 1990;

- October 1988 revision for decedents who died after October 22, 1986, and before January 1, 1990;

- November 1987 revision for decedents who died after December 31, 1981, and before October 23, 1986; and

- November 1981 revision for decedents who died before January 1, 1982.

The latest form at this writing, the August 1993 revision.

Supplemental Documents

Certain documents may be required to be filed with Form 706, such as:

- Certified copy of the will, if any;

- Form 712 if an insurance policy is listed, to be inserted following Schedule D;

- Form 706CE in triplicate for each foreign death tax for which credit is claimed (this form must be filed before credit can be allowed);

- Death certificate;

- Instruments creating a trust or power of appointment;

- State certification of payment of death taxes (not required in California if death occurred after June 9, 1982, since California no longer has an inheritance tax); and

- Forms 709 and 708-A, where required.

Nonresident Decedents

Regardless of the size of the gross estate, the following documents should be filed:

- Copy of the inventory of property and schedule of liabilities, claims against the estate, and expenses of administration filed with the foreign court of probate jurisdiction, certified by a proper court official;

- Certified copy of the return filed under the foreign inheritance, estate, legacy, succession, or other death tax if the estate is subject to such a foreign tax, certified by a property official of the foreign tax department; and

■ Certified copy of any will.

After Form 706 Is Filed

The schedule that follows is meant to serve as a "rule of thumb," since the time schedule of the IRS can change for various reasons.

After Form 706 is filed, three or four months usually elapse before it is received in the IRS's district office. In the four to five months after that receipt, the district office accepts the return and issues closing letters. If the return is assigned for examination, the examination period should not exceed three months before the taxpayer is contacted. If more than one year passes after Form 706 is filed and no word has been received from the IRS, the district office should be contacted.

§ 8.3 When to File Estate Tax Return (706)—Extensions of Time— Payment of Taxes

Form 706 is due nine months after the date of death. This due date must be calendared in the office tickler system. If there is no numerically corresponding day in the ninth month, the last day of the ninth month is the due date. If the due date falls on Saturday, Sunday, or legal holiday, the due date is the next succeeding weekday that is not a legal holiday.

Within a few months after the decedent has died, it should be apparent whether an extension of time is going to be required. It may be impossible or impractical to pay the tax within the nine-month period, as where **liquid assets** are insufficient and a sale of real property will be necessary. Form 4768 is used to request the extension (see Figure 8–2). The reason for requesting the extension must be stated. An extension of time to file Form 706 may not be granted for more than six months unless the personal representative is abroad (IRC § 6081).

Form 4768 should be filed with the Internal Revenue Service in sufficient time for the application to be considered and the reply to be

---

TERMS

liquid assets† Assets that are easily convertible into cash.

Form **4768**

(Rev. May 1993)

Department of the Treasury
Internal Revenue Service

**Application for Extension of Time To File a Return
and/or Pay U.S. Estate
(and Generation-Skipping Transfer) Taxes**

(For filers of Forms 706, 706-A, and 706-NA)

OMB No. 1545-0181
Expires 5-31-96

Note: Use Form 2758 to request an extension for Forms 706GS(D) and 706GS(T).

Part I	Identification

Decedent's first name and middle initial	Decedent's last name	Date of death
Name of executor	Name of application filer (if other than the executor)	Decedent's social security number
Address of executor (Number, street, and room or suite no.)		Estate tax return due date
City, state, and ZIP code		

Part II	Extension of Time To File (Sec. 6081)

You must attach your written statement to explain in detail why it is impossible or impractical to file a reasonably complete return within 9 months after the date of the decedent's death.

Extension date requested

Part III	Extension of Time To Pay (Sec. 6161)

You must attach your written statement to explain in detail why it is impossible or impractical to pay the full amount of the estate (or GST) tax by the return due date. If the taxes cannot be determined because the size of the gross estate is unascertainable, check here ▶ ☐ and enter "-0-" or other appropriate amount on Part IV, line 3. You must attach an explanation.

Extension date requested

Part IV	Payment To Accompany Extension Request

1 Amount of estate and GST taxes estimated to be due **1**
2 Amount of cash shortage (complete Part III) **2**
3 Balance due (subtract line 2 from line 1) (Pay with this application.) **3**

Signature and Verification

If filed by executor—Under penalties of perjury, I declare that I am an executor of the estate of the above-named decedent and that to the best of my knowledge and belief, the statements made herein and attached are true and correct.

....
Executor's signature   Title   Date

If filed by someone other than the executor—Under penalties of perjury, I declare that to the best of my knowledge and belief, the statements made herein and attached are true and correct, that I am authorized by the executor to file this application, and that I am (check box(es) that applies):

☐ A member in good standing of the bar of the highest court of (specify jurisdiction) ▶ ....
☐ A certified public accountant duly qualified to practice in (specify jurisdiction) ▶ ....
☐ A person enrolled to practice before the Internal Revenue Service.
☐ A duly authorized agent holding a power of attorney. (The power of attorney need not be submitted unless requested.)

....
Filer's signature (other than the executor)   Date

Part V	Notice to Applicant—To be completed by the Internal Revenue Service

1 The application for extension of time to file (Part II) is:
☐ Approved
☐ Not approved because ....
....
☐ Other ....
....

2 The application for extension of time to pay (Part III) is:
☐ Approved
☐ Not approved because ....
....
☐ Other ....
....

Internal Revenue Service official	Date	Internal Revenue Service official	Date

For Paperwork Reduction Act Notice, see instructions on the back of this form.   Cat. No. 41984P   Form **4768** (Rev. 5-93)

FIGURE 8–2 Form 4768: Application for Extension of Time to File a Return and/or Pay U.S. Estate (and Generation-Skipping Transfer) Taxes

made before the estate tax due date. The sooner it is filed the better. The form should be filed no later than two months before the due date if feasible, and thirty days before at the absolute minimum. Applications filed after the due date will not be considered except for certain section 6166 or 6166A elections (closely held businesses).

The following is a sample of language to be used in the request for extension of time to file Form 706:

> Because of the difficulty in obtaining appraised valuations for all of the estate assets and because of litigation pending in the estate, preparation of a correct return by the due date is not possible. Payment is being made herewith of the estimated tax and a request is hereby made for an extension of time of _____ days, or until such later time as may be granted, in which to prepare and file the return.

If the application is for an extension of time to file the return only, the amount of tax estimated must be shown on the "balance due" line in part III of Form 4768 and a check or money order payable to the Internal Revenue Service must be included. The decedent's Social Security number should be written on the check or money order. The estate tax return must then be filed before the expiration of the period granted for extension of time to file and cannot be amended thereafter, although supplemental information that would result in a different amount of tax can be subsequently filed.

Form 4768 also is used when applying for an extension of time to pay the estate tax. If requesting only an extension of time to pay the tax, two copies should be filed. If an extension of time to file the return is also being requested, four copies should be filed.

The granting of an extension of time to file Form 706 does not extend the time to pay the tax, nor does it relieve the estate from liability for interest on the balance due during the period of extension. Interest is charged on the tax underpaid or postponed and accrues at specified rates that are subject to change periodically [see IRC § 6621(b)].

The time for payment of the tax can be extended for a reasonable period not to exceed twelve months from the date payment is due [IRC § 6161(a)(1)]. For a showing of reasonable cause, the time may be extended for up to ten years or, if installment payments are made under section 6166, not beyond a date twelve months after the due date for the last installment [IRC § 6161(a)(2)(B)].

Examples of "reasonable cause" for extension can be found on page 2 of Publication 448. Briefly stated, they are as follows:

- The estate has enough liquid assets to pay the tax when due but they are located in several jurisdictions and are not within the personal representative's immediate control, so that with due diligence they cannot be readily collected.

- Most of the estate's assets consist of rights to receive payments in the future, such as annuities, copyright royalties, contingent fees, and accounts receivable, that do not provide enough cash to pay the tax, and the estate cannot borrow against these assets without loss to the estate.

- The estate includes a claim to substantial assets that cannot be collected without a lawsuit, and therefore, the amount of the gross estate cannot be determined at the time the tax is due.

- A reasonable effort to convert the decedent's assets (other than a closely held business) into cash has been made, but estate would have to borrow at an interest rate higher than generally available to have sufficient funds to pay the tax, provide a reasonable allowance for the surviving spouse and dependent children during the administration of the estate, and satisfy claims that are due and payable.

Penalties

Internal Revenue Code section 6651 provides for penalties for both late filing and late payment unless there is reasonable cause for delay. Late filing and late payment should not occur under normal circumstances, and the legal assistant should be alert to prevent such a happening.

Penalties also are provided for willful attempt to evade payment of tax and for underpayment of estate taxes of $1,000 or more attributable to valuation understatements (IRC § 6660) and underpayment of generation-skipping transfer taxes.

If the estate tax is not paid and an extension of time is not granted by showing reasonable cause, a penalty is charged.

Extensions of Time—Reversionary or Remainder Interest

Special rules exist where the estate includes a reversionary or remainder interest. An election may be made to postpone the payment of the tax attributable to that interest until six months after the termination of the precedent interest. This election is made by checking lines 3 and 4, respectively, of part 3, Elections by the Executor, and attaching the required supplemental statements. At the end of the extension period, for reasonable cause shown, additional time to pay may be granted up to three years [IRC §§ 6163(a), (b)].

Extensions of Time—Closely Held Business

The provisions for payment of tax on closely held businesses have been liberalized. **Closely held business** includes a **proprietorship**, or a **partnership** in a trade or business with no more than fifteen partners or stockholders or where twenty percent or more of the capital assets or voting stock is included in determining the decedent's gross estate. The partnership or **corporation** must be carrying on a trade or business at the time of the decedent's death. Property owned through a corporation, partnership, estate, or trust is regarded as proportionally owned by or for the shareholders, partners, or beneficiaries who have a present interest. A person is treated as a beneficiary only if he or she has a present interest. A **present interest** means the beneficiary has a right to the income (IRC § 6166).

Provision is made for installment payments on closely held businesses, with interest being paid annually on the deferred tax. The ratio of the tax that the closely held business bears to the adjusted gross estate must be determined first, as the tax on that interest is the maximum tax that may be deferred. The personal representative may elect to pay the estate tax attributable to that interest in installments. Under the installment method, the personal representative may elect to defer the payment of the principal (the estate tax), but not the interest, up to five years from the original due date for paying the tax. After the first payment is made, the remaining installment payments must be made at least yearly. There can be no more than ten installment payments. Interest on the unpaid portion of the tax is not deferred and must be paid with each installment payment.

This election by the personal representative must be made by the due date for filing the return (or the date to which filing is extended). The

---

TERMS

closely held business†   A corporation in which all the stock is owned by a few persons or by another corporation and is not traded on a stock exchange; sometimes also referred to as a closely held corporation.

proprietorship†   A business owned by one person.

partnership†   An undertaking of two or more persons to carry on, as co-owners, a business or other enterprise for profit; an agreement between or among two or more persons to put their money, labor, and skill into commerce or business, and to divide the profit in agreed-upon proportions.

corporation†   An artificial person, existing only in the eyes of the law, to whom a state or the federal government has granted a charter to become a legal entity, separate from its shareholders, with a name of its own, under which its shareholders can act and contract and sue and be sued.

present interest†   An interest that is vested, as opposed to a future interest.

election may be in letter form and must contain the following information:

- The decedent's name and taxpayer identification number as they will appear on the estate tax return;
- The total amount of tax to be paid in installments;
- The date chosen to make the first installment payment;
- The number of annual installments (including the first for paying the tax;
- The properties shown on the estate tax return qualifying as interest in a closely held business identified by schedule and item number); and
- Reasons the estate qualifies for installment payments (IRS Publication 448).

A copy of the election should be attached to the copy of the estate tax return when it is filed.

If the election is made when the return is filed, it applies to the tax originally due and "certain deficiencies." If the election is not made when the return is filed, only the deficiencies, not the tax, may be paid in installments.

Protective Elections

The personal representative may make a "protective election" under certain conditions. (See IRS Publication 448, Sept. 1984, p. 4); see also IRC § 6601(j) for provisions on the four-percent rate on certain portion of estate tax extended under section 6166). This method is available only where the value of the interest in the closely held business is more than thirty-five percent of the value of the gross estate (less expenses, indebtedness, taxes, and losses). The maximum amount that can be paid in installments is that part of the estate tax attributable to the closely held business, and the decedent must have been a United States citizen or resident at the date of his or her death.

An interest held by the decedent in two or more closely held businesses is treated as an interest in a single closely held business if twenty percent of the total value of each separate business is included in the estate.

SIDEBAR

For an excellent article relating to Internal Revenue Code sections 303 and 6166, see "Pitfalls for the Fiduciary in Estate Tax Deferrals Under IRS Section 6166 and Stock Redemptions Under IRC Section 303," *State Bar Estate Planning Trust and Probate News,* Spring 1984 (vol. 6, no. 1).

Payment of Federal Estate Taxes

When paying the tax after an extension of time has been granted, a copy of Form 4768 must be attached to Form 706. If the amount paid differs from the balance due as shown on the return, the difference should be explained in an attached statement. If prior payments have been made or certain marketable United States Treasury bonds (such as flower bonds) have been redeemed to pay the estate tax, a statement also should be attached including these facts.

If the decedent made a gift within three years before death in an amount sufficient to require the filing of a gift tax return, the thirty-five percent of adjusted gross estate requirement must be met when including or not including the gift in the gross estate. Gifts of life insurance also must be brought back into the estate [IRC § 2035(d)(4)].

Checks should be made payable to the Internal Revenue Service. The decedent's name, Social Security number, and "Form 706" should be written on the check to assist the IRS in posting the payment.

Personal Representative's Duty

The Internal Revenue Service provides a penalty for late filing of Form 706. In one instance, where a return was filed three months late because of a clerical oversight, Internal Revenue Service assessed a late filing penalty. The United States Supreme Court reportedly confirmed the penalty, stating that the personal representative has an unambiguous duty to file the estate tax return on time.

§ 8.4 Tax Assessment Period and Release from Personal Responsibility

The federal estate tax must be assessed within three years after the date the return is filed or, if the tax is payable by stamp, at any time after the tax became due and before the expiration of three years after the date on which any part of such tax was paid (IRC § 6501). This assessment period can be reduced to eighteen months under certain circumstances by making a request for prompt assessment [see IRC § 6501(d)]. Form 4810 is available for this purpose, or you may use your own format. The estate remains liable for the tax during the three-year assessment period (or eighteen months if shortened).

Personal Liability

The personal representative or fiduciary of the estate may apply to the Internal Revenue Service for determination of the estate tax and for discharge from personal liability under Internal Revenue Code section 2204. The determination must be made within nine months after the request or the filing of the return, whichever is later. Within nine months, the personal representative must be notified of the amount of the tax and, upon payment, shall be entitled to a receipt or writing showing the discharge (IRC § 2204).

§ 8.5   Form 56—Notice Concerning Fiduciary Relationship

Form 56, obtainable from the IRS, is one of the first tasks to be taken care of by the personal representative. The legal assistant should see that it is completed and filed with the Internal Revenue Service in the area in which the return is to be filed (Reg. 301.6903-2) within thirty days after appointment. (See Figure 8–3.)

When the fiduciary relationship terminates, that is, when all the duties of the personal representative have been performed and the estate is closed or ready to be closed, a written notice of the termination with satisfactory evidence thereof should be filed with the Internal Revenue Service.

§ 8.6   Valuation of Estate

The value of estate property is the fair market value of the property as of the date of death. However, the personal representative sometimes has a choice between the value as of date of death and the value on the alternate valuation date. (See the discussion below regarding the alternate valuation date.)

If an appraisal has been made by a probate referee in California, ordinarily that appraisal is used in the federal estate tax return and accepted by the Internal Revenue Service. If there is a sizeable holding of real property, commercial property, farm land, or closely held stock, the Internal Revenue Service will need to be satisfied with the basis of the valuation or an audit may result.

Since the unlimited marital deduction has been in effect many estates pay no estate tax if the decedent is survived by a spouse. A personal

Form **56**
(Rev. July 1994)

Department of the Treasury
Internal Revenue Service

Notice Concerning Fiduciary Relationship

(Internal Revenue Code sections 6036 and 6903)

OMB No. 1545-0013

Part I   Identification

Name of person for whom you are acting (as shown on the tax return)	Identifying number	Decedent's social security no.

Address of person for whom you are acting (number, street, and room or suite no.)

City or town, state, and ZIP code (If a foreign address, enter city, province or state, postal code, and country.)

Fiduciary's name

Address of fiduciary (number, street, and room or suite no.)

City or town, state, and ZIP code	Telephone number (optional) ( )

Part II   Authority

1   Authority for fiduciary relationship. Check applicable box:

a(1) ☐ Will and codicils or court order appointing fiduciary. Attach certified copy . . (2) Date of death ....

b(1) ☐ Court order appointing fiduciary. Attach certified copy . . . . (2) Date (see instructions) ....

c   ☐ Valid trust instrument and amendments. Attach copy

d   ☐ Other. Describe ▶ ....

Part III   Tax Notices

Send to the fiduciary listed in Part I all notices and other written communications involving the following tax matters:

2   Type of tax (estate, gift, generation-skipping transfer, income, excise, etc.) ▶ ....

3   Federal tax form number (706, 1040, 1041, 1120, etc.) ▶ ....

4   Year(s) or period(s) (If estate tax, date of death) ▶ ....

Part IV   Revocation or Termination of Notice

Section A—Total Revocation or Termination

5   Check this box if you are revoking or terminating all prior notices concerning fiduciary relationships on file with the Internal Revenue Service for the same tax matters and years or periods covered by this notice concerning fiduciary relationship . ▶ ☐
Reason for termination of fiduciary relationship. Check applicable box:

a ☐ Court order revoking fiduciary authority. Attach certified copy.

b ☐ Certificate of dissolution or termination of a business entity. Attach copy.

c ☐ Other. Describe ▶

Section B—Partial Revocation

6a   Check this box if you are revoking earlier notices concerning fiduciary relationships on file with the Internal Revenue Service for the same tax matters and years or periods covered by this notice concerning fiduciary relationship . . . . ▶ ☐

b   Specify to whom granted, date, and address, including ZIP code, or refer to attached copies of earlier notices and authorizations ▶ ....

Section C—Substitute Fiduciary

7   Check this box if a new fiduciary or fiduciaries have been or will be substituted for the revoking or terminating fiduciary(ies) and specify the name(s) and address(es), including ZIP code(s), of the new fiduciary(ies) . . . . ▶ ☐

Part V   Court and Administrative Proceedings

Name of court (If other than a court proceeding, identify the type of proceeding and name of agency)	Date proceeding initiated

Address of court	Docket number of proceeding

City or town, state, and ZIP code	Date	Time	a.m. p.m.	Place of other proceedings

I certify that I have the authority to execute this notice concerning fiduciary relationship on behalf of the taxpayer.

Please Sign Here ▶

Fiduciary's signature	Title, if applicable	Date
Fiduciary's signature	Title, if applicable	Date

For Paperwork Reduction Act and Privacy Act Notice, see back page.   Cat. No. 163751   Form **56** (Rev. 7-94)

FIGURE 8–3   Form 56: Notice Concerning Fiduciary Relationship

representative may be tempted to overstate the value of an asset on the estate tax return to obtain a higher basis in case the asset is sold or donated to charity. A deliberate overstatement is subject to penalty for negligence or fraud (IRC § 6653). Underpayment of income tax because of a valuation overstatement is also subject to penalty (IRC § 6659).

Where the estate has a substantial interest in mineral rights, an independent appraisal by a geologist is best and not as likely to be questioned on review by IRS engineers.

Rights to receive income in the future (for example, royalties) do not carry today's value and should be discounted.

Alternate Valuation Date

The law regarding alternate valuation dates was changed by the Tax Reform Act of 1984. It applies to estates of decedents dying after July 18, 1984. Under that law, an alternate valuation date may not be elected unless it will decrease both (1) the value of the gross estate and (2) the total net estate and generation-skipping taxes due after application of all allowable credits [IRC § 2032(c)]. Internal Revenue Code section 2032(d) provides that such an election shall be made by the personal representative on the return of the tax imposed. Once the election is made, it is irrevocable. No election may be made if the return is filed more than one year after the time prescribed by law (including extensions) for filing the return.

An election to value the decedent's property on the date six months after the decedent's death cannot be made for only part of the property of the estate. The election applies to all the property. For example, a personal representative cannot value appreciating real property as of the date of death but use the alternate valuation date six months later for stocks that are declining in value. If a substantial percentage of the assets of an estate consist of depreciating stock, the alternate valuation date should be selected as long as the tax savings that result will not be offset by the value of other assets that are appreciating within the six-month period.

If a personal representative elects the alternate valuation date and distributes, sells, exchanges, or otherwise disposes of any estate property within six months after the decedent's death, the value of the property will be the value as of the date it is distributed, sold, exchanged, or otherwise disposed of.

At one time California had no provision for alternate valuation. If an alternate date were chosen for federal estate tax purposes, the estate had to deal with two sets of valuations in accounting and income tax reporting. Since the California inheritance tax has been repealed, this problem no longer exists except in estates where the decedent died prior to June 9, 1982, the effective date of the repeal.

If the alternate valuation date is used, any property, interest, or estate that is affected by mere lapse of time, including **patents**, estates for the lives of persons other than the decedent, **remainders**, and **reversions**, is valued as of the date of the decedent's death, although an adjustment is made for any difference in value not due to mere lapse of time as of six months after the decedent's death or, if earlier, as of the date of its disposition. When the alternate valuation method is used, the values of life estates, remainders, and similar interests are calculated by using the age of the recipients on the date of the decedent's death. Valuation of annuities, life estates, terms for years, remainders, and reversions is discussed on page 11 of IRS Publication 448 (August 1992).

If the alternate valuation date is not adopted, the alternate value is not shown in the schedule columns headed "alternate value." If the alternate valuation date is adopted, the schedules will show the value both at the date of death and on the alternate valuation date. The alternate valuation date should be specified, as there may be more than one such date, for example, where a parcel of real property is sold within the six-month period after death.

§ 8.7 Deductions and Taxes

The personal representative may elect to take deductions from the estate on either Form 706 or the fiduciary income tax return. The decedent's final income tax return also must be considered. Choosing the return on which to take deductions is one of the most important services to the estate, since making the wrong choice can lead to financial loss to the estate. Special care must be exercised by both the attorney and the legal assistant in this area.

TERMS

patent† The exclusive right of manufacture, sale, or use granted by the federal government to a person who invents or discovers a device or process that is new and useful.

remainder† An estate in land to take effect immediately after the expiration of a prior estate (known as the particular estate), created at the same time and by the same instrument.

reversion† A future interest in land to take effect in favor of the grantor of the land or his heirs after the termination of a prior estate he has granted; in other words, the returning of the property to the grantor or his heirs when the grant is over.

SIDEBAR

Before the repeal of the California inheritance tax, consideration had to be given to Form IT-22 when deciding how to take deductions. This is still a consideration if the estate is one where the decedent died before the repeal of the inheritance tax, that is, on or before July 9, 1982.

Any deductible item paid before death is taken on the decedent's final return, the 1040. Items paid after death are taken on the fiduciary tax return, the 1041. If a surviving spouse takes all of the decedent's estate, deductions for which there is a choice are probably better taken on the fiduciary income tax return than the 706, since there is an unlimited marital deduction for surviving spouses, which means that no estate tax would be payable on any amount transferred to the surviving spouse.

Shifting deductions is not difficult. When the 706 is filed, either refrain from claiming any deductions or include the following statement on Schedule J:

Commissions, fees and expenses of administration paid may be taken as deductions against income for income tax purposes. The fact that said expenses are itemized here constitutes neither an election to take these deductions against income for income tax purposes nor an election to take them as deductions in computing the federal estate tax.

Deductions that can be taken on both the 706 and the 1041 returns are as follows:

- Real property taxes;
- Interest on debts accrued to decedent's date of death;
- Certain deductible business expenses;
- Legitimate income deductions;
- Deductible legal fees;
- Investment expenses; and
- State income tax on income received prior to the date of death.

The deductions on which an election must be made, as between the 706 and the 1041, are as follows:

- Unpaid medical expenses;
- Expenses of decedent's last illness;
- Personal representative's or administrator's commissions;
- Attorneys' fees;
- Casualty losses;

- Miscellaneous deductible administration expenses incurred after decedent's death (including court costs, accountants' fees, and appraisers' fees);

- Expenses for preservation and maintenance of real property subject to administration (including cost of storing and maintaining property if immediate distribution to beneficiaries is impossible but only for a reasonable period and not including outlays for additions or improvements); and

- Expenses of real property sales where the sales are necessary to pay the decedent's debts, the expenses of administration, or taxes; to preserve the estate; or to effect distribution [Reg. 20.2053-3(d)(2)].

The following deductions may be taken against income tax only:

- State income taxes on income of the estate;

- Interest on an indebtedness incurred after the decedent's date of death; and

- Interest on estate tax deficiencies.

Funeral expenses may be taken on the estate tax return only, not on an income tax return.

§ 8.8   Completing the 706

An instruction booklet for Form 706 is issued by the Internal Revenue Service. The booklet on which the following is based was revised in October 1991. When completing a 706, the legal assistant should always check the most recent booklet.

Practical Tips for Completing the 706

Read the instructions for the 706 before completing the return. The most complete return possible should be filed. If the IRS asks for yet more information, they should be given all they need.

Following are some particular considerations:

- A copy of any trust instrument referred to should be attached, as well as a copy of the will and any other documents needed, such as canceled checks, copies of 1040s and 1041s, escrow statements, and appraisals;

- Any heir's claim against an estate must be valid and not an attempt to avoid the tax;

- The fact that all debts paid by the estate existed at the time of death, that is, they had not already been paid by the decedent, should be verified;

- Any payments made to heirs for services to the decedent are reported as income, and heirs should be so instructed;

- Any tax-free bequests to a charity or spouse for obscure contingencies should be examined;

- Proof should be obtained from anyone who claims they own property in the decedent's safe-deposit box;

- The word *discount* should not be used to explain an asset valuation, as it is a signal to the IRS for careful scrutiny of the value;

- If the estate had more than one appraisal made, the IRS auditors would like to see all of them;

- If the decedent owned a fractional interest in an asset, he or she may have made unreported gifts;

- If the decedent inherited property, it should be traced;

- Whether the California estate tax (pickup tax) and the marital deduction has been claimed must be determined;

- Discounted promissory notes may be held by family members;

- The 709s should match the 706s;

- Any complicated charitable trust computation or will contest should be double-checked, and any computation on a prior transfer trust if it is sizeable should be provided (worksheets should be attached);

- Section 6701 (aiding and abetting) applies to attorneys and appraisers;

- **Negligence** is defined as a disregard for the rules and regulations of the IRS, and the penalty is five percent of the entire underpayment, even if only five percent is due to negligence (applies after December 31, 1986);

- On real estate, the assessor's parcel number, the acreage, and the address of property rather than a lengthy **metes and bounds** description should be given; and

---

TERMS

negligence†   The failure to do something that a reasonable person would do in the same circumstances, or the doing of something a reasonable person would not do.

metes and bounds†   A property description, commonly in a deed or mortgage, that is based upon the property's boundaries and the natural objects and other markers on the land.

- If there are after-discovered assets, the return should be located and it should be determined whether it is being audited.

Schedule A: Real Estate

All real property belonging to the decedent should be listed on this schedule. The descriptions of real property listed here should correspond to the descriptions in the inventory. A complete legal description of the property is best included as well as a designation of the type of real property, that is, unimproved (without buildings thereon) or improved (with buildings thereon), family residence, commercial, or rental property. The street address of improved property should be given, since the referee will need this when making an appraisal. If the property is unimproved, the location should be given.

If the decedent had only an interest in the property, the value of the entire property should not be given, but only the value of the decedent's interest in it. For example:

> Single family dwelling located at 205 Dunham Street, Sacramento, California, described as the North one-half of the East one-half of Lot 3, and the West 20 feet of the North one-half of Lot 4 in the block bounded by M and N, 24th and 25th Streets, of the City of Sacramento, according to the map or plan thereof.
>
> | | |
> |---|---:|
> | Value of property | $120,000 |
> | Trust deed | –50,000 |
> | | $70,000 |

When property is subject to a loan, the full value of the property is not taxable, but only the **equity of redemption** value, that is, the total value minus the amount of the loan outstanding against it. The amount of the indebtedness on the mortgage is either listed on Schedule K or subtracted as shown above. Only the amount of the encumbrance attributable to the decedent's interest should be shown, not the entire amount. If the decedent's estate is not liable for the mortgage, only the value of the equity of redemption should be given, and then the indebtedness is not deducted on Schedule K.

The value of real estate should not be reduced for homestead or other exemption. The basis of the appraisal should be stated as: "Value based on

---

TERMS

equity of redemption†   The right of a mortgagor who has defaulted upon his mortgage payments to prevent foreclosure by paying the debt in full.

appraisal, copy of which is attached." If a probate referee is not making an appraisal, the valuation can be substantiated by documents such as an independent appraisal. Data also may be obtained from real estate brokers about comparable sales in the area. An explanation of how the values were determined should be attached, along with a copy of any other document supporting the valuation. The legal assistant might check the latest tax statement for an indication of value.

The value of any interest in real estate of the decedent held as a tenant in common should be listed on Schedule A. If the decedent had contracted to purchase real property, the full value of the property should be reported, and the unpaid part of the purchase price is listed on Schedule K.

If the decedent owned rental property, rent that had accrued but was unpaid at the date of death should be included on Schedule A.

There are two ways of listing community property assets:

1. As "Community property, one-half interest in," and so on, and including one-half its value; or

2. At full value, at the end of the page, with an entry such as: "Less surviving spouse's community property one-half interest in items [here list numbers of the items that are community property]," and under the value column, subtracting one-half the *total* value listed.

Joint tenancy interests may be listed on Schedule A, as where real property is held in joint tenancy between husband and wife but the contention is made that the property is actually community property. If it is listed on Schedule A, a statement such as "Real property held in joint tenancy for convenience only" should be included.

Schedule B: Stocks and Bonds

Schedule B lists stocks and bonds. Municipal bonds exempt from federal income taxes, including public housing bonds, are not exempt from estate tax and must be included unless specifically exempted by an estate tax provision of the Internal Revenue Code.

For stocks, the following should be indicated:

■ Number of shares;

■ Whether common or preferred issue;

■ Par value where needed for identification;

■ Price per share;

■ Exact name of corporation;

■ Principal exchange upon which sold, if listed on an exchange; and

- CUSIP (Committee on Uniform Security Identification Procedure) number, if available.

The CUSIP number is assigned to all stocks and bonds traded on major exchanges and many unlisted securities and is usually printed on the stock certificate. If it does not appear on the certificate, it may be obtained through the company's transfer agent.

For bonds, the following should be indicated:

- Quantity and denomination;

- Name of obligor;

- Date of maturity;

- Interest rate;

- Interest due date;

- Principal exchange if listed on an exchange CUSIP number, if available; and

- The company's principal office if the stock or bond is unlisted.

A broker can be helpful in determining values at the date of death. For United States government bonds, the bank's bond department may be of help.

Valuation of Stocks and Bonds

Stocks and bonds are listed at their fair market value, which is the mean (midpoint) between the highest and lowest selling prices quoted on the valuation date (date of death or alternate valuation date). For example, if the high was $10 and the low $5, the mean would be $7.50, the midpoint. If there were no sales on the valuation date but there were sales on dates within a reasonable period both before and after that date, the fair market value is determined by taking a weighted average of the means between the highest and lowest sales on those dates. "The average is to be weighted inversely by the respective numbers of trading days between the selling dates and the valuation date" (Reg. § 20.2031-2). (See Reg. § 20.2031-2 and IRS Publication 448 for specific examples.)

When selling prices or bid and asked prices are not available, the following should be taken into consideration: for bonds, the soundness of the security, the interest yield, the date of maturity, and other relevant factors; for stock, the net worth of the company, prospective earning power and dividend-paying capacity, and other relevant factors. This holds true for stock that is not actively traded or is closely held, which presents a more difficult problem.

A financial statement for the five years preceding the valuation date should be submitted with the return (see IRC § 2031), along with financial and other data, including balance sheets, particularly the one nearest to the valuation date; statements of the net earnings or operating results; and dividends paid for each of the five years immediately before the valuation date. Offers of purchase also show fair market value.

Certain marketable U.S. Treasury Bonds issued before March 4, 1971, called **flower bonds**, may be redeemed at par plus accrued interest in payment of the estate tax at any Federal Reserve bank, the office of the Treasurer of the United States, or the Bureau of the Public Debt. (See Rev. Rul. 69-489, 1969-2 C.B. 172, 69-18, 1969-2 C.B. 300.)

If estate, inheritance, legacy, or succession taxes are paid to a foreign country with respect to any stocks or bonds listed in the schedule, group them together and label them under the heading "Subjected to Foreign Death Taxes."

List separately any interest and dividends on each stock or bond. Also include as separate items any dividends that have not been collected at death but are payable to the decedent or estate because the decedent was a stockholder of record on the date of death. Where a dividend has been declared on a share of stock but is not yet payable to stockholders, it may be selling ex-dividend. If stock held by the decedent is being traded on an exchange and selling ex-dividend on the date of death, the amount of the dividend should not be included as a separate item but should be added to the ex-dividend quotation in determining the fair market value of the stock on the date of death. Dividends declared on stock before the date of death but payable to stockholders of record on a date after death are not includible in the gross estate for federal estate tax purposes.

Schedule C: Mortgages, Notes, and Cash

Schedule C must be completed and filed with the return if the estate contains any mortgages, notes, or cash. Items should be grouped in categories and listed in the following order: (1) mortgages; (2) promissory notes; (3) contracts by the decedent to sell land; (4) cash in possession; and (5) cash in banks, savings and loan associations, and other types of financial organizations. Credit union accounts are included.

Notes payable to the decedent are listed on this schedule. A note secured by a deed of trust on real property should include a brief descrip-

---

TERMS

flower bonds   Certain U.S. Treasury obligations that may be used to pay federal estate taxes, in which event they are redeemable at part.

tion of the property securing the note. Unpaid principal on notes should be shown, as well as the balance in bank accounts and any accrued interest. The interest rate should be indicated, and some attorneys add the date last posted. The legal assistant should check with the attorney about the preferred method of the law firm.

Any cash, in the possession of the decedent at the time of death, however small in amount, should be included. The legal assistant should be aware of this and specifically inquire about it if not previously done.

Schedule D: Insurance on Decedent's Life

If there was any insurance on the decedent's life, whether or not included in the gross estate, this schedule must be completed. Every policy must be listed, including insurance on the decedent's life receivable by or for the benefit of the estate and insurance to be used to pay the estate tax and any other taxes, debts, or charges enforceable against the estate. Insurance receivable by beneficiaries other than the estate must be listed if the decedent possessed at death any incidents of ownership in a policy. "Incidents of ownership" include:

- power to change the beneficiary;

- power to surrender or cancel the policy;

- power to assign the policy or to revoke an assignment;

- power to pledge the policy for a loan;

- power to obtain from the insurer a loan against its surrender value; and

- reversionary interest (whether arising by express terms of policy, other instrument, or operation of law), but only if its value exceeded five percent of the value of the policy immediately before the decedent's death.

Reversionary interest, as used here, includes the possibility that the policy or its proceeds may return to the decedent or the estate or be subject to a power of disposition by the decedent.

If a married decedent was the owner of record of an insurance policy on his or her life that is not payable to a named beneficiary, the premiums were probably paid out of earnings of the decedent or the decedent and

---

TERMS

reversionary interest†   A future interest, i.e., the right to the future enjoyment of a reversion.

another party, which would make the policy community property. In such a case, the survivor automatically has a one-half interest in the benefits of the policy. If an insurance policy is payable to a named beneficiary, normally it will not go to probate. [See Civil Code §§ 5118, 5119; see also *Patillo v. Norris* 65 Cal. App. 3d 209 (1976).]

If all policy proceeds are not included in the gross estate, an explanation must be given. If any policy on the decedent's life is not included on Form 706 for any reason, an explanation should be given (IRC § 2042; Reg. § 20.2042-1). A National Service Life Insurance Policy (the so-called GI insurance) is deemed to be separate property, although premiums are often paid from community property funds.

Any insurance that the decedent owned on the life of another should be included. The amount of the cash surrender value of the policy on the date of the decedent's death should be obtained from the insurance company.

Form 712 should be included for each policy reported. The form may be obtained from the insurance company or the Internal Revenue Service. The form will show the proceeds paid and to whom they were paid and will show separately dividends and interest. The name of the beneficiary should be shown, as well as any outstanding loan against the policy and any accrued interest on the loan. This may be inserted following Schedule D. (For Form 712, see Figure 8–4.)

Schedule E: Jointly Owned Property

If the decedent owned any joint property at the time of death, whether or not included in the estate, Schedule E must be filed. The full value of the property should be entered. Jointly owned property includes all property of whatever kind or character, whether real estate, personal property, or bank accounts, and whether held by the decedent as a joint tenant with right of survivorship or as a tenant by the entirety. (Jointly owned Totten trusts also are included if they are payable to the estate.) A brief explanation of how the joint ownership was acquired should be included.

A joint interest is a qualified joint interest if the decedent and the surviving spouse held the interest as (a) tenants by the entirety or (b) as joint tenants with right of survivorship, if the decedent and the spouse are the only joint tenants. If the decedent and the surviving spouse had an agreement that the property was community property, the legal assistant should consult with the attorney to determine whether a copy of the agreement should be attached. If the interest meets the criteria, it should be entered in part I of Schedule E. If it does not meet the criteria, it is entered in part II. All joint interests not entered in part I must be entered in part II (see the instructions for part II in the booklet).

FIGURE 8–4 Form 712: Life Insurance Statement

Form 712 (Rev. 8-94)   Page **2**

Part II   **Living Insured**
(File With United States Gift Tax Return, Form 709. May Be Filed With United States Estate Tax
Return, Form 706 or Form 706-NA, Where Decedent Owned Insurance on Life of Another)

SECTION A—General Information

33 First name and middle initial of donor (or decedent)	34 Last name	35 Social security number

| 36   Date of gift for which valuation data submitted . . . . ▶ | |
| 37   Date of decedent's death for which valuation data submitted . . . . ▶ | |

SECTION B—Policy Information

38 Name of insured	39 Sex	40 Date of birth

41   Name and address of insurance company

42 Type of policy	43 Policy number	44 Face amount	45 Issue date

46 Gross premium		47 Frequency of payment

48 Assignee's name		49 Date assigned

50 If irrevocable designation of beneficiary made, name of beneficiary	51 Sex	52 Date of birth, if known	53 Date designated

54   If other than simple designation, quote in full. (Attach additional sheets if necessary.)

55   If policy is not paid up:

  a   Interpolated terminal reserve on date of death, assignment, or irrevocable designation of beneficiary . . . .

  b   Add proportion of gross premium paid beyond date of death, assignment, or irrevocable designation of beneficiary . . . .

  c   Add adjustment on account of dividends to credit of policy. . . . .

  d   **Total** (add lines a, b, and c) . . . .

  e   Outstanding indebtedness against policy . . . .

  f   Net total value of the policy (for gift or estate tax purposes) (subtract line e from line d) . . . . .

56   If policy is either paid up or a single premium:

  a   Total cost, on date of death, assignment, or irrevocable designation of beneficiary, of a single-premium policy on life of insured at attained age, for original face amount plus any additional paid-up insurance (additional face amount $ _____)

    (If a single-premium policy for the total face amount would not have been issued on the life of the insured as of the date specified, nevertheless, assume that such a policy could then have been purchased by the insured and state the cost thereof, using for such purpose the same formula and basis employed, on the date specified, by the company in calculating single premiums.)

  b   Adjustment on account of dividends to credit of policy . . . .

  c   **Total** (add lines 56a and 56b). . . . .

  d   Outstanding indebtedness against policy . . . .

  e   Net total value of policy (for gift or estate tax purposes) (subtract line 56d from line 56c) . . . .

The undersigned officer of the above-named insurance company hereby certifies that this statement sets forth true and correct information.

Signature ▶	Title ▶	Date of Certification ▶

🔁 *Printed on recycled paper*

*U.S. Government Printing Office: 1994 — 301-628/00246

FIGURE 8–4   *(continued)*

benefits. Similar benefits under the Railroad Retirement Act likewise are not includible (Rev. Rul. 81-182, 1981-28 (IRB 6); Rev. Rul. 67-277).

Schedule G: Transfers During Decedent's Life

Detailed instructions are given in the booklet accompanying the 706 and should be studied by the legal assistant completing the 706. Schedule G must be completed if the decedent made any of the transfers described below in (1) through (5) or if the answer is "yes" to questions 11 or 12a of part 4, General Information:

1. Certain gift taxes. Item A calls for the inclusion in the estate of the amount of gift taxes paid by the decedent or the spouse within three years before the date of death and refers to Internal Revenue Code section 2035(c). Any 709s filed by the decedent within three calendar years from the date of death should be examined, as well as those of the decedent's spouse, to determine the gifts made within the three-year period before death. The date of the gift, not the date of payment of the gift tax, determines whether a gift tax paid is included in the gross estate under this rule;

2. Other transfers within three years before death [IRC § 2035(a)];

3. Transfers with retained life estate (IRC § 2036);

4. Transfers taking effect at death (IRC § 2037); and

5. Revocable transfers [IRC §§ 2035(d), 2038].

SIDEBAR

Transfers within three years from the date of death are brought back into the estate under the Internal Revenue Code to determine whether the estate qualifies for the purposes of (1) section 303(b) (relating to distributions in redemption of stock to pay death taxes), (2) section 2032A (relating to special valuation of certain farm property, and so on, and real property), and (3) subchapter C of chapter 64 (relating to lien for taxes). See instructions on the form for further details about the types of transfers. In the description column, the name of the transferee, the date of the transfer, and a complete description of the property should be listed. Valuation is as of the date of the decedent's death or, if alternate valuation is adopted, according to Internal Revenue Code section 2032. If the transferee made additions or improvements to the property, the increased value resulting therefrom should not be included on Schedule G. If only a part of the value is included, the value of the whole is entered in the description and what part is included must be explained.

- judgments;

- reversionary or remainder interests;

- shares in trust funds;

- household goods and personal effects, including wearing apparel;

- farm products and growing crops;

- livestock;

- farm machinery;

- automobile (check Blue Book for value);

- claims (such as for a refund of income taxes or the amount actually received); and

- insurance on the life of another. (Form 712 must be attached for each policy.)

The full economic value of any insurance policy should be reported. Sometimes the surrender value of the policy exceeds its replacement cost, making the true economic value greater than the amount shown on line 56 of Form 712. In such event, the full economic value is stated. (See Rev. Rul. 78-137, 1978-1 C.B. 280 for details.)

The value placed on household furniture and personal effects is sometimes too high. The fair market value of used furniture is not very high in relation to its original cost. Furniture ordinarily depreciates very quickly. Personal effects usually have small resale value. If an automobile has been sold, its value is its sale price.

Interest in Business

If the decedent owned an interest in a partnership or unincorporated business, a statement of assets and liabilities for the valuation date and for the preceding five years should be attached. **Goodwill** should be accounted for. In general, methods used to value close corporations are followed (see instructions to Schedule B).

The lump-sum death benefit paid by Social Security to the decedent's spouse is not includible in the gross estate, nor are the spouse's monthly

---

TERMS

goodwill† The benefit a business acquires, beyond the mere value of its capital stock and tangible assets, as a result of having a good reputation and the respect of the public.

benefits. Similar benefits under the Railroad Retirement Act likewise are not includible (Rev. Rul. 81-182, 1981-28 (IRB 6); Rev. Rul. 67-277).

Schedule G: Transfers During Decedent's Life

Detailed instructions are given in the booklet accompanying the 706 and should be studied by the legal assistant completing the 706. Schedule G must be completed if the decedent made any of the transfers described below in (1) through (5) or if the answer is "yes" to questions 11 or 12a of part 4, General Information:

1. Certain gift taxes. Item A calls for the inclusion in the estate of the amount of gift taxes paid by the decedent or the spouse within three years before the date of death and refers to Internal Revenue Code section 2035(c). Any 709s filed by the decedent within three calendar years from the date of death should be examined, as well as those of the decedent's spouse, to determine the gifts made within the three-year period before death. The date of the gift, not the date of payment of the gift tax, determines whether a gift tax paid is included in the gross estate under this rule;

2. Other transfers within three years before death [IRC § 2035(a)];

3. Transfers with retained life estate (IRC § 2036);

4. Transfers taking effect at death (IRC § 2037); and

5. Revocable transfers [IRC §§ 2035(d), 2038].

SIDEBAR   Transfers within three years from the date of death are brought back into the estate under the Internal Revenue Code to determine whether the estate qualifies for the purposes of (1) section 303(b) (relating to distributions in redemption of stock to pay death taxes), (2) section 2032A (relating to special valuation of certain farm property, and so on, and real property), and (3) subchapter C of chapter 64 (relating to lien for taxes). See instructions on the form for further details about the types of transfers. In the description column, the name of the transferee, the date of the transfer, and a complete description of the property should be listed. Valuation is as of the date of the decedent's death or, if alternate valuation is adopted, according to Internal Revenue Code section 2032. If the transferee made additions or improvements to the property, the increased value resulting therefrom should not be included on Schedule G. If only a part of the value is included, the value of the whole is entered in the description and what part is included must be explained.

Any transfers made by the decedent during his or her life must be reported, whether or not believed to be subject to tax. If any transfers do not fit the categories described above, a statement should be attached describing the transfers and listing the date of the transfer, the amount or value, and the type of transfer.

Schedule H: Powers of Appointment

Powers of appointment created after October 21, 1942, are includible in the estate. A complete copy of the power of appointment should be attached. See Publication 448 for rules relating to powers of appointment created before October 21, 1942.

A general power of appointment is a power exercisable in favor of the decedent, his or her estate, creditors, or creditors of estate, except a power that is limited by an ascertainable standard relating to health, education, support, or maintenance of the decedent, or a power exercisable by the decedent only in conjunction with the creator of the power or a person who has a substantial interest in the subject property that is adverse to the exercise of the power.

This schedule should include, as part of the gross estate, (a) the value of property for which the decedent possessed a general power of appointment at the date of death and (b) the value of property for which the decedent possessed a general power of appointment that he or she exercised before death by disposing of it in such a way that if it were a transfer of property owned by the decedent, the property would be includible in the decedent's gross estate.

A part of a power is considered a general appointment if the power may be exercised only in conjunction with another person and also is exercisable in favor of the other person. The part to include is figured by dividing the value of the property by the number of persons, including the decedent, in favor of whom the power is exercisable.

A power of appointment created by a will is generally considered created on the date of death (when created after October 21, 1942). A power of appointment created by an inter vivos instrument is considered created on the effective date of the instrument. If the holder of a power creates a second power, the second power is considered created at the time of exercise of the first power.

Schedule I: Annuities (IRC § 2039)

For estates of decedents dying after December 31, 1982, there is a $100,000 exclusion. Even though the combined annuities exceed $100,000, they may be partially or wholly excludable if contributions were made by someone other than the decedent or the decedent's employer. If the annuity is excluded, enter the amount under "description" and explain the computation made.

The instructions for the 706 contain a detailed discussion of annuities and their inclusion in this schedule and should be read in their entirety. In general, annuities and pensions are subject to the estate tax to the extent of the decedent's contributions. The value is the amount of the payment receivable after the decedent's death by the beneficiary. Only that part of the value of the annuity receivable by the surviving beneficiary that the decedent's contribution to the purchase price of the annuity or agreement bears to the total purchase price should be included. In the example given in the instructions, if the value of the survivor's annuity was $20,000 and the decedent contributed three-fourths, the amount includible is $15,000. Contributions by the decedent's employers, unless made to a qualified pension plan, retirement annuity, or other qualified arrangement, are treated as though they were made by the decedent where they are made because of his or her employment. Probably it will be necessary to write directly to the company. Annuities that the decedent was receiving that terminated at the decedent's death need not be reported.

See line 3 of "elections" on page 2 of the 706 and the 706 instructions for lump-sum distributions from an approved plan to a beneficiary. If the election is not made on line 3, the full amount of the lump-sum distribution will be included. Otherwise, if the election is made on line 3, the portion attributable to employer contributions will be excluded, subject to the $100,000 limitation (see IRC § 2039).

In describing the annuity, the name and address of the grantor of the annuity should be given, and whether the annuity is under an approved plan should be specified. If the annuity is payable out of a trust or other fund, the description should fully identify it. The duration of the term of the annuity and date on which it began are to be included. If the annuity is payable for the life of someone other than the decedent, the date of birth and sex of that person should be included.

This schedule includes **IRAs** and **Keogh accounts**, as well as death benefits that have not been assigned to anyone but are payable to the

---

TERMS

IRA (dividend retirement account)† Under the Internal Revenue Code, individuals who are not included in an employer-maintained retirement plan may deposit money (up to an annual maximum amount set by the Code) in an account for the purchase of retirement annuities.

Keogh account† The type of retirement plan that self-employed professionals and individuals or partners in an unincorporated business activity may set up under the Internal Revenue Code to obtain the tax advantages available to employees under a qualified pension plan.

estate. Death benefits that have been assigned to a specific beneficiary are not includible in the decedent's estate. The Internal Revenue Service, however, is reportedly contending that a taxable gift occurs at the time of assigning such rights or benefits. Deferred compensation also is included in this schedule and may be classified as "income in respect of a decedent."

Schedule J: Funeral Expenses and Expenses Incurred in Administering Property Subject to Claims

This schedule must be filed if a deduction is claimed on item 11 of part 5 of the recapitulation. The names and addresses of persons to whom the expenses are payable and the nature of the expenses are listed.

Reasonable amounts for funeral expenses that are actually expended by the estate are allowable and are listed under A. Reasonable expenses for a tombstone, monument, or mausoleum; a burial lot and its future care; and transportation to the place of burial are deductible. If the decedent or anyone else prepaid the funeral expenses, they are not deductible (IRC § 20.2053-2). In community property states like California, local law determines whether the community property is liable for funeral expenses. In California, the decedent's estate is liable for the funeral expenses without regard to the surviving spouse's ability to pay (Prob. Code § 11446; Health & Safety Code § 7101 *et seq*.). Death benefits received from sources such as the Social Security Administration or the Veterans Administration must be deducted from the cost of the funeral expenses.

Commissions and fees paid or reasonably expected to be paid to personal representatives and attorneys are listed on this schedule under administration expenses, although attorneys' fees for litigation between beneficiaries are not deductible. Whether the commissions and fees are estimated, agreed upon, or paid is indicated by crossing out the inapplicable language.

"Miscellaneous administration expenses" include expenses such as court costs, accounting fees, appraisers' fees, certified copies, bond premiums, notarial fees, Social Security taxes, interest paid on mortgages, liability insurance, and costs incurred in the collection of assets and payment of debts. Expenses necessarily incurred in preserving and distributing the estate are deductible, including the cost of storing or maintaining property of the estate when immediate distribution is impossible. Expenses of administration that may or may not be deductible are mileage for the personal representative and phone calls not designated as long-distance calls. Local probate rules must be checked to determine the policy of local courts. Some courts, for example, consider charges for copying documents to be part of overhead. Administration expenses may be taken on either Form 706 or the fiduciary income tax return, but not on both. A determination will have to be made about which of these will give the greater tax advantage.

If any real property was sold and the sale was necessary to raise cash for debts, to preserve the estate, or to effect distribution, the expenses of sale may be charged. Again, however, such expenses may not be taken as a deduction on both Form 706 and the fiduciary income tax return, so a determination will have to be made about the better tax advantage.

Trustees' commissions are not expenses of administration and are not deductible except to the extent a trustee performs services with respect to property subject to claims normally performed by a personal representative. The phrase *property subject to claims* is defined in Internal Revenue Code section 2053(c)(2) as property includible in the gross estate that under the law would bear the burden of payment of the deduction in the final adjustment and settlement of the estate [see § 20.2053-1(c) for examples]. Certain kinds of property, such as certain real property and insurance, are not subject to claims and should be listed not on this schedule but on Schedule L. Expenses incurred in administering property not subject to claims may be allowed as deductions only if they would be allowed as deductions were the property being administered subject to claims and if they were paid before the expiration of the period of limitation for assessment provided in Internal Revenue Code section 6501.

Schedule K: Debts of Decedent and Mortgages and Liens

If deductions are claimed on either line 12 or 13 of the recapitulation and the gross estate is more than $600,000, this schedule must be completed. It is divided into two parts, one for debts of the decedent and the other for mortgages and liens.

Only valid debts owed by the decedent at the time of death are listed as debts. If the amount of the debt is disputed or in litigation, only the amount the estate concedes to be valid should be deducted, and the fact that the claim is contested should be indicated. Expenses of last illness, such as hospital and medical bills, can be listed here, as well as debts owed by the decedent in connection with his or her separate property and debts for which the community property is liable, such as utilities, department store accounts, and credit card accounts. Unpaid gift and income taxes may be taken as a deduction on this schedule.

A property tax deduction is limited to taxes accrued before the date of the decedent's death. The first installment of property taxes ordinarily becomes payable on December 10, and the second on April 10, since taxes are applicable to the fiscal year ending on July 1. Both installments may be made at the same time if made before December 10.

Federal taxes on income received by the decedent during his or her lifetime are deductible. Taxes on income received after death cannot be deducted.

Under mortgages and liens should be listed obligations secured by mortgages or other liens on property included in the gross estate at its full value or at a value undiminished by the amount of the mortgage or lien. Such obligations may not be listed on this schedule, however, if they have already been subtracted to offset the value of property on other schedules. The description of the mortgage or lien should include the schedule and item number where the property is reported. The name and address of the mortgage, payee, or obligee, and the date and term of the mortgage, note, or other agreement establishing the debt, should be included, as well as the face amount, unpaid balance, rate of interest, and date to which the interest was paid before the decedent's death. If a relative loaned the decedent money and the decedent gave a notice, the same information is given but with a notation of this fact.

Schedule L: Net Losses During Administration and Expenses Incurred in Administering Property Not Subject to Claims

If deductions are claimed on either item 16 or 17 of part 5, recapitulation, this schedule must be filed.

Losses

To the extent not reimbursed by insurance, losses from thefts, fires, storms, shipwrecks, or other casualties that occur pending the administration of the estate may be deducted. The loss sustained should be described in detail, including the amount of any insurance collected. The appropriate schedule and item number should be referenced if the property is included in the gross estate. If the loss is not claimed on Forms 1040 and 1041, this fact should be indicated. If alternate valuation is elected, the amount by which the value of an item is reduced to include it in the gross estate is not deducted.

Consideration should be given to the advantages of taking the loss on the income tax form or the estate tax form, as the loss may not be taken on both.

Expenses Incurred in Administering Property Not Subject to Claims

To be deductible, the expenses must be incurred in administering property not subject to claims that is included in the gross estate. For example, they may be incurred in collecting assets or transferring or clearing title to other property that is included in the decedent's gross estate for estate tax purposes but not included in the probate estate. Deductible expenses are limited to those that result from settling the decedent's interest in the property or vesting good title in the beneficiaries. Such expenses include expenses incurred in connection with joint tenancy property, including attorneys' fees.

These expenses often are incurred in connection with a trust of the decedent. They may be allowed as deductions to the extent they would be allowed if the property involved were subject to claims. They must be paid before the period of limitations for assessment of Internal Revenue Code section 6501 expires—that is, if there is no fraud, within three years after the 706 estate tax return is due (nine months after death) or is filed (if time is extended), whichever is later. Care should be taken to make certain any deductible item is paid within this period if possible.

Schedule M: Bequests to Surviving Spouse

If the total gross estate exceeds $600,000, this schedule must be completed and filed if a deduction on line 18 of the recapitulation for bequests to the surviving spouse is claimed. Schedule M was formerly called "Marital Deduction." The marital deduction is the amount of the deduction from the gross estate of the value of property included in the gross estate that passes, or has passed, to the surviving spouse. (The unlimited marital deduction is discussed in Chapter 13.)

It is necessary to distinguish between the law on marital deductions for estates where the decedent died before January 1, 1982, and for those where the decedent died after December 31, 1981.

Before 1982

In post-1976 estates, the maximum estate tax marital deduction is the greater of (a) $250,000 or (b) fifty percent of the value of the decedent's adjusted gross estate. Prior to 1977 and the Tax Reform Act of 1976, the marital deduction was fifty percent of the adjusted gross estate.

The gross estate is simply the value of all the property to the extent of the decedent's interest at the time of his or her death. The adjusted gross estate is the gross estate less deductions for administration and funeral expenses, claims against the estate, any obligations to which the property included in the gross estate is subject (if the value in the estate is undiminished by the indebtedness), casualty and theft losses, and the amount of the value of community property held at death or transferred by the decedent during life and any insurance proceeds of policies on the life of the decedent to the extent they were purchased with community funds. The value is also reduced by an amount "that bears the same ratio to the total allowable deductions for expenses, indebtedness, taxes and losses that the value of the total gross estate reduced by" the items just mentioned (the decedent's community property interest) bears to the value of the entire gross estate.

On line 1, if property passes to the surviving spouse as the result of a qualified disclaimer, "yes" should be checked and a copy of the disclaimer should be attached. All property interests passing from the decedent to the surviving spouse that are included in the gross estate are listed in this schedule (see Form 706 instructions under the schedule M heading).

Certain interests passing to the surviving spouse are characterized as **terminable interests**, that is, interests that terminate or fail after the passage of time or on the occurrence or nonoccurrence of some contingency. Examples of such interests are life estates, annuities, estates for terms of years, and patents. Ownership of a bond, note, or other contractual obligation that will not have the effect of an annuity for life or for a term when discharged is not considered a terminable interest. Nondeductible terminal interests should not be listed (see Form 706 instructions under the Schedule M heading).

Some attorneys attach a separate page with a computation, showing how they arrived at the value of the bequest to the surviving spouse. Other attorneys prefer not to attach such a page, so the legal assistant should inquire about the attorney's preference. If such a page is not attached, language can be used to reference the item. For example, an entry might read: "Bequest under paragraph ___ of decedent's will," along with the amount. If a will or trust disposes of a particular item, the specific paragraph of the will or trust should be referenced.

After 1982

The Economic Recovery Tax Act initiated an unlimited marital deduction for transfers to surviving spouses where the decedent died after December 31, 1981, with exceptions for certain terminable interests. A marital deduction is allowed for a joint and survivor annuity where only the donor spouse and donee spouse have a right to receive payments before the death of the last spouse. **Qualified terminable interest property** as defined in Internal Revenue Code section 2056(b)(7) may be deducted. (See the discussion of unlimited marital deductions in Chapter 13.)

TERMS

terminable interest† An interest in property that ends with the death of the person who holds the interest or upon the happening of some named event.

qualified terminable interest property† An interest that is less than absolute in property that ends with the death of the person who holds the interest or upon the happening of some named event.

Schedule N: Section 2032A Valuation

This schedule must be completed when an election is made to value certain farm and closely held business property at its special use value, in which event question 2 on page 2 under "Elections by the Executor" is answered "yes." The special use valuation election creates a potential liability for recapture of tax under Internal Revenue Code section 2032A(c), and therefore, the name of each qualified heir who receives an interest in such property must be listed. If there are more than eight qualified heirs, an additional sheet should be used, following the same format. The respective values received by each heir are listed in the columns entitled "Fair market value" and "Special use value."

A notice of election must be completed and attached. The contents of the notice of election are specified in detail in the instructions. An agreement to the special valuation by persons with an interest in the property also must be executed by all parties who have an interest in the property [IRC § 2032A(a)(1)(B) and (d)(2)]. An **interest in property** is defined in the instructions.

Qualified heirs must consent to personal liability in the event of early disposition or early cessation of the qualified use [IRC § 2032A(c)(6)]. Persons other than qualified heirs must consent to the collection of any additional estate tax imposed under Internal Revenue Code section 2032A(c) from the qualified property, and the consent must be in a binding form.

A **protective election** may be made, in which event Schedule N need not be completed, and the notice of election and agreement to special valuation need not be attached. Instead, "protective election" is written across Schedule N, and a notice of protective election is attached. The contents of the notice are described in the 706 instructions for Schedule N.

Schedule O: Charitable, Public, and Similar Gifts and Bequests

If the total gross estate exceeds $600,000 and a deduction is claimed on line 19 of the recapitulation, this schedule must be completed. A **charitable deduction** for property transferred by the decedent during life

---

TERMS

interest in property†   A right, claim, share, or title in property.

protective election†   An election that provides protection to the person making that choice.

charitable deduction†   A tax deduction from federal income tax to which a taxpayer is entitled, within the limitations imposed by the Internal Revenue Code, for contributions or gifts made to a tax-exempt charitable organization.

or by will to a qualified charitable institution may be claimed. (See IRS Publication 448 for details.) Included are corporations organized and operated exclusively for religious, charitable, scientific, literary, or educational purposes.

If for any reason the estate tax is payable in whole or in part from a bequest, legacy, or devise that otherwise would be allowed as a charitable deduction, the amount of same is reduced by the amount of the taxes.

If the residue passes to a charity under a will and the gross estate is more than $600,000, a copy of the computation as to value, and reduction for taxes, must be described. See instructions for further details regarding the contents of the computation.

If charitable transfer is made by will, attach a certified copy of the order admitting the will to probate and a copy of the will. If transfer is by another written instrument, attach a copy (a certified copy if of record, if not, a verified copy).

The charitable deduction may be allowed for amounts transferred by a qualified disclaimer. To be qualified, the property must meet the conditions of Internal Revenue Code section 2518, explained in Publication 448.

Schedule P: Credit for Foreign Death Taxes

If the total gross estate exceeds $600,000 and a credit is claimed on line 16 of the tax computation, this schedule must be completed. A Form 706CE to support any credit claimed must be attached regardless of the amount of the estate. See Form 706 instructions for this schedule regarding when credit for foreign death taxes is allowable.

Schedule Q: Credit for Tax on Prior Transfers

If a credit for prior transfers is claimed (line 17 of the tax computation), this schedule must be completed. If the decedent received property from a transferor who died within ten years before or two years after the decedent's death, a credit is allowable for the federal estate tax paid by the transferor's estate with respect to the transfer.

Where the transferor predeceased the decedent, the maximum percent that is allowed as a credit depends upon the number of years elapsing between dates of death and is determined using the following table:

Period of Time

Exceeding	Not Exceeding	Percent Allowable
—	2 years	100
2 years	4 years	80
4 years	6 years	60
6 years	8 years	40
8 years	10 years	20
10 years	—	none

A worksheet is found in the instructions for computing this credit (see the Form 706 instructions for completing the worksheet).

The property transferred does not need to be identified in the estate of the decedent or be in existence on the date of the decedent's death. If the decedent was the transferor's surviving spouse, no credit is allowable for the property to the extent a marital deduction was allowed to the transferor's estate on the property.

If claiming a credit for tax on prior transfers on Form 706NA, the recapitulation should be completed before computing the credit on Schedule Q.

Property is defined in the Form 706 instructions and includes any interest of which the decedent received the beneficial ownership. Such property includes property over which the decedent received a general power of appointment but does not include interests to which he or she received only a bare legal title, such as that of a trustee. It may include property such as annuities, life estates (including those where the life tenants die shortly after the decedent), terms for years, remainder interests (contingent or vested), and any other interest that is less than complete ownership.

Schedules R and R-1: Generation-Skipping Transfer Tax

Schedule R is used to compute the generation-skipping tax payable by the estate, and Schedule R-1 is used to compute the generation-skipping tax payable by certain trusts that are includible in the estate. The tax is imposed only on "direct skips" occurring at the time of death of the decedent. The property interests includible are in Schedule A-1. The "skip

---

TERMS

property† The right of a person to possess, use, enjoy, and dispose of a thing without restriction, i.e., not the material object itself, but a person's rights with respect to the object.

persons" must be determined (see Chapter 15). Details are given in the instructions.

"Trust" here includes life estates with remainders, terms for years, and insurance and annuity contracts.

Every individual is allowed a generation-skipping transfer tax exemption of $1,000,000 (see IRC §§ 2601–2663).

Attachments

A copy of the inventory should be submitted with Form 706, along with a copy of any trust agreement, the 712 form, the death certificate, and the Social Security numbers of the beneficiaries. A copy of any instrument, trust or otherwise, making a transfer must be attached. If the copy is of a public record, the copy should be certified or otherwise verified. A certified or verified copy of the instrument granting the power and of any instrument by which the power was exercised or released, even if it is contended that the power is not a general power of appointment and not otherwise includible in the estate, must be attached.

§ 8.9   Estate Tax Rates

The estate tax rates are found in Internal Revenue Code section 2001. The Unified Transfer Tax Rate Schedule, in effect in February 1995, for decedents dying and gifts made after 1983 was as follows:

Unified Rate Schedule

Column A Taxable amount over	Column B Taxable amount not over	Column C Tax on amount in column A	Column D Rate of tax on excess over amount in column A (percent)
$ 0	$ 10,000	$ 0	18
10,000	20,000	1,800	20
20,000	40,000	3,800	22
40,000	60,000	8,200	24
60,000	80,000	13,000	26
80,000	100,000	18,200	28
100,000	150,000	23,800	30
150,000	250,000	38,800	32
250,000	500,000	70,800	34
500,000	750,000	155,800	37
750,000	1,000,000	248,300	39

1,000,000	1,250,000	345,800	41
1,250,000	1,500,000	448,300	43
1,500,000	2,000,000	555,800	45
2,000,000	2,500,000	780,800	49
2,500,000	3,000,000	1,025,800	53
3,000,000	—	1,290,800	55

The benefits of the graduated rates for transfers exceeding $10,000,000 have been phased out, and the taxes are calculated differently. Tax books should be consulted.

Since estate tax laws (and other tax laws) change frequently, the legal assistant is cautioned to check on the latest tax law in computing any tax.

§ 8.10 Sample Form 706

Facts upon which the sample Form 706 (see Appendix B) is based are about as simple as possible, but if the beginner reads the accompanying material for the schedules at the same time and follows the form with the computation of the tax, this sample should serve its purpose. Each estate is different and involves various considerations. The facts of the sample estate are as follows.

Kenneth K. Bell died on January 7, 19__, at Mercy Hospital in Sacramento, California. Until his death, he resided with his wife and son at 145 Perry Avenue, Sacramento, California. His family consists of his wife, Clarice Bell, and one son, Kerry Bell, who is past the age of twenty-one. The decedent is also survived by his brother, Morton Bell.

The decedent had a will dated November 15, 19__. Under the terms of his will, the decedent left to his brother, Morton Bell, his yellow gold diamond ring. To his son, Kerry Bell, the decedent left his one-half interest in his 1985 Mercedes automobile, SL Engine No. LS057D807. His wife, Clarice Bell, received his one-half interest in their home at 145 Perry Avenue, the house he owned at 9020 Boykin Way, oil paintings by Matt Discall, the Lincoln Continental automobile, the household furnishings and personal effects, and all the residue of the estate.

All the decedent's property was community property except for the yellow gold diamond ring and the house at 9020 Boykin Way, which were the decedent's separate property. Any taxes were to be paid out of the residue of the estate, and the beneficiaries waived bond.

The schedules are included in Appendix B. Those that did not need to be completed for this sample are included in blank so that each schedule can be examined by the student.

§ 8.11 Miscellaneous Matters

Generation-Skipping Tax

A generation-skipping tax is imposed on every generation-skipping transfer. See the discussion on irrevocable trusts in Chapter 14.

Orphan's Exclusion

Former Internal Revenue Code section 2057 (enacted by the Tax Reform Act of 1976) provided for a deduction from estate tax where the defendant left no surviving spouse but was survived by a minor child who had no known parent. The deduction was limited to $5,000 per year multiplied by the number of years under twenty-one that the child's age was on the date of death of the decedent. The Economic Recovery Tax Act of 1981 (ERTA), section 427, repealed this exclusion for estates of decedents dying after December 31, 1981.

An orphan's exemption was introduced in California effective September 26, 1977, that applies to estates of decedents dying before June 8, 1982. The exemption provision equals $10,000 ($5,000 before 1981) times the number of years between the child's age and twenty-one years if the child was under eighteen when orphaned and the decedent left no surviving spouse so that the child had no known parent [Rev. & Tax. Code § 13801(b)].

Annuities

Annuities are a device for estate planning that offers security and a guaranteed income. The return on investment, however, is not apt to be as high as that on some other types of investments. The money paid for premiums is taken out of the estate and, therefore, is not taxable for estate tax purposes after death.

There are two basic types of annuities, the commercial annuity and the **straight life annuity**. The latter makes payments during the decedent's lifetime and terminates upon death. The annuity that contracts to pay a certain amount for life and terminates at death leaves nothing to tax, and therefore, an estate tax is avoided. On a joint and survivor

---

TERMS

straight life annuity† A yearly payment of a fixed sum of money until the death of the annuitant.

annuity, however, where the insurance company pays a fixed periodic amount during the decedent's life and then the remainder to be a designated survivor upon the decedent's death, an estate tax is payable on the present value of payments to be made after the annuitant's death. This type of annuity is often arranged so that payments are continued until the death of both annuitants to make certain of having sufficient income if one outlives available capital. The commercial annuity provides protection against an early death, as a refund of payments may be made in that event.

The general rule for annuities is that gross income includes any amount received as an annuity, whether for a fixed period or during one or more lives, under "an annuity, endowment, or life insurance contract" [IRC § 72(a); see IRC § 72 for Federal income tax law on annuities]. Annuity payments are taxable as income in part: the part of the payment that is a return on capital is not taxed, but the part that is interest is taxed as ordinary income.

The transfer of an annuity contract is a taxable gift, but it is regarded as a present interest, and therefore, the annual exclusion (now $10,000) is available.

Life Insurance

If a life insurance policy owned by a decedent has a named beneficiary, the proceeds will go directly to the named beneficiary and will not be included in the gross estate. A life insurance policy payable to the estate of the decedent also will not be included in the gross estate for probate purposes if it had been placed in an irrevocable life insurance trust.

Flower Bonds

Flower bonds have long been used to pay federal estate taxes. Flower bonds are certain U.S. Treasury bonds that are redeemable at par (face) value plus accrued interest when used to pay federal estate taxes, although they may not have reached their maturity date at the date of death. The estate's basis in the bond is increased to its estate tax value, that is, par value (IRC § 1014). The estate, therefore, does not recognize any gain on the bond. The bonds are called "flower bonds" because they "blossom" into full or par value upon their owner's death. On the other hand, a surviving spouse's one-half interest in such a bond is not stepped up to the estate tax value, but is the fair market value of the interest on the federal estate tax valuation date. (See Ann F. Neuhoff, 75 T.C. 36 (1980); Rev. Rul. 76-68, 1976-1 C.B. 216.)

For other purposes, these bonds are not exactly attractive to buy, since they have a low interest rate, and their maturity date may be several years in advance. They usually sell at a discount, however, sometimes for as much as twenty to thirty percent less. A mathematical computation of flower bond yields and comparable obligations is necessary to determine whether it is prudent to purchase flower bonds. [(See *Estate Planning, Trust and Probate* (Winter 1985), p. 9, published in the State Bar of California.)]

To redeem flower bonds, they must be presented for payment of the tax (together with Form PD 1782, Application for Redemption at Par of the United States Treasury Bonds Eligible for Payment of Federal Estate Tax) to any Federal Reserve Bank or Branch or to the Bureau of Public Debt, Division of Securities Operation, Washington, D.C. 20226 (see Rev. Proc. 69-18, 1969-2 C.B. 300). A certified copy of the death certificate must accompany the form. If the estate is not being administered, Form PD 1646, Application for Disposition of Registered Securities (or Interest Thereon) Without Administration of Deceased Owner's Estate, should be filed with Form PD 1782 unless it is executed by the surviving joint tenant or trustee liable for the tax in an amount not less than the face value of and accrued interest on the bonds presented.

The form calls for the date of **redemption**, name and date of death of the decedent, and an exact description of the bond including interest rate, maturity year, denomination, serial number, and exact inscription on the bond. Proof must be presented that the bond was owned by the decedent at death. Other information about the estate and its representative also must be furnished.

Flower bonds were issued before March 4, 1971. The following issues of bonds are eligible to be used in payment of the federal estate tax:

Series	Dated	Due
3's 1995	2/15/55	2/16/95
3½'s 1990	2/14/58	2/15/90
3½'s 1998	10/3/60	11/15/98
4¼'s 1987–92	8/15/62	8/15/92
4's 1988–93	1/17/63	2/15/93
$4^1/_8$'s 1989–94	4/18/63	5/15/94

Not all bonds held in trust qualify for redemption. Bonds held in trust are redeemable only "(a) if the trust actually terminated in favor of the decedent's estate, or (b) if the trustee is required to pay the decedent's Federal estate tax under the terms of the trust instrument or otherwise, or

---

TERMS

redemption† The recovery of pledged property by payment of what is due or by the performance of some other condition.

(c) to the extent the debts of the decedent's estate, including costs of administration, State inheritance and Federal estate taxes, exceed the assets of his estate without regard to the trust estate" [31 C.F.R. 306.28(b)(iii), Dep't of Treasury Cir. No. 300, 4th Rev., Mar. 9, 1973].

Care must be taken, therefore, in drafting trusts and wills. The will should not provide for payment of all death taxes from the residuary estate, and if appropriate, the trust should provide that the trustee pay all the taxes or, in the alternative, as much of the tax as requested by the executor to pay.

Bonds must be received by the Federal Reserve Bank or Branch or the Bureau of the Public Debt prior to the redemption dates, but no sooner than three months before those dates. It is suggested that the bonds be submitted for redemption one month prior to the date desired for redemption. If they are received after the specified redemption date, they are redeemed as of the date received, and no further interest accrues on the bonds.

Inquiries about redemptions may be made to the Bureau of the Public Debt, Division of Loans and Currency, Treasury Department, Washington, D.C. 20226. It has been held that where Treasury Bonds can be used to pay federal estate taxes, their value is at least par value. If the bonds cannot be used to pay federal estate taxes, their value is market price. Revenue Ruling 69-489, 1969-2 C.B. 172, provides in part:

> To the extent marketable United States Treasury bonds owned at death may be applied at par in payment of Federal estate taxes the par value thereof or the mean between their highest and lowest quoted selling price at the time of his death (and accrued interest to the date of death), whichever is higher, constitutes their "value" or "unfair market value" within the above cited Code and regulations. Such bonds are, therefore, includible at such value in a decedent's gross estate for Federal estate purposes. As to bonds in excess of the amount which may be so applied, such mean quoted selling price thereof (and accrued interest to the date of death) will be the value at which they are includible in a decedent's gross estate for Federal estate tax purposes.

Where community property is used to fund a trust, a special problem results, for bonds held as community property may be redeemed only to the extent of the decedent's one-half interest. In this event, the trustee should be given authority to partition some of the community property and use a spouse's share to purchase redeemable Treasury bonds for a separate account. This avoids buying twice as many bonds as are needed for the tax.

The forms that may be required to be attached to the application for redemption (Form PD 1782) are as follows:

1. Schedule T, Schedule of United States Treasury Bonds Held in Trust Submitted for Redemption at Par in Payment of Federal Estate Tax.

This form is needed if the bonds are held in a trust. The first four questions of the schedule detail the circumstances under which a bond held in trust is eligible for redemption at par to pay the federal estate tax.

2. Schedule C, Schedule of United States Treasury Bond Held as Community Property Submitted for Redemption at Par in Payment of Federal Estate Tax. This form is needed if the decedent was a resident in a community property state such as California.

3. Form PD 1646, Application for Disposition of Registered Securities (or Interest Thereon) Without Administration of Deceased Owner's Estate. This form is needed if the application is not made by a surviving joint owner and where there is no probate estate and a personal representative has not been, and will not be, appointed.

4. Form 48-1, Request for Denominational Exchange. This form is required if the bonds exceed the amount of federal estate tax. The form prescribes the manner of titling the lower denominational bonds. This is not a Public Debt form.

If the bonds are held by a brokerage house, the legal assistant will want to work with the broker to coordinate the redemption. The broker may require additional documentation and copies of the documents. Both the bonds and the forms have to be submitted at the same time.

It has been suggested that the bonds in excess of the amount needed for tax be retained in the estate. If an audit should result in additional estate tax, the bonds could be redeemed to pay it. If they had been sold, the additional value of the bonds would be included in the federal estate tax return whether or not they had been retained and were available. The bonds might have been sold at less than face value, and if included at par tax would have to be paid on that value.

The Bureau of Public Debt has not been willing to accept at par value flower bonds purchased after a decedent became comatose even if they were purchased under a power of attorney. Its position has been challenged, and some courts have held that these bonds have to be accepted for redemption. The Second Circuit Court of Appeals has agreed with this latter view in *United States v. Manny*, 645 F.2d 163 (1981), where the court said that the account was at most **voidable**, and not **void**. The court said:

TERMS

voidable† Avoidable; subject to disaffirmance; defective but valid unless disaffirmed by the person entitled to disaffirm.

void† Null; without legal effect, although strictly speaking, a transaction that is void is a transaction that, in law, never happened.

A comatose person is mentally incompetent while his coma continues and we think the law of New York is clear that, when an agent under a power of attorney acts during the mental incapacity of a principal who has not been adjudicated incompetent and for whom no court-appointed committee or conservator has been designated, the act is at most voidable, and not void.

United States v. Manny, 645 F.2d at 166.

CHAPTER 9

GIFT TAXES

A **gift** of real property, cash, or stock is not taxable, but the person receiving the gift immediately becomes the owner, and any income from the gift is taxable. If real property produces income, that income is taxable; if cash is deposited in a savings account and produces interest, that interest is taxable; and dividends paid on stock given as a gift are taxable income to the recipient. A gift paid out of income from an estate or complex trust, however, is exempt from taxation if it is paid in not more than three installments (IRC § 663(a)(1); Reg. 1.1.663(a)–1).

Although a recipient of a gift pays no taxes on the gift, the donor of the gift is in an entirely different situation, and a number of tax laws are called into play.

§ 9.1 Federal Gift Tax—Three-Year Rule

Since the enactment of the Economic Tax Recovery Act of 1981, for the estates of decedents who died on or after December 31, 1981, gifts made within three years of death (with certain exceptions discussed elsewhere in this chapter) will not be included in the decedent's estate. Internal Revenue Code section 2035, subsection (a), reads:

> (a) Inclusion of Gifts Made by Decedent.—Except *as provided in subsection (b)*, the value of the gross estate shall include the value of all property to the extent of any interest therein of which the decedent has at any time made a transfer, by trust or otherwise, during the three-year period ending on the date of the decedent's death.

This act, enacted October 4, 1976, as amended, applied in estates of decedents dying after December 31, 1976, except that it did not apply to transfers made before January 1, 1977.

Subsection (b) of section 2035, however, was added by the Economic Tax Recovery Act of 1981 and later amended. Subsection (b) excepts from inclusion in the gross estate any gifts made to a donee during a calendar year if the decedent was not required by section 6019 [other than by reason of section 6019(2)] to file any gift tax return for that year with respect to gifts to such donee. Section 2035(b) is particularly advantageous if the gift made within those three years before death has appreciated substantially within those three years, since the value of the asset will not be included

---

TERMS

gift† A voluntary transfer of property by one person to another without any consideration or compensation.

in the decedent's estate and, therefore, will not be subject to estate tax, assuming the estate is large enough to incur a federal estate tax.

Disadvantage

The disadvantage of the three-year rule is that a stepped-up basis to date of death is applicable only to property included in the estate. If that same appreciating real property were sold after death, substantial income tax savings might result because of a higher stepped-up basis. Such appreciating property, then, probably should not be given away before death. Sometimes "death bed" gifts, that is, gifts made when the donor is expected to die very soon, are made. It may be seem better that such gifts be made in cash or, if in real property, that real property that is not appreciating in value be given.

History of Three-Year Rule

Most estates with which the legal assistant will become involved at this point are apt to be those where the decedent died after December 31, 1981, but since a legal assistant may work on some estates where death occurred at an earlier date, history of the three-year rule could be helpful. The legal assistant should proceed with caution, as the rule varied from time to time, and there are special rules covering certain transitional periods.

Commencing in 1941 and up to January 1, 1977, transfers of property made within three years of the date of death and "in contemplation of death" were included in the decedent's estate. Any transfer made within three years of the date of death was assumed to have been made in contemplation of death unless the transfer could be shown not to have been prompted by the thought of death, depending upon the decedent's intent. Transfers made to avoid death taxes or as a substitute for a disposition by will were prohibitive. The result was a great deal of litigation over whether transfers actually had been made in contemplation of death.

The law was amended effective January 1, 1977, by the Tax Reform Act of 1976, to include in the decedent's estate all transfers made within three years of the decedent's death for which a gift tax return was required to be filed, except gifts not exceeding the annual exclusion (then $3,000 except for insurance). Such transfers were treated as if they had never been made, and the value of the gift and any gift taxes paid upon the gift were added back into the net value of the estate. This eliminated all the disputes and litigation with the Internal Revenue Service over the decedent's intent. The value of the gift was the value as of the date of death, not as of the date the gift was made. This was known as the **gross-up rule** and prevented any reduction in the estate by gift taxes paid shortly before death.

A transitional rule provided that transfers made before January 1, 1977, but within three years of the date of death were to be treated as having been made in contemplation of death and had to be included in the decedent's estate.

§ 9.2   Unified Gift and Estate Taxes

The Tax Reform Act of 1976 also introduced the unified estate and gift tax concept, so that generally the tax would be the same on any transfer whether made by way of gift during a lifetime or upon death. It seemed that the new three-year rule, therefore, would have little tax impact. The new rule, however, did make a significant difference where the property gifted increased in value appreciably between the date of making the gift (which could be as much as three years earlier) and the date of death.

Gifts made prior to 1977 were not included in the amount of transfers. Reduction for prior tax was correspondingly limited. Special rules apply to gifts made between September 8, 1976, and January 1, 1977. A limitation is placed on the unified credit for gift taxes for gifts made before July 1, 1977.

Since the enactment of the Tax Reform Act of 1976, generally speaking, any transfer after 1976, whether by gift or from the estate after death, results in the same tax, that is, gifts and estate are taxed the same, the gifts on a cumulative basis. Upon death, the amount of gifts are added back into the estate and taxed. Credit is allowed for tax previously paid on the gifts. Instead of a lifetime $30,000 exemption for gifts and $60,000 exemption for an estate, a credit is allowed against the tax computed to be due, as follows in the unified gift and estate tax schedule applicable since December 31, 1976:

TERMS

gross-up rule   The rule that required the adding back into an estate of the gift tax paid on gifts made within three years of the date of death.

In the case of decedents dying during	Amount of tax credit	No tax on cumulative transfers (gifts and estate) not exceeding
1977	$ 30,000	$120,666
1978	34,000	134,000
1979	38,000	147,333
1980	42,500	161,563
1981	47,000	175,625
1982	62,800	225,000
1983	79,300	275,000
1984	96,300	325,000
1985	121,800	400,000
1986	155,800	500,000
1987 and thereafter	192,800	600,000

Annual Exclusion

Value of Lifetime Gifts

The shifting of income is probably the best reason for making a lifetime gift. Presumably, the donor is in a high tax bracket or would not be considering making a gift. For example, a donor may have a son or daughter who would inherit the property under will or at law and who is not in as high an income tax bracket as the donor and, therefore, would not have to pay as high an income tax on the property if they owned it. The three-year rule holds true for gifts made within the three years prior to January 1, 1982. The three-year rule also still applies to transfers of property that would have been included in the decedent's gross estate under the pertinent sections if the decedent had retained it, to wit: (1) transfers with a retained life estate (IRC § 2036), (2) transfers taking effect at death (IRC § 2037), (3) revocable transfers (IRC § 2038), (4) transfers of powers of appointment (IRC § 2041), and (5) life insurance payable to an estate (IRC § 2042).

Ordinarily a donor will not retain a life estate in property he or she does not want taxed in his or her estate. Any transfer out of the estate should not have been made within three years of death (IRC § 2036). The same is true of transfers where the donee will not gain possession or enjoyment of the property until the donor's death. Any such transfer should not have been made within three years of death (IRC § 2037) and the same tax situation applies to a revocable trust. A revocable trust ordinarily is not used to reduce the donor's estate. An **irrevocable trust** can be used, but only if the donor survives more than three years after making the irrevocable trust [IRC § 2038(a)(1)]. Similarly, the donor must survive for more than three years the transfer of any insurance policy, whether or not the policy is an irrevocable insurance trust, although the policy may be included in the estate under section 2042 in any event. The annual gift tax exclusion does not apply to the value of insurance policies, and there may be other considerations regarding insurance (IRC § 2042).

There are special situations, in estates of decedents dying after 1981, where gifts (over and above the amount of the annual exclusion) made within three years of the date of death continue to be subject to the three-year rule and must be included as part of the decedent's gross estate. The Internal Revenue Code section 2035(d) lists the following such situations:

- Distribution in redemption of corporate stock to pay death taxes [IRC § 303(b)];

- Special use valuation of certain farm property, and so on, and real property (IRC § 2032);

- Deferral and installment payment of estate tax where the estate consists largely of interest in a closely held business (IRC § 6166); and

- Property subject to liens for taxes (subchapter C of Internal Revenue Code chapter 64).

Under these Internal Revenue Code provisions, a decedent spouse's estate may qualify for special redemption, valuation, and deferral of tax, and to determine whether this is the case, gifts made to the spouse within three years of the date of death are included in the gross estate. The estate qualifies only if the value of certain types of the decedent's assets exceed specified percentages of the value of the estate. Deathbed transfers, therefore, are prevented from being made to spouses who qualify under these provisions.

Gift Tax Returns

For transfers made on or before June 22, 1936, see Internal Revenue Code section 2038(a)(2).

TERMS

irrevocable trust†   A trust in which the settlor permanently gives up control of the trust property.

During the period 1941 to January 1, 1977, annual gifts of $3,000 per donee could be made without incurring any tax and were not added back into the estate. Spouses who consented to split their gifts could give up to $6,000 per donee per year without incurring a gift tax. There was a lifetime exemption from tax on gifts of $30,000 ($60,000 for estates).

As of January 1, 1982, the Economic Recovery Tax Act of 1981 (ERTA) increased the amount to $10,000 per donee. A husband and wife can give $20,000 to each donee per year out of community property or out of separate property. Gift splitting is allowed, although a return has to be filed if gifts are split, even if the $20,000 limit per donee is not exceeded. In addition to the $10,000 exclusion per donee, amounts paid for tuition or medical care directly to the educational institution or the health care provider are not considered transfers or gifts [IRC § 2503(e)].

Under ERTA, federal gift tax returns are filed on an annual, rather than a quarterly, basis for gifts made after December 31, 1981. If an extension of time to file an income tax return is granted, the time for filing any gift tax return is automatically extended to the same date. Gift tax returns for the year of the decedent's death must be filed on the due date for the decedent's estate tax return, including any extensions.

For the federal gift tax return (Form 709), see Figure 9–1.

§ 9.3 Powers of Appointment

The subject of powers of appointment is complex, and a full knowledge of the uses and pitfalls in this area is beyond the scope of this book. The legal assistant, however, needs some basic knowledge of this subject.

A **power of appointment**, as defined in the Internal Revenue Code, is a "power of appointment which is exercisable in favor of the decedent, his estate, his creditors, or the creditors of his estate." Exceptions are listed in subdivisions (A), (B), and (C) of section 2041(b) of the Internal Revenue Code.

A power of appointment may be either general or special. General powers of appointment, however, are voided because they can have adverse effects on income taxes, gift taxes, or estate taxes (see IRC §§ 678, 2514(c), 2041). Powers of appointment are often used in trusts.

○ TERMS

power of appointment† The ability to act for another that includes an interest in the subject of the action.

Form **709**
(Rev. November 1993)

Department of the Treasury
Internal Revenue Service

United States Gift (and Generation-Skipping Transfer) Tax Return

(Section 6019 of the Internal Revenue Code) (For gifts made after December 31, 1991)

Calendar year 19 ....

▶ See separate instructions. For Privacy Act Notice, see the Instructions for Form 1040.

OMB No. 1545-0020
Expires 5-31-96

Part 1—General Information

1 Donor's first name and middle initial	2 Donor's last name	3 Donor's social security number
4 Address (number, street, and apartment number)		5 Legal residence (Domicile) (county and state)
6 City, state, and ZIP code		7 Citizenship

		Yes	No
8	If the donor died during the year, check here ▶ ☐ and enter date of death................................, 19		
9	If you received an extension of time to file this Form 709, check here ▶ ☐ and attach the Form 4868, 2688, 2350, or extension letter		
10	Enter the total number of separate donees listed on Schedule A—count each person only once . . . . ☐		
11a	Have you (the donor) previously filed a Form 709 (or 709-A) for any other year? If the answer is "No," do not complete line 11b .		
11b	If the answer to line 11a is "Yes," has your address changed since you last filed Form 709 (or 709-A)?		
12	Gifts by husband or wife to third parties.—Do you consent to have the gifts (including generation-skipping transfers) made by you and by your spouse to third parties during the calendar year considered as made one-half by each of you? (See instructions.) (If the answer is "Yes," the following information must be furnished and your spouse must sign the consent shown below. If the answer is "No," skip lines 13–18 and go to Schedule A.)		
13	Name of consenting spouse **14** SSN		
15	Were you married to one another during the entire calendar year? (see instructions)		
16	If the answer to 15 is "No," check whether ☐ married ☐ divorced or ☐ widowed, and give date (see instructions) ▶		
17	Will a gift tax return for this calendar year be filed by your spouse?		
18	Consent of Spouse—I consent to have the gifts (and generation-skipping transfers) made by me and by my spouse to third parties during the calendar year considered as made one-half by each of us. We are both aware of the joint and several liability for tax created by the execution of this consent.		

Consenting spouse's signature ▶   Date ▶

Part 2—Tax Computation

1	Enter the amount from Schedule A, Part 3, line 15	1		
2	Enter the amount from Schedule B, line 3	2		
3	Total taxable gifts (add lines 1 and 2)	3		
4	Tax computed on amount on line 3 (see Table for Computing Tax in separate instructions). . .	4		
5	Tax computed on amount on line 2 (see Table for Computing Tax in separate instructions). .	5		
6	Balance (subtract line 5 from line 4)	6		
7	Maximum unified credit (nonresident aliens, see instructions)	7	192,800	00
8	Enter the unified credit against tax allowable for all prior periods (from Sch. B, line 1, col. C) .	8		
9	Balance (subtract line 8 from line 7)	9		
10	Enter 20% (.20) of the amount allowed as a specific exemption for gifts made after September 8, 1976, and before January 1, 1977 (see instructions)	10		
11	Balance (subtract line 10 from line 9)	11		
12	Unified credit (enter the smaller of line 6 or line 11)	12		
13	Credit for foreign gift taxes (see instructions)	13		
14	Total credits (add lines 12 and 13)	14		
15	Balance (subtract line 14 from line 6) (do not enter less than zero)	15		
16	Generation-skipping transfer taxes (from Schedule C, Part 3, col. H, total)	16		
17	Total tax (add lines 15 and 16)	17		
18	Gift and generation-skipping transfer taxes prepaid with extension of time to file	18		
19	If line 18 is less than line 17, enter BALANCE DUE (see instructions)	19		
20	If line 18 is greater than line 17, enter AMOUNT TO BE REFUNDED	20		

Under penalties of perjury, I declare that I have examined this return, including any accompanying schedules and statements, and to the best of my knowledge and belief it is true, correct, and complete. Declaration of preparer (other than donor) is based on all information of which preparer has any knowledge.

Donor's signature ▶   Date ▶

Preparer's signature
(other than donor) ▶   Date ▶

Preparer's address
(other than donor) ▶

Attach check or money order here.

For Paperwork Reduction Act Notice, see page 1 of the separate instructions for this form.   Cat. No. 16783M   Form **709** (Rev. 11-93)

FIGURE 9–1   Form 709: United States Gift (and Generation-Skipping Transfer) Tax Return

Form 709 (Rev. 11-93)   Page **2**

SCHEDULE A	Computation of Taxable Gifts

Part 1—Gifts Subject Only to Gift Tax. *Gifts less political organization, medical, and educational exclusions—see instructions*

A Item number	B • Donee's name and address • Relationship to donor (if any) • Description of gift • If the gift was made by means of a trust, enter trust's identifying number and attach a copy of the trust instrument • If the gift was of securities, give CUSIP number	C Donor's adjusted basis of gift	D Date of gift	E Value at date of gift
1				

Part 2—Gifts That are Direct Skips and are Subject to Both Gift Tax and Generation-Skipping Transfer Tax. You must list the gifts in chronological order. *Gifts less political organization, medical, and educational exclusions—see instructions. (Also list here direct skips that are subject only to the GST tax at this time as the result of the termination of an "estate tax inclusion period." See instructions.)*

A Item number	B • Donee's name and address • Relationship to donor (if any) • Description of gift • If the gift was made by means of a trust, enter trust's identifying number and attach a copy of the trust instrument • If the gift was of securities, give CUSIP number	C Donor's adjusted basis of gift	D Date of gift	E Value at date of gift
1				

Part 3—Taxable Gift Reconciliation

1	Total value of gifts of donor (add column E of Parts 1 and 2)	1	
2	One-half of items ....attributable to spouse (see instructions)	2	
3	Balance (subtract line 2 from line 1)	3	
4	Gifts of spouse to be included (from Schedule A, Part 3, line 2 of spouse's return—see instructions) . .	4	
	If any of the gifts included on this line are also subject to the generation-skipping transfer tax, check here ▶ ☐ and enter those gifts also on Schedule C, Part 1.		
5	Total gifts (add lines 3 and 4)	5	
6	Total annual exclusions for gifts listed on Schedule A (including line 4, above) (see instructions) . . .	6	
7	Total included amount of gifts (subtract line 6 from line 5)	7	

Deductions (see instructions)

8	Gifts of interests to spouse for which a marital deduction will be claimed, based on items .... of Schedule A	8			
9	Exclusions attributable to gifts on line 8	9			
10	Marital deduction—subtract line 9 from line 8	10			
11	Charitable deduction, based on items ....to...........less exclusions	11			
12	Total deductions—add lines 10 and 11			12	
13	Subtract line 12 from line 7			13	
14	Generation-skipping transfer taxes payable with this Form 709 (from Schedule C, Part 3, col. H, Total) .			14	
15	Taxable gifts (add lines 13 and 14). Enter here and on line 1 of the Tax Computation on page 1 . . .			15	

(If more space is needed, attach additional sheets of same size.)

FIGURE 9–1   *(continued)*

Form 709 (Rev. 11-93)   Page **3**

| SCHEDULE A | Computation of Taxable Gifts (continued) |

16 Terminable Interest (QTIP) Marital Deduction. (See Instructions for line 8 of Schedule A.)

If a trust (or other property) meets the requirements of qualified terminable interest property under section 2523(f), and

    a. The trust (or other property) is listed on Schedule A, and

    b. The value of the trust (or other property) is entered in whole or in part as a deduction on line 8, Part 3 of Schedule A,

then the donor shall be deemed to have made an election to have such trust (or other property) treated as qualified terminable interest property under section 2523(f).

    If less than the entire value of the trust (or other property) that the donor has included in Part 1 of Schedule A is entered as a deduction on line 8, the donor shall be considered to have made an election only as to a fraction of the trust (or other property). The numerator of this fraction is equal to the amount of the trust (or other property) deducted on line 10 of Part 3. The denominator is equal to the total value of the trust (or other property) listed in Part 1 of Schedule A.

    If you make the QTIP election (see instructions for line 8 of Schedule A), the terminable interest property involved will be included in your spouse's gross estate upon his or her death (section 2044). If your spouse disposes (by gift or otherwise) of all or part of the qualifying life income interest, he or she will be considered to have made a transfer of the entire property that is subject to the gift tax (see Transfer of Certain Life Estates on page 3 of the instructions).

17 Election out of QTIP Treatment of Annuities

☐ ◄ Check here if you elect under section 2523(f)(6) **NOT** to treat as qualified terminable interest property any joint and survivor annuities that are reported on Schedule A and would otherwise be treated as qualified terminable interest property under section 2523(f). (See instructions.) Enter the item numbers (from Schedule A) for the annuities for which you are making this election ►

| SCHEDULE B | Gifts From Prior Periods |

If you answered "Yes" on line 11a of page 1, Part 1, see the instructions for completing Schedule B. If you answered "No," skip to the Tax Computation on page 1 (or Schedule C, if applicable).

A Calendar year or calendar quarter (see instructions)	B Internal Revenue office where prior return was filed	C Amount of unified credit against gift tax for periods after December 31, 1976	D Amount of specific exemption for prior periods ending before January 1, 1977	E Amount of taxable gifts

1 Totals for prior periods (without adjustment for reduced specific exemption)	**1**	
2 Amount, if any, by which total specific exemption, line 1, column D, is more than $30,000	**2**	
3 Total amount of taxable gifts for prior periods (add amount, column E, line 1, and amount, if any, on line 2). (Enter here and on line 2 of the Tax Computation on page 1.)	**3**	

(If more space is needed, attach additional sheets of same size.)

FIGURE 9–1 *(continued)*

Form 709 (Rev. 11-93)
Page **4**

SCHEDULE C — Computation of Generation-Skipping Transfer Tax

Note: Inter vivos direct skips that are completely excluded by the GST exemption must still be fully reported (including value and exemptions claimed) on Schedule C.

Part 1—Generation-Skipping Transfers

A Item No. (from Schedule A, Part 2, col. A)	B Value (from Schedule A, Part 2, col. E)	C Split Gifts (enter ½ of col. B) (see instructions)	D Subtract col. C from col. B	E Nontaxable portion of transfer	F Net Transfer (subtract col. E from col. D)
1					
2					
3					
4					
5					
6					

If you elected gift splitting and your spouse was required to file a separate Form 709 (see the instructions for "Split Gifts"), you must enter all of the gifts shown on Schedule A, Part 2, of your spouse's Form 709 here.	Split gifts from spouse's Form 709 (enter item number)	Value included from spouse's Form 709	Nontaxable portion of transfer	Net transfer (subtract col. E from col. D)
In column C, enter the item number of each gift in the order it appears in column A of your spouse's Schedule A, Part 2. We have preprinted the prefix "S-" to distinguish your spouse's item numbers from your own when you complete column A of Schedule C, Part 3.	S-			
	S-			
	S-			
	S-			
	S-			
In column D, for each gift, enter the amount reported in column C, Schedule C, Part 1, of your spouse's Form 709.	S-			
	S-			
	S-			
	S-			

Part 2—GST Exemption Reconciliation (Code section 2631) and Section 2652(a)(3) Election

Check box ▶ ☐ if you are making a section 2652(a)(3) (special QTIP) election (see instructions)

Enter the item numbers (from Schedule A) of the gifts for which you are making this election ▶ ....

1	Maximum allowable exemption	1	$1,000,000
2	Total exemption used for periods before filing this return	2	
3	Exemption available for this return (subtract line 2 from line 1)	3	
4	Exemption claimed on this return (from Part 3, col. C total, below)	4	
5	Exemption allocated to transfers not shown on Part 3, below. You must attach a Notice of Allocation. (See instructions.)	5	
6	Add lines 4 and 5	6	
7	Exemption available for future transfers (subtract line 6 from line 3)	7	

Part 3—Tax Computation

A Item No. (from Schedule C, Part 1)	B Net transfer (from Schedule C, Part 1, col. F)	C GST Exemption Allocated	D Divide col. C by col. B	E Inclusion Ratio (subtract col. D from 1.000)	F Maximum Estate Tax Rate	G Applicable Rate (multiply col. E by col. F)	H Generation-Skipping Transfer Tax (multiply col. B by col. G)
1					55% (.55)		
2					55% (.55)		
3					55% (.55)		
4					55% (.55)		
5					55% (.55)		
6					55% (.55)		
					55% (.55)		
					55% (.55)		
					55% (.55)		
					55% (.55)		

Total exemption claimed. Enter here and on line 4, Part 2, above. May not exceed line 3, Part 2, above		Total generation-skipping transfer tax. Enter here, on line 14 of Schedule A, Part 3, and on line 16 of the Tax Computation on page 1	

(If more space is needed, attach additional sheets of same size.)

U.S. Government Printing Office: 1993 — 301-829/80256

FIGURE 9–1 *(continued)*

Internal Revenue Code section 2053(b) states that the possibility of a present interest in property that has been transferred being diminished by the exercise of a power of appointment shall be disregarded in applying that subsection, if no part of such interest will at any time pass to any other person. A special rule prevents application of the annual gift tax exclusion of $10,000 to powers of appointment granted under a trust created before September 12, 1981, that has not since been amended and is exercisable after 1981, if the power of appointment refers to the gift tax exclusion under section 2053(b) and the state involved has not enacted an applicable statute construing such a power of appointment as referring to the increased gift tax exclusion [ERTA § 441(c)]. California no longer imposes a gift tax and incorporates the federal law by reference in any event.

§ 9.4 California Gift Taxes

California imposed a gift tax commencing in 1939 and continuing until it was repealed by vote of the people on June 8, 1982. No California gift tax has been imposed on a gift made since that date.

SIDEBAR

If a legal assistant is working on an estate involving gifts made before June 8, 1982, the tax law in existence on the date of the gift applies. Since most legal assistants are now dealing with estates where the decedent died after June 8, 1982, the law and procedure before that time are not set out here. For more information regarding the prior law, see *California Paralegal's Guide* (Fourth Edition) by the author.

The California gift tax applied to gifts to each donee separately, rather than to the aggregate as does the federal law. The annual exclusion in California was at $3,000 per year. Gift splitting of spouses was not permitted, so $3,000 per year was the maximum that a married couple could give to any one donee without incurring a tax. There were, however, specific exemptions.

A gift tax return had to be filed if gifts to any one donee exceeded $3,000 in a calendar year (before July 29, 1967, it was $4,000). A gift tax return also had to be filed if the gift of a future interest was made, regardless of its value. The return had to be filed with the State Controller each quarter, by the fifteenth day of the second month following the end of the calendar quarter.

CHAPTER 10

DISPOSITION OF ESTATES WITHOUT ADMINISTRATION

Procedures are provided for the collection and transfer of small estates and for the passage of property to the surviving spouse without administration. These procedures include: (1) small estate set-asides; (2) court orders determining succession to real property; (3) affidavits for real property of small value; (4) joint tenancy terminations; and (4) proceedings under the **Independent Administration of Estates Act**. This chapter discusses these proceedings in detail.

Not all of these procedures are available in any given estate. The procedure chosen depends upon the value and character of the estate and other circumstances. For example, the joint tenancy termination may be considered only if the decedent's property was held by the decedent as a

---

TERMS

Independent Administration of Estates Act ‥An act that gives the executor or administrator the option of administering the estate in a simplified manner and with a minimum of court supervision.

joint tenant. The decedent cannot affect the joint tenancy by a disposition in his or her will. Administration under the Independent Administration of Estates Act is available only if the decedent's will does not provide that the estate not be administered under the provisions of this article.

The experienced legal assistant must review the assets of the estate and roughly estimate their value, look at the heirs and beneficiaries and their interests, and examine the debts and liabilities of the estate before forming an opinion about the best procedure. The attorney must make the ultimate decision if a choice is to be made.

§ 10.1 Collection or Transfer of Small Estates Without Administration

Real and Personal Property Valued Under $60,000 (Prob. Code § 13100 *et seq.*)

Probate Code section 13111 provides a special affidavit procedure for establishing title to personal property, not real property, where the gross value of the real and personal property in the estate, with certain exclusions, does not exceed $60,000. When fixing the value of the property, the probate referee, if one has been appointed, is to use the date of the decedent's death as the date of valuation.

After the death of the decedent, forty days must elapse before this procedure may be used. The reason for the delay is to give creditors time to make themselves known and to lessen the chances for someone to obtain the property by forgery or fraud.

The successor of the decedent, as defined in Probate Code section 13006, may do any of the following without procuring letters of administration or awaiting probate of the will:

- Collect any particular item of property that is money due the decedent;

- Receive any particular item of property that is tangible personal property of the decedent; and

- Have any particular item of property that is evidence of a debt, obligation, interest, right, security, or chose in action belonging to the decedent transferred, whether or not secured by a lien on real property (Prob. Code § 13100).

This procedure may be used only if no proceeding for administration of the decedent's estate is pending or has been conducted in California.

Use of this procedure, however, does not preclude later proceedings for administration.

Exclusions from Value

In determining the value of the estate, the following items may be excluded:

- Any property held by the decedent as a joint tenant;

- Multiple-party accounts, whether or not the sums on deposit are community property, to the extent the sums belong after death to a **P.O.D. payee** or beneficiary (see Prob. Code § 5101 for definitions);

- Certain specified vehicles, vessels, mobile homes, manufactured homes, commercial coaches, truck campers, and floating homes;

- Amounts due the decedent for service in the armed forces; and

- Salary or other compensation owed to the decedent for personal services from any employment (Prob. Code § 13050).

Liability of the Holder

The holder of the property may rely on the statements in the affidavit or declaration and has no duty to inquire into the truth of any statement. Receipt by the person holding the decedent's property of the affidavit or declaration constitutes sufficient acquittance for payment of money or delivery or change of registered ownership of the property and discharges the holder from further liability (Prob. Code § 13106).

The contents of the affidavit are listed in Probate Code section 13101. A certified copy of the decedent's death certificate is to be attached to the affidavit or declaration.

Reasonable proof of the identity of the person executing the affidavit or declaration shall be provided to the holder of the decedent's property (Prob. Code § 13104). The persons executing the affidavit or declaration must be entitled to have the property described in it paid, delivered, or transferred to them (see Prob. Code § 13105).

TERMS

P.O.D. payee† The recipient of funds from a P.O.D. (payable on death) account, which is an account payable to a person, upon request, during that person's lifetime and payable, after that person's death, to one or more named payees.

Inventory and Appraisement

If the estate includes any real property, an inventory and appraisement of the real property must accompany the affidavit or declaration. The inventory and appraisement shall be made by a probate referee selected by the affiant or declarant from those referees appointed by the Controller under Probate Code section 8900 to appraise property in the county in which the real property is located.

Liability for Debts

The person to whom the property is transferred is personally liable for the decedent's debts to the extent of the fair market value of the property. Persons who fraudulently secure payment or delivery are liable [Prob. Code § 13110(b)]. An action to impose liability is barred three years after presentation of the affidavit or declaration or the discovery of the fraud, whichever is later (see Prob. Code § 13111). Probate Code section 13554, added in 1990, makes it clear that Code of Civil Procedure section 353 (the general one-year statute of limitations) is applicable to all causes of action against a decedent for the decedent's debts (see also Prob. Code § 551, added in 1990).

The following is a sample declaration:

DECLARATION FOR TRANSFER OF PERSONAL PROPERTY WITHOUT ADMINISTRATION (PROBATE CODE SECTION 13100)

I, _____, declare as follows:

1. I am _____, the successor in interest of the decedent (as defined in Probate Code section 13006), _____, who died in the City of _____, _____ County, California, on _____, 19___.

2. No other person has a right to the interest of the decedent in the described property.

3. At least forty (40) days have elapsed since the death of the decedent, as shown in the certified copy of the decedent's death certificate attached to this declaration.

4. No proceeding is now pending or has been conducted in California for the administration of the decedent's estate.

5. The gross value of the decedent's real and personal property in California, excluding the property described in Probate Code section 13050, does not exceed sixty thousand dollars ($60,000).

6. The following account, to wit: the current balance in checking account No. _____ in the (name and address of bank), (name of city),

California (zip code), constitutes a portion of the property in the decedent's estate.

7. The decedent died without a will, and under section 6402 of the California Probate Code, I am the decedent's sole heir at law and the successor of the decedent (as defined in Probate Code section _____) to the decedent's interest in the described property.

8. Pursuant to the facts set forth above and section 13100 *et seq.* of the California Probate Code, I request that the (description of property) be paid (or "transferred" or "delivered") to the declarant.

I declare under penalty of perjury under the laws of the State of California that the foregoing is true and correct.

Executed at _____, California, this ___ day of _____, 19___.

§ 10.2 Court Order Determining Succession to Real Property—Value Under $60,000 (Prob. Code § 13150 *et seq.*)

This law became effective July 1, 1987. The procedure may be used only where there is no California estate proceeding.

If a decedent leaves real property and the gross value of his or her real and personal property in California (excluding that described in Probate Code section 13050) does not exceed $60,000, and forty days have elapsed since the date of death, the successor in interest to real property may file a petition for a court order determining succession, without procuring letters of administration or awaiting probate of a will. The successor in interest also may file such a petition if the personal representative consents in writing to the procedure. The contents of the petition are specified in Probate Code section 13152.

The small estate set-aside makes the entire estate available for the support of the surviving spouse and minor children. The family takes the estate over the rights of those who otherwise would take all or a portion under a will or by intestate succession.

Judicial Council forms of the petition to determine succession to real property and the order determining succession to real property may be used. (See Figures 10–1 and 10–2.)

ATTORNEY OR PARTY WITHOUT ATTORNEY *(Name and Address)*:

TELEPHONE NO.:

FOR COURT USE ONLY

ATTORNEY FOR *(Name)*:

SUPERIOR COURT OF CALIFORNIA, COUNTY OF

STREET ADDRESS:

MAILING ADDRESS:

CITY AND ZIP CODE:

BRANCH NAME:

MATTER OF (NAME):

DECEDENT

PETITION TO DETERMINE SUCCESSION TO REAL PROPERTY
(Estates $60,000 or Less)

CASE NUMBER:

HEARING DATE:

DEPT.:   TIME:

1. **Petitioner** *(name of each)*:

   requests a determination that the real property described in this petition is property passing to petitioner and that no administration of decedent's estate is necessary.

2. Decedent *(name)*:
   a. Date of death:
   b. Place of death *(city, state)*:

3. At least 40 days have elapsed since the date of decedent's death.

4. a. ☐ Decedent was a resident of this county at the time of death.
   b. ☐ Decedent was not a resident of California at the time of death. Decedent died owning property in this county.

5. Decedent died ☐ intestate ☐ testate and a copy of the will and any codicil is affixed as attachment 5 or 12a.

6. a. No proceeding for the administration of decedent's estate is being conducted or has been conducted in California.
   b. No administration of decedent's estate is necessary in California.

7. Proceedings for the administration of decedent's estate in another jurisdiction
   a. ☐ have not been commenced.
   b. ☐ have been commenced ☐ and completed.
      (Specify state, county, court, and case number):

8. The gross value of all real and personal property in decedent's estate located in California as shown by the inventory and appraisal attached to this petition, excluding the property described in Probate Code section 13050 (joint tenancy, property passing to decedent's spouse, etc.), does not exceed $60,000. *(Attach an inventory and appraisal as attachment 8.)*

9. a. The decedent is survived by
   (1) ☐ spouse ☐ no spouse as follows: ☐ divorced or never married ☐ spouse deceased
   (2) ☐ child as follows: ☐ natural or adopted ☐ natural adopted by a third party ☐ step ☐ foster
       ☐ no child
   (3) ☐ issue of a predeceased child ☐ no issue of a predeceased child
   b. Petitioner ☐ has no actual knowledge of facts ☐ has actual knowledge of facts   reasonably giving rise to a parent-child relationship under Probate Code section 6408(b).
   c. ☐ All surviving children and issue of predeceased children have been listed in item 14.

10. *(Complete if decedent was survived by (1) a spouse but no issue (only a or b apply); or (2) no spouse or issue. Check the first box that applies)*:
   a. ☐ The decedent is survived by a parent or parents who are listed in item 14.
   b. ☐ The decedent is survived by a brother, sister, or issue of a deceased brother or sister, all of whom are listed in item 14.
   c. ☐ The decedent is survived by other heirs under Probate Code section 6400 et seq., all of whom are listed in item 14.

11. The legal description of decedent's real property in California passing to petitioner and decedent's interest in the property are stated in attachment 11. *(Attach the legal description of the real property and state decedent's interest.)*

(Continued on reverse)

Form Approved by the
Judicial Council of California
DE-310 [Rev. January 1, 1989]

PETITION TO DETERMINE SUCCESSION TO REAL PROPERTY
(Probate)

Probate Code, § 13151

FIGURE 10–1   Petition to Determine Succession to Real Property form

ATTORNEY OR PARTY WITHOUT ATTORNEY *(Name and Address)*:　TELEPHONE NO　　*FOR RECORDER'S USE ONLY*

☐ Recording requested by and return to:

ATTORNEY FOR *(Name)*:

SUPERIOR COURT OF CALIFORNIA, COUNTY OF

STREET ADDRESS:

MAILING ADDRESS:

CITY AND ZIP CODE:

BRANCH NAME:

MATTER OF (NAME):

DECEDENT

ORDER DETERMINING SUCCESSION TO REAL PROPERTY (Estates $60,000 or Less)	CASE NUMBER.

1. Date of hearing:　　　Time:　　　Dept.:　　Rm.:　　　*FOR COURT USE ONLY*

THE COURT FINDS

2. All notices required by law have been given.
3. Decedent died on *(date)*:
   a. ☐ a resident of the California county named above.
   b. ☐ a nonresident of California and left an estate in the county named above.
   c. ☐ intestate ☐ testate.
4. At least 40 days have elapsed since the date of decedent's death.
5. No proceeding for the administration of decedent's estate is being conducted or has been conducted in California.
6. The gross value of decedent's real and personal property in California, excluding property described in Probate Code section 13050, does not exceed $60,000.
7. Each petitioner is a successor of decedent (as defined in Probate Code section 13006) and a successor to decedent's interest in the real property described in item 9a because each petitioner is
   a. ☐ (will) a beneficiary who succeeded to the property under decedent's will.
   b. ☐ (no will) a person who succeeded to the property under Probate Code sections 6401 and 6402.

THE COURT FURTHER FINDS AND ORDERS

8. No administration of decedent's estate is necessary in California.
9. a. The following described real property is property of decedent passing to each petitioner *(give legal description)*:
   ☐ described in attachment 9a.

   b. Each petitioner's **name** and specific property interest ☐ is stated in attachment 9b ☐ is as follows *(specify)*:

10. ☐ Other *(specify)*:

Date:

　　　　　　　　　　　　　　　　　　JUDGE OF THE SUPERIOR COURT

11. ☐ Number of pages attached:　　　☐ Signature follows last attachment

Form Approved by the
Judicial Council of California
DE-315 (Rev. January 1, 1989)

ORDER DETERMINING SUCCESSION TO REAL PROPERTY
(Probate)

Probate Code. § 13154

FIGURE 10–2　Order Determining Succession to Real Property form

Inventory and Appraisement

An inventory and appraisement, made as set forth in Chapter 9 of Division 3 (commencing with Probate Code section 8850 *et seq.*), shall be attached to the petition but shall exclude the property described in Probate Code section 13050. The petitioner may appraise the assets a personal representative can appraise under Probate Code section 8901.

If the petitioner's claim is based upon the decedent's will, a copy of the will is attached to the petition.

Notice of Hearing

The clerk sets the petition for hearing. Not less than fifteen days before the hearing, notice must be personally served or mailed, postage prepaid, to each of the persons named in the petition pursuant to Probate Code section 13152, addressed to the person's residence or mailing address as set forth in the petition, or if not known to any petitioner, the county seat of the county where the proceedings are pending (Prob. Code § 1220). The court's order is conclusive on all persons.

The person receiving the property under the court's order is personally liable for the unsecured debts of the decedent to the extent of the fair market value of the property at the date of death, less any liens and encumbrances.

Attorneys' Fees

Attorneys' fees are by agreement unless there is a dispute, in which event the court will fix the fee. If no agreement is made and a dispute arises, a petition may be filed with the court in the same proceeding requesting the court to determine the fee. The court may likewise resolve any dispute concerning the meaning of any agreement entered into (Prob. Code § 13157).

§ 10.3 Affidavit Procedure—Real Property Valued at $10,000 or Less (Prob. Code § 13200 *et seq.*)

No sooner than six months after the date of death, any person or persons claiming real property not in excess of a gross value of $10,000 may file an affidavit, in the superior court of the decedent's domicile at the date of death, or if the decedent was not domiciled in California at the date of death, in any county in which the real property is located. The contents of the affidavit are contained in Probate Code section 13200.

All the decedent's successors must sign the affidavit. A separate notary public's certificate of acknowledgment is needed for each person executing the affidavit. If a person executing the affidavit claims under the will of decedent, a copy of the will also must be attached.

A fee is charged for filing the affidavit and issuing one certified copy. The court clerk files the affidavit and attachments and furnishes a certified copy of the affidavit without the attachments to the successor for recording in the county in which the real property is located.

This law became effective July 1, 1987. The procedure is not available if a probate proceeding is pending, although later proceedings for administration are not precluded. A form has been prescribed by the Judicial Council. (See Figure 10–3.)

Inventory and Appraisement

An inventory and appraisement of the real property, made by a probate referee selected by the affiant, and excluding the real property described in Probate Code section 13050, shall be attached to the affidavit [Prob. Code § 13200(c)].

Liability

Unsecured debts of the decedent may be enforced against the designated successor to the extent of the fair market value of the property, less any liens and encumbrances. The successor has the same defenses that would have been available to the decedent. If fraud is proved, the person is liable for three times the fair market value. Liability is barred five years after issuance of the certified copy. (See Prob. Code §§ 13206, 13207.)

Attorneys' Fees

Attorneys' fees are by agreement, but the court shall determine the fees if there is no agreement or if a dispute arises (Prob. Code § 13157).

ATTORNEY OR PARTY WITHOUT ATTORNEY *Name and Address:* *(After recording return to)*   TELEPHONE NO   FOR COURT USE ONLY

ATTORNEY FOR *(Name)*

SUPERIOR COURT OF CALIFORNIA, COUNTY OF

STREET ADDRESS:

MAILING ADDRESS:

CITY AND ZIP CODE:

BRANCH NAME:

MATTER OF (NAME):

                                                        DECEDENT

AFFIDAVIT RE REAL PROPERTY OF SMALL VALUE
($10,000 or Less)

CASE NUMBER:

FOR RECORDER'S USE ONLY

1. Decedent *(name)*:   died on *(date)*:
2. Decedent died at *(city, state)*:
3. At least six months have elapsed since the date of death of decedent as shown in
   the certified copy of decedent's death certificate attached to this affidavit. *(Attach
   a certified copy of decedent's death certificate.)*
4. a. ☐ Decedent was domiciled in this county at the time of death.
   b. ☐ Decedent was not domiciled in California at the time of death. Decedent
         died owning real property in this county.
5. a. The following is a legal description of decedent's real property claimed by the
      declarants *(copy description from deed or other legal instrument)*:
      ☐ described in an attachment labeled "Attachment 5a."

   b. Decedent's interest in this real property is as follows *(specify)*:

6. Each declarant is a successor of decedent (as defined in Probate Code section 13006) and a successor to decedent's interest in
   the real property described in item 5a, and no other person has a superior right, because each declarant is
   a. ☐ (will) a beneficiary who succeeded to the property under decedent's will. *(Attach a copy of the will.)*
   b. ☐ (no will) a person who succeeded to the property under Probate Code sections 6401 and 6402.
7. Names and addresses of each guardian or conservator of decedent's estate at date of death
   ☐ none ☐ are as follows* *(specify)*:

8. The gross value of all real property in decedent's estate located
   in California as shown by the inventory and appraisal, excluding
   the real property described in section 13050 of the Probate
   Code (joint tenancy, property passing to decedent's spouse,
   etc.), does not exceed $10,000.

9. An inventory and appraisal of decedent's real property in California is attached. The inventory and appraisal was made by a probate referee appointed for the county in which the property
   is located. *(You may use Judicial Council form DE-160.)*
10. No proceeding is now being or has been conducted in Califor-
    nia for administration of decedent's estate.

(Continued on reverse)

*You must personally serve or mail a copy of this affidavit with attachments to each person named in item 7.

Form Adopted by the
Judicial Council of California
DE 305 (Rev. January 1, 1989)

AFFIDAVIT RE REAL PROPERTY OF SMALL VALUE
(Probate)

Probate Code § 13200

FIGURE 10–3   Affidavit Re Real Property of Small Value form

§ 10.4 Small Estates Set-Aside—Value of $20,000 or Less (Prob. Code § 6600 *et seq.*)

Probate Code section 6602, which became effective July 1, 1987, provides for the filing of a petition setting aside the decedent's estate to the surviving spouse and minor children if the net value of the estate, over and above all liens and encumbrances as of the date of death, and over and above the value of any probate homestead interest set apart under section 6520, does not exceed $20,000. The contents of the petition are found in Probate Code section 6604. A sample petition is provided here. (See Figure 10–4.)

The petition may be filed independently or concurrently with a petition for probate of the will or for administration, at any time prior to the entry of an order of final distribution. No additional fee is charged for filing the petition if proceedings for administration of the estate are pending.

The petition may be filed by any of the following persons:

1. Person named in the will as executor;
2. Surviving spouse of the decedent;
3. Guardian of minor child of the decedent (approval of the court in which a guardianship proceeding is pending is not required);
4. Child of the decedent who was a minor at the time the decedent died;
5. Personal representative of the decedent, if appointed.

Notice of Hearing

If no proceedings are pending at the time of filing the petition and petitions are not joined, the petitioner must give fifteen days' notice of the hearing by mail to each heir and devisee and to each person named as executor who is not petitioning, if known to the petitioner. A copy of the petition is mailed with the notice of hearing to the surviving spouse, each child, and each nonpetitioning devisee (Prob. Code § 6607). If, on the other hand, the petition is filed with the petition for probate of will, the notice of hearing is given pursuant to Probate Code section 8003 and shall be included in the notice of hearing required by that section. If the petition is filed with a petition for administration, notice of hearing is given pursuant to Probate Code section 441 and shall be included in the notice required by that section.

If proceedings for probate of will or administration are pending when the petition is filed and the hearing on the petition for probate of will or administration is set for a day more than fifteen days after the filing of the

[TITLE OF COURT AND CAUSE]

PETITION FOR ORDER TO SET ASIDE SMALL ESTATE
NOT EXCEEDING $20,000
(PROBATE CODE SECTION 6600 *ET SEQ.*)

TO THE SUPERIOR COURT OF THE STATE OF CALIFORNIA FOR THE COUNTY OF _____.

I, the undersigned declarant, state:

I

No proceeding for the administration of the above estate is pending.

or

II

Decedent died ("testate" or "intestate") in the County of _____, State of California; decedent at the time of death was a resident of _____ County, California.

III

The names, ages, residences, and relation to the decedent of the heirs and devisees, so far as known to the petitioner, are as follows:

IV

The decedent left an estate, the total net value of which, over and above all liens and encumbrances at the date of death and the value of any homestead interest set apart out of the decedent's estate under Probate Code section 6520, does not exceed the sum of $20,000, and Probate Code section 6600 is applicable.

V

A list of all liens and encumbrances on the property of the estate at the date of death of the decedent is as follows:

Description   Amount

VI

A specific description of each item and the estimated value of the decedent's estate, with a list of all the liens and encumbrances thereon, as of the date of death of the decedent, follows:

VII

A specific description of any of the decedent's real property located outside California that passed to the surviving spouse and minor children of the decedent, or any one or more of them, under the will of the decedent or by intestate succession, and the value thereof, follows:

VIII

A specific description of any of the decedent's real property described in Probate Code section 6600, subdivision (b), that passed to the surviving spouse and minor children of the decedent, or any one or more of them, and the value thereof, follows:

IX

Pursuant to Probate Code section 6520, the court made an order on _____, _____, setting apart out of the decedent's estate a probate homestead to _____ of the following property, of the value of $_____.

FIGURE 10–4
Petition for Order to Set Aside Small Estate form

FIGURE 10–4
(continued)

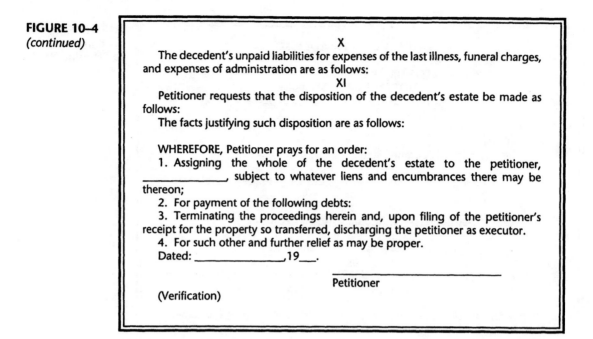

X

The decedent's unpaid liabilities for expenses of the last illness, funeral charges, and expenses of administration are as follows:

XI

Petitioner requests that the disposition of the decedent's estate be made as follows:

The facts justifying such disposition are as follows:

WHEREFORE, Petitioner prays for an order:

1. Assigning the whole of the decedent's estate to the petitioner, _____, subject to whatever liens and encumbrances there may be thereon;

2. For payment of the following debts:

3. Terminating the proceedings herein and, upon filing of the petitioner's receipt for the property so transferred, discharging the petitioner as executor.

4. For such other and further relief as may be proper.

Dated: _____,19___.

_____
Petitioner

(Verification)

petition, the petition shall be set for hearing at the same time. If the hearing on the petition for probate of will or administration is not set for a day more than fifteen days after the filing of the petition, the petition shall be set for hearing at least fifteen days after the date of its filing, and if the petition for probate of will or administration has not been heard, that petition shall be continued until that date and heard at the same time unless the court otherwise orders (Prob. Code § 6607). In either case, notice of the hearing shall be given as required by Probate Code section 1220.

Inventory and Appraisement

The personal representative, or the petitioner if none has been appointed, must file with the clerk an inventory and appraisement in the form set forth in Probate Code section 8802 prior to the hearing of the petition. The personal representative or the petitioner may appraise the assets that a personal representative can appraise under section 8901. (See Prob. Code § 6608.)

Court Orders

The court is given discretion in making the order. It may consider the needs of the surviving spouse and minor children, liens and encumbrances, claims of creditors, the needs of heirs or devisees, the intent of the decedent, and other relevant considerations (Prob. Code § 6609).

Remarriage

If the surviving spouse has remarried at the time of the hearing, it shall be presumed that the needs of the surviving spouse do not justify the setting aside of the small estate, or any portion of it, to the surviving spouse. This presumption affects the burden of proof (Prob. Code § 6609).

Liability

The court may make any orders necessary for the payment of any liabilities for expenses of last illness, funeral charges, and unpaid expenses of administration.

Title vests absolute. There are no further proceedings unless additional property is discovered. The court's order is conclusive on all persons. The persons in whom title vests are personally liable, for one year after the court's order except for actions then pending, for the unsecured debts of the decedent to the extent of the fair market value of the property, less any liens and encumbrances, the homestead interest, and the value of any other property set aside under Probate Code section 6510 (property exempt from enforcement of money judgment for surviving spouse and minor children) and section 6520 (probate homestead).

Actions for personal liability are barred to the same extent as claims under section 9000 *et seq.* except in regards to the following:

- Creditors who commence proceedings for enforcement prior to the time for filing or presenting claims;

- Creditors who have or secure an acknowledgment in writing that the person is liable for the debts; and

- Creditors who file a timely claim in the proceedings for administration of the estate [Prob. Code § 6611(e)].

If a petition under Probate Code section 6600 *et seq.* is filed with a petition for probate of will or administration and the court determines not to make an order under section 6609, the court acts on the petition for probate of will or administration as if a petition under this chapter had not been filed (Prob. Code § 6612).

Attorneys' Fees

Attorneys' fees under this chapter are by agreement. If there is no agreement and a dispute about the reasonableness of the attorney's fee, or if there is an agreement and a dispute concerning the meaning of that agreement, a petition may be filed in the same proceeding requesting the court to determine the fee.

§ 10.5 Collection by Affidavit of Compensation Owed to Deceased Spouse (Prob. Code §§ 13600–13606)

Probate Code section 13600 permits the surviving spouse, or the guardian or conservator of the estate of the surviving spouse, to collect salary or other compensation owed by an employer for personal services of the deceased spouse, including compensation for unused vacation, up to $5,000. If there is more than one employer, not more than a total of $5,000 can be collected form all of them. This section applies regardless of whether there is a will or a petition for letters of administration. Proof of identity (as provided in Probate Code section 13104) of the surviving spouse or the guardian or conservator must be provided to the employer. The employer may rely in good faith on the statements in the affidavit or declaration.

Probate Code section 13601 sets forth the contents of the affidavit to collect compensation owed to the decedent. A sample form is provided here. (See Figure 10–5.)

§ 10.6 Passage of Property to Surviving Spouse Without Administration (Prob. Code § 13500 *et seq.*)

This law became effective July 1, 1987, and applies to all estates, regardless of when the deceased spouse died. Probate Code sections 639 to 658 were repealed, except that the repeal of former section 649.2 does not affect any sale, lease, mortgage, or other transaction or disposition of real property made prior to July 1, 1987, to which that section applied. On and after July 1, 1987, a reference in any statute or written instrument, including a will or trust, to a provision of former Probate Code sections

DECLARATION FOR COLLECTION OF COMPENSATION OWED TO DECEASED SPOUSE PURSUANT TO PROBATE CODE SECTIONS 13600–13606

I,_____, declare:

1. The name of the decedent is _____, who died in the City of _____, County of _____, State of California, on _____, 19___.

2. The declarant (or affiant) is the surviving spouse of the decedent.

or

2. The declarant (or affiant) is the guardian or conservator of the estate of the surviving spouse of the decedent.

3. The surviving spouse of the decedent is entitled to the earnings of the decedent under the decedent's will or by intestate succession and no one else has a superior right to the earnings.

4. No proceeding is now being or has been conducted in California for administration of the decedent's estate.

5. Sections 13600 to 13606, inclusive, of the California Probate Code require that the earnings of the decedent, including compensation for unused vacation, not in excess of $5,000 net, be paid promptly to the declarant or affiant.

6. Neither the surviving spouse, nor anyone acting on behalf of the surviving spouse, has a pending request to collect compensation owed by another employer for personal services of the decedent under sections 13600 to 13606, inclusive, of the California Probate Code.

7. Neither the surviving spouse, nor anyone acting on behalf of the surviving spouse, has collected any compensation owed by an employer for personal services of the decedent under sections 13600 to 13606, inclusive, of the California Probate Code, except for the sum of _____ dollars ($_____), which was collected from _____.

8. The declarant (or affiant) requests that he (or she) be paid the salary or other compensation owed by you for personal services of the decedent, including compensation for unused vacation, not to exceed $5,000 net (less the amount of $_____ that was previously collected).

9. The declarant (or affiant) declares (or affirms) under penalty of perjury under the laws of the State of California that the foregoing is true and correct.

Executed at _____, California, this _____ day of _____, 19___.

_____
Declarant

FIGURE 10–5
Declaration for Collection of Compensation Owed to Deceased Spouse form

202 through 106 or 630 through 658 shall be deemed to be a reference to the comparable provision of the new law. Only a few substantive changes and additions, however, were made in the law applying to surviving spouses.

When a husband or wife dies intestate leaving property that passes to the surviving spouse under Probate Code section 6401, or dies testate and by his or her will devises all or part of his or her property to the surviving spouse, the property passes to the survivor subject to the provisions of Probate Code Chapter 2 (commencing with section 13540) and Chapter 3 (commencing with section 13550), and no administration is necessary. Property of the decedent subject to administration under section 13500 *et seq.* is the following:

- Property passing to someone other than the surviving spouse under the decedent's will or by intestate succession;

- Property disposed of in trust under the decedent's will; and

- Property in which the decedent's will limits the surviving spouse to a qualified ownership.

For the purposes of this section, a devise conditioned on the spouse surviving the decedent by a specified period of time is not a qualified ownership interest if the specified period of time has elapsed.

Election by Surviving Spouse

An election may be made by the surviving spouse, personal representative, or guardian of the estate—or by the conservator of the estate of the surviving spouse or, if the spouse's death soon follows the decedent's, the spouse's executor—to administer under Probate Code Division 7 (commencing with section 7000) the one-half of community property that belongs to the decedent under section 100, the one-half of the quasi-community property that belongs to the decedent under section 101, and the separate property of the decedent, and also the one-half of community property that belongs to the surviving spouse under section 100 and the one-half of the quasi-community property that belongs to the surviving spouse under section 101 (Prob. Code § 13502). The election must be in writing specifically evidencing the election and be filed in the estate administration within four months after the issuance of the letters testamentary or of administration, or within such further time as the court may allow on a showing of good cause, and before entry of an order under Probate Code section 13656.

This election relieves the surviving spouse of liability for the debts of the decedent. The election may be worded according to the following sample form:

[TITLE OF COURT AND CAUSE]

ELECTION BY SURVIVING SPOUSE UNDER

PROBATE CODE SECTION 13502

_____, as surviving spouse of the above-named decedent, hereby elects under the provisions of Section 13502 of the California Probate Code to have both (his or her) interest and that of decedent in their community property and the quasi-community property (and the quasi-community property and the separate property of decedent) administered in the above estate proceeding.

Dated: _____, 19___.

An election also may be made for transfer of the property to the trustee under the will of the deceased spouse or existing trust identified by the will of the deceased spouse, to be administered by the trustee (Prob. Code § 13503). Community property held in revocable trust, however, is governed by the provisions in the trust for disposition at death (Prob. Code § 13504). The election must be in writing and be filed in the estate proceedings.

§ 10.7 Right of Surviving Spouse to Dispose of Real Property (Prob. Code § 13540 *et seq.*)

The surviving spouse, personal representative, guardian of estate, or conservator of the estate of the surviving spouse may dispose of community real property or quasi-community real property forty days after the death of the spouse, unless a notice has been recorded by someone other than the spouse claiming an interest in the property, as provided in Probate Code section 13541 (Prob. Code § 13540). Such a notice must describe the property, set forth the name or names of the owner of record title, and contain a statement that an interest is claimed by a named person under the will of the deceased spouse (Prob. Code § 13541). The attorney may wish to petition the court for instructions. The attorney should consider how the handling of the estate would be affected if the surviving spouse were to die before the estate was closed.

If the surviving spouse elects to take under these sections without probate administration, a petition is filed pursuant to Probate Code section 13540 *et seq.* If a probate administration is not already pending, the spousal petition may, but need not, be joined with a petition for probate of will or for letters of administration (Prob. Code § 13653).

The surviving spouse is personally liable for the debts of the deceased spouse chargeable against the property described in Probate Code section 13551 to the extent provided by that section. The surviving spouse is not liable if all the property is administered under Probate Code Division 7, commencing with section 7000.

The Judicial Council forms for the spousal petition and order may be used only where the decedent died after January 1, 1985. (See Forms 10–6 and 10–7.) If the decedent died before January 1, 1985, the estate is governed by the law that would have applied if the changes in the Probate Code had not been made.

Inventory and Appraisement (Prob. Code § 13659)

Except as provided in Probate Code section 13658 (unincorporated business), no inventory and appraisal is required. However, within three months after the filing of any petition under Chapter 5, or within such further time as the court or judge for reasonable cause may allow, the petitioner may file with the clerk of the court an inventory and appraisal in the form set forth in Probate Code section 8802. The appraisal shall be made as set forth in Part 3 commencing with section 8800 of Division 7.

The petitioner may appraise the assets that an executor or administrator can appraise under section 8901.

Notice of Hearing on 13650 Petition—No Joinder

If proceedings for administration are pending or no proceeding is pending, and if the petition under Probate Code section 13650 is not filed with the petition for probate of will or administration, the clerk sets the petition for hearing and the petitioner gives notice. The hearing shall be set for not less than fifteen nor more than thirty days after the petition is filed. If the petitioner so requests at the time of filing, the hearing shall be set for a day not less than thirty nor more than forty-five days after the petition is filed. Better practice may be to not set the petition for hearing until the referee has completed any appraisal requested, which may avoid a continuance.

At least fifteen days prior to hearing, the petitioner personally serves a notice of hearing on the petition or mails notice, postage prepaid, to each heir of the decedent, so far as known or reasonably ascertainable to the petitioner, and to each devisee and executor named in any will being offered for probate. In addition, if the will may involve a testamentary trust of property for charitable purposes, other than a charitable trust with a designated trustee resident in California, or a devise for charitable purposes without an identified devisee, a notice of hearing, accompanied

ATTORNEY OR PARTY WITHOUT ATTORNEY *(Name and Address)*:

TELEPHONE NO.:

FOR COURT USE ONLY

ATTORNEY FOR *(Name)*:

SUPERIOR COURT OF CALIFORNIA, COUNTY OF

STREET ADDRESS:

MAILING ADDRESS:

CITY AND ZIP CODE:

BRANCH NAME:

ESTATE OF (NAME):

DECEDENT

SPOUSAL PROPERTY PETITION

CASE NUMBER:

HEARING DATE:

DEPT.:   TIME:

1. **Petitioner** *(name)*:
   requests
   a. ☐ determination of property passing to the surviving spouse without administration (Probate Code, § 13500).
   b. ☐ confirmation of property belonging to the surviving spouse (Probate Code, §§ 100 and 101).
   c. ☐ this petition be joined with the petition for probate or administration of the decedent's estate.
   d. ☐ immediate appointment of a probate referee.

2. **Petitioner is**
   a. ☐ surviving spouse of the decedent.
   b. ☐ personal representative of *(name)*:   , surviving spouse.
   c. ☐ guardian of the estate or conservator of the estate of *(name)*:   surviving spouse.

3. **Decedent died on** *(date)*:
   a. ☐ a resident of the California county named above.
   b. ☐ a nonresident of California and left an estate in the county named above.
   c. ☐ intestate   ☐ testate and a copy of the will and any codicil is affixed as attachment 3c or 6d. *(Attach will.)*

4. a. *(Complete in all cases)* The decedent is survived by
   (1) ☐ child as follows: ☐ natural or adopted   ☐ natural adopted by a third party   ☐ step   ☐ foster
       ☐ no child
   (2) ☐ issue of a predeceased child   ☐ no issue of a predeceased child
   b. Petitioner ☐ has no ☐ has actual knowledge of facts reasonably giving rise to a parent-child relationship under Probate Code section 6408(b).
   c. ☐ All surviving children and issue of predeceased children have been listed in item 7.

5. *(Complete only if no issue survived the decedent. Check only the first box that applies.)*
   a. ☐ The decedent is survived by a parent or parents who are listed in item 7.
   b. ☐ The decedent is survived by a brother, sister, or issue of a deceased brother or sister, all of whom are listed in item 7.

6. a. Administration of all or part of the estate is not necessary for the reason that all or a part of the estate is property passing to the surviving spouse.
   b. ☐ The legal description of the deceased spouse's property that petitioner requests to be determined as passing to the surviving spouse is set forth in attachment 6b,[1] and includes the trade or business name of any unincorporated business or an interest in any unincorporated business the deceased spouse was operating or managing at the time of death.
   c. ☐ The legal description of the community or quasi-community property petitioner requests the court to confirm to the surviving spouse as belonging to the surviving spouse under Probate Code sections 100 and 101 is set forth in attachment 6c.
   d. The facts upon which the petitioner bases the allegation that the property described in attachments 6b and 6c is property that should pass or be confirmed to the surviving spouse are stated in attachment 6d.[2]

(Continued on reverse)

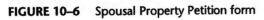

Form Approved by the
Judicial Council of California
DE-221 [Rev. July 1, 1987]

SPOUSAL PROPERTY PETITION
(Probate)

See reverse for footnotes.
Probate Code, § 13650

FIGURE 10–6   Spousal Property Petition form

ESTATE OF (NAME): _____ CASE NUMBER: _____

_____ DECEDENT

7. The names, relationships, ages, and residence or mailing addresses of all persons checked in items 4 or 5 and all other heirs and devisees of the decedent, so far as known to petitioner, including stepchild and foster child heirs and devisees to whom notice is to be given ☐ are listed below ☐ are listed in attachment 7.

NAME AND RELATIONSHIP	AGE	RESIDENCE OR MAILING ADDRESS

8. The names and address of all persons named as executors in the decedent's will or appointed as personal representatives ☐ are listed below ☐ are listed in attachment 8 ☐ none.

9. ☐ The personal representative is the trustee of a trust that is a devisee under decedent's will. The names and addresses of all persons interested in the trust who are entitled to notice under Probate Code section 13655(b)(2) are listed in attachment 9.

10. A petition for probate or for administration of the decedent's estate
   a. ☐ is being filed with this petition and published notice will be given.
   b. ☐ was filed on (date):
   c. ☐ has not been filed and is not being filed with this petition.

11. ☐ Number of pages attached:

I declare under penalty of perjury under the laws of the State of California that the foregoing is true and correct.
Date:

▶

....   _____
(TYPE OR PRINT NAME)   (SIGNATURE OF PETITIONER)

¹ See Probate Code, § 13658 for required filing of a list of known creditors of a business and other information in certain instances. If required, include in attachment 6b.
² See Probate Code, § 13651(b) for the requirement that a copy of the will be attached in certain instances. If required, include in attachment 3c or 6d.

DE-221 [Rev. July 1, 1987]

SPOUSAL PROPERTY PETITION
(Probate)

Page two

FIGURE 10–6 (continued)

ATTORNEY OR PARTY WITHOUT ATTORNEY *(Name and Address)*:	TELEPHONE NO.:	*FOR COURT USE ONLY*
ATTORNEY FOR *(Name)*:		

SUPERIOR COURT OF CALIFORNIA, COUNTY OF
STREET ADDRESS:
MAILING ADDRESS:
CITY AND ZIP CODE:
BRANCH NAME:

ESTATE OF (NAME):

DECEDENT

SPOUSAL PROPERTY ORDER

CASE NUMBER:

1. Date of hearing: Time: Dept.:   Room:

THE COURT FINDS

2. All notices required by law have been given.

3. Decedent died on *(date)*:
   a. ☐ a resident of the California county named above.
   b. ☐ a nonresident of California and left an estate in the county named above.
   c. ☐ intestate ☐ testate.

THE COURT FURTHER FINDS AND ORDERS

4. a. ☐ The property described in attachment 4a is property passing to the surviving spouse,
      (name):   , and no administration of it is necessary.
   b. ☐ See attachment 4b for further order respecting transfer of the property to the surviving spouse.

5. ☐ To protect the interests of the creditors of *(business name)*:

   an unincorporated trade or business, a list of all its known creditors and the amount owed each is on file.
   a. ☐ Within *(specify)*:   days from this date, the surviving spouse shall file an undertaking in the amount of
      $, upon condition that the surviving spouse pay the known creditors of the business.
   b. ☐ See attachment 5b for further order protecting the interests of creditors of the business.

6. a. ☐ The property described in attachment 6a is property that belongs to the surviving spouse,
      (name):   , under Probate Code sections 100 and 101, and the surviving
      spouse's ownership is hereby confirmed.
   b. ☐ See attachment 6b for further order respecting transfer of the property to the surviving spouse.

7. ☐ All property described in the Spousal Property Petition that is not determined to be property passing to the surviving spouse
   under Probate Code section 13500, or confirmed as belonging to the surviving spouse under Probate Code sections 100
   and 101, shall be subject to administration in the estate ☐ described in attachment 7.
8. ☐ Other *(specify)*:

Date:

_____
JUDGE OF THE SUPERIOR COURT

9. ☐ Number of pages attached: ☐ Signature follows last attachment

Form Approved by the
Judicial Council of California
DE-226 [Rev. July 1, 1987]

SPOUSAL PROPERTY ORDER
(Probate)

Probate Code. § 13656

FIGURE 10–7   Spousal Property Order form

by a copy of the petition and the will, shall be served on the Attorney General (Prob. Code §§ 8110, 8111).

Notice of hearing of a petition for administration also shall be published before the hearing. The first publication shall be fifteen days before the hearing, and there shall be three publications in a newspaper published once a week or more often, with at least five days between the first and last publication dates, not counting the publication dates. Publication shall be in a newspaper of general circulation in the city where decedent resided at the time of death, or where the decedent's property is located if the court has jurisdiction under section 7052 (not domiciled in California at the time of death). If there is no such newspaper, the decedent did not reside in a city, or the property is not located in a city, then publication shall be in a newspaper of general circulation in the county in which the decedent resided or the property is located. If there is no such newspaper, then publication shall be in a newspaper published nearest to the county seat of the county in which the decedent resided or the property is located that is circulated within the area of the county in which the decedent resided or the property is located (Prob. Code §§ 8120, 8121).

Probate Code section 8122 covers situations in which notice is published in good faith but inadvertently may not satisfy section 8121.

Proof of service of a copy of the petition and a notice of hearing must be filed prior to the hearing.

Notice of Hearing on Combined Petitions (13650 Petition and Petition for Probate of Will)

If the 13650 petition is joined with a petition for probate of will administration, notice of hearing is given as prescribed by Probate Code section 8003 and shall be included in the notice required by that section. Notice of hearing on the petition for probate of will or administration shall be given at least fifteen days prior to the date of the hearing, and a copy of the 13650 petition shall be personally served upon, or mailed postage prepaid, to all persons entitled to notice under section 13655.

Liability

Probate Code section 649.4 covers the surviving spouse's liability to creditors. Generally speaking, the surviving spouse is personally liable for the debts chargeable to community property to the amount of the community property taken. The surviving spouse also is liable for any action brought under section 205 for any contract entered into by the deceased spouse. Such an action may be brought before the expiration of the statute of limitations on the contract or four months after the death, whichever is later (Code Civ. Proc. § 353.5).

Attorneys' Fees

Attorneys are to be allowed a reasonable fee for their services, subject to approval by the court (Prob. Code § 910).

§ 10.8 Allocation of Debts Between Estate and Surviving Spouse

The new laws permitting informal probate of community property posed problems regarding responsibility for debts. Legislation was passed as a means of achieving an equitable apportionment of debts between spouses and their property.

Probate Code section 11440 provides for the filing of a petition by the personal representative, the surviving spouse, or a beneficiary, prior to the filing of a petition for final distribution, for an order allocating the responsibility for those debts payable by the estate and, in whole or in part, by the surviving spouse. The petition must include a statement of all the debts of the decedent and the surviving spouse known to the petitioner that are alleged to be subject to allocation and must indicate whether they have been paid in whole or in part or are unpaid. The petition should state why the debts should be allocated, the proposed allocation, and the basis for allocation alleged by the petitioner (Prob. Code § 11441). If the petition shows that allocation would be affected by the value of the separate property of the surviving spouse and community property not administered, and the surviving spouse has not furnished an inventory, the court must issue an order to show cause why such information should not be furnished (Prob. Code § 11442).

The personal representative and the surviving spouse may provide for allocation by agreement, and if the court determines that the agreement substantially protects the rights of persons interested in the estate, that allocation will be ordered by the court. Otherwise, the court will apportion according to California law and make an order directing payment as provided in Probate Code section 11444(b). Apportionment will vary according to the facts surrounding the debts in each situation.

Notice of the hearing on such a petition, together with a copy of the petition and order to show cause, is served under Probate Code section 1220 fifteen days prior to hearing on the personal representative, to persons who have given notice of appearance in person or by attorney (if by attorney, notice shall be mailed to the attorney), and to persons who have requested special notice under section 1250 (Prob. Code § 11443).

§ 10.9 Independent Administration of Estates Act (Prob. Code §§ 10400–10600)

The Independent Administration of Estates Act, enacted in 1974, applies to estates of decedents dying on or after July 1, 1975, and may be used in estates of persons dying before that date if no letters were granted before July 1, 1975 (Prob. Code § 591 *et seq.*). Unless the decedent's will provides that the estate shall not be administered under the provisions of the Independent Administration of Estates Act, an executor or administrator has the option of proceeding to administer the estate under this act (Prob. Code, § 10404). A special administrator may be granted authority under the act if he or she is appointed with, or granted, the powers of a personal representative. (See Prob. Code § 10406.)

Under the Independent Administration of Estates Act, the court provides minimal supervision. The executor or administrator must file a petition for authority under the act. Once the petition is granted, the procedure for administration of the estate is simplified. If no real property is being sold, no further court appearance may be required until the hearing on the final account, which may be waived, and the petition for final distribution. This simplification should operate to reduce extraordinary fees. Statutory fees are not affected by the act.

The printed form of the regular petition for probate may be used, with the appropriate boxes checked. The box in the title labeled "Authorization to Administer Under the Independent Administration of Estates Act" should be checked, as well as boxes 2c and 5.

Unless restricted by will, the petition may ask for either limited authority, as defined in Probate Code section 10403, or full authority. Full authority means all the powers granted under the act. Some powers may be exercised without court supervision and without notice, while others may require either supervision or notice, or both. (See Prob. Code §§ 10500 *et seq.*) These powers are in addition to any other powers in the Probate Code or case law.

Notice of Hearing on Petition

If the petition for appointment under this act is included in the petition for letters, notice of hearing is given in the same manner as applicable to a petition for letters. If a separate petition for authority is filed under Probate Code section 10450, notice is given as provided by

Probate Code section 1220, at least fifteen days before the date set for hearing to each known heir and devisee whose interest in the estate would be affected by the petition and each person named as executor in the will. Where a petition for probate is pending at the time the petition is filed, the notice of hearing must include in its caption and in the body references to both the petition and the application.

For the form of the notice of hearing on the petition, see Figure 10–8.

Court Supervision

After obtaining authority under this act, the personal representative may seek court approval of any action taken during the course of administration. Court approval is required, however, with respect to the following actions:

1. Allowance of the personal representative's commissions;
2. Allowance of attorneys' fees;
3. Settlement of accounts;
4. Preliminary and final distributions and discharge;
5. Sale of property of the estate to the personal representative or his or her attorney;
6. Exchange of property of the estate for property of the personal representative or his or her attorney;
7. Grant of an option to purchase property of the estate to the personal representative or his or her attorney;
8. Allowance, payment, or compromise of a claim of the personal representative or his or her attorney against the estate;
9. Compromise or settlement of a claim, action, or proceedings by the estate against the personal representative or his or her attorney; and
10. Extension, renewal, or modification of the terms of a debt or other obligation of the personal representative or the attorney for the personal representative, owing to or in favor of the decedent or the estate (Prob. Code § 10501).

If only limited authority has been granted, court supervision is required for the following actions:

1. Sale, exchange, or grant of an option to purchase real property; and
2. Borrowing money with the loan secured by an encumbrance on real property (Prob. Code § 10501).

ATTORNEY OR PARTY WITHOUT ATTORNEY *(Name and Address)*:

TELEPHONE NO.:

FOR COURT USE ONLY

ATTORNEY FOR *(Name)*:

SUPERIOR COURT OF CALIFORNIA, COUNTY OF

STREET ADDRESS:

MAILING ADDRESS:

CITY AND ZIP CODE:

BRANCH NAME:

SACRAMENTO SUPERIOR COURT
720 9th ST.
SACRAMENTO, CA 95814

ESTATE OF (NAME):

DECEDENT

NOTICE OF HEARING
(Probate)

CASE NUMBER:

This notice is required by law. This notice does not require you to appear in court, but you may attend the hearing if you wish.

1. NOTICE is given that *(name)*:

(representative capacity, if any):

has filed *(specify):* *

2. You may refer to the filed documents for further particulars. *(All of the case documents filed with the court are available for examination in the case file kept by the court clerk.)*

3. A HEARING on the matter will be held as follows:

Date: Time: Dept.:   Room:

Address of court ☐ shown above ☐ is:

. . . .
(TYPE OR PRINT NAME)

☐ Attorney or party _____
(SIGNATURE)

Date:

☐ Clerk, by _____ , Deputy

4. This notice was mailed on *(date)*:   at *(place)*:

(Continued on reverse)

* Do not use this form to give notice of hearing of the petition for administration *(see Probate Code, § 8100)*.

Form Approved by the

NOTICE OF HEARING

Probate Code, §§ 1211, 1215, 1216, 1230

FIGURE 10–8   Notice of Hearing form

ESTATE OF (NAME):

CASE NUMBER:

DECEDENT

CLERK'S CERTIFICATE OF ☐ POSTING ☐ MAILING

I certify that I am not a party to this cause and that a copy of the foregoing Notice of Hearing (Probate)

1. ☐ was posted at (address):

   on (date):

2. ☐ was served on each person named below. Each notice was enclosed in an envelope with postage fully prepaid. Each envelope was addressed to a person whose name and address is given below, sealed, and deposited with the United States Postal Service
   at (place): _____ California,
   on (date):

Date: _____ Clerk, by _____ , Deputy

PROOF OF SERVICE BY MAIL

1. I am over the age of 18 and not a party to this cause. I am a resident of or employed in the county where the mailing occurred.
2. My residence or business address is (specify):

3. I served the foregoing Notice of Hearing (Probate) on each person named below by enclosing a copy in an envelope addressed as shown below AND
   a. ☐ depositing the sealed envelope with the United States Postal Service with the postage fully prepaid.
   b. ☐ placing the envelope for collection and mailing on the date and at the place shown in item 4 following our ordinary business practices. I am readily familiar with this business' practice for collecting and processing correspondence for mailing. On the same day that correspondence is placed for collection and mailing, it is deposited in the ordinary course of business with the United States Postal Service in a sealed envelope with postage fully prepaid.

4. a. Date mailed: b. Place mailed (city, state):

5. ☐ I served with the Notice of Hearing (Probate) a copy of the petition or other document referred to in the notice.

   I declare under penalty of perjury under the laws of the State of California that the foregoing is true and correct.

Date:

▶ _____

....
(TYPE OR PRINT NAME)   (SIGNATURE OF DECLARANT)

NAME AND ADDRESS OF EACH PERSON TO WHOM NOTICE WAS MAILED

FIGURE 10–8 (continued)

Notice of Proposed Action

Some powers are exercisable only after giving a **notice of proposed action** (see Prob. Code §§ 10510–10520, 10530–10538). A printed form has been prepared by the Judicial Council. (See Figure 10–9.)

Powers exercisable without giving notice of proposed action are specified in Probate Code sections 10550 through 10564. Notice also need not be given to any person who consents in writing to the proposed action or who waives notice. The Judicial Council has issued a form for waiver of notice of proposed action.

Contents of Notice of Proposed Action

The notice of proposed action is required by Probate Code section 10585 to contain:

1. Name and mailing address of the personal representative;
2. Person and telephone number to call to get additional information;
3. Action proposed to be taken and a reasonably specific description of that action;
4. Date on which the action is proposed to be taken; and
5. When the proposed action involves the sale or exchange of real property or the grant of an option to purchase real property, the material terms of the transaction, including, if applicable, the sale price and the commission to be paid.

Service of Notice of Proposed Action

The legal assistant has the responsibility to see that proper notice is given and proof of service filed. Probate Code section 10586 provides that notice of the proposed action shall be mailed or personally delivered to each person required to be given notice not less than fifteen days before the date specified in the notice on or after which the proposed action is to be taken. If mailed, the notice shall be sent to the person's last known address. (See Prob. Code §§ 1215, 1216.)

Notice shall be given to each known devisee and heir whose interest in the estate is affected by the proposed action and to each person who has filed a request for special notice pursuant to section 1250, as well as to the Attorney General if any portion of the estate is to escheat to it and

---

notice of proposed action†   The formal notice that informs a person that an action will be taken if no objections to it are forthcoming.

ATTORNEY OR PARTY WITHOUT ATTORNEY *(Name and Address)*:   TELEPHONE NO.:   FOR COURT USE ONLY

ATTORNEY FOR *(Name)*:

SUPERIOR COURT OF CALIFORNIA, COUNTY OF

    STREET ADDRESS:

    MAILING ADDRESS:

    CITY AND ZIP CODE:

    BRANCH NAME:

ESTATE OF (NAME):

                                         DECEDENT

| | CASE NUMBER: |

NOTICE OF PROPOSED ACTION
Independent Administration of Estates Act
Objection—Consent

NOTICE: If you do not object in writing or obtain a court order preventing the action proposed below, you will be treated as if you consented to the proposed action and you may not object after the proposed action has been taken. If you object, the personal representative may take the proposed action only under court supervision. An objection form is on the reverse. If you wish to object, you may use the form or prepare your own written objection.

---

1. The personal representative (executor or administrator) of the estate of the deceased is *(names)*:

2. The personal representative has authority to administer the estate without court supervision under the Independent Administration of Estates Act (Probate Code section 10400 et seq.)
   a. ☐ with full authority under the act.
   b. ☐ with limited authority under the act (there is no authority, without court supervision, to (1) sell or exchange real property or (2) grant an option to purchase real property or (3) borrow money with the loan secured by an encumbrance upon real property).

3. On or after *(date)*: _____ , the personal representative will take the following action without court supervision *(describe in specific terms here or in Attachment 3)*:
   ☐ The proposed action is described in an attachment labeled Attachment 3.

4. ☐ **Real property transaction** *(Check this box and complete item 4b if the proposed action involves a sale or exchange or a grant of an option to purchase real property.)*
   a. The material terms of the transaction are specified in item 3, including any sale price and the amount of or method of calculating any commission or compensation to an agent or broker.
   b. $ _____ is the value of the subject property in the probate inventory. ☐ No inventory yet.

   NOTICE: A sale of real property without court supervision means that the sale will NOT be presented to the court for confirmation at a hearing at which higher bids for the property may be presented and the property sold to the highest bidder.

(Continued on reverse)

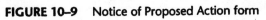

Form Approved by the
Judicial Council of California
DE-165 (Rev. July 1, 1988)

NOTICE OF PROPOSED ACTION
Objection—Consent
(Probate)

Probate Code, § 10580 et seq

FIGURE 10–9   Notice of Proposed Action form

ESTATE OF (NAME):

DECEDENT

CASE NUMBER:

5. If you OBJECT to the proposed action
   a. Sign the objection form below and deliver or mail it to the personal representative at the following address *(specify name and address)*:

   -OR-
   b. Send your own written objection to the address in item 5a. *(Be sure to identify the proposed action and state that you object to it.)*
   -OR-
   c. Apply to the court for an order preventing the personal representative from taking the proposed action without court supervision.

   d. NOTE: Your written objection or the court order must be received by the personal representative before the date in the box in item 3, or before the proposed action is taken, whichever is later. If you object, the personal representative may take the proposed action only under court supervision.

6. If you APPROVE the proposed action, you may sign the consent form below and return it to the address in item 5a. If you do not object in writing or obtain a court order, you will be treated as if you consented to the proposed action.

7. If you need more INFORMATION, call *(name)*:
   (telephone): (   )

Date:

. . . .
(TYPE OR PRINT NAME)

▶

_____
(SIGNATURE OF PERSONAL REPRESENTATIVE OR ATTORNEY)

OBJECTION TO PROPOSED ACTION

☐ I OBJECT to the action proposed above in item 3.

NOTICE: Sign and return this form (both sides) to the address in item 5a. The form must be received before the date in the box in item 3, or before the proposed action is taken, whichever is later. *(You may want to use certified mail, with return receipt requested. Make a copy of this form for your records.)*

Date:

. . . .
(TYPE OR PRINT NAME)

▶

_____
(SIGNATURE OF OBJECTOR)

CONSENT TO PROPOSED ACTION

☐ I CONSENT to the action proposed above in item 3.

NOTICE: You may indicate your consent by signing and returning this form (both sides) to the address in item 5a. If you do not object in writing or obtain a court order, you will be treated as if you consented to the proposed action.

Date:

. . . .
(TYPE OR PRINT NAME)

▶

_____
(SIGNATURE OF CONSENTER)

DE-165 (Rev. July 1, 1988)

NOTICE OF PROPOSED ACTION
Objection—Consent
(Probate)

Page two

FIGURE 10–9 *(continued)*

its interest in the estate is affected (Prob. Code § 10581).

The original notice should be filed with the clerk, with proof of service (personal or by mail) attached. The proof of service should reflect any service by airmail.

Objections to Proposed Action

Objection may be made to any proposed action being taken without court supervision by any of the persons entitled to notice under section 10581 (devisees and legatees whose interest is affected by the proposed action, heirs in intestate estates, the State of California if any portion of the estate **escheats** to it, and persons who file a request for special notice). These persons may do either of the following:

1. They may apply to the court, and the court must grant an order restraining the action without requiring notice to the personal representative and without cause being shown therefor (Prob. Code § 10588). The person objecting must serve the order upon the personal representative as provided in Code of Civil Procedure section 415.10 or section 415.30 or in the manner authorized by court.

2. They may deliver or mail a written objection to the executor or administrator, at the address stated in the notice of proposed action, so that the objection is received before the date specified on or after which the proposed action is to be taken, or before the proposed action is actually taken, whichever is later.

If the personal representative has notice of the issuance of a restraining order or a written objection, he or she may submit the proposed action to the court for approval and may complete that action under an order approved by the court.

Failure to object on the part of anyone receiving notice is a waiver of the right to have the court later review the action taken unless the person who fails to object can establish that the notice of the proposed action was not received before the time to object expired. A person who waives notice of or consents to the proposed action may not object (Prob. Code § 10590).

Title to property conveyed or transferred to bona fide purchasers and third persons acting in good faith who did not have actual notice of the failure of the personal representative to comply with sections 10580(a),

---

TERMS

escheat† The right of the state to take title to property after the death of a person who has not disposed of the property by will and has left no heirs to inherit it.

10581, 10485, 10586, or 10589 is valid. Such persons have no duty to inquire or investigate whether the personal representative has complied with these sections (Prob. Code § 10591).

Distribution

Distribution of such estates is governed by Probate Code section 11600 *et seq.* If the time for claims has expired and all uncontested claims have been paid or sufficiently secured, but the estate is not in a condition to be finally closed and distributed, the administrator or executor may petition for distribution of up to fifty percent of the net value of the estate. Net value of the estate in this context means the excess of value of the assets in all inventories and appraisements on file over the total amount of creditors' claims filed or presented and liens and encumbrances recorded or known to the executor or administrator but not reflected in any creditors' claim filed or presented, excluding death tax liens occasioned by the decedent's death. The petition need not include an accounting except when distributing to a trustee, although the trustee may consent to a distribution without an accounting.

The clerk sets the petition for hearing and gives notice as prescribed in Probate Code section 1220. The court may order notice to be given for a shorter period or dispense with the required notice (Prob. Code § 1004).

SIDEBAR

The legal assistant should consult local rules. Los Angeles County for example, requires that every petition for distribution include a schedule of claims showing the name of the claimant, the amount claimed, the date presented, the date allowed, the amount allowed, and if paid, the date of payment. The date of any rejection of claim must be shown, and the original notice of rejection, with an affidavit of mailing to the creditor, must be filed. A petition for preliminary distribution must show that the estate is solvent. Also, all independent actions taken without court approval must be set forth and described, and an allegation must be made that the fifteen-day notice was duly served and no objections were filed. The original notice with an affidavit attached must be filed with the court.

---

§ 10.10 Transfer of an Automobile from an Estate

Automobiles are frequently held in joint tenancy, particularly between spouses. To transfer an automobile to a distributee, the representative should first obtain the certificate of ownership, which usually is in a safe-deposit box or among other papers of the decedent. The certificate of ownership should be examined. Use of the word *or* creates joint tenancy. Use of the word *and* creates joint tenancy only if the certificate so states [Veh. Code § 4150.5(a) and (c)].

The representative should send a letter to the Department of Motor Vehicles enclosing:

1. The certificate of ownership issued in the name of the decedent, along with a description of the vehicle (make, license number, and engine number). The personal representative should sign the certificate of ownership in his or her official capacity on lines 1 and 2. The name and address of the distributee (lines 5 and 7) should be typewritten. The person receiving the vehicle, the distributee, should sign on line 6;

2. Affidavit for Transfer Without Probate (California Titled Vehicle or Vessels only), and Notice of Release of Liability. (See Figure 10–10.) These forms can be obtained from the Department of Motor Vehicles;

3. Certified copy of letters testamentary or letters of administration, with the will, if any, annexed;

4. Evidence of current registration, which usually can be found in the glove compartment of the car;

5. Evidence of a smog control device if the vehicle is an older model or a foreign car; and

6. The transfer fee.

The automobile may have been previously sold from the estate. If so, a notice of sale or transfer of vehicle form should be filed immediately to avoid liability. Instructions for completing this form appear on its reverse side.

The insurance company should be notified immediately of any change of ownership to avoid any liability for damages caused by the new owner. The legal assistant should either take care of this or make certain the representative does so. A personal check by the legal assistant is advisable to avoid any undesirable consequences.

§ 10.11 Termination of Joint Tenancy

Terminating joint tenancy is not truly a summary procedure or an alternative to formal probate, since formal probate is not ordinarily considered where property is held in joint tenancy. It is, however, a means of "disposing" of a decedent's property, and since a legal assistant will be involved in the termination of joint tenancies, the procedures are included in this chapter.

STATE OF CALIFORNIA
DMV
DEPARTMENT OF MOTOR VEHICLES
A Public Service Agency

NOTICE OF RELEASE OF LIABILITY
(Use to Report Sale or Transfer of Vehicle/Vessel)

READ INSTRUCTIONS ON REVERSE. LIABILITY WILL NOT BE RELEASED IF INFORMATION ON FORM IS ILLEGIBLE, INCOMPLETE OR DOES NOT MATCH OUR RECORDS. KEEP A COPY FOR YOUR RECORDS.

VEHICLE LICENSE NO. OR VESSEL CF NO. | MAKE OF VEHICLE OR VESSEL BUILDER

VEHICLE OR HULL IDENTIFICATION NO.

I sold or transferred my interest in the above described vehicle/vessel on: MONTH DAY YEAR 19
(IF TRANSFER DATE IS NOT PROVIDED, LIABILITY IS NOT RELEASED)
I sold or transferred the above described vehicle/vessel for the amount of: SELLING PRICE $

BUYER
FULL NAME (PLEASE PRINT LAST NAME FIRST IN SPACES BELOW)
ADDRESS CITY STATE ZIP CODE

SELLER
FULL NAME (PLEASE PRINT LAST NAME FIRST IN SPACES BELOW)
SIGNATURE
X
ADDRESS CITY STATE ZIP CODE

ENTER ODOMETER READING HERE: 10ths

FOR DEPARTMENT USE ONLY Your liability for this vehicle has not been released because the information ☐ is illegible ☐ is incomplete ☐ does not match our records.

REG. 138 (REV. 5/87)

FIGURE 10–10(*a*) Notice of Release of Liability form

STATE OF CALIFORNIA
DMV
DEPARTMENT OF MOTOR VEHICLES

AFFIDAVIT FOR TRANSFER WITHOUT PROBATE
CALIFORNIA TITLED VEHICLE OR VESSELS ONLY

VEHICLE OR HULL IDENTIFICATION NO. | VEHICLE LICENSE OR VESSEL CF NO.

FOR MOTORCYCLES ONLY
Engine No.: | MAKE OF VEHICLE OR VESSEL BUILDER

The undersigned states that:

____________________ the owner of the above described vehicle or vessel died on __________ (DATE), in __________ (PLACE OF DEATH)

that said decedent left no other property necessitating probate and no probate proceeding is now being or had been conducted in this state for the decedent estate, that there are no creditors of the deceased whose claims remain unsatisfied, that the undersigned is the heir pursuant to Probate Codes 6401 and 6402, bearing the relationship to the decedent of:

☐ Sole person or persons who succeeded to the property of the decendent.
☐ Conservator or guardian of the property of the sole person or persons who succeeded to the property of the decedent.
☐ Beneficiary under the decedent's last will and testament and has the right to have title to the vehicle transferred to his/her name without probate proceedings.

Truck campers and vessels may be transferred if 40 days have elapsed since the death of the registered or legal owner and applicant is the heir pursuant to Pobate Codes 6401 and 6402.

The person who secures transfer of this vehicle is subject to the provisions of Sections 13109 through 13113 inclusive, of the Probate Code to the same extent as a person to whom transfer of property is made.

Executed at __________ (CITY), __________ (STATE), on __________ (DATE)

I certify under penalty of perjury that the foregoing is true and correct.

SIGNATURE
X | DAYTIME TELEPHONE NO.
( )

REG. 5 (REV. 6/87)

FIGURE 10–10(b) Affidavit for Transfer Without Probate form

In the past, there have been two means of terminating a joint tenancy: (1) by affidavit, and (2) by petition to establish the fact of death. If for any reason a certified copy of the death certificate of the deceased joint tenant cannot be obtained, a petition to establish the fact of death is necessary. In California, section 683.2 was added to the Civil Code in 1984 to provide a third method of severing joint tenancy in real property for deaths occurring after January 1, 1985. This method, termination by deed or written instrument, is discussed below.

SIDEBAR

If there are several pieces of property, a petition may be the easiest method and may cost less, particularly if there are many involved legal descriptions or a number of bank accounts or other personal property. The legal assistant should discuss with the attorney the desirability of probating the joint tenancy property if it appears at all appropriate, for example, where the real property has appreciated in value tremendously. If the property is terminated under the affidavit method, the real property will receive a stepped-up basis only as to one-half, whereas with probate there will be a stepped-up basis of one hundred percent to the date of death. (Stepped-up basis is discussed further in Chapter 12.)

The surviving joint tenant is not liable for the debts of the deceased joint tenant except to the extent the deceased joint tenant encumbered the property.

Affidavit Method of Terminating Joint Tenancy (Prob. Code §§ 210–212)

To terminate the joint tenancy by use of an affidavit, the following items are needed:

1. An affidavit of the surviving joint tenant, which should include a particular description of the real property. This affidavit identifies the person making the affidavit as the same person named in the deed. Any other pertinent facts about the acquisition of the property should be included; and

2. A certified copy of the death certificate of the joint tenant. An additional copy is needed for common or preferred stock.

The affidavit with the certified copy of the death certificate attached are recorded (Prob. Code § 211). A printed form is available from the title companies. A form of affidavit is provided in Figure 10–11.

If death occurred before June 9, 1982, the Division of Tax Administration may require the following related documents:

1. Original and copy of IT-22;
2. Two copies of the will, whether or not used;
3. Original and copy of IT-3, marital property declaration, if applicable;
4. Original and copy of residence declaration, IT-2, if nonresidence is claimed;
5. Two copies of any other schedule, declaration of contribution, and attached exhibits that form a part of the documents by reference; and
6. Copy of any applicable document if copy of appraised values is desired.

The IT-22 and IT-3 forms are reproduced in Figures 10–12 and 10–13. See *California Paralegal's Guide,* Second Edition, by the author for instructions on the completion of the IT-22.

Petition to Establish Fact of Death

A petition is used where there has been a delay in issuing a death certificate or for some reason a certificate is not available. This procedure is not used as often now as it was at one time.

The petition may be filed by the surviving joint tenant or any interested person (Prob. Code § 200). The petition must be verified. A photocopy of the deed in joint tenancy should be attached as an exhibit to the petition.

If the petitioner files an affidavit with the petition stating that he or she has no reason to believe that there is any opposition to, or contest of, the petition, the court may act ex parte, that is, without notice to anyone.

Notice

If notice must be given, the clerk sets the petition for hearing by the court and gives notice by posting at the courthouse of the county in which the proceedings are pending at least fifteen days before the hearing (Prob. Code § 1220). Then the petitioner must mail notice at least fifteen days before the hearing [Prob. Code § 1200.5(b)]. Notice must be given to the executor or administrator if he or she is not the petitioner, any coexecutor or coadministrator not petitioning, and all persons (or their attorneys if they have appeared by attorney) who have requested notice or given notice of appearance in person or by attorney as heir, devisee, legatee, creditor, or otherwise interested person. Proof of the giving of notice shall be made at the hearing (Prob. Code § 1172).

The court may act on the petition and supporting affidavits and render judgment thereon as though the petitioner or affiants were personally present to testify (Prob. Code § 1174).

FIGURE 10–11
Affidavit to
Terminate Joint
Tenancy

AFFIDAVIT TO TERMINATE JOINT TENANCY

STATE OF CALIFORNIA
COUNTY OF SACRAMENTO
    MARY DOE, over age 18, being first duly sworn, deposes and says:
    That JANE JILLIAN, the decedent mentioned in the attached certificate copy of Certificate of Death, is the same person as Jane Jillian, named as one of the parties in that certain deed dated July 9, 1993, executed by Maryanne Daba to Mary Doe and Jane Jillian, as joint tenants, recorded on June 7, 1995, in Book 870587, Page 758, of the Official Records in the Office of the County Recorder of Sacramento County, State of California, concerning the following described real property situated in the City of Sacramento, County of Sacramento, State of California:
    [Insert property description]
    That the value of all real and personal property owned by said decedent at the date of death, including the full value of the property described, did not then exceed the sum of $_____.
    Dated: _____.

_____

Subscribed and sworn
before me this _____ day
of _____, 19___
_____
(Seal)

SIDEBAR

A certified copy of the decree establishing the fact of death should be recorded in each county in which real property is located. The legal assistant should make certain this is done. The legal assistant should obtain the information needed for the petition, such as the names of both joint tenants and the place in which the decedent was a resident at time of death, from the deed granting the joint tenancy. The deed contains its date, the name of the grantor, the book and page number in which it was recorded, the name of the county, and most importantly, the correct legal description of the real property involved. The date of death should be obtained from the death certificate.

A form of the petition for a decree establishing the death of a joint tenant (Prob. Code § 201) is in Figure 10–14. The form for the decree establishing the fact of death used in Los Angeles County is in Figure 10–15.

<u>**SUBMIT IN DUPLICATE**</u>

STATE OF CALIFORNIA

INHERITANCE TAX DECLARATION, FORM IT-22

ANSWER ALL QUESTIONS. If space insufficient, attach sheets of same size showing decedent's name, social security number and question number.

Full Name of Decedent (Show all names ever used)		Date of Death	Social Security No.
			Date of Birth
Place of Death. (Last usual address)	Cause of Death		Length of Last Illness
Attorney for Estate	Address		Telephone No.

Type of Court Proceeding	Case No.	Name of Executor/Administrator, If Any, and Title	
☐ Probate ☐ 650 Petition ☐ Other ☐ None	County and State	Address	Telephone No.

1. RESIDENCE OF DECEDENT AT TIME OF DEATH
   . County _____ State _____

   NOTE: If claimed that decedent was not a California resident, attach completed form IT-2, Declaration Concerning Residence.

2. Did decedent leave a will?   ☐ Yes   ☐ No   If yes, attach copy of will and any codicils.

3a. Was decedent survived by a spouse?   ☐ Yes   ☐ No

3b. Did decedent and surviving spouse ever enter into any written or oral agreement concerning the status of their property as community or separate?   ☐ Yes   ☐ No   If yes, attach copy of agreement or affidavit proving oral agreement and completed form IT-3, Marital Property Declaration.

3c. Does decedent's will dispose of any part or all of surviving spouse's interest in community property?   ☐ Yes   ☐ No   If yes, complete form IT-3, Marital Property Declaration.

4a. JOINT TENANCIES. Did decedent, at date of death, hold any assets. in joint tenance or joint tenancy form? To obtain a release of Inheritance Tax Lien for real estate, it is necessary to submit date of deed, date of recordation and book and page number of record.   ☐ Yes   ☐ No   If yes, list all jointly held personal property (including stocks, bonds, mortgages, checking and savings accounts, etc.) wherever located, and California real estate. Full amount must be shown, although portion has been released or transferred after death, and all assets must be included even if tax release or consent is not required.

Item No.	Name of surviving joint tenant	Relationship to decedent (See Instr. 5)	Description of each asset (See Instruction 7)	Market value at date of death (See Instr. 8)	FOR STATE USE ONLY

4b. Does surviving joint tenant claim contribution to any of the joint tenancy assets?   ☐ Yes   ☐ No   If yes, give full particulars tracing source of funds, values, dates, etc., in attachment. (See Instruction 9)

NOTE: **Survivor's burden of proof of claim of contribution:** All joint tenancies are presumed to have been created from assets originally belonging to the decedent and subject to tax in full to the surviving joint tenant, except to the extent that the survivor can prove that the assets, or a portion, originally belonged to the survivor or that the survivor furnished consideration which was never received from the decedent. (Revenue and Taxation Code Sec. 13671.)

I DECLARE UNDER PENALTY OF PERJURY THAT THIS DECLARATION, INCLUDING ANY ATTACHMENTS, HAS BEEN EXAMINED BY ME AND TO THE BEST OF MY KNOWLEDGE AND BELIEF IS TRUE, CORRECT AND COMPLETE. IF PREPARED BY A PERSON OTHER THAN THE DECLARANT, HIS DECLARATION IS BASED ON ALL INFORMATION OF WHICH HE HAS ANY KNOWLEDGE.

Signature	Date	Address
Relationship to Decedent		
Signature of Person Preparing This Declaration	Date	Address

THE INHERITANCE TAX REFEREE MUST HAVE THIS FORM TO BEGIN DETERMINATION OF THE TAX. Send this form and all attachments to the Inheritance Tax Referee, if one has been appointed, otherwise to STATE CONTROLLER, Division of Tax Administration—Inheritance Tax.

P.O. Box 247   107 South Broadway   785 Market Street
Sacramento 95802   Los Angeles 90012   San Francisco 94103

IT-22 (REV. 1/81)

FIGURE 10–12   California Inheritance Tax Declaration, Form IT-22

5.	ASSETS OUTSIDE CALIFORNIA. Excluding assets listed at item 4a, did decedent own tangible or intangible personal or real property outside of California?	☐ Yes	☐ No	If yes, describe property and give estimated value. (If probate is pending in another state, also attach copy of inventory.)

TRUSTS, LIFE ESTATES, POWERS OF APPOINTMENT

6a.	Was decedent a trustee or beneficiary of a "trustee" bank or savings and loan or similar account?	☐ Yes	☐ No	(See Instructions 7, 8, 11) If yes, attach a list of accounts giving balances at date of death, sources of funds and exact title in which each was held. (See Instruction 9)
6b.	Did decedent enter into a declaration of trust, written or oral, or join in a trust agreement during his lifetime?	☐ Yes	☐ No	If yes, attach copy of trust document or proof of the oral agreement, and a list of trust assets at date of death with estimated market value of each.
6c.	Was decedent beneficiary of a trust not created by him?	☐ Yes	☐ No	If yes, attach copy of trust documents and a list of assets at date of death and estimated market value.
6d.	Was decedent a donee of a power of appointment?	☐ Yes	☐ No	If yes, attach a copy of document creating power of appointment and a list of assets at date of death and estimated market value.

7a. HEIRS, BENEFICIARIES, SURVIVING JOINT TENANTS AND TRANSFEREES.   List all even if there is no court proceeding.

Item No.	Name	Date of Birth	Full Address	Relationship to decedent (See * below and instr. 5)	Approximate value of interest or percentage of estate (See Instr. 10)

* **Relationship must be by blood**, except for surviving spouse, son-in-law, daughter-in-law, adopted or mutually acknowledged child or issue of adopted or mutually acknowledged child. List all others who are not blood relatives as "strangers".
* **Attach blood tracing** for niece, nephew, grandniece, grandnephew, great grandniece or great grandnephew.
* **Adoption or mutual acknowledgment of child.** Affidavit or other proof is required for transferee claiming through adoption or mutual acknowledgment. (Revenue and Taxation Code Sections 13307, 13310)

7b.	Did any beneficiaries named in will predecease decedent?	☐ Yes	☐ No	If yes, list names, and if blood relatives list names of their children.
7c.	Did decedent have any predeceased spouses? (Probate Code Sections 228, 229)	☐ Yes	☐ No	If yes, give name, county of residence and date of death of each.
7d.	Is any divorced spouse a creditor of decedent or his estate or claiming an interest in the estate?	☐ Yes	☐ No	If yes, attach a copy of final decree and any property settlement agreement.
7e.	Is California previously taxed property credit claimed?	☐ Yes	☐ No	If yes, give name, county of residence and date of death of prior decedent. (See Instruction 6)
8.	LIFE INSURANCE. Was there life and/or accident insurance in force on life of decedent?	☐ Yes	☐ No	If yes, list below.

Item No.	Insurance Company	Face amount and type of policy (term, endowment, mortgage, etc.)	Owner of policy (See * below)	Beneficiary receiving proceeds and relationship to decedent (See Instruction 5)	Mode of payment and amount of proceeds received (See * below)

* If owner was other than decedent or total proceeds exceed $50,000, or if decedent irrevocably selected mode of settlement, attach copy of IRS Form 712, obtainable from insurance company.

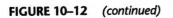

FIGURE 10–12   *(continued)*

ANNUITIES, SUPPLEMENTAL CONTRACTS AND DEATH BENEFITS

9a. Was decedent owner of annuity policies or supplemental contracts? ☐ Yes ☐ No   If yes, list under 9c.

9b. Did decedent have any interest in a "death benefit", "retirement plan", "profit sharing plan" or "stock purchase plan" or were any payments made under such plans by virtue of decedent's death? ☐ Yes ☐ No   If yes, list under 9c.

9c. Item No.	Company, or issuer of annuity, supplemental contract or death benefit	Type of policy or death benefit	Beneficiary and relationship to decedent (See Instruction 5)	Mode of payment	Lump sum or commuted value

9d. Is any item in 9c claimed to be nontaxable? ☐ Yes ☐ No   If yes, explain below or in attachment.

GIFTS AND TRANSFERS

10a. Did decedent transfer, at any time during his life, any real or personal property (stocks, bonds, notes, savings accounts, insurance policies, etc.) for other than money, for less than market value, or without any payment or consideration (including withdrawals or transfers from joint tenancy bank or savings and loan accounts)? ☐ Yes ☐ No   If yes, list under 10b and answer 10c through 10g. (See Instruction 12)

10b. Item No.	Name of transferee and relationship to decedent (See Instruction 5)	Date of transfer	Description of property and estimated market value at date of transfer (See Instructions 7, 8)	Market value at date of death (See Instr. 8)	FOR STATE USE ONLY

10c. Did decedent continue to receive all or part of the income after transfer, or continue to use property (including residing on real estate)? ☐ Yes ☐ No   If yes to 10c, 10d or 10e, explain below or in attachment.

10d. Was deed to any real property listed under 10b recorded after decedent's death? ☐ Yes ☐ No

10e. Was any restriction imposed by decedent on transfer of any property listed under 10b? ☐ Yes ☐ No

10f. Is it claimed that any property listed under 10b is not subject to inheritance tax? ☐ Yes ☐ No   If yes, explain below or in attachment. ("Payment of gift tax" or "exemption under Gift Tax Law" is insufficient.)

10g. Were California gift tax returns filed for any of the transfers listed under 10b? ☐ Yes ☐ No   If yes, identify transfer and give amount of gift tax paid (including penalties and interest).

11a. Did decedent receive any real or personal property by gift, bequest, devise, descent, proceeds of life insurance or joint tenancy survivorship? ☐ Yes ☐ No   If yes, complete 11b and 11c.

11b. Item No.	General description of each asset (See Instruction 15)	Full name and relationship of person from whom received	Date received	Approx. value on date received (See Instr. 16)

11c. IF RECEIVED BY GIFT	Item No.	State of residence of donor at date of gift

FIGURE 10–12   *(continued)*

12. **ASSETS NOT OTHERWISE LISTED.** Assets standing in decedent's name alone, or in bearer form, including real property, stocks, bonds, mortgages, judgments, notes, accounts and loans receivable, cash, business or partnership interests, autos, farm equipment, interests in retirement funds, stock purchase plans or other employee benefits, furniture, furnishings, personal effects, insurance owned by decedent on life of any other persons, amounts due including tax or other refunds, and any other type of property. Also include assets in name of the surviving spouse which are community property. **(Probate cases.** If all property is listed in Inventory and Appraisement, do not list but make reference to Inventory and Appraisement.)

Item No.	Description of assets not otherwise listed (See Instruction 7)	Market value at date of death (See Instr. 8)	FOR STATE USE ONLY

13a. Was probate homestead granted or exempt personal property set aside by probate court? ☐ Yes ☐ No If yes, attach copy of court order.

13b. Was a family allowance ordered by probate court? ☐ Yes ☐ No If yes, attach copy of court order(s).

13c. Has there been litigation affecting the estate as to distribution, entitlement or value? ☐ Yes ☐ No If yes, attach copies of court orders. If litigation is pending, give case title, number, relevant issues and facts.

14. Will Federal Estate Tax Return, Form 706, be filed? ☐ Yes ☐ No If already filed, attach copy of page 1 of Form 706.

Federal Estate Tax	$	☐ Estimated	☐ Paid
Maximum allowable credit for State death taxes	$	☐ Estimated	☐ Determined

ALLOWABLE DEDUCTIONS (See Instruction 13) Any deduction over $1,000 must be itemized.

15a. **All Cases**

Expenses of last illness (paid after death by transferee or estate, net after any insuranceB reimbursement)_____

Funeral expenses (net after burial insurance, social security or other reimbursement)_____

Debts of decedent (if probate, list only allowed claims)_____

Encumbrances on real property (state exact balance for each parcel)_____

Liens or security agreements on personal property (state exact balance for each asset)_____

Taxes, a lien or due and unpaid at death: Income tax (net due at death)_____

Real property (state exact balance for each parcel)_____

Other taxes (itemize and explain)_____

Other deductions (itemize and explain)_____

15b. **Probate Cases Only**

Other debts (itemize and explain)

Ordinary executor's/administrator's commission ☐ Statutory ☐ Other ☐ Not claimed_____

Ordinary attorney's fees ☐ Statutory ☐ Other ☐ Not claimed_____

Costs of administration (filing fees, notices, etc.)_____

15c. **Additional Professional Fees—Probate and Other Court Cases.** (Show basis: tax work, joint tenancy, etc. Include only fees allowed under Revenue and Taxation Code Sections 13988.1)

Executor/Administrator_____

Attorney_____

Accountant_____

Itemization and detail of items under 15a, b, c.

16000-208 9-80 300M CAM Ⓞ OSP

FIGURE 10–12 *(continued)*

STATE OF CALIFORNIA

MARITAL PROPERTY DECLARATION, FORM IT-3

ANSWER ALL QUESTIONS. If space insufficient, attach sheets of same size showing decedent's name, social security number and question number.

Full Name of Decedent				Social Security No.		Date of Death

1. DECEDENT AND SURVIVING SPOUSE WERE MARRIED ON	Date	In City of			In State of	

2. Did decedent own any real or personal property at date of marriage? ☐ Yes ☐ No If yes, list below. (Also attach real property tax bill for year of marriage, if available)

Item No.	General description of each asset (See Instruction 15)	Approximate market value at date of marriage (See Instr. 16)

3. Decedent's occupation at date of marriage	4. Decedent's net worth at date of marriage

5a. Did decedent receive any real or personal property after date of marriage by gift, bequest, devise, descent, proceeds of life insurance or joint tenancy survivorship? ☐ Yes ☐ No If yes, complete 5b, 5c and 5d.

5b. Item No.	General description of each asset (See Instruction 15)	Full name and relationship of person from whom received	Date received	Approx. value on date received (See Instr. 16)

5c. IF CALIFORNIA INHERITANCE TAX DETERMINATION WAS MADE	Name of estate		Court case No. (if any)	County

5d. IF RECEIVED BY GIFT	Item No.	State of residence of donor at date of gift	

6. Are any assets listed under 2 or 5b now on inventory of decedent's estate or included in Inheritance Tax Declaration, Form IT-22? (See Instruction 17) ☐ Yes ☐ No If yes, specify where each such item is shown on inventory or Form IT-22.

7a. Were any assets listed under 2 or 5b transferred to anyone (including decedent's spouse) during decedent's lifetime? (See Instruction 17) ☐ Yes ☐ No If yes, complete 7b and 7c.

7b. ANY SUCH ASSETS SOLD	Item No.	Date of sale	Proceeds received	Subsequent disposition of proceeds	

7c. ANY SUCH ASSETS TRANSFERRED WITHOUT FULL CONSIDERATION	Item No.	Date of transfer	Names & addresses of persons to whom transfers made	Consideration, if any

I DECLARE UNDER PENALTY OF PERJURY THAT THIS DECLARATION, INCLUDING ANY ATTACHMENTS, HAS BEEN EXAMINED BY ME AND TO THE BEST OF MY KNOWLEDGE AND BELIEF IS TRUE, CORRECT AND COMPLETE. IF PREPARED BY A PERSON OTHER THAN THE DECLARANT, HIS DECLARATION IS BASED ON ALL INFORMATION OF WHICH HE HAS ANY KNOWLEDGE.

Signature	Date	Relationship: ☐ Spouse of decedent ☐ Representative of spouse

If not spouse, explain in attachment:
a. Why spouse is not signing,
b. Declarant's relationship or connection with decedent and
c. Basis of knowledge required to provide necessary information.

Address	

Signature of person preparing this declaration	Date	Address

Send this form and all attachments to the Inheritance Tax Referee, if one has been appointed, otherwise to STATE CONTROLLER, Division of Tax Administration—Inheritance Tax.

P.O. Box 247
Sacramento 95802

107 South Broadway
Los Angeles 90012

285 Market Street
San Francisco 94103

IT-3 (REV. 1-81)

FIGURE 10–13 California Marital Property Declaration, Form IT-3

8a. Did decedent and surviving spouse reside outside California during marriage? (See Instruction 18)   ☐ Yes   ☐ No   If yes, complete 8b, 8c and 8d.

8b. States in which resided, including California, after marriage	Inclusive dates (month and year if known)		Combined net worth of spouses upon taking up residence in each state (include value of all assets, including cash)
	From	To	

8c. Does net worth at date of last arrival in California include any separate property of either spouse?   ☐ Yes   ☐ No   If yes, state source and value.

8d. Trace subsequent disposition of combined net worth of spouses after last arrival in California.

9. Brief history of **decedent's** business or occupational career from marriage to death, showing dates. **(See Instruction 19)**

10. Brief history of **surviving spouse's** business or occupational career from marriage to decedent's death, showing dates. **(See Instruction 19)**

11. Did either spouse receive damages or a settlement for a personal injury after September 11, 1957?   ☐ Yes   ☐ No   If yes, show dates, amounts received and subsequent disposition.

12. Did decedent and surviving spouse ever enter into any written or oral agreement concerning the status of their property as community or separate?   ☐ Yes   ☐ No   If yes, attach copy of agreement or affidavit proving oral agreement.

13. Did spouse ever obtain a legal separation (separate maintenance) or an interlocutory divorce?   ☐ Yes   ☐ No   If yes, attach copy of decree and any property settlement agreement.   Date of reconciliation, if any.

14. Give on attachment any additional information bearing upon the separate or community status of decedent's property.

NOTE: *It is vital that all pertinent information be given. Under the inheritance tax law there is no presumption that property acquired after marriage is community property; the burden of proof is upon the person so claiming.* (Revenue and Taxation Code Sections 13556, 13556.5)

FIGURE 10–13   *(continued)*

Termination by Deed or Written Instrument (Where Death Occurred After January 1, 1985)

Civil Code section 683.2 provides that a joint tenant may sever a joint tenancy in real property without the joinder or consent of the other joint tenants by either of the following means:

1. Execution and delivery of a deed that conveys legal title of the interest to a third person, or

2. Execution of a written instrument that evidences the intent to sever the joint tenancy, including a deed that names the joint tenant as transferee, or of a written declaration that the joint tenancy is severed in regard to the interest of the joint tenant.

Severance contrary to a written agreement of the joint tenants is not authorized, but such a severance does not defeat the rights of a purchaser or encumbrancer for value in good faith who did not have knowledge of the written agreement.

Subdivisions (a) and (b) of Civil Code section 683.2 apply to all joint tenancies in real property, whether the joint tenancy was created before, on, or after January 1, 1985, but do not affect the validity of a severance where the death of the joint tenant occurred before January 1, 1985, in which event the law in effect at the time of death determines the validity of the severance. Subdivisions (c) and (d) do not apply to affect a severance of a joint tenancy made before January 1, 1986.

§ 10.12 Joint Tenancy versus Community Property—Carry-over Basis— Stepped-up Basis

One disadvantage of joint tenancy relates to the real property's **carry-over basis**. The carry-over basis, in simple language, is the value attributed to the property upon death.

TERMS

carry-over basis   A basis for tax computation for inherited property by which the gain is computed when the property is sold.

**PETITION FOR DECREE ESTABLISHING
DEATH OF JOINT TENANT**

In the Matter of the Petition
of

to establish fact of death of

_____,

a joint tenant.

To the Superior Court of the State of California, in and for the County of Sacramento:

Petitioner _____ represents as follows:

_____ died on the _____ day of _____, 19___, being at the time a resident of the County of _____, State of California (or, if a nonresident, "owning land in the County of _____, State of California");

Petitioner and said _____ are the same persons named as grantees in the deed whereby there was conveyed to them, as joint tenants, the real property described as follows:

[Insert legal description]

Said deed was dated _____, 19___, and was recorded _____, 19___, in Book _____, Page _____, official records in the office of the Recorder of County, a copy of which deed is hereto attached, marked "Exhibit A" and made a part hereof;

Upon the death of said _____ all interest of said decedent in said real property under the joint tenancy provisions of said deed terminated;

[There are no proceedings pending in any Court in the State of California wherein the amount of inheritance tax payable by reason of the death of said decedent can be ascertained.]

Wherefore, petitioner prays that this petition be set for hearing and that notice thereof be given as required by law; [that a probate referee be appointed to determine what, if any, inheritance tax became payable by reason of the death of said _____]; that upon hearing said petition a decree be made and entered herein decreeing that said _____ died on or about the _____ day of _____, 19___, whereupon the interest of said decedent in said real property under the joint tenancy provisions of said deed terminated.

Dated _____, 19___.

_____

Petitioner

_____

Attorney for Petitioner

[Attach verification and copy of deed]

[Note: Where death occurred after June 8, 1982, the paragraph pertaining to inheritance tax is not needed, nor is the request in the prayer for appointment of a referee.]

[TITLE OF COURT AND CAUSE]

FIGURE 10–14
Petition for Decree Establishing Death of Joint Tenant form

DECREE ESTABLISHING DEATH OF JOINT TENANT

The verified petition of _____ by _____, his/her attorney, to establish the fact of death of _____, deceased, joint tenant in the above-entitled proceeding, in certain property, coming on regularly to be heard on _____, 19___, in Department _____, the Honorable _____, Judge presiding, the Court, after examining the petition and hearing the evidence, and finding that all notices have been duly given as required by law, and that all the facts alleged in said petition are true, and that the [statement regarding inheritance tax*] grants said petition as follows:

It is ORDERED, ADJUDGED AND DECREED that said _____ died on _____, 19___.

The property in which decedent had a life interest is described as follows:

[Description]

Dated: _____

_____
Judge of the Superior Court

*State either: "inheritance tax has been paid as shown by receipt on file herein," or "referees' certificate of no inheritance tax is on file herein," or "inheritance tax, if any, will be determined in the probate proceeding."

Federal Law

The general rule for federal purposes is that to the extent property is in the estate of the decedent, it will have a new basis. Internal Revenue Code section 1014(a) provides that the basis of property in the hands of a person "acquiring the property from a decedent or to whom the property passed from a decedent" shall be the fair market value of the property at the date of the decedent's death, and section 1014(b) provides that property "acquired by bequest, devise, or inheritance, or by the decedent's estate from the decedent," shall be considered to have been acquired from or to have passed from the decedent. At death, then, if property was held by a husband and wife as community property, the entire property receives a stepped-up basis, bringing it up to the value as of the date of death, assuming the property has appreciated in value, which is usually, but not always, the case.

This federal law has been in effect since 1948. One exception occurs for deaths between January 1, 1977, and November 6, 1978, where an election was made by July 31, 1980, to apply carry-over provisions that were repealed in 1980. Federal law was amended in 1976, and a new concept of carry-over basis was introduced for property acquired from a decedent who died after 1976. California conformed to this new law in 1977, although the effective date was later deferred to January 1, 1980. If an election was made for federal purposes, California law deemed it made automatically for state purposes unless the **Franchise Tax Board** was notified otherwise before the end of 1980.

California Law

California income tax law had a special rule from 1953 to 1975 comparable to the federal rule described above, but with different results under the inheritance law as it then read, since ordinarily the community property was not includible in the estate, and its basis was usually its cost. For deaths after 1975 where the decedent's interest went to a third party, the surviving spouse got a stepped-up basis for his or her one-half interest, but not otherwise. On the other hand, under California law, when property is held in joint tenancy, the surviving spouse or surviving joint tenant receives a stepped-up basis to the value as of the date of death on only the one-half that belonged to the decedent. Since the inheritance tax law has been repealed, this applies for income tax purposes, as when a sale is made. The basis of the survivor's one-half interest is cost.

Property held in joint tenancy can be treated in California as community property upon death if the parties made a written agreement before death that the property was being held in joint tenancy for convenience only. The surviving spouse also may declare that the property is community property, though held in joint tenancy, because the parties had an understanding based on their conduct that it was community property. The title companies, however, may not be willing to accept such a declaration. A problem may arise when a sale is made, and a court order may become necessary. The better practice may be for the surviving spouse to make an election under Probate Code 13502 to administer the estate under section 7000 *et seq.*

Significance of Basis

The significance of the basis of property is that if the surviving spouse decides to sell the real property, the higher the value, the less will be the capital gains tax.

Ordinarily, when real property is sold, a capital gains tax, that is, a tax on the gain made on the real property, is levied on the seller. The gain is not simply the difference between the selling and the purchase price. All the depreciation, if any, that the seller has taken during the holding period

---

TERMS

Franchise Tax Board   The state agency that collects and processes California income tax returns.

of the property is now deducted from the purchase price to arrive at the property's adjusted basis. The tax is levied on the difference between the adjusted basis and the selling price. In addition, accelerated depreciation taken is added back under certain circumstances.

When community property goes to a spouse, the spouse receives a new basis on the entire property, or its value as of the date of death, that is usually higher than the purchase price, although this may not be true for persons who purchase real property at inflated prices, as has been the case in recent years. As a matter of fact, unless real property appreciates, the owners can find themselves in a bind when they come to sell. The typical owner who holds a parcel of rental or commercial property for some years has depreciated the property as much as permitted by law and, therefore, has as a base for calculating capital gains at an adjusted price that is much lower than the purchase price. Without this allowance for depreciation, most individuals could not afford to invest in real property. But with property purchased at an inflated price, where the mortgage still has to be paid or assumed upon sale, the seller may not receive enough cash to pay the capital gains tax. Unless he or she has other cash on hand, the financial situation of the seller can be bad.

It can readily be seen, then, that if the surviving spouse receives a stepped-up basis on only one-half of the property because it was held in joint tenancy, the tax benefits will be much less. The amount of capital gains tax imposed varies from time to time. At one time, the capital gains rate was lower than the rate for ordinary income, which made real estate investment more attractive. Currently, capital gains tax is levied on one hundred percent of gains and treated as ordinary income, taxable at the individual's tax rate.

§ 10.13 Delivery of Tangible Personal Property

Probate Code section 330, enacted in 1989, permits the delivery, without a wait of forty days, of a decedent's tangible personal property, including keys, in the possession of a public administrator, government official, law enforcement agency, or hospital or institution in which the decedent died. The property may be delivered to a relative or a conservator or guardian of the estate acting in that capacity at the time of death. Proof of identity is required. A record of the delivery shall be kept for three years.

See Chapter 7 for procedure regarding delivery of tangible personal property in cases where the death occurred before June 9, 1982.

CHAPTER 11

WILLS, INTESTATE SUCCESSION, ESCHEATS, AND UNCLAIMED PROPERTY

§ 11.1 Wills

A will is often thought of as the first matter to be taken care of in estate planning. Without a will, an estate is distributed by the laws of intestate succession. The distribution may be at variance with the wishes of the decedent.

The testator must have testamentary capacity, that is, be mentally capable of knowing what he or she is doing, before a valid will can be made. One of the first decisions is to determine the executor. The surviving spouse may be named, or an adult child or children, a relative, friend, or anyone else. In making this decision, the following matters must be taken into consideration: the size and complexity of the estate, who has the financial expertise to most capably handle the estate, to whom the estate will be left, who is the most reliable person, who already has knowledge of the estate, who can give the estate the time and attention it requires, who can best deal with other heirs if questions arise, and whether any fees or taxes can be saved through the choice of an executor.

If a bank or trust company is selected as executor, its reputation in the legal community and otherwise should be examined. Other considerations are whether its location is convenient for the surviving spouse and other survivors, whether its expense will be offset by its expertise, and how much time will be required to properly manage the assets.

Kinds of Wills

In California, a will may be made using the preprinted statutory form prescribed by Probate Code sections 6240 and 6246. A will also may be typewritten and witnessed, or it may be written in longhand, which is termed a **holographic will**. An oral will, or **nuncupative will**, is no longer recognized in California.

A holographic will is valid if the signature and the material provisions are entirely in the handwriting of the testator. The holographic will also should contain its date of execution in the testator's handwriting. If it does not contain a date and the failure "results in doubt as to whether its

---

TERMS

holographic will†   A will that is entirely written and signed by the testator in his or her own handwriting.

nuncupative will†   A will declared orally by a testator during his or her last illness, before witnesses, and later reduced to writing by a person who was present during the declaration.

provisions or the inconsistent provisions of another will are controlling, the holographic will is invalid to the extent of the inconsistency unless the time of its execution is established to be after the date of execution of the other will" (Prob. Code § 6111). No other writing and no printed or stamped material should be on the document. The statutes do not require that the place where the holographic will is executed be stated in the will, but it is advisable to include it.

A holographic will may not be the best kind of will to use. Controversies are more likely to arise over the intent of the testator. If the will is contested, it may not be interpreted as the testator intended. The language used may not be clear.

Any statement of testamentary intent contained in a holographic will may be set forth either in the testator's own handwriting or as part of a commercially printed will [Prob. Code § 6111(c)]. Probate Code section 6140 provides that the intention of the testator as expressed in the will controls the legal effect of the dispositions made in the will. Section 6140 does not apply if the testator died before January 1, 1985. If the testator's intentions are not expressed in the will, the rules of construction in Probate Code section 6141 *et seq.* apply.

Any extrinsic evidence is admissible to determine whether a document constitutes a will under Probate Code sections 6110 or 6111 or to determine the meaning of the will or a portion thereof if the meaning is unclear (Prob. Code § 6111.5). The Judicial Council has prepared a form for proof of a holographic will.

Review of Wills

Many people go to an attorney to have a will drawn, and once it is finished, they forget about it. This can be a mistake.

In the first place, tax laws change, and the changes can have a substantial post-mortem effect. For example, in recent years the introduction of the unlimited marital deduction has had a significant impact on estate taxes, in many instances signifying the need for a new will or codicils. Secondly, the named executor or trustee may have died, and the will may no longer provide for an alternate executor or trustee because of the death of one or more named persons.

Other changes may require a review of the will. If a testator moves from one state to another, the will should be reviewed in light of the laws of the state to which he or she has moved. A testator may change his or her attitude toward named heirs or beneficiaries and, therefore, may wish to eliminate names or add new ones. A death in the family, a dissolution or separation, a marriage, or a birth may necessitate changes in the will. A major change in financial status can occur, such as a liquidation of assets, a sale of assets, an inheritance or gift, a substantial increase in earnings, or even winning a lottery. Changes in the testator's employment, including retirement, or health also may necessitate a review of the will.

The word processor can be used to expedite the will preparation process. A fact sheet can be given to the client to complete before an interview. This saves a lot of the attorney's time.

See "Word Processing, Client Education and the Simple Will," by Peter G. Seward, in *Legal Economics* (Summer 1978, p. 45). See also the *California Will Drafting Willmaster System*, sold by the California Continuing Education of the Bar (CEB). This is for use in drafting wills on computers. The CEB also publishes a three-volume book called *California Will Drafting Practice*.

Videotaping Execution of Wills

If the execution of a will is videotaped, questions about signatures and whether the testator and his or her witnesses were present should be eliminated. The client can be questioned as it is filmed to demonstrate the soundness of the testator's mind and memory and to lessen any doubts about the testator's capacities. Questioning also may lessen doubts about whether there has been undue influence, although it will not eliminate such doubts, since anyone exercising undue influence presumably would be smart enough not to appear in the videotape.

A form of a will is shown in Figure 11–1 as an example only. It is not to be used in drawing an actual will.

Codicils

If a change needs to be made in a will, the entire will need not be redrawn, although it may be better to do so if substantial changes are being made. A carefully drawn will may be "undone" by a carelessly prepared codicil.

A codicil is an amendment to a will. It may simply add something to the will, or it may change a provision in the will. The beginning of the codicil should refer to the date of the will and may reaffirm the will except as to the changes being made in the codicil.

The legal assistant will find more than one form for codicils, but a sample is provided in Figure 11–2.

FIGURE 11–1
Last Will and
Testament

LAST WILL AND TESTAMENT

I, KENNETH K. BELL, a resident of Sacramento County, California, declare this to be my will.

FIRST: I hereby revoke all wills and codicils I have previously made.

SECOND: I declare that I am married to CLARICE BELL, and all references in this will to "my spouse" are to her.

THIRD: I have one child now living, KERRY BELL, born April 15, 1955. I have no deceased children with issue surviving.

FOURTH: I give my 1985 Mercedes automobile to my son, KERRY BELL.

FIFTH: I give my brother, MORTON BELL, my yellow gold diamond ring, if he survives me, otherwise to my said son, KERRY BELL.

SIXTH: I give my Lincoln Continental automobile, household furnishings, oil paintings by Matt Bonnet, and other tangible personal property of a personal nature, not otherwise disposed of in this will, to my spouse, CLARICE BELL, if she survives me. If my said spouse does not survive me, I give all such personal property to my son, KERRY BELL.

SEVENTH: I give to my spouse, CLARICE BELL, my interest in the property that is our principal residence at the time of my death, and other real property of which I may die possessed; if my said spouse does not survive me, I give all such real property to my son, KERRY BELL.

EIGHTH: I give all the rest, residue and remainder of my estate to my said wife, CLARICE BELL, if she survives me. If my said spouse does not survive me, I give all the rest, residue and remainder of my estate to my said son, KERRY BELL.

NINTH: I appoint my spouse, CLARICE BELL, as executor of this last will and testament, to serve without bond. In the event my wife, CLARICE BELL, serves as executor, I specifically authorize her to sell at either public or private sale, any property belonging to my estate, with or without notice. In the event my said spouse should predecease me, or shall fail or cease for any reason at any time or times to act as executor, then in such event I appoint my son, KERRY BELL, to act as executor, to serve without bond, and specifically authorize him to sell at either public or private sale, any property belonging to my estate, with or without notice.

TENTH: I specifically make no provision for any other person. If any person or persons shall contest this will or object to any of the provisions hereof, I give to such person or persons so contesting or objecting the sum of one Dollar ($1.00) and no more, in lieu of the provisions which I might have made for such person or persons so contesting or objecting.

IN WITNESS WHEREOF, I have hereunto set my hand at Sacramento, California, this _____ day of November, 199___.

s/ Kenneth K. Bell

_____

The foregoing instrument, consisting of three pages, including this page, was signed, published and declared by Kenneth K. Bell to be his last will and testament in our joint presence. At his request and in his presence, and in the presence of each other, we hereby subscribe our names as witnesses to the execution of this will, declaring our belief that said Kenneth K. Bell is of sound

FIGURE 11–1
(continued)

and disposing mind and memory and under no constraint, duress, menace or undue influence whatsoever.

We, individually, declare under penalty of perjury that the foregoing is true and correct and this declaration was executed on November 15, 1991, at Sacramento, California.

_____ Residing at _____
_____

_____ Residing at _____
_____

_____ Residing at _____
_____

FIGURE 11–2
Codicil

CODICIL

I, _____, of the City of Sacramento, County of Sacramento, State of California, do hereby make, publish and declare this codicil to my last will dated the _____ day of _____, 19___.

I hereby revoke and annul paragraph _____ and in lieu thereof I hereby substitute the following:

I hereby ratify and confirm my said will in all other respects.

In witness whereof, I have hereunto set my hand this _____ day of _____, 19___.

_____

The testator declared to us, the undersigned, that this instrument consisting of the number of pages indicated below, including the page signed by us as witnesses, was a codicil to the testator's will and requested us to act as witnesses to it. The testator thereupon signed this codicil in our presence, all of us being present at the same time. We now, at the testator's request, in the testator's presence, and in the presence of each other, subscribe our names as witnesses:

We declare under penalty of perjury under the laws of the State of California that the foregoing is true and correct.

_____ Residing at _____
_____

_____ Residing at _____
_____

_____ Residing at _____
_____

§ 11.2   Intestate Estates Procedure

This section explains the procedure for intestate proceedings in cases in which the decedent did not leave a will. Generally, the same statutes apply to intestate estates as to those in which there is a will to be administered, but with some differences. It is necessary to know the laws relating to intestate succession in order to determine who takes the property in the absence of a will or trust.

Laws of Intestate Succession in General

If a married decedent does not leave a will, the estate is distributed pursuant to the California laws of succession contained in Probate Code section 200 *et seq.*

Community Property and Quasi-Community Property

Upon the death of either a husband or a wife, one-half of the property goes to the surviving spouse, and the other half, if not otherwise disposed of by will, also goes to the surviving spouse (Prob. Code §§ 100, 101, 6401).

A surviving spouse may waive in whole or in part any of his or her rights listed in Probate Code section 141. To be enforceable, the waiver must be in writing and signed by the surviving spouse. The waiver is enforceable unless the court finds either (1) that a fair and reasonable disclosure of the property of the decedent was not provided to the surviving spouse, unless the surviving spouse waived such a fair and reasonable disclosure after advice by independent legal counsel, or (2) the surviving spouse was not represented by independent legal counsel at the time of executing the waiver. A waiver is not enforceable under Probate Code section 142 if the court finds that enforcement of the waiver would be unconscionable under the circumstances existing at the time enforcement is sought. Subdivision (b) of Civil Code section 5103 does not apply if the waiver is enforceable under Probate Code section 143. Any waiver, agreement, or property settlement agreement made prior to January 1, 1985, continues to be determined by the law applicable before January 1, 1985.

Separate Property

If the decedent leaves a surviving spouse but no surviving issue, parent, brother, sister, or issue of a deceased brother or sister, the entire separate property goes to the surviving spouse under the laws of intestate succession. If the decedent leaves a surviving spouse and no issue but leaves a parent or parents or their issue or the issue of either of them, one-half goes to the surviving spouse [Prob. Code § 6401(2)(b)].

If a decedent without a will leaves a surviving spouse and one child or issue of a deceased child, one-half of the property goes to the surviving spouse and one-half goes to the child or issue of a child [Prob. Code § 6401(2)(A)]. If the decedent leaves a surviving spouse and more than one child living, one-third goes to the surviving spouse. [Prob. Code § 6401(3)(A)]. One-third also goes to the surviving spouse where the decedent leaves a surviving spouse, and one child living, and issue of one or more deceased children [Prob. Code § 6401(3)(B)] and where the decedent leaves a surviving spouse and issue of two or more deceased children [Prob. Code § 6401(3)(C)]. Issue of the decedent take equally if they are of the same degree of **kinship**. If they are of unequal degree, those of more remote degree take in the manner provided by Probate Code section 240(a).

If a decedent with no will leaves no surviving spouse and no issue (Prob. Code § 6402), except as provided in Probate Code section 6402.5 (applicable where the decedent had a predeceased spouse who died not more than fifteen years before the decedent), the entire estate passes to the decedent's parent or parents equally [Probate Code § 240(b)]. If there is no parent, the property passes to issue of parents, who take equally if of the same degree of kinship to the decedent. If they are of unequal degree, they take in the manner provided by Probate Code section 240(c). If there is no surviving issue of parents but the decedent is survived by one or more grandparents or issue of grandparents, property passes to the grandparent or grandparents equally, or the issue of grandparents if there is no surviving grandparent, the issue taking equally if of the same degree of kinship or, if of unequal degree or more remote degree, in the manner provided by Probate Code section 240(d). If there is no grandparent or issue of grandparent but the decedent is survived by issue of a predeceased spouse, property passes to such issue, the issue taking equally if of same degree of kinship to the predeceased spouse or, if of unequal degree, those of more remote degree taking as provided by Probate Code section 240(e). If there is no surviving issue of a predeceased spouse but the decedent is survived by next of kin, property passes to the next of kin in equal degree. If two or more collateral kindred in equal degree but claiming through different ancestors exist, those claiming through the nearest ancestor shall be preferred to those claiming through a more remote ancestor [Probate Code § 240(f)]. If no next of kin of the decedent is surviving but the

---

TERMS

kinship†   The circumstance of being related by blood; the fact of being kin.

decedent is survived by the parents of a predeceased spouse or the issue of such parents, property, passes to the parent or parents equally if they are all of some degree of kinship to the predeceased spouse or, if of unequal degree, in manner provided by Probate Code section 240(g).

If the decedent left neither a surviving spouse nor issue but had a predeceased spouse who died not more than fifteen years before the decedent, the portion of the decedent's estate attributable to the decedent's predeceased spouse passes as prescribed by Probate Code section 6402.5. If the decedent leaves no relative to take his or her estate under the laws, the property escheats to the State of California.

SIDEBAR

Additional succession statutes, applicable in other situations, are found in Probate Code section 6400 *et seq.* Probate Code sections 240 through 247 provide for the division of property. Section 240 is applicable where the death of the decedent occurred after January 1, 1985. The law applicable prior to January 1, 1985, continues to apply where the death occurred before January 1, 1985. These sections should be read in their entirety, as well as the Comment of the **California Law Revision Commission.** The diagrams of the commission are reproduced in this text for assistance in interpreting these sections.

Probate Code Sections 240 and 245 (Intestate Distribution System)

For sections applying Probate Code section 240, see Civil Code section 1389.4 and Probate Code sections 6402 and 6402.5. For an example of distribution under Probate Code section 240, see the commission's Comment to section 250.

Probate Code section 245 gives one drafting a will or trust the option of selecting the distribution system provided in section 240, the distribution system used in case of intestate succession. Under section 240, if all the first generation of issue of the deceased ancestor are deceased, the initial division of the property is not made at that generation but, instead, at the first descending generation of issue having at least one living member. (See generally Fellows, Simon & Rau, "Public Attitudes About Property Distribution at Death and Intestate Succession Laws in the United

---

TERMS

California Law Revision Commission   A commission created by the California legislature to make substantive changes in the California laws. Topics may be assigned by the legislature for study, or the commission may respond to suggestions from attorneys, judges, or others.

States," 1978 *Am. B. Found. Research J.* 321, 380.) For example, if there have been four generations of descendants of the deceased ancestor but all the deceased ancestor's children are dead, distribution under section 240 is made as illustrated in Figure 11–3 (brackets indicate those who are dead when distribution is made).

If GGGC-3 in Figure 11–3 were deceased, leaving three surviving children, each of the surviving children would take a one-thirty-sixth share.

The language in Probate Code section 245(a) that "a will, trust, or other instrument that expresses no contrary intention provides for issue or descendants to take without specifying the manner" continues a provision formerly found in section 240. Subdivision (b) of section 245 provides that certain language is not an expression of a contrary intention sufficient to negate the application of section 240. For example, if property in a testamentary trust is to be distributed when the trust terminates to "the descendants of the testator per capita" and, at the time of distribution, the testator's three children survive and one of the surviving children has five children, each of the surviving children takes a one-third share. The five grandchildren of the testator take nothing, since their parent survives. This results from applying the distribution scheme of section 240. Under subdivision (b) of section 247, this scheme is not negated by use of the term **per capita**, since the living members of the designated class ("descendants of the testator") are not all of the same generation. In this context, it is reasonable to assume that the use of the term *per capita* is not

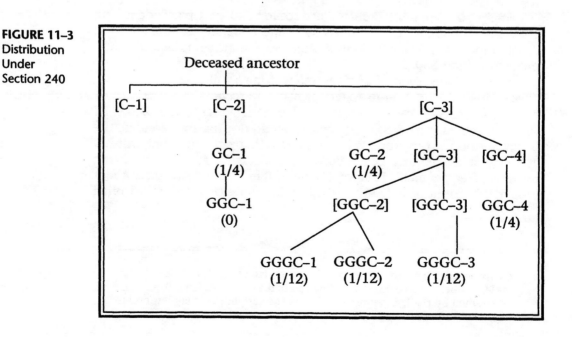

FIGURE 11–3
Distribution
Under
Section 240

intended to provide a share for a class member whose parent or other ancestor is still living and takes a share, although the drafter of the instrument may provide for such a result by appropriately clear language. In order for the testator's grandchildren to take in Figure 11–3, their parent (the testator's child) must be dead at the time of distribution. In such a case, the testator's two living children would each take a one-third share and the five children of the deceased child would share equally in the one-third share their deceased parent would have taken.

Probate Code Section 246 (True Per Stirpes)

Probate Code section 246 gives one drafting a will or trust the option of selecting a pure stirpital representation system. Under such a system, the roots or stocks are determined at the children's generation, whether or not any children are then living. [See generally Fellows, Simon & Rau, "Public Attitudes About Property Distribution at Death and Intestate Succession Laws in the United States," 1978 *Am. B. Found. Research J.* 321, 378–79; see also *Maud v. Catherwood* 67 Cal. App. 2d 636, 155 P. 2d 111 (1945). For example, if there have been four generations of descendants of the deceased ancestor but all the deceased ancestor's children are dead, distribution under section 12461 is made as illustrated in Figure 11–4 (brackets indicate those who are dead when distribution is made).

The terms defined in Probate Code section 246(b) are subject to some other definition that may be provided in the instrument. For example, many wills use "by right of representation" to refer to the distribution pattern for intestate succession, rather than to a pure stirpital distribution pattern under subdivision (a). [See, e.g., Johnston, "Outright Bequests and Devises," in *California Will Drafting* §§ 11.42–.43, at 375 (CEB, 1965)]. In such a case, the definition provided in the instrument controls.

Probate Code Section 247 (Per Capita at Each Generation)

Probate Code section 247 gives one drafting a will or trust the option of selecting the system of per capita at each generation distribution. [See generally Waggoner, "A Proposed Alternative to the Uniform Probate Code's System for Intestate Distribution Among Descendants," 66 Nw. U.L. Rev. 626, 630–31 (1971); Fellows, Simon & Rau, "Public Attitudes

---

TERMS

per capita†   A Latin phrase meaning "by the head," or by the individual; a method of dividing or distributing an estate in which all persons who are equally related to the decedent share equally in the estate.

FIGURE 11–4
True Per
Stirpes
Distribution
Under
Section 12461

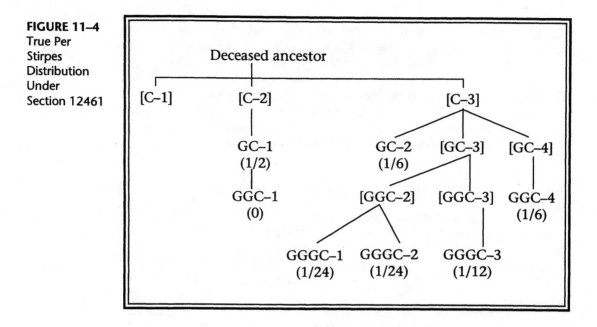

About Property Distribution at Death and Intestate Succession Laws in the United States," 1978 *Am. B. Found. Research J.* 321, 380–382.] For example, if there have been four generations of descendants of the deceased ancestor but all the deceased ancestor's children are dead, distribution under section 247 is made as illustrated in Figure 11–5 (brackets indicate those who are dead when distribution is made).

The relationship to the decedent determined the rate of California inheritance tax attributable to the inherited portion of the estate before the repeal of the tax as of June 8, 1982.

Simultaneous Death

For the purpose of determining whether one person survived another, a proceeding may be brought pursuant to Probate Code sections 230 through 234. (The old law continues to apply in deaths prior to January 1, 1985.) If it cannot be established by clear and convincing evidence that one spouse survived the other, one-half of the community property and one-half of the quasi-community property is distributed as if one spouse had survived and as if that half belonged to that spouse, and the other half is distributed as if the other spouse had survived and as if that half belonged to that spouse (Prob. Code § 103).

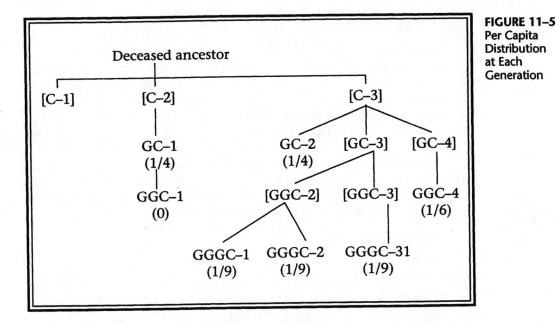

FIGURE 11–5
Per Capita
Distribution
at Each
Generation

Community property held in a **revocable trust** (Civ. Code § 5113.5) is governed by the provisions, if any, in the trust for disposition upon death. If an insured and a beneficiary under a policy of life or accident insurance die and it cannot be established by clear and convincing evidence that the beneficiary survived the insured, the proceeds are treated as if the insured survived the beneficiary (Prob. Code § 224). If an insurance policy is community or quasi-community property of an insured and his or her spouse and there is no alternative beneficiary except the estate or the personal representatives of the insured, the proceeds are distributed as community property under Probate Code section 103 (Prob. Code § 224).

Probate Code section 6403 provides that for purposes of intestate succession, a person who fails to survive a decedent by one hundred and twenty hours is deemed to have predeceased the decedent unless application of this rule would result in the property escheating to the state. Nor does this amendment apply if the person whose time of death determines the disposition of the property died before January 1, 1990.

TERMS

revocable trust† A trust in which the settlor does not give up the right to revoke.

Procedure in Intestate Estates

The procedure in intestate estates is substantially the same as that in estates where there is a will. The petition for probate becomes a petition for letters of administration rather than letters testamentary by a check in the appropriate box on the form. The other printed forms (the order for probate, the letters, and so on) are used to appoint either an executor or administrator. Again, the appropriate boxes on each form must be checked.

The petition for letters of administration must state the facts essential to give jurisdiction. The petitioner must allege that he or she is a resident of the United States. Probate Code section 422(a) lists the order of priority by which persons are entitled to letters as follows:

1. The surviving spouse;
2. Children;
3. Grandchildren;
4. Other issue;
5. Parents;
6. Brothers and sisters;
7. Issue of brothers and sisters;
8. Grandparents;
9. Issue of grandparents;
10. Children of a predeceased spouse;
11. Other issue of a predeceased spouse;
12. Other next of kin;
13. Parents of a predeceased spouse;
14. Issue of parents of a predeceased spouse;
15. Conservator or guardian of estate acting in that capacity at the time of death who has filed a first account and is not acting as conservator or guardian for any other person;
16. Public administrator;
17. Creditors; and
18. Any other person (Prob. Code § 8461; see Prob. Code § 8469).

Under Probate Code section 8462, the surviving spouse, a relative of the decedent, or a relative of a predeceased spouse of the decedent has priority under section 8461 *only* if the surviving spouse or relative either (a) is entitled to succeed to all or part of the estate, or (b) takes under the will or is entitled to succeed to all or part of the estate of another deceased person who is entitled to succeed to all or part of the estate of the decedent.

If the persons having priority fail to claim appointment, the court may appoint any person who claims appointment (Prob. Code § 8468).

The same form of notice used in probating a will, the notice of the petition to administer the estate, is used in intestate estates. The hearing on the petition is set and notice is published pursuant to Probate Code section 8121, the same as in a testate estate. The petitioner must mail this notice to the heirs named in the petition at least fifteen days before the hearing, either to each heir's residence or mailing address as set forth in the petition or to the county seat of the county in which the proceedings are pending (Prob. Code § 8110). The clerk is furnished with the notices and stamped, addressed envelopes for this purpose. The mailed notice also shall advise the person receiving the notice of the right to request special notice pursuant to Probate Code section 1250.

The forms used in the testate estate are reproduced here to illustrate how they would be completed for the intestate estate. (See Figures 11–6, 11–7, 11–8, 11–9, and 11–10.)

§ 11.3 Family Allowance

If the decedent leaves a spouse or minor children, or adult children who are physically or mentally incapacitated from earning a living and were dependent in whole or in part upon the decedent for support, who need money to live on before the estate is distributed, the petition should contain a request to the court to grant payment of a monthly amount as a family allowance. Such persons are entitled to a reasonable allowance out of the estate as is necessary for their maintenance according to their circumstances during the progress of the settlement of the estate. The court also has discretion to grant an allowance to a parent who was dependent in whole or part upon the decedent [Prob. Code § 6540(b)].

The family allowance may not continue for more than one year after the granting of letters. It takes precedence to all other expenses except funeral charges, expenses of the last illness, and expenses of administration. The court may grant it effective as of the date of death of the decedent.

The inventory need not be on file before the family allowance is granted, but after the inventory is filed, the allowance may be modified upon ex parte petition of any person interested or after notice of hearing pursuant to Probate Code section 1220. Notice of the hearing on the petition for allowance must be given to all legatees or devisees and, in case of intestacy, to all known heirs of the decedent, and to all persons (or their attorney if they have appeared by attorney) who have requested special notice as provided by Probate Code section 1250 or who have given notice

ATTORNEY OR PARTY WITHOUT ATTORNEY *(Name and Address)*

ALBERT TREAT
Attorney at Law   (415) 334-6040   TELEPHONE NO.
101 Bond St.
San Francisco, CA 94102

ATTORNEY FOR *(Name)*: **Ralph Rampart**

SUPERIOR COURT OF CALIFORNIA, COUNTY OF   SAN FRANCISCO

STREET ADDRESS: **400 Van Ness Ave.**

MAILING ADDRESS:

CITY AND ZIP CODE: **San Francisco, CA 94102**

BRANCH NAME:

ESTATE OF (NAME):
KAREN RAMPART, also known as KAREN RUTH RAMPART,
    DECEDENT

FOR COURT USE ONLY

PETITION FOR		
	☐	Probate of Will and for Letters Testamentary
(For deaths after December 31, 1984)	☐	Probate of Will and for Letters of Administration with Will Annexed
	☒	Letters of Administration
	☐	Letters of Special Administration
	☐	Authorization to Administer Under the Independent Administration of Estates Act ☐ with limited authority

CASE NUMBER: **240458**

HEARING DATE: **March 13, 19**

DEPT.   TIME. **9:30 a.m.**

(Signature of attorney or party without attorney) ▶ *albert Treat*

1. Publication will be in *(specify name of newspaper)*:
   a. ☒ Publication requested.
   b. ☐ Publication to be arranged.
2. Petitioner *(name of each)*:   **Ralph Rampart**
   requests
   a. ☐ decedent's will and codicils, if any, be admitted to probate.
   b. ☒ *(name)*: **Ralph Rampart**
      be appointed (1) ☐ executor   (3) ☒ administrator
         (2) ☐ administrator with will annexed   (4) ☐ special administrator
      and Letters issue upon qualification.
   c. ☐ that ☐ full ☐ limited authority be granted to administer under the Independent Administration of Estates Act.
   d. ☒ bond not be required for the reasons stated in item 3d.
      ☐ $_____ bond be fixed. It will be furnished by an admitted surety insurer or as otherwise provided by law. *(Specify reasons in Attachment 2d if the amount is different from the maximum required by Probate Code, § 8482.)*
      ☐ $_____ in deposits in a blocked account be allowed. Receipts will be filed. *(Specify institution and location)*:

3. a. Decedent died on *(date)*: **Jan. 5, 19** . at *(place)*: **San Francisco**
      ☒ a resident of the county named above.
      ☐ a nonresident of California and left an estate in the county named above located at *(specify location permitting publication in the newspaper named in item 1)*:
   b. Street address, city, and county of decedent's residence at time of death:
      67 Marin St., City and County of San Francisco
   c. Character and estimated value of the property of the estate
      (1) Personal property . . . . $ **90,000.**
      (2) Annual gross income from
         (i) ☒ real property . . . . $ **16,000.**
         (ii) ☒ personal property . . . . . . $ **7,200.**
            Total . . . . $ **113,200.**
      (3) Real property: $ **250,000.** *(If full authority under the Independent Administration of Estates Act is requested, state the fair market value of the real property less encumbrances.)*
   d. ☐ Will waives bond. ☐ Special administrator is the named executor and the will waives bond.
      ☐ All beneficiaries are adults and have waived bond, and the will does not require a bond. *(Affix waiver as Attachment 3d.)*
      ☒ All heirs at law are adults and have waived bond. *(Affix waiver as Attachment 3d.)*
      ☐ Sole personal representative is a corporate fiduciary.

(Continued on reverse)

Form Approved by the
Judicial Council of California
DE 111 (Rev. July 1, 1989)

PETITION FOR PROBATE

Probate Code §§ 8002, 10450

FIGURE 11–6   Petition for Letters of Administration

ESTATE OF (NAME):
KAREN RAMPART, also known as KAREN RUTH RAMPART,
DECEDENT

CASE NUMBER: 240458

3. a. [X] Decedent died intestate.
    [ ] Copy of decedent's will dated: _____ [ ] codicils dated: _____ are affixed as Attachment 3e.
      [ ] The will and all codicils are self-proving (Probate Code, § 8220).

Attach a typed copy of a holographic will and a translation of a foreign language will.

  f. Appointment of personal representative (check all applicable boxes)
    (1) Appointment of executor or administrator with will annexed
      [ ] Proposed executor is named as executor in the will and consents to act.
      [ ] No executor is named in the will.
      [ ] Proposed personal representative is a nominee of a person entitled to Letters. (Affix nomination as Attachment 3f(1).)
      [ ] Other named executors will not act because of [ ] death [ ] declination [ ] other reasons (specify in Attachment 3f(1)).
    (2) Appointment of administrator
      [X] Petitioner is a person entitled to Letters. (If necessary, explain priority in Attachment 3f(2).)
      [ ] Petitioner is a nominee of a person entitled to Letters. (Affix nomination as Attachment 3f(2).)
      [X] Petitioner is related to the decedent as (specify):   spouse
    (3) [ ] Appointment of special administrator requested. (Specify grounds and requested powers in Attachment 3f(3).)
  g. Proposed personal representative is a [X] resident of California [ ] nonresident of California (affix statement of permanent address as Attachment 3g) [X] resident of the United States [ ] nonresident of the United States.
4. [ ] Decedent's will does not preclude administration of this estate under the Independent Administration of Estates Act.
5. a. The decedent is survived by
    (1) [X] spouse [ ] no spouse as follows: [ ] divorced or never married [ ] spouse deceased
    (2) [X] child as follows: [X] natural or adopted [ ] natural adopted by a third party [ ] step [ ] foster
      [ ] no child
    (3) [ ] issue of a predeceased child [X] no issue of a predeceased child
  b. Petitioner [ ] has no actual knowledge of facts [ ] has actual knowledge of facts reasonably giving rise to a parent-child relationship under Probate Code section 6408(b).
  c. [X] All surviving children and issue of predeceased children have been listed in item 8.
6. (Complete if decedent was survived by (1) a spouse but no issue (only a or b apply); or (2) no spouse or issue. Check the first box that applies):
  a. [ ] The decedent is survived by a parent or parents who are listed in item 8.
  b. [ ] The decedent is survived by issue of deceased parents, all of whom are listed in item 8.
  c. [ ] The decedent is survived by a grandparent or grandparents who are listed in item 8.
  d. [ ] The decedent is survived by issue of grandparents, all of whom are listed in item 8.
  e. [ ] The decedent is survived by issue of a predeceased spouse, all of whom are listed in item 8.
  f. [X] The decedent is survived by next of kin, all of whom are listed in item 8.
  g. [ ] The decedent is survived by parents of a predeceased spouse or issue of those parents, if both are predeceased, all of whom are listed in item 8.
7. (Complete only if no spouse or issue survived the decedent) Decedent [ ] had no predeceased spouse [ ] had a predeceased spouse who (1) [ ] died not more than 15 years before decedent owning an interest in real property that passed to decedent,
  (2) [ ] died not more than five years before decedent owning personal property valued at $10,000 or more that passed to decedent,
  (3) [ ] neither (1) nor (2) apply. (If you checked (1) or (2), check only the first box that applies):
  a. [ ] The decedent is survived by issue of a predeceased spouse, all of whom are listed in item 8.
  b. [ ] The decedent is survived by a parent or parents of the predeceased spouse who are listed in item 8.
  c. [ ] The decedent is survived by issue of a parent of the predeceased spouse, all of whom are listed in item 8.
  d. [ ] The decedent is survived by next of kin of the decedent, all of whom are listed in item 8.
  e. [ ] The decedent is survived by next of kin of the predeceased spouse, all of whom are listed in item 8.
8. Listed in Attachment 8 are the names, relationships, ages, and addresses of all persons named in decedent's will and codicils, whether living or deceased, and all persons checked in items 5, 6, and 7, so far as known to or reasonably ascertainable by petitioner, including stepchild and foster child heirs and devisees to whom notice is to be given under Probate Code section 1207.
9. [1] Number of pages attached:

Date:
► _____
(SIGNATURE OF PETITIONER*)

► *Ralph Rampart*
(SIGNATURE OF PETITIONER*)

I declare under penalty of perjury under the laws of the State of California that the foregoing is true and correct.
Date: January 18, 19 .
............Ralph Rampart............
(TYPE OR PRINT NAME)

► *Ralph Rampart*
(SIGNATURE OF PETITIONER)

* All petitioners must sign the petition. Only one need sign the declaration.
DE 111 (Rev July 1, 1989)   **PETITION FOR PROBATE**   Page two

FIGURE 11–6   *(continued)*

Estate of KAREN RAMPART, also known as KAREN RUTH RAMPART, Deceased.

ATTACHMENT 1

NAME	RELATIONSHIP	AGE	MAILING ADDRESS
ROBERT RAMPART	Spouse	Adult	202 Alhambra Blvd. San Francisco, CA 9410
MARIA RAMPART	Daughter	Adult	202 Alhambra Blvd. San Francisco, CA 9410
ALICE HARMAN	Sister	Adult	303 Royston Way San Francisco, CA 9412

FIGURE 11–6 *(continued)*

ATTORNEY OR PARTY WITHOUT ATTORNEY *(Name and Address)*:

ALBERT TREAT
Attorney at Law
101 Bond St.
San Francisco, CA 94102

TELEPHONE NO.: (415) 334-6040

ATTORNEY FOR *(Name)*: Ralph Rampart

FOR COURT USE ONLY

SUPERIOR COURT OF CALIFORNIA, COUNTY OF

STREET ADDRESS: 400 Van Ness Ave., Room 317

MAILING ADDRESS:

CITY AND ZIP CODE: San Francisco 94102

BRANCH NAME:

ESTATE OF (NAME):

KAREN RAMPART, also known as KAREN RUTH RAMPART,
DECEDENT

NOTICE OF PETITION TO ADMINISTER ESTATE

OF *(name)*: KAREN RAMPART, also known as KAREN
RUTH RAMPART

CASE NUMBER: 240458

1. To all heirs, beneficiaries, creditors, contingent creditors, and persons who may otherwise be interested in the will or estate, or both, of *(specify all names by which decedent was known)*:

    KAREN RAMPART, also known as KAREN RUTH RAMPART

2. A PETITION has been filed by *(name of petitioner)*: Ralph Rampart
   in the Superior Court of California, County of *(specify)*: San Francisco

3. THE PETITION requests that *(name)*: Ralph Rampart
   be appointed as personal representative to administer the estate of the decedent.

4. ☐ THE PETITION requests the decedent's WILL and codicils, if any, be admitted to probate. The will and any codicils are available for examination in the file kept by the court.

5. ☒ THE PETITION requests authority to administer the estate under the Independent Administration of Estates Act. (This authority will allow the personal representative to take many actions without obtaining court approval. Before taking certain very important actions, however, the personal representative will be required to give notice to interested persons unless they have waived notice or consented to the proposed action.) The independent administration authority will be granted unless an interested person files an objection to the petition and shows good cause why the court should not grant the authority.

6. ☐ A PETITION for determination of or confirmation of property passing to or belonging to a surviving spouse under California Probate Code section 13650 IS JOINED with the petition to administer the estate.

7. A HEARING on the petition will be held

    on *(date)*: March 13, 19__, at *(time)*: 9:30 a.m. in Dept.: Room: 336

    located at *(address of court)*: 400 Van Ness Avenue, San Francisco

8. IF YOU OBJECT to the granting of the petition, you should appear at the hearing and state your objections or file written objections with the court before the hearing. Your appearance may be in person or by your attorney.

9. IF YOU ARE A CREDITOR or a contingent creditor of the deceased, you must file your claim with the court and mail a copy to the personal representative appointed by the court within four months from the date of first issuance of letters as provided in section 9100 of the California Probate Code. The time for filing claims will not expire before four months from the hearing date noticed above.

10. YOU MAY EXAMINE the file kept by the court. If you are a person interested in the estate, you may file with the court a formal Request for Special Notice of the filing of an inventory and appraisal of estate assets or of any petition or account as provided in section 1250 of the California Probate Code. A Request for Special Notice form is available from the court clerk.

11. ☐ Petitioner ☒ Attorney for petitioner *(name)*: Albert Treat

    (address): 101 Bond St., San Francisco, CA 94102

    ▶ *Albert Treat*
    (SIGNATURE OF ☐ PETITIONER ☒ ATTORNEY FOR PETITIONER)

12. This notice was mailed on *(date)*: 2/23/ at *(place)*: San Francisco , California.
    (Continued on reverse)

NOTE: If this notice is published, print the caption, beginning with the words NOTICE OF PETITION, and do not print the information from the form above the caption. The caption and decedent's name must be printed in at least 8-point type and the text in at least 7-point type. Print the case number as part of the caption. Print items preceded by a box only if the box is checked. Do not print the *italicized* instructions in parentheses, the paragraph numbers, the mailing information, or the material on the reverse.

Form Approved by the
Judicial Council of California
DE 121 (Rev. July 1, 1989)

NOTICE OF PETITION TO ADMINISTER ESTATE
(Probate)

Probate Code § 8100

FIGURE 11-7 Notice of Petition to Administer Estate

ESTATE OF (NAME):	CASE NUMBER:
─KAREN RAMPART, also known as KAREN RUTH RAMPART DECEDENT	240458

PROOF OF SERVICE BY MAIL

1. I am over the age of 18 and not a party to this cause. I am a resident of or employed in the county where the mailing occurred.

2. My residence or business address is *(specify)*: 101 Bond St., San Francisco, CA 94102

3. I served the foregoing **Notice of Petition to Administer Estate** on each person named below by enclosing a copy in an envelope addressed as shown below AND

   a. ☒ **depositing** the sealed envelope with the United States Postal Service with the postage fully prepaid.

   b. ☐ **placing** the envelope for collection and mailing on the date and at the place shown in item 4 following our ordinary business practices. I am readily familiar with this business' practice for collecting and processing correspondence for mailing. On the same day that correspondence is placed for collection and mailing, it is deposited in the ordinary course of business with the United States Postal Service in a sealed envelope with postage fully prepaid.

4. a. Date of deposit: February 23, 19   b. Place of deposit *(city and state)*: San Francisco, California

5. ☐ I served with the Notice of Petition to Administer Estate a copy of the petition and other documents referred to in the notice.

I declare under penalty of perjury under the laws of the State of California that the foregoing is true and correct.

Date: February 23, 1989

...... Mona Consuelo ....   ▶ *Mona Consuelo*
(TYPE OR PRINT NAME)   (SIGNATURE OF DECLARANT)

NAME AND ADDRESS OF EACH PERSON TO WHOM NOTICE WAS MAILED

Robert Rampart
202 Alhambra Blvd.
San Francisco, CA 94107

Maria Rampart
202 Alhambra Blvd.
San Francisco, CA 94107

Alice Harman
303 Royston Way
San Francisco, CA 94127

DE-121 [Rev. July 1, 1989]   **NOTICE OF PETITION TO ADMINISTER ESTATE**   Page two
                                        (Probate)

FIGURE 11–7   *(continued)*

ATTORNEY OR PARTY WITHOUT ATTORNEY (Name and Address):
ALBERT TREAT
Attorney at Law
101 Bond St.
San Francisco, CA 94102

TELEPHONE NO.: 334-6040

ATTORNEY FOR (Name): Ralph Rampart

FOR COURT USE ONLY

SUPERIOR COURT OF CALIFORNIA, COUNTY OF
STREET ADDRESS: 400 Van Ness Ave.
MAILING ADDRESS:
CITY AND ZIP CODE: San Francisco, CA 94102
BRANCH NAME:

ESTATE OF (NAME):
KAREN RAMPART, also known as KAREN RUTH RAMPART,
DECEDENT

ORDER FOR PROBATE

ORDER APPOINTING
- [ ] Executor
- [ ] Administrator with Will Annexed
- [X] Administrator [ ] Special Administrator
- [X] Order Authorizing Independent Administration of Estate
  - [X] with full authority [ ] with limited authority

CASE NUMBER: 240458

1. Date of hearing: Mar.13,19 Time: 9:30 am Dept/Rm: 336 Judge:

THE COURT FINDS

2. a. All notices required by law have been given.
   b. Decedent died on (date):
      (1) [X] a resident of the California county named above
      (2) [ ] a nonresident of California and left an estate in the county named above
   c. Decedent died
      (1) [X] intestate
      (2) [ ] testate and decedent's will dated:
          and each codicil dated:
          was admitted to probate by Minute Order on (date):

THE COURT ORDERS

3. (Name): Ralph Rampart
   is appointed personal representative:
   a. [ ] Executor of the decedent's will
   b. [ ] Administrator with will annexed
   c. [X] Administrator

   d. [ ] Special Administrator
      (1) [ ] with general powers
      (2) [ ] with special powers as specified in Attachment 3d
      (3) [ ] without notice of hearing

   and letters shall issue on qualification.

4. a. [X] Full authority is granted to administer the estate under the Independent Administration of Estates Act.
   b. [ ] Limited authority is granted to administer the estate under the Independent Administration of Estates Act (there is no authority, without court supervision, to (1) sell or exchange real property or (2) grant an option to purchase real property or (3) borrow money with the loan secured by an encumbrance upon real property).

5. a. [X] Bond is not required.
   b. [ ] Bond is fixed at: $ to be furnished by an authorized surety company or as otherwise provided by law.
   c. [ ] Deposits of: $ are ordered to be placed in a blocked account at (specify institution and location):
          and receipts shall be filed. No withdrawals shall be made without a court order.

6. [X] (Name): JOHN DOE is appointed probate referee.

Date: March 13, 19

Merton Tigron
JUDGE OF THE SUPERIOR COURT

7. [0] Number of pages attached:

[ ] Signature follows last attachment.

Form Approved by the
Judicial Council of California
DE-140 Rev July 1 1988

ORDER FOR PROBATE

Probate Code, § 329

FIGURE 11–8 Order for Probate

Name, Address and Telephone No. of Attorney(s)	Space Below for Use of Court Clerk Only
ALBERT TREAT Attorney at Law 101 Bond St. San Francisco, CA 94102 334-6040	

Attorney(s) for Representative(s) Administrator

SUPERIOR COURT OF CALIFORNIA, COUNTY OF ...SAN FRANCISCO.................

STATE OF CALIFORNIA	CASE NUMBER
Estate of	240458
KAREN RAMPART, also known as KAREN RUTH RAMPART,	
	ORDER APPOINTING REFEREE
DECEASED MINOR CONSERVATEE	

IT IS HEREBY ORDERED that   JOHN DOE,

a disinterested person, be, and he is appointed Referee to appraise the property of the above entitled estate in accordance with Section 605 of the Probate Code, at its fair market value at the date of the death of the decedent or, as the case may be, at the date of the appointment of the conservator or Guardian.

Dated: March 13 ,19

Merton Myron
Judge/Commissioner of the Superior Court

F1331-REV.   ORDER APPOINTING REFEREE

P-14

FIGURE 11–9   Order Appointing Referee

ATTORNEY OR PARTY WITHOUT ATTORNEY *(Name and Address):*
ALBERT TREAT
Attorney at Law
101 Bond St.
San Francisco, CA 94102

TELEPHONE NO.: 334-6040

FOR COURT USE ONLY

ATTORNEY FOR *(Name):*

SUPERIOR COURT OF CALIFORNIA, COUNTY OF SAN FRANCISCO
STREET ADDRESS: 400 Van Ness Ave., Room 336
MAILING ADDRESS:
CITY AND ZIP CODE: San Francisco, CA 94102
BRANCH NAME:

ESTATE OF (NAME):
KAREN RAMPART, also known as KAREN RUTH RAMPART,
DECEDENT

LETTERS

| ☐ TESTAMENTARY | ☒ OF ADMINISTRATION |
| ☐ OF ADMINISTRATION WITH WILL ANNEXED | ☐ SPECIAL ADMINISTRATION |

CASE NUMBER: 240458

LETTERS

1. ☐ The last will of the decedent named above having been proved, the court appoints *(name):*

   a. ☐ Executor
   b. ☐ Administrator with will annexed

2. ☐ The court appoints *(name):*
   RALPH RAMPART

   a. ☒ Administrator of the decedent's estate
   b. ☐ Special administrator of decedent's estate
      (1) ☐ with the special powers specified in the Order for Probate
      (2) ☐ with the powers of a general administrator

3. ☐ The personal representative is authorized to administer the estate under the Independent Administration of Estates Act ☒ with full authority ☐ with limited authority (no authority, without court supervision, to (1) sell or exchange real property or (2) grant an option to purchase real property or (3) borrow money with the loan secured by an encumbrance upon real property).

WITNESS, clerk of the court, with seal of the court affixed.

Date: March 13, 1989

Clerk, by *Nelson Gilchrist* , Deputy

(SEAL)

AFFIRMATION

1. ☐ PUBLIC ADMINISTRATOR: No affirmation required (Prob. Code, § 1140(b)).

2. ☒ INDIVIDUAL: I solemnly affirm that I will perform the duties of personal representative according to law.

3. ☐ INSTITUTIONAL FIDUCIARY *(name):*

   I solemnly affirm that the institution will perform the duties of personal representative according to law.
   I make this affirmation for myself as an individual and on behalf of the institution as an officer.
   (Name and title):

4. Executed on *(date):* March 13, 1989
   at *(place):* San Francisco   , California.

▶ *Ralph Rampart*
(SIGNATURE)

CERTIFICATION

I certify that this document is a correct copy of the original on file in my office and the letters issued the personal representative appointed above have not been revoked, annulled, or set aside, and are still in full force and effect.

(SEAL)

Date: March 13, 19
Clerk, by
Nelson Gilchrist
(DEPUTY)

Form Approved by the
Judicial Council of California
DE 150 [Rev. July 1, 1988]

LETTERS
(Probate)

Probate Code, §§ 463, 465, 501, 502, 540
Code of Civil Procedure, § 2015.6

FIGURE 11–10 Letters of Administration

of appearance in person or by attorney. The cost of the proceeding is an expense of administration.

The amount requested should be justified, that is, fixed expenses such as rent and needs and other resources should be shown. The person receiving the allowance may avoid any possible stay of payment by executing and filing an undertaking in double the amount of payment or payments (Prob. Code § 6545).

Form for the ex parte petition for family allowance and the order for family allowance are shown in Figure 11–11. These forms are examples only and must be modified to fit the facts of the case.

§ 11.4 Escheats

Unclaimed property means all property unclaimed, abandoned, escheated, or distributed to the state—property to which the state is or will become entitled if it is not claimed. **Permanent escheat** is the absolute vesting of title to such property after all claims are barred by judicial determination (Code Civ. Proc. § 1300). When an estate in California is unclaimed by any heir entitled to the estate, it escheats to the State of California, that is, it becomes the property of the State of California.

The legal assistant usually will not be called upon to work on escheat matters unless the assistant happens to work in that section of the Attorney General's office that handles these matters, in which case he or she would be expected to know a good deal more than that which is included here. Legal assistants should at least be aware of the facts and circumstances under which an estate can escheat to the State of California and know where to find more information in the codes.

In view of the number of estates that escheat to the State of California, it seems likely that a substantial number of the decedents had living relatives entitled to take the decedent's property under the law of intestacy, or that some of them had made wills that either were not found or were not delivered up. For example, in fiscal year 1994–1995, California reportedly received $18,860,508 in 7,170 unclaimed estates of decedents. The annual average is reportedly between $2,500,000 and $3,000,000.

TERMS

unclaimed property All property that is abandoned, escheated, or distributed to the state.

permanent escheat The absolute vesting of title in the state to unclaimed property.

SUPERIOR COURT OF CALIFORNIA, COUNTY OF SACRAMENTO

Estate of　)
　　　　　)
　　　　　)　　　　　　CASE NO.
　　　　　)　　　　　　EX PARTE PETITION FOR
　　　　　)　　　　　　FAMILY ALLOWANCE
　　　　　)
Deceased.)

　　Petitioners _____ and _____ respectfully represent:

　　1. Petitioners are the duly appointed, qualified and acting executors under decedent's will. The decedent is survived by _____, his wife, and has no minor children.

　　2. _____ died on _____, 19___, and his estate is pending administration in this Court.

　　3. An inventory and appraisement has not yet been filed in this estate.

　　4. Pursuant to the provisions of Probate Code section 6540, the surviving spouse is a person entitled to the payment of a family allowance from the assets of decedent's estate pending administration.

　　5. Petitioners are informed and believe, and thereon allege, that the estate assets consist of real and personal properties, including stocks and cash, producing an annual income in excess of $10,000. Petitioners are further informed and believe, and therefore allege, that the estate has assets in excess of its liabilities.

　　6. A reasonable allowance out of the principal and income of the estate is necessary for the maintenance of the surviving spouse. According to her circumstances, a reasonable allowance is $_____ per month. _____ average monthly expenses for necessities are set forth and attached hereto in Exhibit A. The surviving spouse has no maintenance from other sources except [Social Security benefits ($_____), rental income ($_____), and interest income ($_____), or use other appropriate language], for a total of $_____ per month.

　　7. No request for special notice has been filed.

　　WHEREFORE, petitioners pray for an order of this Court directing the personal representatives of the estate to pay to _____ the sum of $_____ per month from income and/or principal, which sum shall be paid monthly from the day of death up to the filing of the inventory, or six months, whichever is sooner, or until further order of this Court, and for such other orders as the Court shall deem proper.

　　Dated: _____, 19___.

　　　　　　　　　　　　　　　_____
　　　　　　　　　　　　　　　Attorney(s) for Petitioner

　　　　　　　　　　　　　　　VERIFICATION
　　I, _____, declare:
　　I am one of the petitioners in the above-entitled matter. I have read the foregoing Ex Parte Petition for Family Allowance, and it is true of my own

FIGURE 11-11
Ex Parte Petition for Family Allowance form and Order for Family Allowance form

FIGURE 11–11
(continued)

knowledge except for matters stated to be on information and belief, and as to those matters I believe it to be true.

I declare under penalty of perjury under the laws of the State of California that the foregoing is true and correct.

Executed at _____, California, this _____ day of _____, 19___.

_____

On a separate sheet of paper, prepare a list of monthly expenses, and attach as Exhibit A.

ESTATE OF _____, DECEASED.

MONTHLY EXPENSES

for

_____

[List the expenses]

TOTAL $_____

EXHIBIT A

[Prepare an Order for Family Allowance, the text of which might read as follows:]

The petition of _____ and _____, executors of the will of the above-named decedent, for an order for family allowance in the amount of $_____ per month to _____, the surviving spouse, is granted. The allowance is payable from income and/or principal, is payable from the day of death up to the filing of the inventory or six months, whichever is sooner, or until further order of this Court.

Dated: _____, 19___.

_____

Judge of the Superior Court

Sometimes heirs have not been in communication with the decedent, do not know of the decedent's death, or are not aware that they have an interest in the estate.

Petition for Distribution of Escheated Estate

If there are no known heirs, the property is distributed directly to the State of California at the close of the estate and then held by the State Treasurer for five years from the date of the decree of distribution. Within this five-year period, any person may claim entitlement to the estate or any part thereof (Code Civ. Proc. § 1300 *et seq.*). If no such person appears, the property vests absolutely in the state, and claims are forever barred (Prob. Code § 1320).

The executor or administrator of the estate must petition for distribution to the State of California. At least fifteen days before the hearing, notice of the hearing on the petition must be served on the devisees and legatees whose interests are affected by the petition, on heirs of the decedent in intestate estates, and on the State of California if any portion of the estate is to escheat to the State. In addition, at least thirty days before the hearing, the State Controller must be served, personally or by mail, with a copy of the petition for distribution, together with the notice of the hearing thereon, specifying the date of the hearing, and a copy of the latest account filed (Prob. Code § 1027).

Petition for Recovery of Escheated Estate

Within five years after the date of entry of judgment, an escheat proceeding may be filed showing claim or right to the money or property or proceeds thereof (Code Civ. Proc. § 1355), although if the amount is less than $1,000, the claim may be presented directly to the State Controller (Code Civ. Proc. § 1352). The proceeding is initiated by filing a petition for recovery of escheated estate against the State of California. The heirs are the petitioners, and the State Controller is the respondent. The name of the estate is part of the title for reference.

The Attorney General and the State Controller must be served with a copy of the petition at least thirty days before the hearing on the petition. Some attorneys suggest giving a forty-five-day notice. Certified copies of any vital statistics should be included (Prob. Code § 1027). Proof of service is submitted with the petition and notice of hearing to the Attorney General.

In most cases, the Attorney General does not make an appearance but furnishes a "no contest" letter stating that no opposition will be made after examining proof (birth certificates, declarations, and so on), in which event the court usually grants the prayer for judgment in favor of the heirs. If the Attorney General's office files an answer, the matter has to be placed on the master calendar.

After the court makes its order, a certified copy of the judgment and an endorsed copy of the order fixing the inheritance tax, if any, must be presented to the Unclaimed Property Division of the State Controller. A copy of the order also is sent to the Attorney General. A probate referee must be appointed, and in order fixing inheritance tax must be filed if the estate is one still subject to the inheritance tax, that is, if the decedent died on or before June 9, 1982. The tax is due nine months after death. A copy of the petition and proposed judgment are submitted to the referee.

If no one petitions within the five-year period, the property is permanently escheated to the state without further proceedings, except that infants and persons of unsound mind have the right to appear and file claims within the time limited or within one year after their respective disabilities cease (Code Civ. Proc. § 1441). Persons who purchase from the state in good faith and for a valuable consideration during this period are protected under this code section. Infants and persons of unsound mind have the right of recourse to the proceeds of any sale or other disposition by the State as provided under the code.

Abandoned bank accounts draw interest while on deposit pursuant to Code of Civil Procedure section 1513. The state does not pay interest on the estates held upon later distribution to the heirs in an escheat proceeding.

Unclaimed Property Law

Chapter 7 of the Code of Civil Procedure, sections 1500 through 1582, is cited as the "Unclaimed Property Law." The conditions for escheat of intangible personal property are in section 1510. Banking and financial organizations are required to make reasonable efforts to notify any customer by mail that his or her deposit, account, shares, or other interest will escheat to the state not less than six nor more than twelve months before the time of payment to the State Controller. Notice is not required for interests less than $25, and no service charge may be made for notice on these items. (See Code Civ. Proc. § 1513.5.) The interests must be unclaimed, as specified, for a period of seven years.

Payment or delivery of the property is made to the State Controller as provided by section 1532. The property is held by the State Controller in perpetuity, that is, indefinitely. At the end of five years the property is subject to being permanently escheated but only by judicial action by the Attorney General pursuant to Code of Civil Procedure section 1410 or section 1420, or under section 1415 by publication if the property is valued at $1,000 or less. After such action is taken, a second five-year period begins. Only after this second five-year period has passed without claim being filed may the property be permanently escheated. Then the Attorney General files. Usually a number of these cases are filed at the same time. These proceedings are called **omnibus escheat proceedings**.

In Sacramento County, escheat proceedings are heard in the probate department. Legal assistants should always check the local rules of practice.

TERMS .

---

omnibus escheat proceedings Proceedings in which the Attorney General presents a number of cases of unclaimed property that is ready to be permanently escheated to the state.

CHAPTER 12

ESTATE PLANNING

§ 12.1 The Role of the Paralegal in Estate Planning

Good **estate planning** requires a knowledge of estate administration and tax laws that affect estates, trusts, real property, and income taxes. Some paralegals are not called upon or expected to do estate planning, but a growing number of firms involve paralegals in this area to a high degree. The amount of involvement may depend on the firm's probate workload, the expertise of the paralegal, the confidence of the employing attorney in the paralegal, and the attorney's willingness to delegate.

The complexity of the estate planning field is increasing, not decreasing. As paralegals continue to gain knowledge through training, experience, and continuing education seminars, attorneys should more and more value their skills. A job description for the paralegal in the estate planning area can be found in *Estate Planning and Drafting* (Second Edition) by Regis W. Campfield (Commerce Clearing House). Appendix 4 describes the estate planning system of a small firm and includes practices and procedures that would be useful in any firm. The following is taken from a job description for a legal assistant in a large California law firm that includes estate planning duties.

I. CLASSIFICATION:

The position of Legal Assistant is a full-time position. The individual assigned to this position will receive benefits afforded supervisory and paraprofessional personnel as outlined in the Policy and Procedures Manuals.

II. MAJOR DUTIES:

The Legal Assistant will assist attorneys of the firm by performing numerous tasks, including:

a. Prepare and file pleadings and documents required by the court in the course of administering a probate estate, conservatorship or guardianship.

b. Work with attorneys in preparation of federal and California estate tax returns, determining tax liabilities, income tax planning, selection of fiscal year and planning cash requirements of estates. Maintain an up-to-date knowledge of various elections available on a federal estate tax

---

return, and the documents and procedures for making each election.

c. Coordinate and confer with personnel in the Probate Division of various county Superior Courts to determine the status of petitions scheduled for hearing and to discuss issues of probate procedure.

d. Coordinate and confer with accountants on matters of estate income and death taxes; with real estate agents on sales of real property; and with stockbrokers on sales and transfers of estate assets.

e. Research title to assets and obtain information regarding stock values, stock dividends, real property descriptions and taxes as required to complete inventory of estate assets and related death tax forms.

f. Prepare court accountings for estates, trusts, guardianships and conservatorships.

g. Recommend distribution plans for estate assets. Assist clients in the transfer of title to various assets upon completion of administration of the estate.

h. Maintain a personal working relationship with clients; answer general procedural questions and assist clients in preparing and obtaining financial information for accountings and income/death tax documents.

i. Perform legal research in contested probate matters and in income/death tax areas related to estate administration.

j. Research tax regulations and tax law changes, Probate Code provisions and related cases as well as local probate rules and procedures in various counties. Maintain a working knowledge of yearly Probate Code changes resulting from the seven-year rewrite of the Probate Code, including new forms and procedures.

k. Draft correspondence, opinion letters, research memoranda, pleadings and orders pertaining to probate and estate planning.

l. Participate in client interviews and meetings with attorneys and clients, accountants, real estate brokers, trust officers and IRS estate tax attorneys.

m. Analyze planning requirements and draft trusts, wills, property agreements, trust extracts, powers of attorney and related estate planning documents.

n. Prepare charts using computer graphics software to illustrate the course and operation of individual estate plans.

o. Review and amend the master forms for trusts, wills and related documents.

p. Accomplish other duties as required and requested by supervisory personnel.

III. SUPERVISION AND GUIDANCE REQUIRED:

The Legal Assistant shall be directly supervised by a senior Corporate/Tax Section attorney. The individual shall be responsible for managing his/her own workload and accomplishing all assigned work in a timely manner. Finished work is reviewed by the appropriate attorney for content, compliance with policies and procedures and legal sufficiency.

IV. KNOWLEDGE, SKILLS AND ABILITIES REQUIRED:

a. Basic knowledge and understanding of the organization and functions of the Corporate/Tax Section and of the firm.

b. Basic knowledge of case law, statutes and other regulations required to perform duties in the corporate/tax area.

c. Basic knowledge of basic principles, concepts and methodology used in legal research.

d. Ability to independently exercise discretion and judgment.

e. Ability to identify, evaluate and extract pertinent information from a wide variety of sources and documents.

f. Ability to analyze and interpret complex issues and determine, as appropriate, alternate courses of action.

g. Ability to communicate effectively and to deal professionally with others using tact and discretion.

h. Ability to work effectively under pressure.

i. Basic knowledge of computers to include word processing and automated research software.

j. Possession of an Associate Degree or completion of two years of formal study from an accredited college or university. Two years of progressive experience in the legal profession may be substituted.

k. Possession of a Paralegal Certificate desired.

l. One to three years previous experience in the legal profession required.

V. PERSONAL CONTACTS:

This position requires that the individual perform effectively, considerately and professionally when in contact with the attorneys and support personnel of the firm, clients and others outside of the firm.

The paralegal, whether in estate planning or other probate work, operates under at least the general supervision of the attorney, who bears the ultimate responsibility to the client. What is done or not done in the field of estate planning, however, can be of immense significance to the client. The responsibility is not one to be taken lightly.

The client who consults an attorney in estate planning often does not know what questions to ask, and the attorney must offer guidance. Most clients cannot appreciate the expertise involved, but do look at the cost. Time is needed to get all the facts necessary to give good legal advice, and time means expense. In gathering the facts, the experienced, well-trained probate paralegal can help to cut this expense for the client.

Estate planning can be improved if the family members who may be beneficiaries are involved in the planning. The testators can be better advised if the desires and financial status of beneficiaries are known. On the other hand, the testators may not want the beneficiaries to know what they are doing, and often beneficiaries are not interested until it is too late. Involvement of beneficiaries can start some controversies, even before death. In this connection, the legal assistant can be valuable. As the legal assistant becomes acquainted with the client and his or her family (often the beneficiaries), he or she may be told more of intrafamily relationships than the attorney is told, perhaps because the client can more closely identify with the legal assistant.

This chapter on estate planning and the chapters following on trusts will familiarize the paralegal with the terminology and the general principles that anyone working in the probate field needs to understand. The probate paralegal, as well as the attorney, must keep current on all the legal developments. In this field, particularly, a team approach is valuable.

§ 12.2 Estate Planning—Generally

Maximizing an estate requires time and attention. Preparation of a will is certainly important, but it is only a first step. In an era when tax laws are changing annually, any will must be reviewed in light of the new laws or much can be lost. New tax laws may provide opportunities to pass an estate during the testator's lifetime, as through gifts, or to wipe out arrangements already in existence. For example, the law increasing the annual exclusion for gifts to donees from $3,000 to $10,000 ($20,000 for a couple agreeing to split the gift, requiring filing of a return) is a matter for consideration by those with money they do not expect to need.

Wills After ERTA

The Economic Recovery Tax Act (ERTA), enacted in 1981, has affected many wills, trust agreements, and estate planning in general. Wills often need to be updated. A will may need a codicil or redrafting, or a new trust agreement may be needed, or provisions eliminated. All wills drawn before 1981 should be reviewed.

There are two schools of thought about whether attorneys have a duty to notify their clients. Notification can involve substantial time and expense, and some attorneys are concerned that clients may misinterpret a contact as a solicitation on the attorney's part. On the other hand, the attorney is in the best position to know that laws have changed and that a will should be reviewed. The average layperson is not aware of all the new laws, and thousands of dollars in taxes may be paid by a client unnecessarily because of that lack of knowledge.

Each attorney must make a decision about policy in this area. Some offices send out general form letters covering new laws without spending time analyzing each client's particular situation. Such a letter may suggest that the client make an appointment in the near future.

See the material on review of wills in Chapter 11.

Unlimited Marital Deduction

Under the Tax Reform Act of 1976, the surviving spouse was entitled to an exemption from estate tax of $250,000 or one-half of the decedent's adjusted estate, whichever was greater, under Internal Revenue Code section 2056(c). For deaths that occurred prior to 1977, no marital deduction was available to an estate consisting entirely of community property. A transition rule kept in effect the marital deduction of the greater of $250,000 or fifty percent of the adjusted gross estate for wills executed before September 13, 1981, to specifically indicate an intent to adopt an unlimited marital deduction. Under the Economic Recovery Tax Act of 1981, effective for estates of decedents who die after December 31, 1981, an unlimited marital deduction for estate and gift taxes for transfers to surviving spouses is available. The amount that a spouse can leave his or her surviving spouse is unlimited, the surviving spouse pays no tax on any size estate, and any estate taxes may be deferred until the death of the surviving spouse. This deduction applies to both separate and community property.

In spite of the unlimited marital deduction, when planning for an estate, the size of the estate and the relationship of the heirs or devisees should be considered. In a larger estate, certain kinds of living trusts and other kinds of trusts may avoid estate tax in certain circumstances and should be considered.

Terminable Interests

A terminable interest is one that will terminate or fail with the lapse of time or on the occurrence or failure to occur of some contingency. Generally, no marital deduction is allowed with regard to transfers of terminable interests between spouses. The Economic Recovery Tax Act of 1981, however, allows a marital deduction for qualified terminable interest property in estates of decedents dying after December 31, 1981. The interests transferred may be either separate or community property.

The executor must make an election to treat the assets as nontaxable, that is, as a qualifying income interest for life [IRC § 2056(b)(7)(B)(II)], in order for the interests to be qualified terminable interests for which the marital deduction is allowed. The election to qualify the trust for the marital deduction may be made by the executor of the deceased spouse's estate at the time of filing the estate tax return (Form 706). Once made, such an election is irrevocable [IRC § 2056(b)(7)(B)(v)].

The following conditions must be satisfied for the interests to be considered qualified terminable interests:

- The property must pass to the spouse from the decedent, and the surviving spouse must be entitled to all of the income from the property for life [IRC § 2056(b)(7)(B)(iv)];

- The income interest cannot be granted for a term of years, there must be no remarriage provision, and a life estate cannot end if a specified event occurs;

- Payments of income must be made at least annually but may be made at more frequent intervals; and

- No person, including the spouse, may have the power to appoint any part of the trust or property producing the income to anyone other than the surviving spouse during the spouse's life.

Retention of any powers over all or a portion of the trust is allowed if they cannot be exercised until after the spouse's death. *Property* includes an interest in property, and the trustee may have the power to invade corpus for the benefit of the spouse. For estates of decedents dying after December 31, 1981, a transfer made during life or upon death may also qualify for the unlimited marital deduction if the spouse granted an annuity or unitrust interest in a qualified charitable remainder trust [IRC § 2056(b)(8)]

A trust that qualifies for the marital deduction under Internal Revenue Code section 20.2056(e)-2(b) is called an *estate trust*. A fiduciary is neither required to make nor prohibited from making the election regarding qualified terminable interests.

§ 12.3 Disclaimers

A **disclaimer** renounces a right to a bequest in a will or benefits conferred by law. One may wonder why anyone would refuse a gift. Usually the purpose is to avoid estate or gift taxes, or possibly a generation-skipping transfer tax, either for the benefit of the person disclaiming or for the benefit of persons close to the person disclaiming. A disclaimer also could have been used to avoid the California inheritance tax when it was still in effect.

Although the disclaimer is an after-death "estate planning" tool, it is best if preplanned, that is, planned before death. Otherwise, as a practical matter, it may not be available. If preplanned, the survivor may be able to disclaim all rights if that seems to be the best thing to do under the circumstances at the time of death.

To have a valid disclaimer, the disclaimant may not direct the transfer once the disclaimer is made. The asset disclaimed must go to whomever it would otherwise go to under the law without any direction on the part of the disclaimant.

Federal Law Disclaimers

The Tax Reform Act of 1976 provided the first federal disclaimer statute, effective for transfers creating an interest in the person disclaiming made after December 31, 1976. The disclaimer of an interest must be received by the transferor of the interest, his or her legal representative, or the holder of the legal title to the property to which the interest relates within nine months after the later of the date on which the transfer creating the interest is made (date of death) or, in the case of a minor, the day the disclaimant attains age twenty-one [IRC § 2518(b)]. The disclaimer must be in writing, and the refusal must be irrevocable and unqualified.

The disclaimant is treated as though he or she never received the transfer. The property disclaimed does not constitute a taxable gift as long as the disclaimer is made before the property interest or any of its benefits is accepted. For example, if a will left interest in an apartment house to the decedent's surviving spouse and the surviving spouse took the property and tried to manage it but found it was too much to handle, and so decided to let her children who otherwise would have taken the property

---

TERMS

disclaimer†   The refusal to accept, or the renunciation of, a right or of property.

have it, the surviving spouse could not then disclaim the property, even within the nine-month period.

If a generation-skipping transfer is involved, the nine-month period commences upon a taxable termination or a taxable distribution [IRC § 2518(a) and the regulations for section 2518; see also IRC § 2045.]

California Disclaimers

California disclaimer statutes are found in Probate Code section 275 *et seq.* Unlike the federal law, with its flat nine-month limit after the date of transfer regardless of whether one knows there is an interest to be disclaimed, California Probate Code section 279 requires a disclaimer to be filed within a "reasonable time" after the person able to disclaim acquires knowledge of the interest.

Probate Code section 279 states that in the case of the interests enumerated therein, a disclaimer is conclusively presumed to have been filed within a reasonable time if it is filed within nine months after the death of the creator of the interest or within nine months after the interest becomes "indefeasibly vested," whichever occurs later. The interests enumerated include interests created by will, by intestate succession, pursuant to exercise or nonexercise of a testamentary power of appointment, by surviving the depositor of a Totten trust account or P.O.D. account, by life insurance, by surviving the death of a joint tenant, under an employee benefit plan, and by an individual retirement account, annuity contract, or bond.

In the case of interests created by inter vivos gift or trust, power of appointment, or succession to a disclaimed interest, the disclaimer is conclusively presumed to have been filed within a reasonable time if filed within nine months after the latest of the following times: time of creation, time first knowledge of the interest is acquired, or time the interest becomes indefeasibly vested.

Regarding interests other than those described above, Probate Code section 279, subdivision (d), provides that a disclaimer is conclusively presumed to have been filed within a reasonable time if filed within nine months of the time the first knowledge of the interest is identified by the person disclaiming or the time the interest becomes indefeasibly vested.

Probate Code section 295 provides that if as a result of a disclaimer or transfer, an interest is treated under federal law as never having been transferred to the beneficiary, then the disclaimer or transfer is effective as a disclaimer under the California law.

Some questions have been posed about the application of the federal and California disclaimer laws. For further information, see "California Disclaimers—Can You Give Up Without Making It a Federal Case?" in

Estate Planning, Trust & Probate News (official publication of The State Bar of California, Spring 1984).

A valid disclaimer, once made, is irrevocable.

Disclaimers and Joint Tenancy

Postmortem planning generally is inhibited by a joint tenancy. The Internal Revenue Service has reasoned that a qualified disclaimer cannot be made after acceptance of ownership of property and that acquiescence in the creation of a joint tenancy is an acceptance of an interest. When a joint tenancy is created, each tenant owns an undivided interest in the entire property and has a right of survivorship to take all the property. The result may be different where the person disclaiming the property was totally unaware of the joint tenancy and, therefore, had not "accepted" it before the decedent's death (Rev. Rul. 83-35, 1983-9 IRB 6).

§ 12.4   Titles to Real Property

Joint Tenancy

Whether property is joint tenancy property is indicated by how title to the real property is held, which is determined by the language on the deed. For spouses, the language is usually something like "Jane Doe and Richard Doe, husband and wife, as joint tenants." In the past, title to property was placed in the names of the parties (husband and wife) as joint tenants because the parties were not aware of the consequences and when asked how they wanted to take title, they chose joint tenancy. Sometimes the title company suggested it in the absence of other instructions.

One reason for taking title to property as joint tenants is that property held in joint tenancy is not subject to probate, although this reason has lost some of its validity with changes in tax and probate laws. It is true that assets held in joint tenancy are not properly part of an estate and not listed in the inventory and appraisement and that the representative need not account for such property. Avoiding probate, however, does not avoid federal estate taxes, and it did not avoid California inheritance taxes before June 9, 1982, when the California inheritance tax was repealed. The joint tenancy property, therefore, is listed separately in any inheritance tax affidavit and any federal estate tax return (Form 706) required to be filed.

Alternative Ways to Hold Title

The legal assistant should be knowledgeable about the following alternative ways of holding title to real estate:

1. Spouses—Community Property. Where the parties are husband and wife, the language might be "Jane Doe and Richard Doe, husband and wife, as community property."

2. Tenants in Common. Two or more persons may own property as tenants in common. Each owns an undivided interest in the property that may be equal or in proportion to the contribution of each to the purchase price, or as otherwise agreed upon. The language on the deed may read "Jane Doe, Richard Roe, and Alice Wonder, as tenants in common." If the language "as tenants in common" is omitted, a tenancy in common is usually presumed. If a dispute arises about the tenants' respective interests, a partition suit is necessary.

3. Tenancy by the Entirety. This form of title holding, available only to spouses, does not exist in California because California is a community property state. The language in such a deed would read "Jane Doe and Richard Doe, as tenants by the entirety." Title vests in the survivor unless both spouses agree otherwise. The legal assistant may encounter this deed if a decedent or client owns out-of-state property.

§ 12.5 Bank Accounts

Joint Tenancy Accounts

Bank accounts of spouses are frequently set up as joint tenancy accounts. Where a bank account is held in joint tenancy, either person in whose name the account stands may withdraw the entire account without the other's signature. This is not always understood and can lead to problems. A surviving spouse is entitled to withdraw the money in a joint tenancy account without limit. (See *Perkins v. West*, 122 Cal. App. 2d 585 (1954); see also Prob. Code § 5302, which expressly authorizes payment from P.O.D. accounts as well as Totten trust accounts.)

Trustee Accounts

Another type of bank account should be mentioned in passing. A trustee account, or Totten trust account, is not as well known or utilized as it might be. Money held by "Jane Doe as Trustee for Alice Wonder" goes outright to Alice Wonder upon Jane's death, without probate. Jane retains full control of the account and has the right to change the ownership on the account at any time up to her death. Alice Wonder has no right to withdraw any of the money while Jane is living. The money in the account is subject to any estate tax that may be payable.

Payable-on-Death (P.O.D.) Accounts

An account may be set up to be payable upon death to a named beneficiary. Upon death, the financial institution may transfer the balance in the account to the beneficiary, and the financial institution is discharged from any claims for the amounts so paid out unless, prior to payment, the financial institution was served with a court order restraining payment. (See Prob. Code §§ 5401–5405; see also Prob. Code § 56000, which relates to instruments other than wills, such as insurance policies, promissory notes, mortgages, and other enumerated instruments that provide for payment upon death.)

§ 12.6 Carry-over Basis and Stepped-up Basis

Federal law now requires that in estates of decedents dying after December 31, 1981, one-half the value of the property held as joint tenants with right of survivorship by the decedent and any other person, or as tenants by the entirety with the spouse, is assumed to belong to each, and one-half is included in the estate of the first to die without regard to the consideration furnished by either spouse [IRC § 2040(b)]. Consequently, under federal law, a new basis at death is available for only one-half of the property [IRC § 2040(a)]. Under California law, joint tenancy property receives no step-up in basis on either half.

Joint Tenancy—Nonspousal

In the case of property held in joint tenancy by persons other than spouses, the contribution tracing rules apply with respect to survivorship interests and determine the basis.

Gifts Within One Year of Date of Death

If a decedent who dies after December 31, 1981, had acquired property by gift within one year of the date of death and that property passes to the original donor or the donor's spouse on the decedent's death, the property will not receive a step-up in basis at the time of death but will have the adjusted basis of the property in the hands of the decedent immediately before his or her death [IRC § 1014(e)].

Redemptions

In estates where the decedent dies after December 31, 1981, if the decedent's interest in a closely held business exceeds thirty-five percent (formerly fifty percent) of his or her gross estate, the stock in that closely held business may be redeemed to pay any estate taxes imposed and the amount of funeral and administration expenses allowable as deductions for the estate (IRC § 303). If the decedent had an interest in two or more closely held businesses and twenty percent or more of the total value of each business is included in determining the value of the decedent's gross estate, the interest is treated as an interest in a single closely held business [IRC § 6166(c)].

CHAPTER 13

TRUST ADMINISTRATION

§ 13.1   Introduction

The Role of the Paralegal in Trust Administration

The role of the legal assistant in estate planning varies from office to office, depending upon the experience and competency of the particular legal assistant and the attorney's willingness to delegate in this area. The legal assistant who is knowledgeable about trusts in general, both revocable and irrevocable, can be valuable to the attorney, for trusts are one of the devices used in estate planning. Although the paralegal may not deal directly with the drafting and administration of trusts, most probate paralegals will find that trusts are part of the administration of some of the estates they are handling, particularly in firms that are heavily involved with trust work.

Competence in the field of estate planning requires extensive knowledge of tax laws, which are constantly changing, and of developments in the investment field, which in recent years has been in a constant state of flux. Continuing education through seminars, journals, tax digests, and books is a must not only for attorneys but also for paralegals.

The trust is basically a means of providing for one person to legally hold property for the benefit of another. The trust instrument is a written instrument. The legal assistant, after consultation with the attorney and client, should be able to prepare at least a rough draft of a revocable or irrevocable trust. As with other legal documents, the attorney bears the ultimate responsibility for proper preparation of the trust.

Many questions arise and must be answered in setting up and administering a particular trust. Each trust setting must be analyzed before a trust is established.

§ 13.2   Considerations in Establishing a Trust

The estate planner today has many things to consider in establishing a trust. Tax laws have become increasingly complex. Other considerations involve life insurance, ownership of properties, designations of beneficiaries, annuities, employee benefits and compensation, charitable giving, and income-splitting among the family members.

The principal reason for a trust may be to save taxes, both income and estate taxes. A trust can avoid probate and its consequent cost, delays, and lack of privacy. Trusts provide privacy of transfer. They are not a matter of court record and are not filed in an estate proceeding. On the other hand, probate records may be viewed by anyone who wants to take the time to go to the courthouse. A trust also provides financial management for persons who are minors, infirm, or simply lacking in the expertise to handle money matters competently. They can protect against mismanagement, waste, and misuse of funds. The purposes of trusts are discussed at greater length in the chapters on revocable and irrevocable trusts that follow.

The good trust manager knows his or her beneficiaries and their needs. This is important in deciding whether the trust needs income or growth or both, how much liquidity is required, and whether a tax shelter is desirable. A good trust manager will choose competent investment people to pick any stocks, bonds, or other securities.

There are several types of trusts, for example, the testamentary trust that is created by will, the revocable trust such as a living or inter vivos trust, and the irrevocable trust, such as the Clifford trust. These trusts are described in detail in the following chapters.

The Probate Code sections relating to administration of estates of decedents are found in sections 9000 through 11446, disposition of estates without administration in Division 8, sections 13000 through 13660; passage of property to the surviving spouse without administration in Division 8, Part 2, sections 13250 through 13660; and most of the new trust laws in Division 8, section 15000 *et seq.* The new laws became operative July 1, 1987, and apply to all trusts whether they were created before, on, or after July 1, 1987. The new laws also apply to all proceedings concerning trusts commenced before July 1, 1987, unless the court finds that a particular provision would substantially interfere with the effective conduct of the proceedings or the rights of the parties and other interested persons, in which event the particular provision does not apply and prior law applies. Civil Code section 5110.150 relates to community property transferred in trusts and likewise applies to transfers made before, on, or after July 1, 1987.

Pursuant to Probate Code section 17200 *et seq.,* the jurisdiction of the superior court may be invoked for a number of purposes without the trust becoming subject to the continuing jurisdiction of the court. Among the purposes for which a petition may be filed are the following:

- Determining questions of construction of a trust instrument;

- Determining the existence or nonexistence of any immunity, power, privilege, duty, or right;

- Determining the validity of a trust provision;

- Ascertaining beneficiaries and determining to whom property shall pass or be delivered upon final or partial termination of the trust, to the extent the determination is not made by the trust instrument;

- Settling the accounts and passing upon the acts of the trustee, including the exercise of discretionary powers;

- Instructing the trustee;

- Compelling the trustee to report information about the trust or account to the beneficiary if (a) the trustee has failed to submit a requested report or account within sixty days after written request of the beneficiary, and (b) no report or account has been made within six months preceding the request;

- Granting powers to the trustee;

- Fixing or allowing payment of the trustee's compensation;

- Appointing or removing a trustee;

- Accepting the resignation of a trustee;

- Compelling redress of a breach of the trust by any available remedy;

- Approving or directing the modification or termination of the trust;

- Approving or directing the combination or division of trusts;

- Amending or conforming the trust instrument in the manner required to qualify a decedent's estate for the charitable estate tax deduction under federal law in any case in which all parties interested in the trust have submitted a written agreement to the proposed changes or written disclaimer of interest;

- Authorizing or directing transfer of a trust or trust property to or from another jurisdiction;

- Directing transfer of a testamentary trust subject to continuing court jurisdiction from one county to another;

- Approving removal of a testamentary trust from continuing court jurisdiction; and

- Reforming or excusing compliance with the governing instrument of an organization pursuant to Section 16105.

The court may dismiss a petition, however, when it appears that it is not reasonably necessary to protect the interests of a trustee or of beneficiaries (Prob. Code § 17202).

Notice of Hearing

Notice of hearing on such a petition must be given for at least thirty days before the hearing. Notice must be given to all trustees, all beneficiaries entitled to notice, and to the Attorney General if the petition relates to a charitable trust, subject to the jurisdiction of the Attorney General unless the Attorney General waives notice (Prob. Code § 17203).

Choice of Fiduciary

Great care should be exercised in the choice of a fiduciary. The person must be trustworthy, a person of integrity, and someone well-versed and experienced in financial matters. The person also must be willing to act and take on the responsibility and must have the time to devote to the work that needs to be done.

The attorney should determine if other trusts are already in existence and whether the grantor owns property in more than one state, in which case ancillary administration in more than one state may be necessary. Generally speaking, it is better to have only one trustee to handle all the properties, but special assets such as a family farm or a small business may require an additional trustee who has the expertise required for a particular type of management.

Community Property

In California, both spouses have control of the community property. When such property is transferred to a trust, it should retain its character and remain identifiable, particularly to obtain a stepped-up basis on the death of one spouse. The trust must be carefully drafted to this end.

The trust should define the scope of the spouses' respective powers of revocation and powers to make, and the effects of making, withdrawals of **corpus** and distribution of income. The disposition to be made of the trust corpus upon either spouse becoming incompetent, dissolution, or the death of either spouse must be set forth. In addition, the trust should define the effect of a subsequent consent of the nonsettlor spouse, or his or her waiver or refusal to consent, and the effects of trust distributions and of the death of the settlor spouse on the rights of the nonsettlor spouse.

TERMS

corpus† A Latin term meaning "the body"; the subject matter or capital of a trust or estate, or the principal of a fund, as distinguished from the income or interest.

Selection of Assets

Consideration should be given to omitting income-producing assets from a trust if the income is to be distributed at the death of the grantor to persons in a higher income tax bracket. If not transferred to the trust, these assets can remain in the estate during the period of probate and possibly be taxed at a lower rate. Knowledge of the financial situation and tax situation of the beneficiaries is more important now than ever because of the changes in the tax laws.

Miscellaneous Pointers

As in probate estates, all the names by which the trustee is known should be used, for example, as "Ivan M. Trustworthy, also known as Ivan Trustworthy, also known as I. M. Trustworthy." Amendments to trusts would read, "Amended Mary Doe Trust Executed July 8, 1985."

Annuities that are part of a trust are not subject to federal estate taxes, provided the language of the trust does not require the trustee to make those funds available to the representative of the estate.

§ 13.3 Powers of Appointment

The California law relating to powers of appointment is found in Civil Code section 1380.1 *et seq.* The exercise of a power of appointment is not void solely because it is more extensive than authorized by the power but is valid to the extent the exercise was permissible under the power (Prob. Code § 1389.1 *et seq.*).

Internal Revenue Code section 2041(b)(1) defines a "general power of appointment" as a power that is exercisable in favor of the decedent or the decedent's estate, creditors, or creditors of the estate. The section lists some exceptions, including the "power to consume, invade, or appropriate property for the benefit of the decedent, which is limited by an ascertainable standard relating to the health, education, support, or maintenance of the decedent." This exception to the powers included in a general power of appointment has generated questions about whether the power is limited by an ascertainable, objective standard. The consensus seems to be that the language creating the power should be exactly as set forth in the statute. The regulations contain examples of acceptable provisions. Internal Revenue Code Regulation 20.2041-1(c)(2), for example, reads as follows:

(2) <u>Powers limited by an ascertainable standard</u>. A power to consume, invade, or appropriate income or corpus, or both, for the benefit of the decedent which is limited by an ascertainable standard relating to the health, education, support, or maintenance of the decedent is, by reason of section 2041(b)(1)(A), not a general power of appointment. A power is limited by such a standard if the extent of the holder's duty to exercise and not to exercise the power is reasonably measurable in terms of his needs for health, education, or support (or any combination of them). As used in this subparagraph, the words "support" and "maintenance" are synonymous and their meaning is not limited to the bare necessities of life. A power to use property for the comfort, welfare, or happiness of the holder of the power is not limited by the requisite standard. Examples of powers which are limited by the requisite standard are powers exercisable for the holder's "support," "support in reasonable comfort," "maintenance in health and reasonable comfort," "support in his accustomed manner of living," "education, including college and professional education," "health," and "medical, dental, hospital and nursing expenses and expenses of invalidism." In determining whether a power is limited by an ascertainable standard, it is immaterial whether the beneficiary is required to exhaust his other income before the power can be exercised.

For federal estate tax purposes, property under a general power of appointment is included in the taxable estate of the donee, but property subject to a limited power is not included in the donee's estate. A provision for "maintenance, comfort, and happiness" was held limited by an ascertainable standard in *Estate of Brantingham v. United States* 631 F.2d 542, 545 (7th Cir. 1980), but the Internal Revenue Service reportedly believes the holding is incorrect and has said that it will not follow it. (See Rev. Rul. 82-63, 1982-1.)

CHAPTER 14

TRUSTS

§ 14.1   Revocable Trusts

What Is a Revocable Trust?

A trust means a "written voluntary express trust," with additions thereto, wherever and whenever created [Prob. Code § 82(a)]. The title and provisions should state whether the trust is revocable or irrevocable. The law varies from state to state but under Probate Code section 15400, unless a trust is expressly made irrevocable by the trust instrument, the trust is revocable by the settlor. The better practice is to make it clear on its face. Where a trust is held to be irrevocable because the trust fails to specify that it is revocable, even though the settlor's intent was to make a revocable trust, the results can be damaging.

A revocable trust is the same as a revocable gift. If a person gave a car to a friend but kept the title in his or her own name and told the friend he or she might want it back sometime, the gift is revocable. If a trust in writing is set up for someone else's benefit but retains the right to revoke it, that is, to take the trust money or assets back without the consent of the person for whom the trust is set up or anyone else, the trust is revocable. It is important that a trust that is meant to be irrevocable specifically provide that it is irrevocable. Otherwise, income may be taxable to the grantor. [See *Appeal of Blake and Alice Hale* CCH Cal. Tax Rep. 16.392.481 (1960).]

The revocable trust, unlike the irrevocable trust, ordinarily triggers no gift tax because the gift is not completed. The income from the revocable trust will be taxed to the grantor while he or she is living. Upon the grantor's death, the trust property is taxed in the grantor's estate. After the grantor's death, the beneficiaries of the trust or the trust itself must pay the tax on any income earned by the trust. Unless the surviving spouse retains the power of revocation over his or her share of the community property in a trust, however, after the surviving spouse's death, he or she may be deemed to have made a taxable gift with regard to the remaining trust.

The grantor will be taxed on the income of the trust as long as he or she controls the enjoyment of the property of the trust. A grantor also may be taxed on the income of the trust if he or she retains certain administrative powers that enable the grantor to obtain benefits from the trust that he or she otherwise could not obtain. The principal distinction, then, between the revocable trust and the irrevocable trust is that the grantor retains control of a revocable trust and may alter or revoke it altogether, whereas with an irrevocable trust, the grantor loses control and the trust is permanent, that is, it may not be revoked.

A revocable trust can be reached by creditors to the extent of the value of the assets in the trust over which the settlor has retained the power of revocation if the estate is insufficient to pay the creditors' claims (Prob. Code § 18200). The trust also is liable for the expenses of administration if the settlor's estate is insufficient (Prob. Code § 18201).

Advantages and Disadvantages

Advantages

The assets of a revocable inter vivos trust are not subject to probate. The assets must actually be transferred into the name of the trustee, however, or they may have to be probated. The assets granted to the trust stand in the name of the trust. The assets are simply reregistered in the name of the trust.

The obvious reason for avoiding probate is the expense. A trust cuts the costs of settling the estate. The fees of an executor are either eliminated entirely if all property of the decedent is in a trust, or reduced if part of the decedent's property is probated.

The value of the property in trust is not included in determining the amount of the statutory fees for probate. In California, an attorney's fee and a personal representative's fee are statutory. The attorney and the personal representative or executor also may be awarded extraordinary fees by the court.

After the death of the grantor, a trust set up as a revocable living trust is more difficult to challenge than a will, since it was already in operation before the death of the decedent, which gives it added strength. Having a trust, however, does not preclude the necessity for a will. If a **pour-over will** is created, assets excluded from the trust can "pour over" into the trust after death. The will often is created at the same time as the trust.

The person who sets up a revocable trust has the advantage of being able to observe the ability of the trustee he or she has chosen to manage the trust and judge whether the trustee will act in a manner to his or her liking. After death, no change of management is necessary as happens in probate.

Another advantage of the trust is that upon the death of the grantor, the extent of the grantor's assets and the distribution made of them are private, at least for the most part. Knowledge of the holdings of the trust

---

TERMS

pour-over will A will in which property "pours over" from the will to an existing trust of the decedent.

becomes available only to a limited number of persons, such as the bank involved, the trustee, and so on. This information, however, becomes available to those persons during the grantor's lifetime, whereas with probate, the information is not available until after the decedent's death. The inventory and appraisement in an estate is a public record that anyone can inspect at the county courthouse if they have an interest.

If a federal estate tax return (Form 706) needs to be filed, the assets of the trust will have to be included, and a copy of the instrument creating the trust must accompany the form. This is not filed with the probate record of the estate and open to inspection by the public, however, like the will which must be filed with a county clerk and becomes a public document upon filing, open for inspection. Succeeding probate documents filed also become public documents.

A trust is frequently set up to provide for someone, probably a relative, who if given a lump sum of money might be expected to immediately spend it. So a trust instrument is set up providing for monthly payments and use of the principal, or corpus, of the trust for only certain designated purposes or needs such as medical needs, maintenance, education, or general welfare. Money also may be set aside for the future education of children or grandchildren. They may be minors or mentally incompetent and, therefore, unable to handle their own affairs. A trust also can provide for possible illness or temporary incapacity. If an elderly person with substantial assets becomes unable to handle his or her financial affairs, a living trust can avoid the necessity of a conservatorship, since a trustee is immediately available. The trust is a good alternative to a guardianship or conservatorship.

One possibility is a charitable trust. With such a trust, the income is paid to a charity.

Real property owned by a trust gets a value based on its fair market value at the date of death, not the original cost, which cuts the capital gains tax. A declaration can be made by the parties that everything is community property to establish the foundation for taking a stepped-up basis. In California, a community property state, the basis of the surviving spouse's one-half of the community property is increased to the fair market value at the date of death, for federal purposes, unless the property is held in joint tenancy or has been transferred into a living trust.

Disadvantages

There are legal fees involved in setting up a trust, and there are costs involved in operating a trust, that must be measured against probate costs. An annual trustee's fee will be charged, if the trustee is other than the grantor, and there is an attorney's fee for setting up the trust initially. Most large banks offer trust services, but some have minimum amounts, and the fees for administering the trusts may seem steep. A smaller account may be better placed in a smaller institution.

The **living trust** carries no tax benefits for estate tax purposes, as the property of the trust is included in the value of the estate.

The income of a trust is taxable to the grantor, although separate ID and tax return is not required if the grantor is the trustee.

Possession and enjoyment of trust property is restricted, and other limitations may be imposed by trust ownership. For example, the right to set aside property for a spouse or minor children under Probate Code section 6510 is lost. Also, Probate Code section 6540, providing for a family allowance, applies to estates, not to revocable trusts. There is no statute that provides for a family allowance out of a revocable trust.

It is not always wise to avoid probate. Informal probate procedures, with lesser costs, are available in some estates. For example, if the only reason for the revocable trust is to avoid probate, it may serve no purpose if the value of the real property and the personal property do not exceed $60,000, since a petition for a court order to succeed to the property may be filed under Probate Code section 13150 *et seq.* It should be remembered that probate expenses are deductible on any federal estate tax return, so the probate costs are only a percentage of the actual cost. This will not apply, however, if the estate is not large enough to require the filing of a Form 706 or if no tax is payable. Probate in general has been simplified, and some advantages available under the Probate Code are lost if a trust is used. The cost of setting up a living trust and administering it may exceed the cost of an informal probate procedure.

If claims of creditors against the entire community property is a problem, the surviving spouse may be able to avoid personal liability for the claims by electing to probate the decedent's one-half interest in the community property. On the other hand, by submitting the entire community property to probate, the property does not have to be split up into undivided interests, and an interruption in management of the property may be avoided.

Funded and Unfunded

The trust may be funded or unfunded. A **funded trust** has assets, while the **unfunded trust**, such as an insurance policy assigned to the trust, an

---

TERMS

living trust A trust created in one's lifetime; same as an inter vivos trust.
funded trust A living trust that holds property that has been transferred to it.
unfunded trust A trust without any property in it.

insurance policy that designates a beneficiary, or a pension and profit-sharing account designating a beneficiary, has few or no assets.

Typically, a pour-over trust is created to serve the purpose of a pour-over will. Where the will provides that the assets of the estate, or certain assets, will be transferred upon death into a trust, the trust has no assets until after the death of the testator. The pouring over of assets after death to such a trust is authorized by the Uniform Testamentary Additions to Trusts Act (Prob. Code § 6300). The terms of the trust must be set forth in a written instrument other than the will, executed before or concurrently with the testator's will, and must not have been revoked or terminated before the death of the testator.

In California, under Probate Code section 6321, it is sufficient to create a valid trust if an insurance, annuity, or endowment contract designates as a primary or contingent beneficiary, payee, or owner a trustee named or to be named in the will of the person entitled to designate the beneficiary, payee, or owner (Prob. Code § 6321).

The funded trust, then, operates during the lifetime of the grantor, while the unfunded trust usually comes into operation upon the death of the grantor. Some states, however, do not recognize a trust unless it is funded. For this reason, attorneys may choose to fund the trust with at least a nominal amount, such as $100.

The assets transferred to the trust should be described clearly so that there will be no question about the assets being transferred. A full legal description should be given of any real property being transferred. If the client is to make the transfer, he or she should be given a written letter of instructions regarding the transfer of the assets to the trust. Failure to provide such a letter potentially could be malpractice. It is prudent to follow up and make sure the client has actually made the transfer. Care also should be taken that no asset to be transferred is prohibited from transfer for any reason and that transfer will have no untoward effect.

Assets of the estate that have not actually been transferred into the revocable inter vivos trust will have to be probated. The expense and difficulty of probating the remaining estate will depend upon the nature and extent of those assets. The Independent Administration of Estates Act may be available, and if the property consists only of community property, the property may be transferred under Probate Code section 13656. (See Chapter 10.)

Tax Aspects of the Revocable Trust

The rules governing the taxation of revocable trusts can be complicated. This text provides a brief overview of taxability in general, and refers to some of the more common rules. The material will not make the legal assistant a tax expert by any means, but will provide some general knowledge.

A grantor is taxed on future income that he or she assigns to a trust, even if the grantor has no control over the trust, in the same way that a bondholder who assigns a right to interest on a bond may be taxed on that interest even though he does not control the bond. The grantor would not be taxed on the interest on the bond, however, if he or she gave or sold the bond to the trust. In other words, the property producing the income must be transferred to the trust to avoid tax on the income from that property.

The income of any portion of the trust is attributed to the grantor if he or she has a reversionary interest in either the corpus or the income therefrom if the value of that interest exceeds five percent of the value of the trust [IRC § 673(a)]. A grantor is treated as the owner if he or she has a reversionary interest in either the corpus or income if the grantor's interest will take effect in possession or enjoyment within ten years [IRC § 673, Reg. § 1.673(a)-l]. The grantor is not taxed on the trust income even though it is used for the maintenance of a person other than the grantor's spouse to whom he or she owes a legal obligation of support or for payment of his or her legal obligations except to the extent such income is so applied or distributed [IRC § 677(b); Reg. § 1.677(b)-l]. The grantor is taxed on capital gain added to trust corpus if the corpus reverts to the grantor upon termination of the trust [Reg. §§ 1.671.-3(b)(2), 1.677(a)-l(g)].

In short, a grantor is treated as the owner of any portion of a trust in which he or she retains a reversionary interest in either the corpus or income if, at the inception of that portion of the trust, the grantor's interest will or may reasonably be expected to take effect in possession or enjoyment within ten years from the date of transfer of that portion of the trust [IRC § 673; Reg. § 1.673(a)-l]. If, however, the reversion takes effect only upon the death of the beneficiary, the income will not be taxed. Also excepted is a transfer in trust made after April 22, 1969, of a reversionary interest in a charitable trust that meets the requirements of section 673(b). [See Reg. 1.673(b)-l.]

If a person other than the grantor has the power to vest the corpus of the trust or income of the trust in himself or herself, he or she may be taxed on its income [IRC §§ 678(a), Reg. § 1.678(a)-l]. For instance, where a father sets up a trust for the benefit of his children, but his wife may at any time take the trust property, the wife is taxed on its income as if she were the owner unless she renounces or disclaims within a reasonable period of time [IRC § 678(a), Reg. § 1.678(d)-l].

In *Estate of Friedman*, 94 Cal. App. 3d 667 (1979), the court ruled that the husband's power to invade and consume corpus in his uncontrolled discretion was not limited by an ascertainable standard relating to his own health, education, support, or maintenance and was a general power of appointment. The court held that uncontrolled discretion meant that the husband was not held to a standard of reasonableness but only to one of good faith, and "such standard not being reasonably measurable in terms of the purposes specified, was not ascertainable" (94 Cal. App. at 667). In other words, a general power of appointment occurs when a trustee has a power under the trust agreement to invade and consume, in his or her uncontrolled discretion, the corpus of the trust and is not limited by an ascertainable standard relating to his or her own health, education, support, or maintenance. **Uncontrolled discretion** means the trustee is not held to a standard of reasonableness, but only to one of good faith.

California Civil Code section 16081, however, provides that where a trust instrument confers absolute, sole, or uncontrolled discretion upon a trustee, the trustee shall act in accordance with fiduciary principles and shall not act in bad faith or in disregard of the purposes of the trust. The section further provides that a person who is a beneficiary of a trust and who holds a power to take or distribute income or principal to or for his or her own benefit pursuant to a standard shall exercise that power reasonably and in accordance with the standard, notwithstanding the trustor's use of terms such as *absolute, sole,* or *uncontrolled.* California Civil Code section 196 provides that a "father and mother of a child have an equal responsibility to support and educate their child in the manner suitable to the child's circumstances, taking into consideration the respective earnings or earning capacities of the parents."

The income is reported on a separate statement attached to Form 1041, not on Form 1041 itself (Reg. § 1.671-4). Income from a trust that is distributed to a beneficiary, however, is taxed to that beneficiary. Further, income is taxed to the beneficiary if it is required by the trust to be distributed to him or her by the trustee, whether or not the trustee actually distributes it. If distributions to the beneficiary exceed the trust's distributable net income, the beneficiary becomes subject to the throwback rules. In short, the excess is taxed as if distribution actually was made in the year the income accumulated in the trust. Form 4970 is used for computation of tax.

If a "United States person" transfers property to a foreign trust that has a United States beneficiary, he or she is treated as the owner of that portion (IRC § 679) and must file an information return [IRC §§ 6048(c), 6677(a)]. Under Internal Revenue Code section 212, the expenses incurred in setting up family estate trusts are not deductible.

TERMS

uncontrolled discretion   The trustee is not held to a standard of reasonableness, but only to one of good faith.

California Taxation of Revocable Trusts

The taxation of estates, trusts, beneficiaries, and decedents shall be determined in accordance with subchapter i of Chapter 1 of subtitle A of the Internal Revenue Code sections 641 through 692 except as otherwise provided in the Revenue and Taxation Code (Rev. & Tax. Code § 17731). Until 1983, California law was self-contained, although it duplicated many provisions of the federal law. Since 1983, California law incorporates much of the federal law by reference and "deals only with the differences between California and Federal law." Any federal regulations issued are applicable to California unless California has issued its own regulations or the federal regulations conflict with California law.

If an election is a proper federal election, it is deemed to be a proper election for California purposes unless California law or regulations otherwise provide. The federal election is furnished to the Franchise Tax Board upon request. If the taxpayer wishes to make an election for federal purposes but not for California, or vice versa, it has been suggested that the taxpayer explain that in a timely notice to the Franchise Tax Board.

The 1983 conformity legislation (effective for taxable years on or after January 1983) specifies that certain provisions of federal law do not apply in California, although they may be incorporated in California law. Some of the subjects covered by these provisions are foreign trusts, **nonresident aliens**, and tax on generation-skipping transfers. The federal conformity law references to *three years* (limitation periods, and so on) should be modified to *four years*.

Where the grantor of a revocable trust is not a California resident, the income of the trust derived from sources within California is taxed to the grantor. The remainder of the income is taxed to the trust or to the beneficiaries under the rules regarding taxability of trust income.

Revocable Life Insurance Trusts

A life insurance trust is quite simple. The person insured becomes the grantor of the trust, and the grantor names the trustee, who might be a bank's trust department or a knowledgeable friend or family member, as beneficiary of the life insurance policy in the trust. A trust agreement is drawn up that provides instructions to the trustee for investment of the proceeds and distribution of the income and principal. Upon the death of the insured, the trustee collects the proceeds.

TERMS

nonresident aliens†   A person who is neither a citizen nor a resident of the United States.

Advantages of the revocable life insurance trust are that it can be changed or terminated at any time. Special instructions can be given to the trustee, such as the power to invade the principal if a family emergency or illness occurs or the education of a child or grandchild requires payment. Another advantage is that the proceeds of the policy, unless payable to the estate of the insured or unless the insured has incidents of ownership that he or she gave away within three years of the date of death, are paid directly, in cash, to the named beneficiary and do not become part of the insured's estate and thus subject to probate. If the decedent owned a policy on someone else's life, however, the value of the policy is included in the estate. The valuation of the policy is complex and is determined by the company that issued the policy. If the decedent did not have all incidents of ownership in the policy, that is, the insured had retained an incident of ownership, the policy is not considered transferred but becomes a taxable gift, and the annual exclusion is available.

A life insurance trust is especially beneficial if there are minor children, because a guardianship can be avoided. The trustee can manage the proceeds until the children are of age and able to handle the funds. Employee death benefits can be made payable to the same trust, and the will can provide for a pouring over of certain assets into the trust.

If the trustee of a life insurance trust is experienced in investments and financial matters, the insured can be more certain of prudent management. The life insurance trust also provides privacy.

Marital Deduction

The inception of the federal estate tax occurred in 1916. There are both community property states and common law states. In the community property states, if the estate consisted of a husband's earnings during marriage, only one-half of the estate was subject to the estate death tax. But if the wages were earned in a common law state, all of the earnings were taxed. This inequality prompted a change in the law in 1942 that called for all of such earnings to be included in the gross estate of the husband, but if the wife died first, one-half was to be included in her estate because of a provision calling for the inclusion of community property over which the decedent held a power of testamentary disposition. This was unpopular in community property states and did nothing for those in common law states. The Revenue Tax Act of 1948 attempted to equalize the effects of the estate tax.

Before 1976, the amount that could be inherited tax free did not exceed $60,000. As inflation increased, the purchasing power of the dollar decreased, and the $60,000 estate tax exemption no longer accomplished what originally had been intended. The Tax Reform Act of 1976 increased the amount that could be inherited without paying tax for estates of persons dying after December 31, 1976. The $60,000 exemption was replaced by a new unified credit to be phased in over five years. The unified gift and estate tax schedule, now in effect, is as follows:

Where decedent died during	Amount of tax credit	No tax on cumulative transfers (gifts and estate) not exceeding
1977	$30,000	$120,666
1978	34,000	134,000
1979	38,000	147,333
1980	42,500	161,563
1981	47,000	175,625
1982	62,800	225,000
1983	79,300	275,000
1984	96,300	325,000
1985	121,800	400,000
1986	155,800	500,000
1987 and thereafter	192,800	600,000

The table above shows that by 1981, a $47,000 credit in effect increased the $60,000 exemption (amount of estate that could pass tax free) to $175,625. The amount in estates of decedents dying after 1987 has been increased to $600,000.

In addition, a maximum estate marital deduction to the surviving spouse has been increased. In estates of decedents dying after December 31, 1976, and before January 1, 1982, an estate could deduct as a marital deduction either $250,000 or fifty percent of the amount of the adjusted gross estate, whichever was greater. This deduction had been limited to one-half of the adjusted gross estate. An adjustment was made, however, for the marital deduction previously (but post-1976) claimed for gifts. The first $100,000 gift made by a spouse after 1976 was not a taxable gift, the second $100,000 was fully taxable, and all amounts over $200,000 were subject to a fifty percent marital deduction. In other words, an adjustment was required where gifts to a spouse were under $200,000, since a tax would have been paid on the second $100,000 and a $250,000 marital deduction allowed.

The Unlimited Marital Deduction

The Economic Recovery Tax Act of 1981 was passed to apply to federal estate taxes for decedents dying on or after January 1, 1982. Under this law, estates of decedents dying on or after January 1, 1982, are to be transferred to surviving spouses free of estate and gift taxes, with some exceptions in regard to terminal interests. Section 403 of this act contains a provision referred to as the unlimited marital deduction that places no limit on the amount transferred to a surviving spouse, whether of community or separate property (other than certain terminable interests), without being taxed. Under this law, on the surviving spouse's death, the estate is taxed only if it exceeds the allowable exemptions, which have been phased in each year to a maximum of $600,000.

Marital Deduction Trust

The **marital deduction trust** is one in which a spouse creates a trust for the surviving spouse to pay income for life. The surviving spouse is given a general power of appointment to direct that on his or her death, the principal be paid to persons designated by him or her. The assets in the trust qualify for the federal estate tax marital deduction. If created during the lifetime of the spouse, the trust qualifies for the federal gift tax marital deduction.

Nonmarital Trust

When it appears not to be advantageous to take the unlimited marital deduction, a spouse may create a trust for his or her surviving spouse that will pay the surviving spouse income and principal for life. An amount equal to the unified estate and gift tax exemption is "carved out" of the estate. When the surviving spouse also dies, the trust will not be included in the surviving spouse's estate.

Bypass Trust

A **bypass trust** is typically used to avoid taxes that may be due on the death of the surviving spouse, that is, on the second death. In California and other community property states, the husband and the wife each own one-half of the community property. Therefore, the wife always has an estate, assuming that there is at least some community property, regardless of whether she has been drawing a salary. She may or may not own separate property. The tax situation has changed since 1982.

After 1980 and before 1982, for example, if a husband died and the value of his one-half of community property was $500,000, his wife would

---

TERMS

marital deduction trust   A trust created for a spouse that will pay income for life to the surviving spouse.

bypass trust   A trust intended to save the "second tax," that is, the tax on the death of the second spouse to die.

have paid taxes on that $500,000, which would have amounted to $55,000. After deducting the unified credit then in effect, $47,000, a tax of $108,800 would have been due. But then when the wife subsequently died (after 1980 but before 1982), her estate would be taxed on $1,000,000, the $500,000 from her husband and $500,000 of her own half of the community property. The tax would have been $345,800, but after deducting the unified credit of $47,000, her estate would have been taxed an additional $298,800. The total tax on both estates would have been $407,600 ($108,800 plus $298,800). (Note that this illustration ignores other possibilities such as the wife spending some of the money, administration expenses, prior gifts, and so on.)

The second tax in the example above could have been avoided if the husband had set up a bypass trust. By his will, he could have provided that his one-half of the community property be placed in trust for his wife for life, the remainder after her death to go to his lineal descendants. By the use of this bypass trust, the tax results would have been the same upon the husband's death, but on his wife's subsequent death (after 1980 and before 1982), only her one-half of the estate, $500,000, would have been taxed, upon which the tax would have been $155,800 less the unified credit of $47,000, or $108,800. The total tax on both estates, then, would have been $217,600 ($108,800 plus $108,800).

The problem becomes more complicated when there is separate property. Suppose the wife in the above illustration had $300,000 in separate property. Many times the separate property, for one reason or another, becomes so commingled that it is virtually impossible to distinguish separate and community property, although many spouses who have assets of their own keep them clearly apart. If the wife made gifts of part of the $300,000 to her husband to equalize their holdings, the tax results would have been the same. But since her husband died first, she would have paid taxes on money that was originally her own and on which she would not have needed to pay any tax.

In estate planning, there is no way to predict which spouse will die first. Sometimes people assume that because one is much older, or not in good health, that one will be the first to die. It does not necessarily happen that way, and many undesirable results have occurred when estate planning was predicated on that assumption.

Pour-over Will or Trust

The term pour-over will is used to describe a will in which the testator, after disposing of certain specific assets, provides for the remainder of his or her property to "pour over" into a trust after his or her death. The personal property of the testator, such as household furniture and jewelry and his or her residence, usually is not placed in the trust. The testator retains ownership and control of the property during his or her lifetime. The trust may be funded or unfunded. Only a minimal amount of property need be placed in the trust. If the trust is unfunded, only nominal assets are placed in the trust.

A-B Trust

The **A-B trust** was used in California mainly to equalize the holdings of married persons in order to take full advantage of the marital deduction. With the advent of the unlimited marital deduction, this trust is no longer as useful.

As an example, the wife's share of the community property would be placed in Trust A and the husband's share in Trust B. The terms could provide that the wife receive the income from both trusts with the principal to be used only for emergencies, or that she receive the income from only Trust A, while the income would accumulate in Trust B at possibly a lower income rate.

Q-Tip Trust

The **qualified terminable interest property (Q-Tip) trust** came into being with the Economic Recovery Tax Act of 1981 (ERTA), which permitted the life estate of a surviving spouse in qualified terminable interest property to qualify for the marital deduction. The trust may pay income to a surviving spouse, and principal if needed, and also provide for an eventual gift to a charity, and still qualify as a Q-Tip trust.

A Q-Tip trust may be desirable in a second marriage where a spouse wants to provide for the surviving spouse during his or her lifetime but wants the remaining property to go to the issue of a previous marriage.

TERMS

A-B trust   A trust used mainly in California to equalize the holdings of married persons in order to take full advantage of the marital deduction.

qualified terminable interest property (Q-Tip) trust   A trust that permits the life estate of a surviving spouse in qualified terminable interest property to qualify for the marital deduction and that may pay income, and principal if needed, to a surviving spouse and also provide for an eventual gift to a charity.

Family Pot Trust

In a **family pot trust** all the money is kept together, and not divided into shares. Such a trust may not be set up until after the death of the surviving spouse. Then the assets may be distributed out of probate to the trust, which may have been established by a will.

If a family pot trust is set up for a specific purpose, such as providing education for all the children, when it has served its purpose, the remaining money may be distributed to the children. Distribution may be made when the children all reach a certain age or at various ages. Sometimes when the youngest child reaches age twenty-one, the remaining money is divided into equal shares for the children. Sometimes the children are given the optional power to withdraw a certain percentage at various ages, for example, starting at age twenty-one or twenty-five, then at age thirty, and then the balance at age thirty-five. If the children leave the money in the trust, however, they have the benefits of a ready-made trust without any expense and with professional management, and they have readily identifiable separate property.

Sample Revocable Trust

The following revocable trust is not set forth as a model form to follow in drafting such a trust, but only as a sample to give the reader an idea of what such a trust might look like.

TRUST AGREEMENT

GEORGE STEINWAY and ELLEN STEINWAY, husband and wife, the Trustors, hereby transfer and assign to Wells Fargo Bank, N.A., the Trustee, the property described in Exhibit "A" attached, in trust upon the following terms:

FIRST: Community property of the Trustors transferred to this trust and the proceeds thereof shall continue to be community property under the laws of California, subject to the provisions of this trust.

SECOND: The Trustee may accept additions to the trust from any source. Additions to the trust received after the death of the first Trustor to die shall be irrevocable unless otherwise provided in the instrument of transfer or this agreement.

THIRD: The Trustee shall have no greater powers over community

---

TERMS

family pot trust A trust set up after the death of the surviving spouse that keeps all the money together, rather than dividing it into shares.

property subject to this trust than those possessed by the Trustors under California Civil Code sections 5125 and 5127. This limitation shall terminate on the death of either Trustor.

FOURTH: During the Trustors' joint lifetimes, either Trustor may revoke as to all or any part of the Trustors' community property held in the trust by a written instrument signed by either Trustor and delivered to the Trustee and the other Trustor, and both Trustors may amend this trust agreement by a written instrument signed by both Trustors and delivered to the Trustee, provided, the duties and compensation of the Trustee may not be changed without the Trustee's consent. A Trustor may at any time revoke as to all or any part of any separate property the revoking Trustor has contributed to the trust by a written instrument signed by the revoking Trustor and delivered to the Trustee. Upon revocation, community property shall continue to be community property of the Trustors under the laws of the State of California. Upon the death of the first Trustor to die, the Marital Deduction Trust and the Residuary Trust shall be irrevocable.

FIFTH: During the joint lifetimes of the Trustors, the Trustee shall pay the net income of community property held in the trust to the Trustors for the account of the community. The Trustee shall pay the net income from separate property held in the trust to the Trustor who contributed such separate property to the trust. During the joint lifetimes of the Trustors, the Trustee may also pay to or apply for their benefit as much of the trust principal as the Trustee in its absolute discretion deems necessary for the care and comfortable support of the Trustors in their accustomed manner of living, charging first community property for these purposes so long as it is readily available for these purposes in the judgment of the Trustee.

SIXTH: Upon the death of the first Trustor to die, the Trustee shall segregate the surviving Trustor's share of the community and quasi-community property and the surviving Trustor's separate property held in this trust and allocate such property to the Survivor's Trust. The balance of the trust estate shall be allocated to the Marital Deduction Trust and to the Residuary Trust in the manner set forth below.

SEVENTH: The Trustee shall pay to or apply for the benefit of the surviving Trustor so much of the income and principal of the Survivor's Trust as it deems advisable for his/her health, comfort and support in his/her accustomed manner of living, and for payment of tax liabilities. Any undistributed income shall be accumulated and added to principal. The Trustee shall exercise its discretion liberally for the benefit of the surviving Trustor, bearing in mind that providing for his/her comfort and welfare is the primary purpose of this trust. The Trustee's discretion to make payments of principal or income shall be absolute, and the Trustee may, but shall not be required to, take into consideration other income or resources known by the Trustee to be available to the surviving Trustor, and the Trustee may accept as final and conclusive the written statement of the surviving Trustor as to other income or resources.

EIGHTH: The surviving Trustor shall have the right to direct the payment of income and principal and the right to withdraw any part or all of the principal of the Survivor's Trust during his/her lifetime by a written instrument signed by him/her and delivered to the Trustee.

NINTH: On the death of the surviving Trustor, the Survivor's Trust shall terminate and the trust property, together with any undisbursed income, shall be distributed as the surviving spouse shall appoint by the last unrevoked instrument in writing other than a will signed by him/her and delivered to the Trustee during his/her lifetime. Any appointment made is revocable by a signed writing delivered to the Trustee during the surviving Trustor's lifetime. Any property of the Survivor's Trust that is not effectively appointed shall be added to the principal of the Residuary Trust hereinafter established.

TENTH: The Trustee shall allocate to the Marital Deduction Trust an amount equal in value to the maximum allowable marital deduction as finally determined for federal estate tax purposes, diminished by the value for such purposes of all other items in the Trustor's gross estate that pass or have passed to or for the benefit of the Trustor's spouse under other provisions of the Trustor's will or otherwise in such manner as to qualify for and be allowed as a marital deduction, but no greater amount than is necessary to reduce to the smallest amount possible the federal estate tax payable as a result of the Trustor's death, taking into account all other deductions and the unified credit and the credit for state death taxes. The credit for state death taxes shall be taken into account in determining the amount to be allocated to the marital share only to the extent that it does not cause an increase in the amount of death taxes payable to any state.

ELEVENTH: Only assets that qualify for the marital deduction shall be allotted to the Marital Deduction Trust. The Trustee is specifically authorized to satisfy said share in cash or in kind or partly in each; provided, however, that any assets transferred in kind to satisfy said share shall be valued for that purpose at their fair market values determined as of the date or dates of their respective transfers. This trust shall carry with it (as income and not as principal) its proportionate share of all net income received.

In establishing and administering the Marital Deduction Trust, the Trustee shall not exercise any discretionary power in any manner that would disqualify this trust for the marital deduction.

TWELFTH: The Trustee shall pay the entire net income of this trust to the Trustor's surviving spouse or apply it for his/her benefit in quarterly or more frequent installments so long as he/she shall live.

The Trustee is authorized in its sole and absolute discretion at any time and from time to time to distribute to or for the benefit of said spouse from the principal of this trust (even to the point of completely exhausting same) such amounts as it may deem advisable to provide adequately for his/her health, maintenance and support. In determining the amounts of principal to be so disbursed, the Trustee shall take into consideration any other income that the Trustor's spouse may have from any other source, but not the spouse's capital resources, and the Trustee may accept as final and conclusive the written statement of the beneficiary receiving payment as to other income or resources.

THIRTEENTH: The Trustor directs his/her Executor to qualify this trust for the marital deduction. The Trustor exonerates his/her Executor from all liability for such election and directs that no beneficiary shall have any claim against his/her Executor or his/her estate by reason of the exercise of his/her Executor's judgment in this respect.

FOURTEENTH: Upon the death of the Trustor's spouse, the assets of the Marital Deduction Trust shall pass in the same manner as the assets of the Residuary Trust created hereunder. The accumulated and accrued income shall be payable to The Trustor's spouse's estate.

FIFTEENTH: On the death of the Trustor's spouse, the Trustee shall be authorized to withhold distribution of an amount of property sufficient, in its judgment, to cover any liability that may be imposed on the Trustee for estate or other taxes until such liability is finally determined.

SIXTEENTH: On the death of the Trustor's spouse, this trust shall terminate and the Trustee shall distribute the remaining trust estate to the Trustor's then surviving issue by right of representation.

SEVENTEENTH: The Trustee may, in its sole and absolute discretion, pay to the estate of the Trustor from the principal of the trust fund prior to its division such amounts as may be needed to pay all or any part of the Trustor's debts, funeral expenses and administration expenses of his/her estate. The Trustee shall pay to the Trustor's estate or the appropriate tax authorities all estate and inheritance taxes that may become payable by reason of the Trustor's death in respect of all property comprising the Trustor's gross estate for death tax purposes, whether or not such property passes under this Agreement, under the Trustor's will or otherwise, it being intended that all such death taxes be borne by the Residuary Trust to the extent that the assets thereof are sufficient for that purpose.

EIGHTEENTH: In addition to those powers now or hereafter conferred by law, in managing the trust estate, the Trustee shall have full power, with or without notice and without the necessity of obtaining the order of any court therefor, (1) to sell at public or private sale (for cash or on terms); (2) to lease (without restriction or limitation as to term); (3) to borrow, mortgage, secure by deed of trust, hypothecate; (4) to lease or contract with reference to oil, gas or other minerals or natural resources and mineral rights and mineral royalties that may be part of the Trustor's estate, with full power to mine and drill therefor, upon such terms as it may deem advisable; (5) to partition, exchange or otherwise dispose of any of the Trustor's property; (6) to retain all stocks, bonds, securities and any other property that may constitute a part of the Trustor's estate, including stock of Wells Fargo Bank, N.A.; (7) to vote, and give proxies to vote, any securities, including stock of Wells Fargo Bank, N.A., having voting rights; (8) to purchase assets from and make loans, secured or unsecured, to the Executor or other representative of the Trustor's estate; (9) to invest and reinvest the trust estate in such property, real or personal, including limited partnerships and common trust funds maintained by the Trustee, as it may deem advisable without being restricted by statutory limitations on trust investments; (10) to do and perform any and all acts and things deemed by it necessary or advisable in the management of the trust estate.

NINETEENTH: The Trustors may, by an instrument in writing delivered to the Trustee, direct that any one or more of the following modifications of the Trustee's investment powers shall be effective and may at any time revoke any such direction by an instrument in writing delivered to the Trustee:

a. As long as the Trustors are living and not, in the absolute judgment of the Trustee, disabled from managing property properly, the Trustee shall consult with them if they shall be reasonably available and obtain their written approval before exercising any of the investment powers set forth in Paragraph Eighteenth. If the Trustors shall withhold approval of any proposal made by the Trustee, notwithstanding the actual or anticipated effect thereof on the trust estate, the Trustee shall not be liable or accountable in any manner for failing to act in the absence of such approval.

b. During the joint lifetimes of the Trustors and as long as the Trustors are not, in the absolute judgment of the Trustee, disabled from managing property properly, the Trustors shall have the power by an instrument in writing delivered to the Trustee to direct the Trustee in the exercise of any one or more of the investment powers set forth in Paragraph Eighteen. The Trustee shall not be liable or accountable for complying with such directions, and shall have no duty to review, initiate action or make recommendations with respect to investments acquired or retained pursuant to such directions, but shall at all times have the foregoing powers set forth herein and provided by law with respect to the other assets of the trust.

c. During the joint lifetimes of the Trustors and as long as they are not, in the absolute judgment of the Trustee, disabled from managing property properly, all power over and responsibility for the administration of the trust and the trust property, including its management, disposition and investment, is reserved to the Trustors. The Trustee shall have no duty other than to hold title to and provide custodial and bookkeeping services for property delivered to it and otherwise to deal with the trust property as instructed in writing by the Trustors, and notwithstanding the actual or anticipated effect thereof on the trust estate, the Trustee shall not be liable or accountable in any manner for failing to act in the absence of written instructions from the Trustors or for complying with their written instructions. After the death of the first of the Trustors to die, or if the Trustors become disabled, in the absolute judgment of the Trustee, from managing property properly, the Trustee shall have full power and authority to exercise the foregoing powers set forth herein and any other administrative powers conferred by law on Trustees.

In determining whether the Trustors are under a disability, the Trustee may rely upon any information believed by it to be correct, and the Trustee shall be fully protected for acts done by it, or for failure to take any action, in good faith reliance upon such information. Any person transacting business with the Trustee may conclusively rely upon the affidavit of an officer of the Trustee that it has authority to act under this provision.

TWENTIETH: The Trustee shall have the power, exercisable in its sole discretion, to receive additional property from any source and add it to and commingle it with any trust estate held under the Trustor's will.

TWENTY-FIRST: The validity and construction of this agreement shall be controlled by the laws of the State of California.

IN WITNESS WHEREOF, the Trustors GEORGE STEINWAY and ELLEN STEINWAY, have executed this agreement this _____ day of June, _____.

§ 14.2 Irrevocable Trusts

Another means of estate planning is the irrevocable trust. An irrevocable trust is categorized as an inter vivos trust or a living trust, as is a revocable trust. California Civil Code section 15400 provides that every voluntary trust shall be revocable unless expressly made irrevocable by the instrument creating the trust. Therefore, the irrevocable trust must contain language such as the following: "This trust is irrevocable and shall not be altered, amended, or revoked by any person." *Irrevocable* means exactly that. The donor should proceed on the assumption that, once made, the trust cannot be undone.

Probate Code sections 15403 through 15412, however, has established rules for the modification and termination of irrevocable trusts. If all beneficiaries consent, modification or termination can be compelled unless the court determines that the purpose of the trust outweighs the reason for termination. The trust cannot be terminated if it contains a spendthrift clause [Prob. Code §§ 15300 *et seq.*, 15403 (b)].

Why an Irrevocable Trust?

The objective of the irrevocable trust is the same as that of other trusts: to transfer legal ownership and management of property to a trustee for the purposes specified in the agreement creating the trust. In an irrevocable trust, the donor essentially makes a gift or gifts, usually with tax saving objectives, whether of income tax, estate taxes, or inheritance or gift taxes. An outright gift would be simpler, and might be more to the liking of the donee, but would not provide the donor the same opportunity for tax planning. Nor would a revocable trust accomplish the same results.

The trustor may have reasons other than tax savings for setting up the trust. The trustor may not have confidence in the ability of the donee to manage the property, in which case the trustee can choose an older person or more experienced person with expertise in property management. Or the trustor may want to be free of the burden of managing the property. The donees may be very young children or minors who do not have the experience and mature judgment to manage substantial sums of money. Also, where there are multiple beneficiaries, the donor can leave to the trustee's discretion how and when the gifts shall be apportioned among them.

Although the donor must pay a gift tax when setting up the trust, the property is out of the donor's estate when he or she dies and is not subject to estate taxes or probate. Aside from the costs of probate, some persons prefer that their holdings not be made a matter of public record available to the general public.

Why Not an Irrevocable Trust?

As noted above, once the gift is made, the donor cannot undo it. This price is too high for many people. It means giving up all control of the assets and enjoyment of any of the benefits. Donors should be certain they will not want or need the assets. If a time comes when they do need them, the assets may be gone. Donors, including parents, are unwise to count on the donees to return the assets or take care of the donors and their needs.

There are administrative costs involved in setting up a trust and keeping it going. Records must be kept and income tax returns filed. The trustee's task may be made difficult by donees who do not agree with the trustee or among themselves, especially if the trustee has the power to "sprinkle" income to the beneficiaries, that is, to pay out to them according to their needs. Naturally, the trustee's ideas about their needs may not coincide with those of the beneficiaries.

Despite the most careful draftsmanship, the beneficiaries and the donor may ultimately become unhappy with the results of the trust. All eventualities cannot be foreseen.

Tax Planning Considerations for Irrevocable Trusts

The trust should define the terms used in the trust to be certain they mean what the donor intended them to mean, rather than risk someone misinterpreting them. *Income,* for example, as well as other terms, should be clearly defined.

Annual Exclusion

The donor can give to as many donees as he or she wishes the sum of $10,000 each year without incurring any tax. No gift tax return need be filed if the $10,000 per donee amount is not exceeded. For example, a donor can give outright $10,000 each to thirty-five donees, or $350,000, without filing a return or incurring a tax. But if the donor gives one donee $15,000, the donor must file a federal gift tax return and pay a gift tax on $5,000.

A donor can make the same gifts through an irrevocable trust with the same tax consequences, but the gift to the trust must qualify as a present interest under IRC section 2503(b). To give a present interest, the gift must be outright and the donee must have absolute present control of the money or property given. If the beneficiary under the trust has a present right to the income from the trust, the gift is one of present interest. "An unrestricted right to the immediate use, possession, or enjoyment of property or the income from property (such as a life estate or term certain) is a present interest in property" (Reg. § 25.2503-3). A present interest stands in contradistinction to a future interest, which does not qualify for the annual exclusion.

Future interest is defined in Regulation section 25.2503-3(a) as including

> reversions, remainders, and other interests or estates, whether vested or contingent, and whether or not supported by a particular interest or estate, which are limited to commence in use, possession or enjoyment at some future date or time. The term has no reference to such contractual rights as exist in a bond, note (though bearing no interest until maturity), or in a policy of life insurance, the obligations of which are to be discharged by payments in the future. But a future interest or interests in such contractual obligations may be created by the limitations contained in a trust or other instrument of transfer used in effecting a gift.

TERMS

---

future interest†   An estate or interest in land or personal property, including money, whether vested or contingent, that is to come into existence at a future date.

An outright gift in a trust to A, without any restrictions, is a gift of a present interest. But if the gift is to A for life, with the remainder to B, the gift to B is a future interest. Any deferred or contingent right is a gift of future interests. If the trustee has discretion to either make the gift to the donee or accumulate income in the trust, the gift is of future interests. If A has a right to all the income of the trust but the trustee has the power to pay principal only, the gift remains a present interest as long as the trustee does not have the power to give it to any other person [IRC § 2503(b); see Reg. § 25.2503.3]. The trust agreement must require that the income from the trust be either paid, credited, or distributed to the beneficiary. Then the donee pays the income tax, and presumably the donee is in a lower income tax bracket than the donor. Otherwise, the income is taxable to the beneficiary if distributed, or to the trust, as a separate entity taxpayer. [See IRC § 2642(c), as amended by the Technical and Miscellaneous Revenue Act of 1988; *Estate Planning and California Probate Reporter*, Vol. X, No. 4, p. 108, (Feb. 1989).]

Accumulation of Income

The annual exclusion for a gift of a present interest is lost if the trustee is given the power to accumulate income without the concurrent power to pay it out.

Effect of Donor Control

The donor who tries to retain control over the trust risks defeating its purpose. A donor does not escape tax if he or she retains rights over the trust income or property that (1) cause the income to be taxed or (2) make the trust taxable for estate tax purposes at the donor's death. To avoid taxation to the donor, then, the trust must be irrevocable, which means that title cannot revert to the donor, nor can the donor and a **nonadverse party** have the power to revest title in the donor (IRC § 676). A nonadverse party is any party who is not an adverse party [IRC § 672(b)], and an **adverse party** is any party having a substantial beneficial interest in a trust who would be adversely affected by the exercise or nonexercise of the power he or she possesses respecting the trust [IRC § 672(a)]. A person having a

---

TERMS

nonadverse party Any party who is not an adverse party.

adverse party Any party having a substantial beneficial interest in a trust who would be adversely affected by the exercise or nonexercise of the power he or she possesses respecting the trust.

general power of appointment over the trust property is deemed to have a beneficial interest in the trust.

The trustee of an irrevocable trust, in order to avoid taxation, cannot have the power to distribute income to the donor or the donor's spouse, to hold or accumulate income for future distribution to the donor or the spouse, or to apply the payment of premiums on policies of life insurance on the donor or spouse (except for policies irrevocably payable to charities), regardless of whether the income is actually distributed, accumulated, or applied to life insurance premiums. Under Internal Revenue Code section 677(b), if the income of a trust is in fact distributed or applied for the support or maintenance of a beneficiary (other than the donor's spouse after October 10, 1969) who the donor is legally obligated to support or maintain, the income is taxed to the donor. Also, under Internal Revenue Code section 2041, the property may be included in the estate of the donor.

The power of the independent trustee to sprinkle income is another power that a donor of an irrevocable trust cannot hold. Such a power, if held by the donor, especially in a trust with the power to accumulate income, may result in taxability to the donor under Internal Revenue Code section 2036 unless the power is tested by an ascertainable standard.

Powers of Appointment—General and Special

A power of appointment is the power given by a donor to any person to decide who is to receive the property given by the donor and how it is to be divided among those persons. A power of appointment is defined in Regulation 20.2042.1(c) as any power of appointment "exercisable in favor of the decedent, his estate, his creditors, or the creditors of his estate, except (i) joint powers, to the extent provided in 20.2041-2 and 20.2041-3, and (ii) certain powers limited by an ascertainable standard, to the extent provided in subparagraph (2) of this paragraph." For example, a man frequently leaves property to his wife with a general power of appointment to decide who is to get what is left of it upon her death. In default of his wife's exercising that right, he may provide that the remaining property go to charities or other named persons. The husband (donor) remains the maker of the gift, and the wife (donee of the power of appointment) is merely his agent. She herself does not make a gift. If the husband gives the wife a general power of appointment, she may leave the property to anyone. If he gives her only a special power of appointment, she can divide the property only among a specified group of individuals, such as children, nieces, and nephews.

Giving the donee a special power of appointment avoids a completed gift. An example of such a provision follows.

B. Upon the death of a child the trust share shall terminate and vest in and be distributed to one or more persons in the class consisting of the child's surviving issue and spouse, or if no issue survives such child, to one or more persons, excluding the child's estate, his or her creditors and the creditors of his or her estate, and upon such limitations and estates as such child shall appoint by an instrument in writing other than a will delivered to the Trustee during the child's lifetime or by a will or codicil specifically referring to and exercising this limited testamentary power of appointment. Any trust property not validly appointed under this paragraph shall vest in and be distributed to the child's then living issue, by right of representation, and if there are no descendants of the child then living, the Trustee shall distribute the balance of the trust in and to my then living issue, by right of representation, provided the share of any person for whom a trust is then being administered under this will shall be added to such trust for administration and distribution.

Disclaimers and Powers of Appointment

A general power of appointment is the equivalent of owning the property, since a person holding such property can take it for himself or herself. Therefore, such property can be taxed in the gross estate of the person holding that power unless it is renounced by a disclaimer within nine months after its discovery.

California Probate Code section 279 governs the time for filing disclaimers. A disclaimer must be filed within a reasonable time, as defined by that section, after the person able to disclaim acquires knowledge of the interest. Under subsection (a)(3) of that section, interests resulting from the exercise or nonexercise of a nontestamentary power of appointment are deemed created by the donee of the power for purposes of California Probate Code Chapter 2. On the other hand, holding a special power of appointment does not cause the property to be included in the gross estate.

A power in a trust is not deemed to be a general power of appointment if it is limited by an "ascertainable standard" relating to the "health, education, support or maintenance" (or any combination thereof) of the decedent. *Support* and *maintenance* are synonymous and are not limited to the bare necessities of life. Powers limited by the requisite standard are powers exercisable for the holder's "support," "support in reasonable comfort," "support in his accustomed manner of living," "education, including college and professional education," "health," and "medical, dental, hospital and nursing expenses and expenses of invalidism" [Reg. 20.2041-1(c)(2)]. It is immaterial whether the beneficiary is required to exhaust his or her other income before the power can be exercised. A power to use profit for the "comfort, welfare, or happiness" of the donee is not an ascertainable standard [Reg. 20.2041-1(c)(2)].

The drafter of the trust should be careful not to add any words to the permissible ones of "health, education, maintenance, or support." Adding only one word may, and frequently has, caused the income to be taxed to the donor. The donor is not taxed under federal law, however, if the donor's power is exercisable only while the beneficiary is under the age of twenty-one (or in California, under the age of eighteen). If the donor is not a California resident, he or she is taxed on the income only to the extent it is derived from sources in California.

Distributable net income (DNI) is the amount of income on which the beneficiaries of an estate or trust are actually taxed, that is, their taxable income.

Sprinkling Power and Sprinkling Trusts

Sprinkling power pertains to a clause within a trust. Trusts containing such clauses are referred to as **sprinkling trusts** or **discretionary trusts**. A distinction is made, however, between sprinkling power, referring to a trust sprinkling income only by an ascertainable standard, and sprinkling trust, referring to distributions of both principal and income.

Under a sprinkling trust, the trustee must be an independent trustee. The trustee has power to exercise his or her own discretion in the distribution of both income and principal to the persons specified under the trust agreement. The donor must not have any control over the distributions, although limited investment control by the donor is permitted. Guidelines from the donor are permissible to help the trustee carry out the intentions of the donor and also may avoid arguments among the beneficiaries.

The power of the independent trustee to sprinkle income is a power that a donor cannot hold. A sprinkling power simply means that the trustee has discretion in the distribution of income only and that the discretion is limited by an "ascertainable standard," or in the language of Internal Revenue Code Section 674(d), "a reasonably definite external

---

TERMS

distributable net come (DNI)   The amount of income on which the beneficiaries of an estate or trust are actually taxed, that is, their taxable income.

sprinkling power   A trustee's power to distribute income that is limited by an ascertainable standard, or a reasonably definite external standard that is set forth in the trust instrument.

sprinkling trust†   A trust whose income the trustee may distribute among its beneficiaries as, when, and in the amounts he or she chooses.

discretionary trust†   A trust in which broad discretion is vested in the trustee and is to be exercised by him or her in carrying out the purposes of the trust.

standard which is set forth in the trust instrument." The trustee may be anyone other than the donor and the donor's spouse who is living with the donor. The trustee is given the power to do whatever he or she deems best when distributing the income, considering tax savings and the needs of the beneficiaries. The income of the beneficiaries may vary from year to year. The trustee may make a distribution that is either desirable or undesirable from a tax viewpoint if the needs of the beneficiaries so require in the trustee's discretion. If a trustee has the power to sprinkle income and distribute according to the beneficiaries' needs and their tax identities, however, transfers to beneficiaries may not be eligible for the annual exclusion as a gift of a present interest unless the trust also provides for *Crummey* withdrawal rights.

Internal Revenue Code section 2503(c) provides that no part of a gift to an individual under twenty-one years of age on the date of transfer shall be considered a gift of a future interest for purposes of the annual exclusion in section 2503(b) if the property and income from it may be expended for the donee before he or she is twenty-one, if property not so expended will pass to the donee upon reaching twenty-one, and if the property will be payable to the donee's estate or as the donee may appoint under a general power of appointment, as defined in section 2514 (c), if the donee dies before the age of twenty-one.

Funding the Trust

The assets transferred to the trust must be income-producing or the donor will not be able to shift income to save taxes and may have to pay a gift tax. Also, an annual exclusion for gifts may not be available if the income interest in the property is not producing income, as the gift becomes one of future interest unless there is also a *Crummey* power. It may be best to give the trustee the power to exchange assets. Assets that are likely to appreciate might be included, as they will then escape being taxed in the donor's estate at a higher value after they have appreciated. But consideration should be given to transferring these assets if the trust is to be a short-term trust or if the donor is expected to die soon.

Care should be taken in transferring appreciated property to a trust where sale of the property is likely to be made within two years. A special tax is imposed on a trust that sells the property within two years after transfer if the fair market value exceeds the price, if any, paid by the trust, and the property is sold at a gain. An amount is imposed that is equal to the tax the transferor would have had to pay if he or she had disposed of the property in the same taxable year in which the trust disposed of it. This special tax, however, is not imposed if the transferor dies within two years of the date of the transfer to the trust [IRC § 644(e)]. Nor does this tax apply to property acquired by the trust from a decedent, a pooled income fund, or a charitable remainder annuity trust or unitrust [IRC § 644(e)].

Since the main purpose of the trust usually is to save taxes, assets should not be transferred if the donor might lose tax benefits. If assets are already tax-sheltered, they probably should not be transferred into a trust, nor should assets be transferred where tax benefits might be lost, such as for percentage depletion assets [see IRC § 613(a)].

Classes of Trusts

Under both California and federal law, trusts are divided into two classes: (1) the simple trust, and (2) the complex trust. Both California law and federal law provide separate rules for taxing the beneficiaries of these two types of trusts. California law conforms closely to federal law.

One difference in California law is that there is no law comparable to the federal "sixty-five-day rule," which permits a trustee to elect to treat any distribution to a beneficiary made within sixty-five days after the end of the year as having been made in the prior year. Also, California law refers to income accumulated before age eighteen rather than twenty-one as under federal law.

Simple Trust

A trust is a **simple trust** only if it (1) requires that the income of the trust be distributed to its beneficiaries, and (2) does not provide for any distribution to a charity. In a simple trust, income is accumulated and distributed annually to the beneficiaries, who pay a tax on the amounts distributed.

Complex Trust

A **complex trust** is any trust other than a simple trust. Such a trust can accumulate income or distribute its income to a charity.

TERMS

simple trust†   A straightforward conveyance of property to one person for the use of another, without further specifications or directions.

complex trust   Any trust other than a simple trust.

Throwback Rule

The throwback rule applies only in complex or accumulation trusts, not in simple trusts. In a complex trust, an **accumulation distribution** occurs when there is an excess after deducting (1) any income required to be distributed currently, (2) amounts distributable at the discretion of the trustee, and (3) deductions for charitable contributions [see IRC, §§ 661(a), 665(a), 665(b), 665(d); Reg. § 1.661(a)-2]. In later years, when distributions are made to the beneficiaries in excess of the distributable net income of the trust in that year, the beneficiaries may be taxed under the **throwback rule** (IRC §§ 665–668).

The purpose is to cause the beneficiaries who receive the income to pay the same tax on it they would have paid if they had received it in the year in which it was accumulated for their benefit.

The reason behind the throwback rule is that permitting a trust to accumulate income in the trust provides too much opportunity to avoid tax. The income accumulated (after payment of a tax by the trust) becomes a part of the corpus, or principal, of the trust. When principal is distributed to a beneficiary, it usually is not taxable income, but a distribution of income is taxable to the beneficiary.

When accumulated income is actually distributed, under the throwback rule, the beneficiary's tax bracket will have to be compared with that of the trust. If the beneficiary would have paid more than the trust paid, he or she will have to pay an extra tax in the amount of the difference. Since accumulating income makes more record-keeping for the trustee, if the beneficiaries are in a higher tax bracket than the trust, it is unlikely there is any reason to accumulate the income rather than distribute it annually.

The throwback rule was changed in 1969 and again under the Tax Reform Act of 1976, which applies to tax years commencing after 1975.

Exceptions

Under the Tax Reform Act of 1976, distributions to persons under twenty-one years of age are excepted from the throwback rule. Special rules

---

TERMS

accumulation distribution Distribution of the excess after deducting (1) any income required to be distributed currently, (2) amounts distributable at the discretion of the trustee, and (3) deductions for charitable contributions.

throwback rule Under this rule, trust income in a complex or accumulation trust that is over and above the ordinary net income is carried back to the distribution year or taxed to the beneficiary as if it had been distributed to the beneficiary in the year accumulated.

apply to beneficiaries of multiple trusts, however, regardless of whether they are under age twenty-one [see IRC §§ 666(e), 667, 6401(b)].

The Tax Reform Act of 1976 repealed the capital gains throwback rule entirely. The repeal is effective for distributions in tax years after 1975. The former rule operated only when an accumulation distribution exceeded the trust's accumulated ordinary income. The gain was thrown back only to tax years after 1968. In other words, since 1976, if the trust makes a sale and keeps the proceeds so that it has to pay a capital gains tax at the end of the year, and later distributes the proceeds, no further **capital gains tax** will be due.

The Tax Reform Act of 1976 made a further change, found in Internal Revenue Code section 665(b), which reads: "If the amounts properly paid, credited, or required to be distributed by the trust for the taxable year do not exceed the income of the trust for such year, there shall be no accumulation distribution for such year." This provision applies to distributions made in taxable years beginning after December 31, 1975. If the trust's accounting income is greater than its distributable net income, this provision will prevent a current year's distribution to a beneficiary from being treated as an accumulation distribution.

Spendthrift Trust

A **spendthrift clause** is added to a trust principally to protect the trust against claims of creditors. The pertinent language of the clause might read in part:

> The trustee shall not recognize any transfer, mortgage, pledge, **hypothecation**, order, or assignment of any beneficiary by way of anticipation of income or principal. The income and principal of any trust hereunder shall not be subject to transfer by operation of law, and shall be exempt from the claims of creditors or other claimants, and from

---

TERMS

capital gains tax†   Income tax upon financial gain resulting from the sale or exchange of capital assets.

spendthrift clause   A protective clause in a trust to prevent creditors from making claims on the beneficiary's interest and to prevent bankruptcy.

hypothecation†   A pledge in which the pledged property remains in the possession of the debtor.

orders, decrees, levies, **attachments**, **garnishments**, executions, and other legal or equitable process or proceedings to the fullest extent permissible by law.

The spendthrift clause may be added because the donor anticipates that a particular donee or donees might incur debts that could become liens on the trust. [See *Johnson v. First National Bank of Jackson,* 386 So. 2d 1112 (Miss. 1980).]

Five-by-Five Power

A power in a trust giving the beneficiary a right to withdraw annually $5,000 or five percent of the total amount of the principal of the trust, whichever is greater, is called a **five-by-five power**. The amount withdrawn is nontaxable, but the power is noncumulative. For example, the beneficiary may not skip the withdrawal one year and take out $10,000 the next year. Either the withdrawal is made or the beneficiary loses the right to make the withdrawal until the following year.

One disadvantage of the five-by-five power is that in the year the holder of the power dies, $5,000 or five percent of the amount of the principal, whichever is greater, will be added into the holder's estate, whether or not the holder actually withdrew the funds during the year in which he or she died, since the holder is held to have a general power of appointment in the year of his or her death to make the withdrawal. The beneficiary also may incur taxation he or she does not desire by virtue of having the power.

The five-by-five power has been used less since the Economic Recovery Tax Act of 1981, which introduced the $10,000 annual exclusion.

TERMS

attachment† The process by which a person's property is figuratively brought into court to ensure satisfaction of a judgment that may be rendered against that person.

garnishment† A proceeding by a creditor to obtain satisfaction of a debt from money or property of the debtor which is in the possession of a third person or is owed by such a person to the debtor.

five-by-five power The power given to a trustee to take from the trust principal an amount not exceeding $5,000 or five percent of the principal, whichever is greater.

Clifford Trust

The **Clifford trust** is an irrevocable trust that is not permanent. Before the Tax Reform Act of 1986, the term of the trust had to be ten years or longer to avoid the donor being regarded as the owner of the trust, in which event the income of the trust would be taxed to the donor and the purpose of the trust defeated. Neither the corpus nor the income could revert to the donor within ten years after the transfer. If the grantor's reversionary interest took effect only on the death of the beneficiary of the income, the grantor was not treated as the owner, regardless of the beneficiary's life expectancy. This applies to trusts made before March 2, 1986.

For trusts made after March 1, 1986, the Tax Reform Act of 1986 provides that the grantor of any portion of a trust in which he or she has a reversionary interest in either the corpus or income therefrom will be treated as the owner if, at the inception of that portion of the trust, the value of the interest exceeds five percent of the value of that portion. An exemption applies for a reversionary interest taking effect upon the death of a minor lineal descendant (under age twenty-one) if the beneficiary has the entire present interest in the trust or a trust portion [IRC § 673 (b)]. Also for trusts made after March 1, 1986, the Tax Reform Act of 1986 enacted a **spousal attribution rule** that treats the grantor as holding a power or interest if the grantor's spouse is living with the grantor at the time of the creation of the power or interest. California law conforms to these amendments.

The Technical and Miscellaneous Revenue Act of 1988 (TAMRA) further expanded the spousal attribution rule to include a spouse who marries a grantor after the creation of the power or interest. Individuals are not to be considered married if they are legally separated under a decree of divorce or separate maintenance. The grantor is also to be treated as the owner if the grantor's spouse is a trustee or more than half the trustees are related to subordinate parties subservient to the wishes of the grantor's spouse [IRC § 672(e)]. California follows most of the 1986 Tax Reform Act, a check of California law should be made regarding whether California has conformed to this 1988 amendment. The laws on trusts change as frequently as the tax laws, so the legal assistant should always check for the latest amendments or changes.

TERMS

Clifford trust A temporary trust for not less than ten years at the expiration of which the donor receives back his or her property.

spousal attribution rule A rule for trusts that treats the grantor as holding a power or interest if the grantor's spouse is living with the grantor at the time of the creation of the power or interest.

This type of trust is used primarily as an income tax-saving device. The donor is usually in a high income tax bracket, or at least a higher bracket than that of the donee who is usually in a low income tax bracket. The income of the trust is taxed to the beneficiary. Typically, a parent establishes this trust for a child. The parent may donate an income-producing asset, the income of which will flow to the child. The trust cannot be used for the benefit of a spouse or for a child whom the donor has a legal obligation to support, but it can be used for an adult child. The income will be taxed to the grantor to the extent the income is used to support the child. State laws must be examined to ascertain the obligations of the donor. This trust also is utilized for aged relatives in a lower income bracket.

The transfer of funds to the Clifford trust is subject to gift taxes, called **unitary transfer taxes**, based on a valuation of the right to receive the property over the ten-year period. Also, the donor has a reversionary interest in the trust. If he or she should die within the ten-year period, the value of that reversionary interest (roughly forty-four percent of its original value) will be included and taxed in his or her gross estate. Discount tables are available in the code to fix the value. If the donor dies after the ten-year period, the trust property will revert to the donor and will be taxed in his or her gross estate.

SIDEBAR

The term **pipe dream trust** has been used to describe the kind of a trust that people would like to have, but that does not exist. Parents or grandparents would like to set up a trust that would save taxes for them while helping their children and lineal descendants, but at the same time, they would like to manage the property, decide when and how much the children take, and also have it for their own use if they have financial reverses or find they need more than anticipated. In reality, trusts are governed by specific laws that must be considered.

For a full discussion of the pipe dream trust see Cohan, *Drafting California Irrevocable Inter Vivos Trusts* (CEB), p. 76, *et seq.*

TERMS

unitary transfer taxes   Gift taxes on the transfer of funds to a Clifford trust based on a valuation of the right to receive the property over a ten-year period.

pipe dream trust   An ideal trust that does not actually exist in which the donors could save taxes while helping their children and lineal descendants and still manage the property, decide when and how much the children would take, and have the assets for their own use should they need them.

Trusts—Minors

Gifts to Minors

Under Internal Revenue Code section 2503(b), the $10,000 exclusion applies to gifts to minors, and such gifts qualify as present interests under section 2503(c) if the property and income may be expended by or for the benefit of the donee before he or she is twenty-one or, if not so expended, pass to the donee when he or she attains the age of twenty-one, or if the proceeds are payable to the estate of the donee, if the donee dies before age twenty-one, or to such person as he or she may appoint under a general power of appointment as defined in section 2514(c) (see Reg. 25.2503-4). An unrestricted power of appointment is deemed safest in order to qualify as a present interest. When the minor reaches age twenty-one, he or she may elect to have the trust continue past age twenty-one.

Not all donors want the donee to have all the principal at age twenty-one. A typical device used in trusts is to give a percentage of the principal at different ages, such as twenty-five, thirty, and so on. The distribution of the corpus at a later age, for example, age twenty-five, is a gift of a future interest.

The section 2503(c) limitation led to the evolution of the so-called *Crummey* trust, which not only retains the present interest exclusion but also permits the distribution of the trust at the ages desired or after death of the primary beneficiary.

Window Minor's Trust

Internal Revenue Code section 2503(c) trusts for minors contemplate that the corpus will be distributed to the minor at age twenty-one but do permit the trust agreement to provide for the donee to extend the trust when he or she reaches age twenty-one. The trust instrument also may provide for the minor to be given an option, within a specified time, to receive the trust corpus. If the minor does not exercise this option, the right lapses and the corpus stays in the trust for the period specified in the trust agreement until the minor is older. This limited time period aspect, based on section 2503(c), is referred to as a **window minor's trust**.

Transfers to the trust after the minor reaches age twenty-one ordinarily are not made because once the minor beneficiary reaches age twenty-one,

---

TERMS

window minor's trust   A trust for minors that contemplates distribution once the minor reaches age twenty-one but that provides for the donee to extend the trust beyond that time.

transfers to a trust for his or her benefit are regarded as gifts of future interests and will not have the benefit of the $10,000 annual exclusion unless other provisions, such as the *Crummey* right of withdrawal, are included in the trust.

Crummey Trusts

The *Crummey* trust stems from the case *Crummey v. Commissioner* 397 F.2d 82 (9th Cir. 1978). The "*Crummey* power" was set out in the following provision of the trust in question:

> THREE. Additions. The Trustee may receive any other real or personal property from the Trustors (or either of them) or from any other person or persons, by lifetime gift, under a Will or Trust from any other source. Such property will be held by the Trustee subject to the terms of this Agreement. A donor may designate or allocate all of his gift to one or more Trusts, or in stated amounts to different Trusts. If the donor does not specifically designate what amount of his gift is to augment each Trust, the Trustee shall divide such gift equally between the Trusts then existing, established by this Agreement. The Trustee agrees, if he accepts such additions, to hold and manage such additions in trust for the uses and in the manner set forth herein. With respect to such additions, each child of the Trustors may demand at any time (up to and including December 31 of the year in which a transfer to his or her Trust has been made) the sum of Four Thousand Dollars ($4,000.00) or the amount of the transfer from each donor, whichever is less, payable in cash immediately upon receipt by the Trustee of the demand in writing and in any event, not later than December 31 in the year in which such transfer was made. Such payment shall be made from the gift of that donor for that year. If a child is a minor at the time of such gift of that donor for that year, or fails in legal capacity for any reason, the child's guardian may make such demand on behalf of the child. The property received pursuant to the demand shall be held by the guardian for the benefit and use of the child.

Three of the children under this trust were minors. The Tax Court held that gifts to the adult child under this trust were of a present interest but denied the annual exclusion of the gifts to the minors because the gifts were of a future interest [*Crummey*, 25 T.C.M. 772 (CCH), 35 T.C.M. ¶¶ 66,

---

TERMS

Crummey **trust**   Name given to a trust stemming from case of *Crummey v. Commissioner*, 397 F.2d 82.

144 (PH) (1966)]. The Ninth Circuit reversed, holding that a guardian could be appointed for the minors, who resided in California, and a timely demand could be made by the guardian so they could take charge of the funds. The trust should provide the minors enough time to permit a guardian to be appointed and to make the withdrawal. Since California law requires a fifteen-day notice, fifteen days is the minimum time. Some attorneys never provide for less than thirty days, and some prefer thirty to sixty days.

Even if the donee is obliged under the trust to demand distribution in writing within a limited period of time or lose the right, the transfer is of a present interest under the *Crummey* doctrine as long as the terms and duration are reasonable.

The Internal Revenue Service has accepted the *Crummey* holding in Rev. Rul. 73-405 (1973-2 C.B. 321). The ruling states: "[I]f there is no impediment under the trust or local law to the appointment of a guardian and the minor donee has a right to demand distribution, the transfer is a gift of a present interest that qualifies for the annual exclusion allowable under section 2503(b) of the Code." (Revenue Ruling 54-91 has been revoked.)

If a *Crummey* trust is created, say, for the benefit of four children, four separate shares should be set up. Then $40,000 may be transferred (or $80,000 if a husband and wife are donors or agree to split gifts) and qualify for the annual exclusion.

In a *Crummey* trust, the beneficiary has a power to withdraw specified amounts for a limited period of time. If this power to withdraw refers specifically to Internal Revenue Code section 2503(b), only $3,000 can be withdrawn if the trust was executed on or before September 12, 1981, and not since amended. The trust may be one that is irrevocable and cannot be amended. In that event, it may be necessary to establish a new trust, in which case contributions to the old trust should be limited to $3,000.

Deciding to Use the *Crummey* Trust

Alternatives to the *Crummey* trust should be considered. An outright gift in the amount of the $10,000 annual exclusion can be made without any trust. A gift may be made to minors under Internal Revenue Code sections 2503(b) and 2503(c). By testamentary trust or devise, a gift can be postponed to the death of the donor. A trust can be set up for a gift of a future interest, which would not qualify for the annual exclusion, but the donor may be willing to pay the tax to accomplish his or her purposes.

California Uniform Transfers to Minors Act

In 1984, the California Uniform Gifts to Minors Act was repealed and the California Uniform Transfers to Minors Act was enacted. The latter act sets forth a method for making gifts to minors that are to be held, managed, and invested by a custodian; expended for the support, maintenance, education, and benefit of the minors; and distributed to the minors at age eighteen (Prob. Code § 3909). In specified instances, the act permits a custodianship to continue after the minor attains the age of eighteen, but not beyond age twenty-one or twenty-five, depending upon the method of transfer that created the custodianship, if there is express provision for the higher age, as specified (Prob. Code § 3920.5). The act also provides for the transfer of property to minors, to be held by a custodian, from parties indebted to minors and authorizes transfers from trusts, estates, and guardianships.

Civil Code section 3914 directs the custodian to pay to or expend for the minor's benefit as much of the custodial property as the custodian deems advisable for the use and benefit of the minor, without court order, without regard to other income or property of the minor that may be applicable or available for that purpose, and without regard to the duty or ability of the custodian or any other person to support the minor.

The act is contained in Probate Code section 3900 *et seq.* and should be read in its entirety.

Generation-Skipping Transfer Tax

Prior to 1977, estate taxes could be avoided by passing property to successive generations through the use of long-term trusts. The amounts of the income to be paid to the beneficiaries were specified, and usually the right to principal for support was limited. For example, a wealthy grandparent would set up a trust providing that the income from the trust be paid to their children for life. When these children died, the income would be paid to the grandchildren. Upon the death of the grandchildren, the principal might have been distributed to the great-grandchildren.

These trusts were subject only to the rule against perpetuities. The most common rule against perpetuities was probably lives in being plus twenty-one years. Some states limited the duration of such trusts. In California, the rule against perpetuities was found in Civil Code section 715.2, which has been repealed. Civil Code section 715 now provides that a lease to commence at a time certain or upon the happening of a future event becomes invalid if its term does not actually commence in possession within thirty years after its execution.

The federal statutes creating and governing the generation-skipping tax enacted by the Tax Reform Act of 1976 are found at Internal Revenue

Code section 2601 *et seq*. The tax as formerly written applied generally to transfers made after June 11, 1976. A generation-skipping tax was not imposed on an irrevocable trust in existence on June 11, 1976, if a transfer was not made out of corpus added to the trust after June 11, 1976, and the testator died before a certain date. On such earlier trusts, then, the only tax consequences were gift taxes on the original transfer into the trust and an estate tax at the death of the great-grandchildren.

The Tax Reform Act of 1986 changed the generation-skipping tax. Chapter 13 of the Internal Revenue Code of 1954 was repealed retroactive to 1976, with a minor exception applying to persons who executed wills before September 25, 1985, and who died before January 1, 1987. The generation-skipping tax was further amended and changed by the Technical and Miscellaneous Revenue Act of 1988. Under this new law, a tax is imposed on every generation-skipping transfer under a trust or trust equivalent. A generation-skipping transfer is defined in Internal Revenue Code section 2611(a) as "(1) a taxable distribution, (2) a taxable termination, and (3) a direct skip." A **trust equivalent** includes any arrangement that, although it is not a trust, has substantially the same effect and may include life estates and remainder estates for years and insurance and annuity contracts (IRC § 2663). The tax is the same amount as the maximum federal estate tax in effect under Internal Revenue Code section 2001 at the time of the taxable distribution, taxable termination, or direct skip, and the inclusion ratio in effect at the time [IRC §§ 2641 (a), (b), 2642(a)].

Exclusions from the tax are found in Internal Revenue Code section 2611(b) and include "any transfer to the extent . . . the transferee in the prior transfer was assigned to the same generation as (or a lower generation than) the generation assignment of the transferee in this transfer." The annual gift tax exclusion of $10,000 per donee and payments for tuition and medical expenses are exempt from the tax. There is also a generation-skipping tax exemption of $1,000,000 for an individual transferor, that he or she may allocate among generation-skipping transfers. This exemption is transferable between spouses. In addition, there is a $2,000,000 exemption for direct gifts to a grandchild if made before 1990 (the so-called "Gallo" exemption). This exemption must be viewed in light of the present gift tax, as gift taxes will have to be paid. However, federal legislation has been introduced to extend the 1990 date indefinitely. Also, there is an

---

TERMS

trust equivalent Any arrangement that, although not a trust, has substantially the same effect as a trust, including life estates and remainder estates for years and insurance and annuity contracts.

exemption for direct skips to grandchildren if the grandchild's parent is deceased at the time of transfer [IRC § 2612(c)].

There must be two lower generations. Who is a **lower generation beneficiary?** The donor's spouse and brothers and sisters are of the same generation, regardless of their actual ages. **Lineal descendants** are younger generation beneficiaries. Children, nieces, and nephews and their spouses are lower generation beneficiaries. Legally adopted children are in the same class. Grandchildren, grandnieces, and grandnephews are a second lower generation. **Nonlineal descendants,** beneficiaries who are not related, are assigned to a generation on the basis of their birthdates. A person born no more than twelve and one-half years before or after the donor's generation is in the same generation. Any beneficiary born more than twelve and one-half years after the donor but not more than thirty-seven and one-half years later is of a younger generation. Thereafter, a lower generation is assigned for each successive twenty-five years [IRC § 2651(d)].

If a donor leaves a trust for a friend who is eleven years younger, with a remainder to a friend who is forty years younger, it is not a generation-skipping trust. If the trust is for a friend who is twenty years younger, with the remainder to a friend who is forty years younger, it is a generation-skipping trust.

Generation-skipping transfers occur whenever there is a taxable distribution from the trust or a taxable termination (by death, lapse of time, exercise or nonexercise, or otherwise) [see IRC § 2613(b)] to a generation-skipping heir.

Taxable Distribution

A **taxable distribution** is any distribution from a trust to a skip person, other than a taxable termination or a direct skip [IRC § 2612(b)]. If both income and principal are distributed in the same taxable year, the income is deemed to go first to the oldest generation [IRC § 2613(a)(2)]. An

---

TERMS

lower generation beneficiary A beneficiary of a generation that is younger than the donor such as children, nieces, and nephews, and their spouses, and grandchildren, grandnieces, and grandnephews.

lineal descendant† A person in the direct line of descent such as one's child, grandchild, or great-grandchild.

nonlineal descendant A beneficiary who is not related but is assigned to a generation on the basis of his or her birthdate.

taxable distribution Any distribution from a trust to a skip person, other than a taxable termination or a direct skip.

individual with a future interest is not considered a younger generation beneficiary in this context.

Taxable Termination

A **taxable termination** means the termination (by death, lapse of time, release of power, or otherwise) of an interest in trust property unless, immediately after termination, a nonskip person has an interest in the property or, at no time after such termination, may a distribution (including a distribution or taxation) be made from a trust to a skip person. A **direct skip** is a transfer subject to a tax imposed on an interest in property transferred to a skip person.

A **skip person** is an individual who is at least two generations younger than the transferor. A **nonskip person** is of the same generation or one generation younger than the transferor. A taxable termination occurs when a present interest of a younger generation beneficiary, who is a member of a generation older than that of any other younger generation beneficiary, terminates. The effective date of the termination is the date of the last termination. No generation-skipping tax is levied if the transfer is subject to an estate or gift tax.

The tax is paid out of the trust property. The trust is entitled to a credit for charitable deductions as specified [IRC § 2602(c)(2)]; for unused portion of the unified credit [IRC § 2602(c)(3)]; for tax on prior transfers [IRC § 2602(c)(4)]; for certain administrative expenses [IRC § 2602(c)(5)]; and for state death taxes as specified [IRC § 2602(c)(5)(B)].

A generation-skipping transfer arrangement includes any arrangement that has substantially the same effect as a trust, though not a trust. Examples are arrangements as to life estates and remainders, estates for

---

TERMS

taxable termination The termination, by death, lapse of time, release of power, or otherwise, of an interest in trust property unless, immediately after termination, a nonskip person has an interest in the property or, at no time after such termination, may a distribution (including a distribution or taxation) be made from a trust to a skip person.

direct skip A transfer subject to a tax imposed on an interest in property transferred to a skip person.

skip person An individual who is at least two generations younger than the transferor.

nonskip person An individual who is of the same generation or one generation younger than the transferor.

years, insurance and annuities, and other arrangements for splitting enjoyment of assets between generations [IRC § 2611(d)].

$250,000 Exclusion

Formerly there was an exclusion of $250,000 on transfers to grandchildren. This exclusion was allowed to any **deemed transferor**. A deemed transferor was the parent of the transferee of the trust property who is most closely related to the grantor of the trust, whether or not the parent was living at the time of transfer. The deemed transferor was the key to the tax. For example, say the donor had five children, and four of his five children had one child each, and the remaining child had four children. If the donor left a life interest to his children and the remainders to his grandchildren, the amount of exclusion was limited by the number of children (5), not the number of grandchildren (8). Thus $1,250,000 ($250,000 × 5) was excludable, not $2,000,000 ($250,000 × 8). The "deemed transferor" concept was eliminated by the Tax Reform Act of 1986.

California's Tax

The California generation-skipping tax is imposed if death occurred after September 26, 1977, and the transferor was a California resident at the time of transfer or the property transferred is real or personal property in California. It is sometimes referred to as a pickup tax, as is California's estate tax. If the federal generation-skipping tax involves property in California and in another state, the California tax would be in proportion to the total federal credit. A federal credit is allowed for up to five percent of the generation-skipping tax paid to California.

TERMS

deemed transferor   A person who is regarded as being the one who transferred the property.

CHAPTER 15

PROBATE ETHICS AND PRACTICE

§ 15.1   Ethics and the Probate Paralegal

There are not two sets of rules of ethics, one for attorneys and one for paralegals. The rules that govern attorneys should be adequate for paralegals. Some of the rules are plain common sense. See the chapter on ethics for legal assistants in *California Paralegal's Guide* (Fourth Edition) by the author, which discusses factors such as competence, integrity, client confidences, and handling of trust funds as they relate to the professional responsibility of the attorney. That chapter also discusses the Code of Ethics and Professional Responsibility of the National Association of Legal Assistants, Inc., the Affirmation of Responsibility of the National Federation of Paralegal Associations, the State Bar of California's Rules of Professional Conduct, and the American Bar Association's Model Rules of Professional Conduct. The legal assistant should read and become familiar with all of these publications.

The American Bar Association's Model Rules of Professional Conduct contains one specific rule [(Rule 1.8(h)] regarding **malpractice**, which reads as follows:

> A lawyer shall not make an agreement prospectively limiting the lawyer's liability to a client for malpractice unless permitted by law and the client is independently represented in making the agreement, or settle a claim for such liability with an unrepresented client or former client without first advising that person in writing that independent representation is appropriate in connection therewith.

The Comment on limiting liability states that this paragraph "is not intended to apply to customary qualifications and limitations in legal opinions and memoranda."

According to Mallen and Levit, there were almost as many reported malpractice decisions between 1970 and 1980 as in the previous history of American jurisprudence [*Legal Malpractice* (Second Edition), p. v]. Malpractice claims can arise out of probate matters as well as in any other field of law. Statistics of the National Legal Malpractice Data Center Study in 1981 show that out of a total of 7,021 malpractice claims, 510 were in estates and trusts (7.3%). Estates and trusts ranked fifth among the various fields in frequency of malpractice claims.

TERMS

malpractice†   The failure of a professional person to act with reasonable care; misconduct by a professional person in the course of engaging in his profession.

§ 15.2 Docketing and Deadline Control

Studies by the National Legal Malpractice Data Center have shown that 26.24% of all claims were attributable to administrative errors, directly related to docket control. Another 15.62% were due to client relations problems, making a total of 41.86% resulting from poor business management. This seems to be a high percentage of problems in areas in which they could be eliminated with relative ease.

A legal assistant must develop a system for complying with all "deadlines, statutory limitations, law and motion matters, trial setting dates, and other dates that must be remembered" (Levit, *Malpractice Prevention Checklist*). The probate legal assistant should set up docket controls where they do not exist and maintain those that do exist in dealing with the clients and keeping them advised. In a larger office, the system devised must be followed by all in the firm. A deadline control system reminds the attorney and staff of dates that require certain action to be taken. There are different systems by which this can be done, but some kind of system is imperative.

Important dates should be recorded and calendared. The legal assistant should establish due dates for each estate when the proceeding is commenced. Estates generally will have the same due dates, but dates may vary somewhat from estate to estate, depending on the size of the estate. For example, if no federal estate tax return needs to be filed, the due date for filing a return need not be calendared. The due dates should be reviewed by the attorney.

Files must be pulled on the due dates. Court dates must be prepared for in advance. More than one person should be aware of the "must do" dates. In a small office, for example, the dates may be recorded on the daily calendars for both the attorney and the legal assistant. One method used is to calendar not only the actual date, but also to calendar the same case a week to three weeks in advance as a reminder to prepare to take the action on the due date.

Depending on memory alone to remember deadlines in a law office is foolhardy. Missed deadlines, such as those for filing and tax payment due dates, may give rise to claims of malpractice. Extensions of time can be obtained in some instances to avoid penalty and interest assessments, but not always. Illness of the attorney, the legal assistant, the secretary, or another member of the staff can result in something not being done on time. Such eventualities must be guarded against with an effective deadline control system.

Although some deadlines may be, strictly speaking, the responsibility of the executor, if that person is inexperienced in probate matters, he or she ordinarily will depend upon the attorney's office for advice.

Statutes of Limitation

One of the most important deadlines is the **statute of limitations deadline.**

It is not always enough just to advise a client about a statute of limitations. The average layperson probably has never heard of a statute of limitations and does not know what it means and may not understand the importance or urgency of the attorney's information. The attorney must not only warn the client of such deadlines but also follow through on the warning.

In *Togstad v. Vesley, Adieu, Miller & Keefe*, 291 N.W.2d 686 (Mich. 1980), a prospective client consulted an attorney about whether he had a medical malpractice claim. Apparently, the attorney expressed doubts or uncertainty about such a claim, and the client left. Sometime later the client consulted another attorney, who was of the opinion that the client had a good medical malpractice claim except for the fact that the statute of limitations had run out by that time. The client sued the first attorney. The situation probably could have been avoided if the first attorney had advised the prospective client of the statute of limitations and the need to seek the advice of other counsel promptly in order to proceed, or if the first attorney had advised the client that the attorney had not determined the statute of limitations and that the client would need legal advice promptly to protect any possible claim.

See the discussion of statutes of limitation in Chapter 5 of *California Paralegal's Guide* (Fourth Edition) by the author.

§ 15.3 Liability to Nonclients— The Privity Test

Prior to 1958, under the **strict privity test** that governed, an attorney could not be held liable to a party who was not his or her client [*Buckley v. Gray*, 110 Cal. 339 (1895)]. In 1958, however, the case of *Biakanja v.*

TERMS

statute of limitations† A federal or state statute prescribing the maximum period of time during which a civil action or criminal prosecution can be brought after the occurrence of the injury or the offense.

strict privity test A test based on privity, which connotes an identity of interest, a close relationship that exists between two parties having some legal right.

Irving (49 Cal. 2d 647) held the opposite of the *Buckley* case. The will involved was denied probate because of improper attestation of the will and, as a result, an intended beneficiary received one-eighth of an estate rather than the entire estate [49 Cal. 2d at 650; see also *Lucas v. Hamm,* 56 Cal. 2d 583 (1961)]. A case may arise because a beneficiary served as a witness to the will, causing a loss or reduction in the inheritance, or because there were an insufficient number of witnesses. Other cases arise due to negligent advice to heirs, executors, and administrators. [See *Pete v. Henderson,* 155 Cal. App. 2d 772 (1957).] A paralegal may subject an attorney to a malpractice suit or disciplinary action through acts of commission, since he or she is performing duties that otherwise might be done by the attorney, or through acts of omission because of lack of knowledge.

§ 15.4 Conflict of Interest

As in other fields of law, a **conflict of interest** problem can arise for an attorney handling probate. An obvious one can occur in a will contest. An attorney may have been representing two persons and suddenly find that they have a will contest. For example, where an attorney has been representing both the **conservator** of a person and the conservator of the estate of the same person and the person dies, if a will contest develops between the two conservators, the attorney may feel that he or she cannot represent either conservator without a conflict of interest problem, particularly if bitter feelings are evidenced.

Attorneys are often drawn into representing persons who are friendly and in agreement at the outset, such as members of a family the attorney has known for years. After the death of a member of the family, the attorney is apt to represent the executor, the fiduciary. If the executor and the family later have adverse interests, the attorney's first duty is to the fiduciary.

A conflict of interest problem is not always self-evident or easily avoided. In estate matters, several beneficiaries may want and expect the attorney to represent them. They may even be offended if the attorney

---

TERMS

conflict of interest† The existence of a variance between the interests of the parties in a fiduciary relationship.

conservator† A person placed in charge of the property of an incompetent person by a court.

declines to do so. If the attorney does agree to represent all of them because it seems practical and will save expense, the attorney should at least keep a record and have an agreement about his or her duties. If the attorney undertakes representation of conflicting parties, however, he or she may be disqualified from representing any of the parties in future litigation and may have to spend considerable time as an unpaid witness in discovery proceedings.

If facts or issues are undisclosed to the attorney, conflicts may later occur. When an attorney finds himself or herself representing clients with adverse interests, the attorney may quickly withdraw unless he or she is satisfied that the conflict has been cured by an agreement between the parties. If there appears to be even a remote possibility that the parties might be in dispute, the safest course of action may be for the attorney to insist on independent counsel.

The legal assistant must be aware of potential problems and conflicts, since information of which the attorney was not aware may come to the legal assistant's attention first. It is probably unwise for an attorney to draw a will for someone and then later represent another person who contests that will, or for an attorney to represent more than one person who is contesting a will. The legal assistant should watch for this possibility.

§ 15.5 Time for Probating Estate

One of the biggest complaints in probate is that an undue amount of time is being taken to probate an estate. In California, there are set time limits for probating an estate. If these time limits cannot be met, the client, usually the executor or administrator, should be advised. If the client is working closely with the legal assistant, he or she will know what is happening and, if the estate cannot be closed, will know why it cannot be closed. Many times, however, the client is not informed about what is happening and does not know what is supposed to happen next. If the client receives no phone call or letter from the attorney's office and it appears that nothing is happening, the client may become annoyed. If heirs are phoning the client and asking for their money, the irritation may grow, especially if the client does not know what to tell them. The legal assistant can be responsible for keeping the probate client informed.

Malpractice claims have arisen from failure to keep the client informed and to calendar deadlines. Writing letters and making phone calls takes time and costs money, but it is good legal practice and the ethical way in which to handle matters. Any necessary delay should be explained to the client, and unnecessary delays should not be allowed to occur.

§ 15.6 Miscellaneous Considerations

Client Satisfaction

Happy, satisfied clients do not file malpractice lawsuits. The time it takes to keep a client happy produces recommendations from the client to other prospective clients and an absence of malpractice actions. Rules of good practice and professional relationships with clients apply to probate as well as to other fields. Thoughtfulness and ordinary courtesy when dealing with clients promotes goodwill.

The legal assistant is usually in the best position to detect client dissatisfaction. First, he or she is apt to be working closely with the client. Also, a client may feel freer and have greater opportunity to express feelings to the legal assistant. The legal assistant should make such feelings known to the attorney.

Tax Pitfalls

An estate can be liable for penalty and interest payments for not paying taxes or for not paying them when due. The legal assistant as well as the attorney should be aware of all dates for paying taxes and see that the taxes are paid. Otherwise, a malpractice claim may follow. If an extension of time to pay is required, the application to extend the time should be made by the attorney's office in plenty of time to have the request considered, not when it is too late to get a reply before action needs to be taken.

The tax consequences to an estate should always be considered. Money can be lost in payment of taxes that could have been saved by a proper knowledge and application of the tax laws. Bad judgment about tax decisions or failure to file an income tax return can result in a substantial loss to a client and constitute a fertile field for malpractice claims. The rules for estimating taxes and the penalties for underestimating them are greater than ever before. Some questions call for considerable knowledge of tax law, which is always changing. If the legal assistant has any question, he or she should inquire of the attorney or the tax accountant who is being consulted in connection with the estate.

Possible tax benefits to beneficiaries should be carefully considered before making distribution of an estate. Timing can make a big difference. Distribution should not be made without a reserve for taxes if there is any possibility of an additional assessment. Once assets are distributed, from a practical standpoint, they may not be recoverable should additional taxes be found owing, and the personal representative may be held liable to pay such taxes himself or herself.

See Chapter 8 on federal estate taxation.

Probate Accounting

An estate may lose money through the improper timing of payment of expenses and the improper taking of deductions where a choice is granted under the law. Money also can be lost through the failure to distinguish between income and principal of receipts and disbursements.

Need to Document

In the probate field, there may not be as many occasions to document, that is, to send a letter to the client, as in other fields. There are occasions, however, when advice is being given that should be verified by a letter. A client is more apt to understand advice set out in a letter than oral advice, and a letter reviewed by the writer after it is written is more apt to state what is really meant. A letter also takes care of any arguments resulting from faulty memory on the part of either the sender or the receiver.

A memo should be written to the file after every telephone call and every conversation. A letter of confirmation should be sent regarding any communication with an adverse person or other entity. Any settlement offer should be communicated to the client in writing, and the client should be fully advised, as the client's views of an acceptable settlement may differ from those of the attorney.

Proofreading

One of the areas in which the legal assistant can be of greatest assistance is in the proofreading of legal documents, particularly in probate where the documents contain legal descriptions of real property and dollar amounts. All documents that pass through the hands of the legal assistant and for which he or she has any responsibility should be read by the legal assistant, even if the secretary has proofread them. The attorney has the final responsibility for all documents and should read them as well. This may seem a waste of time and, therefore, is not always done, but a typographical error can be critical and costly in some cases.

Regarding the method of proofreading, the legal assistant should read from the copy or draft, and not watch the original, unless the person who prepared the original is required to initial the file copy and thus be accountable for any errors.

§ 15.7 Closing the Probate File

Before closing a file, any documents belonging to the client or other persons should be returned. The client should be furnished with copies of any papers he or she might need, for instance, a copy of the decree of discharge. The file should be closed only when no further action in the proceeding is contemplated. If the estate has been distributed, no audit is expected, and no money is on reserve for taxes, the file can be closed. As a matter of policy, however, it may be wise to keep files open for a year or so after everything has been done in case something unexpected occurs. Attorneys have different opinions about how long probate files should be permanently retained. Some shift them to storage or copy them onto microfilm and retain them indefinitely.

APPENDIX A

**FIRST AND FINAL ACCOUNT AND
PETITION FOR STATUTORY
EXECUTOR'S COMMISSION AND
ATTORNEY'S STATUTORY AND
EXTRAORDINARY FEES, FOR
APPROVAL OF PRELIMINARY
DISTRIBUTION, AND FOR FINAL
DISTRIBUTION**

```
 1   ARTHUR ANDREW
     Attorney at Law
 2   123 Sandor Place
     Sacramento, CA 95814
 3   Telephone:  (916) 447-0923

 4   Attorney for Executor

 5

 6

 7

 8                    SUPERIOR COURT OF CALIFORNIA

 9                       COUNTY OF SACRAMENTO

10

11

12   Estate of KENNETH BELL,  )   No. 92457      Dept. No. 17
     also known as           )
13   KENNETH K. BELL,         )   FIRST AND FINAL ACCOUNT AND
                              )   PETITION FOR STATUTORY EXECUTOR'S
14            Deceased.       )   COMMISSION AND ATTORNEY'S STATU-
                              )   TORY AND EXTRAORDINARY FEES, FOR
15                            )   APPROVAL OF PRELIMINARY DISTRIBU-
                              )   TION, AND FOR FINAL DISTRIBUTION
16                            )
                              )
17   _____    )

18

19        CLARICE BELL, as Executor of the will of the above-

20   named decedent, presents her First and Final Account and

21   Petition for Statutory Executor's Commission and Attorney's

22   Statutory and Extraordinary Fees, for Approval of Preliminary

23   Distribution, and for Final Distribution and respectfully

24   represents as follows:

25                               I

26        Kenneth Bell, also known as Kenneth K. Bell, died

27   testate on January 7, 19__ , in the County of Sacramento, State

28   of California, and was a resident of that county.

                                 1
```

II

    The following reconciliation and summary constitutes
the condensed report and account of petitioner for the period
from January 7, 19__, through December 1, 19__. The supporting
exhibits are incorporated in the account and report by reference.

CHARGES

Amount of Inventory and Appraisement	$ 608,951.00
Receipts (Schedule A)	23,512.00
Gain on Sale (Schedule B)	20,000.00
TOTAL CHARGES:	$ 652,463.00

CREDITS

Disbursements (Schedule C)	$ 14,755.43
Preliminary Distributions (Schedule E)	31,000.00
Property on Hand (Schedule D)	606,707.57
TOTAL CREDITS:	$ 652,463.00

III

    Decedent's will dated November 15, 19__, was admitted
to probate by order of this Court dated March 15, 19__. Petitioner qualified as executor of the will, and letters testamentary were issued to petitioner on March 15, 19__; at all
times since then she has been and now is executor of the
decedent's will.

IV

    An Inventory and Appraisement in the amount of
$608,951.00 was filed herein on May 7, 19__, showing the total
value of the estate to be the sum of Six Hundred Eight
Thousand Nine Hundred Fifty-one Dollar ($608,951.00); the
inventory contains all of the assets of the decedent that

2

1   have come to the petitioner's knowledge or into her possession.

2   V

3   Petitioner has performed all duties required of her
4   as executor of the will of decedent with respect to administra-
5   tion of the estate, and the estate is ready for distribution
6   and is in a condition to be closed.

7   VI

8   During the within accounting period petitioner received
9   receipts in the amount of Twenty-three Thousand Five Hundred
10   Twelve Dollars ($23,512.00), as set forth in detail in Schedule
11   A. Petitioner has charged herself with said receipts.

12   VII

13   Pursuant to proper orders of the above-entitled Court,
14   petitioner sold the real property of the decedent located at
15   9020 Boykin Way, Sacramento, California. Said sale resulted
16   in a gain to the estate of Twenty Thousand Dollars ($20,000.00),
17   as set forth in detail in Schedule B, and petitioner has charged
18   herself for the whole amount of said gain.

19   VIII

20   During the period covered by the within account peti-
21   tioner made disbursements in the amount of Fourteen Thousand
22   Seven Hundred Fifty-five and 43/100ths Dollars ($14,755.43), set
23   forth in detail in Schedule C. In each case the amount paid
24   was the amount justly due, the payments were made by petitioner
25   in good faith, and the amount paid was the true amount of the
26   indebtedness over and above all payments and offsets. The
27   estate of the within decedent is solvent and petitioner is
28   entitled to credit for the whole amount of such disbursements.

3

IX

Pursuant to the will of the decedent, the yellow gold diamond ring, having an appraised value of Nine Thousand Dollars ($9,000.00), was distributed to decedent's brother, Morton Bell, and the 1985 Mercedes 459SL Engine No. LS057C807, having an appraised value of Twenty-two Thousand Dollars ($22,000.00), was distributed to decedent's son, Kerry Bell. Petitioner respectfully requests Court approval of said advance distribution and is entitled to credit for the whole thereof.

X

As shown in the foregoing reconciliation and summary as set forth in paragraph I above, petitioner had on hand as of March 31, 19__, cash and property of the value of Six Hundred Six Thousand Seven Hundred Seven and 57/100ths Dollars ($606,707.57), which constitutes all of the money and property with which petitioner is chargeable.

XI

Notice to creditors has been duly given, published and filed, the first publication being made on February 25, 1989. Within thirty days after the completion of publication, on March 26, 19__, an affidavit showing due publication in the manner and form required by law was filed with the clerk of this Court. More than four months have elapsed since the first publication of notice to creditors, and the time for filing or presenting claims has expired.

The following creditors' claims were presented, and filed, approved by petitioner, allowed by the Court and paid from funds of the estate:

4

1	Holy Cross Cemetery	$ 665.00
2	Everland Funeral Home	1,469.72
3		$ 2,134.72

4 All expenses of administration have been paid. No other claims

5 were presented or filed.

6   XII

7   In addition to the creditors' claims which were filed

8 in the estate as set forth above, debts of the decedent were

9 paid by the executor pursuant to Probate Code section 929. Said

10 payments in the amount of Six Hundred Seventy-six and 81/100ths

11 Dollars ($676.81), which are set forth in Schedule C attached

12 hereto, were paid during the creditor's claim period, the debts

13 being justly due and paid in good faith and the amounts paid

14 being the true amounts owed over and above all offsets. The

15 estate is solvent and petitioner respectfully requests approval

16 of the court for payment of said debts.

17   XIII

18   A federal estate tax return was filed and no tax

19 was shown due thereon. The return has not yet been audited.

20 Petitioner has not been released from personal liability for

21 federal estate tax.

22   XIV

23   No California estate tax was due in this estate.

24   XV

25   No requests for special notice have been filed in

26 the within proceeding.

27   XVI

28   All personal property taxes due and payable by the

5

1   estate or by the decedent and all federal and California income

2   taxes accruing against the decedent and the estate to the date

3   of this report, so far as they are known to your petitioner,

4   have been paid by petitioner from funds of the estate.

5   XVII

6   All surplus funds have been invested in income-

7   producing assets during the administration of the estate.

8   XVIII

9   Petitioner is entitled to compensation for her services

10   as executor of the within estate. Based on the estate accounted

11   for of $652,463.00, the statutory commission allotted to the peti-

12   tioner is Fourteen Thousand One Hundred Ninety-nine and 26/100ths

13   Dollars ($14,199.26). The computation of said commission is set

14   forth in Schedule F. Petitioner respectfully requests that she be

15   authorized to pay to herself as said executor said amount as her

16   statutory commission for her ordinary services to the estate.

17   XIX

18   Petitioner has retained Arthur Andrew as attorney

19   for the administration of the estate. The statutory fee to

20   which said attorney is entitled, based upon the estate accounted

21   for as set forth above, is Fourteen Thousand One Hundred Ninety-

22   nine and 26/100ths Dollars ($14,199.26). Petitioner respect-

23   fully requests that she be authorized to pay said amount to

24   said attorney as his statutory attorney's fee for his ordinary

25   services to the executor and to the estate.

26   XX

27   In addition to his regular services to the executor,

28   Arthur Andrew has rendered extraordinary services for which he

6

1   is entitled to reasonable compensation.

2   SERVICES PERFORMED

3   A. Sale of Boykin Way Single Family Dwelling

4   After the death of the decedent the house became

5   unoccupied. The house was broken into and notice was given

6   that the insurance coverage was to be cancelled for that reason.

7   Finally two informal but professional appraisals were obtained

8   to aid in setting an asking price. It was agreed to show the

9   house unfurnished and a broker was selected. It was further

10 agreed that Arthur Andrew would hold keys to supplement access

11 to the house by other interested purchasers or their brokers.

12 Notice of sale was published and the property was sold "as is"

13 pursuant to negotiations for $170,000.00. A return of sale was

14 prepared by Arthur Andrew which was to be heard on March 20,

15 19__. Prior to the purchase, one of the proposed purchasers died

16 and it appeared that the sale could not be completed as origi-

17 nally planned. Prior to this hearing, however, the remaining

18 joint purchasers, with the consent of the executor, nominated

19 a purchaser who completed the transaction at the agreed price

20 and on the original terms. The property was shown to more than

21 twenty different prospects and four different written bids were

22 submitted before one was selected for presentation to this Court.

23 In order to close the escrow, it was necessary to secure a

24 release of the real property sold from the lien of the federal

25 estate tax. Arthur Andrew prepared the necessary application,

26 caused it to be executed and filed. As a result the required

27 release was obtained. More than four days of the time of attor-

28 ney and more than eleven days of the time of paraprofessionals

                                  7

1 were expended in rendering the foregoing services. The services

2 have a reasonable value of Three Thousand Dollars ($3,000.00).

3 B. Tax Returns

4 All state and federal income tax returns, although

5 prepared by other persons, were reviewed prior to filing by

6 Arthur Andrew. Advice and assistance was given to assure the

7 proper coordination of the income tax and death tax returns

8 filed on behalf of the estate.

9 The federal estate tax return was prepared by Arthur

10 Andrew from material supplied by the petitioner. More than

11 one and one-half days of attorney time and over five days of

12 paraprofessional time were required to render the foregoing

13 services. The reasonable value thereof is One Thousand Dollars

14 ($1,000.00).

15 The total reasonable value of said services and the

16 agreed value thereof is Four Thousand Dollars ($4,000.00).

17 Petitioner respectfully requests that she be authorized to pay

18 said amount to Arthur Andrew for his extraordinary services to

19 the executor and to the estate.

20 XXI

21 All debts of the decedent and all expenses of

22 administration including the costs of legal publication have

23 been paid except the executor's commission and attorney's

24 fees requested herein and those miscellaneous minor administra-

25 tion expenses which will be incurred in connection with closing

26 the estate and distributing the assets. Said estate is now

27 in condition to be finally settled and distributed.

28 XXII

8

1   Petitioner respectfully requests that she be author-

2 ized and directed to distribute the residue of the estate

3 pursuant to the terms of the will, subject to a lien for any

4 additional taxes which may be owed by virtue of the decedent's

5 death. Said taxes, if any, are to be paid from the residue

6 pursuant to the terms of decedent's will.

7   WHEREFORE, petitioner prays:

8   1. That the within First and Final Account and

9 Report of Executor, Petition for Statutory Executor's Commission

10 and Attorney's Fees, and Petition for Extraordinary Attorney's

11 Fees and Petition for Final Distribution be set for hearing and

12 that notice of said hearing be given as required by law.

13   2. That the within account and report be approved,

14 allowed and settled in all respects.

15   3. That the advance distribution to decedent's

16 brother, Morton Bell, of the yellow gold diamond ring, having

17 an appraised value of Nine Thousand Dollars ($9,000.00), and

18 to decedent's son, Kerry Bell, of the 1985 Mercedes 450 SL

19 automobile, Engine No. LS057C807, having an appraised value of

20 Twenty-two Thousand Dollars ($22,000.00), be approved.

21   4. That petitioner be authorized and directed to

22 pay to herself as executor Fourteen Thousand One Hundred Ninety-

23 nine and 26/100ths Dollars ($14,199.26) as her statutory com-

24 mission for her ordinary services to the estate as executor.

25   5. That the petitioner be authorized and directed to

26 pay to the attorney for the estate Fourteen Thousand One Hundred

27 Ninety-nine and 26/100ths Dollars ($14,199.26) as his statu-

28 tory attorney's fees for his ordinary services to the estate.

9

6. That petitioner be authorized and directed to pay Four Thousand Dollars ($4,000.00) to Arthur Andrew as extraordinary attorney's fees for extraordinary services to the executor and to the estate.

7. That the payment of debts of the decedent pursuant to Probate Code section 929 in the amount of Six Hundred Seventy-six and 81/100ths Dollars ($676.81), which are set forth in paragraph XII, be approved.

8. That petitioner be authorized to distribute the residue of the estate pursuant to the terms of decedent's will.

9. For such other and further relief as may be proper.

Dated: December 4, 19__.

Clarice Bell
Petitioner

Arthur Andrew
Attorney for Petitioner

STATE OF CALIFORNIA)
) ss.
COUNTY OF SACRAMENTO)

I am the executor of the will of the above-named decedent.

I have read the foregoing First and Final Account and Report of Executor, Petition for Statutory Executor's Commissions and Attorneys' Fees, Petition for Extraordinary Attorneys' Fees and Petition for Final Distribution and know the contents thereof, and the same is true of my own knowledge,

10

1 except as to those matters therein stated upon my information

2 or belief and as to those matters I believe it to be true.

3   I certify under penalty of perjury that the foregoing

4 is true and correct.

5   Executed at Sacramento, California, on December 4,

6 19__.

7 _____

    Clarice Bell

8   Clarice Bell

9

10

11

12

13

14

15

16

17

18

19

20

21

22

23

24

25

26

27

28

11

EXHIBIT A - ACCOUNT

SUMMARY OF ACCOUNT

(From January 7, 19___, to December 4, 19___)

CHARGES

Amount of Inventory and Appraisement	$ 608,951.00
Receipts (Schedule A)	23,512.00
Gain on Sale (Schedule B)	20,000.00
TOTAL CHARGES	$ 652,463.00

CREDITS

Disbursements (Schedule C)	$ 14,755.43
Preliminary Distributions (Schedule E)	31,000.00
Property on Hand (Schedule D)	606,707.57
	$ 652,463.00

12

SCHEDULE A

RECEIPTS

	Principal
<u>Interest on Savings Accounts:</u>	
Pacific Savings Bank, Main Street, Sacramento, California, Cash Management Account #2345	$ 6,018.00
Atlantic Savings & Loan Association, Main Street, Sacramento, California, Savings ACcount #2-022705-8	5,684.00
2-1/2 Year T-Note Certificate #061-00581-4, Better Future Savings and Loan Association, 700 L Street, Sacramento	967.00

		Principal
<u>Stock dividends:</u>		
AT&T 5% preferred stock (CUSIP No. 030177)		
Accrued dividends paid	$6,000.00	
Dividends paid during account period		5,000.00
Pacific Gas and Electric common stock, par $10 each (CUSIP 694308)		
Accrued dividends paid	900.00	
Dividends paid during account period		1,000.00
Rental of property at 9020 Boykin Way, Sacramento - $500 mo. for eight months		4,500.00
<u>Miscellaneous receipts:</u>		
Social Security, special payment		50.00
Blue Shield, payment of claim		150.00
Blue Shield, refund of dues		11.16
Pacific Gas & Electric Co. refund		10.84
Refund on insurance for 145 Perry Avenue, Sacramento		121.00
	$6,900.00	$23,512.00

13

```
 1                            SCHEDULE B

 2                            GAIN ON SALE

 3

 4    Single family dwelling at
      9020 Boykin Way, Sacramento,
 5    California (Inventory item #2):

 6        Appraised at . . . . . . . . . . . . . . . . . . . .$ 150,000.00

 7        Sold at. . . . . . . . . . . . . . . . . . . . . .   170,000.00

 8                              Gain on sale . . . . . . .$  20,000.00

 9

10

11

12

13

14

15

16

17

18

19

20

21

22

23

24

25

26

27

28
```

14

```
1                          SCHEDULE C

2                         DISBURSEMENTS

3    Creditors' Claims Approved by Representative
     and Court and Paid:
4
     1.  Everland Funeral Home        $1,469.72
5
     2.  Holy Cross Cemetery             665.00        $  2,134.72
6
     Debts of decedent paid
7    pursuant to Probate Code
     section 929:
8
     Pacific Gas & Electric Co. -
9    residence utility, 145 Perry
     Avenue                              37.11
10
     Ralph Anderson - January-March
11   gardening, 145 Perry Avenue         60.00

12   Standard Oil - gasoline              9.36

13   Willie Wilde's Pharmacy,
     pharmacy expenses of decedent       62.39
14
     Pacific Bell, residence utility    127.95
15
     Daniel Medical Laboratory,
16   laboratory fees of decedent         20.00

17   Hermione Baker, nursing services,
     January 1-9, 1985                  360.00               676.81
18
     Miscellaneous Administrative Expenses:
19
     Probate referee, appraisal fee     424.60
20
     Filing fee, petition for
21   probate of will                    117.00

22   Publication costs                  150.00

23   Fine Jewelry Co., jewelry
     appraisal                          200.00
24
     Jerrold Charles, preparation
25   of fiduciary returns               150.00

26   R. Bates, notary fees                2.00

27   Miscellaneous Automobile Expenses:

28   Battery                 44.00
                            15
```

1	License	50.00	
2	Storage	54.40	
3	Insurance, NAA	<u>44.50</u>	192.90
4	Home insurance		800.00
5,6	3/2/ . House repairs due to vandalism, paid to Barry Black	<u>540.00</u>	2,576.60
7,8	Expenses of sale of house from 1/7/ to close of escrow, paid outside of escrow:		
9	Broker's fee, Ed Brown	6,000.00	
10	Reconveyance fee	25.40	
11	Forwarding fee	15.00	
12	Title policy fee	490.00	
13	Escrow fee	174.00	
14	Documentary transfer tax	134.75	
15	Recording charges, Order and Release and Reconveyances	11.85	
16,17	Title company's charge for delivery of payoff	<u>5.00</u>	6,856.00
18,19	Real property taxes, 19 - 19 , 145 Perry Avenue, Sacramento home	2,008.65	
20	Credit in escrow	<u>502.75</u>	<u>2,511.40</u>
21	Total		.$14,755.53

22
23
24
25
26
27
28

16

1		SCHEDULE D
2		PROPERTY ON HAND
3	Cash Items:	

1. Cash in Cash Management Account
   #2345 at Pacific Savings Bank,
   Main Street, Sacramento, California $ 96,018.00

2. Savings Account No. 2-022705-8, Atlantic
   Savings & Loan Association, Main Street,
   Sacramento, California   90,684.00

3. 2-1/2 Year T-Note Certificate
   #061-00581-4, 12%, Better Future Savings
   and Loan Association, 700 L Street,
   Sacramento   10,009.75

4. Cash in fiduciary checking account #78905,
   Better Future Savings and Loan Association,
   700 L Street, Sacramento   173,245.82

5. Two original oil paintings by Matt Discall   3,000.00

6. 1984 Continental, Engine No. 7538042   10,000.00

7. Household furniture, furnishings and personal
   effects located at 145 Perry Avenue,
   Sacramento, California   1,750.00

8. 5,000 shares AT&T 5% preferred stock
   (CUSIP No. 030177)   72,000.00

9. 1,000 shares Pacific Gas and Electric Common
   stock, par $10 each (CUSIP 694308)   5,000.00

10. Single family dwelling located at 9020
    Boykin Way, Sacramento, described as the
    West 59.00 feet of the East 590.00 feet of
    Lot 1248, as shown on the "Plat of Elvira,"
    recorded in the office of the County Recorder,
    January 23, 1909, in Book 8 of Maps, Map
    No. 41 –
    Assessor's Parcel No. 006-175-0200   145,000.00

     $ 606,707.57

17

1	SCHEDULE E	
2	PROPERTY DISTRIBUTED	
3	One yellow gold diamond ring	$ 9,000.00
4	One 1985 Mercedes 450 SL Engine No. LS057C807 automobile	22,000.00
5		$ 31,000.00

18

1		SCHEDULE F
2		COMPUTATION OF STATUTORY FEES AND COMMISSIONS
3		
4	Per Inventory and Appraisement	$ 608,951.00
5	Receipts - Schedule A	23,512.00
6	Gain on Sale - Schedule B	20,000.00
7		$ 652,463.00
8		
9		
10		
11		
12	$15,000 at 4%	600.00
13	85,000 at 3%	2,500.00
14	552,463 at 2%	11,049.26
15	$652,463	$14,199.26
16		
17		
18		
19		
20		
21		
22		
23		
24		
25		
26		
27		
28		

APPENDIX B

FORM 706 UNITED STATES ESTATE (AND GENERATION-SKIPPING TRANSFER) TAX RETURN AND SCHEDULES

Form **706**
(Rev. August 1993)

Department of the Treasury
Internal Revenue Service

United States Estate (and Generation-Skipping Transfer) Tax Return

Estate of a citizen or resident of the United States (see separate instructions). To be filed for decedents dying after October 8, 1990. For Paperwork Reduction Act Notice, see page 1 of the instructions.

OMB No. 1545-0015
Expires 12-31-95

Part 1.—Decedent and Executor

1a Decedent's first name and middle initial (and maiden name, if any)	1b Decedent's last name
KENNETH K.	BELL
2 Decedent's social security no.	520 : 21 : 4433

3a Domicile at time of death (county and state, or foreign country)	3b Year domicile established	4 Date of birth	5 Date of death
Sacramento,California	1945	6/15/10	January 7, 19

6a Name of executor (see instructions)
Clarice Bell

6b Executor's address (number and street including apartment or suite no. or rural route; city, town, or post office; state; and ZIP code)

6c Executor's social security number (see instructions)
543 : 22 : 5454

145 Perry Avenue
Sacramento, California 95817

7a Name and location of court where will was probated or estate administered
California Superior Court, Sacramento County, Sacramento, CA

7b Case number
92457

8 If decedent died testate, check here ▶ ☒ and attach a certified copy of the will. 9 If Form 4768 is attached, check here ▶ ☐

10 If Schedule R-1 is attached, check here ▶ ☐

Part 2.—Tax Computation

1	Total gross estate (from Part 5, Recapitulation, page 3, item 10)	1	608,951 00
2	Total allowable deductions (from Part 5, Recapitulation, page 3, item 20)	2	577,951 00
3	Taxable estate (subtract line 2 from line 1)	3	31,000 00
4	Adjusted taxable gifts (total taxable gifts (within the meaning of section 2503) made by the decedent after December 31, 1976, other than gifts that are includible in decedent's gross estate (section 2001(b))	4	—
5	Add lines 3 and 4	5	31,000 00
6	Tentative tax on the amount on line 5 from Table A in the instructions	6	6,220 00
7a	If line 5 exceeds $10,000,000, enter the lesser of line 5 or $21,040,000. If line 5 is $10,000,000 or less, skip lines 7a and 7b and enter -0- on line 7c. **7a**		
b	Subtract $10,000,000 from line 7a **7b**		
c	Enter 5% (.05) of line 7b	7c	0
8	Total tentative tax (add lines 6 and 7c)	8	0
9	Total gift tax payable with respect to gifts made by the decedent after December 31, 1976. Include gift taxes by the decedent's spouse for such spouse's share of split gifts (section 2513) only if the decedent was the donor of these gifts and they are includible in the decedent's gross estate (see instructions)	9	0
10	Gross estate tax (subtract line 9 from line 8)	10	0
11	Maximum unified credit against estate tax **11** 192,800 00		
12	Adjustment to unified credit. (This adjustment may not exceed $6,000. See page 6 of the instructions.) **12**		
13	Allowable unified credit (subtract line 12 from line 11)	13	192,800 00
14	Subtract line 13 from line 10 (but do not enter less than zero)	14	0
15	Credit for state death taxes. Do not enter more than line 14. Compute the credit by using the amount on line 3 less $60,000. See Table B in the instructions and attach credit evidence (see instructions)	15	0
16	Subtract line 15 from line 14	16	0
17	Credit for Federal gift taxes on pre-1977 gifts (section 2012) (attach computation) **17**		
18	Credit for foreign death taxes (from Schedule(s) P). (Attach Form(s) 706CE) **18**		
19	Credit for tax on prior transfers (from Schedule Q) **19**		
20	Total (add lines 17, 18, and 19)	20	0
21	Net estate tax (subtract line 20 from line 16)	21	0
22	Generation-skipping transfer taxes (from Schedule R, Part 2, line 10)	22	0
23	Section 4980A increased estate tax (from Schedule S, Part I, line 17) (see instructions)	23	0
24	Total transfer taxes (add lines 21, 22, and 23)	24	0
25	Prior payments. Explain in an attached statement **25** 0		
26	United States Treasury bonds redeemed in payment of estate tax **26** 0		
27	Total (add lines 25 and 26)	27	0
28	Balance due (or overpayment) (subtract line 27 from line 24)	28	0

Under penalties of perjury, I declare that I have examined this return, including accompanying schedules and statements, and to the best of my knowledge and belief, it is true, correct, and complete. Declaration of preparer other than the executor is based on all information of which preparer has any knowledge.

Clarice Bell
Signature(s) of executor(s)

Nov. 1, 19
Date

Arthur Andersen
Signature of preparer other than executor

123 Sandor Place
Sacramento, CA 95814
Address (and ZIP code)

Nov Nov. 1, 19
Date

Cat. No. 20548R

Form 706 (Rev. 8-93)

Estate of: KENNETH BELL, also known as KENNETH K. BELL

Part 3.—Elections by the Executor

Please check the "Yes" or "No" box for each question.

	Yes	No
1 Do you elect alternate valuation?		x
2 Do you elect special use valuation? . . . . If "Yes," you must complete and attach Schedule A–1		x
3 Do you elect to pay the taxes in installments as described in section 6166? . . . . If "Yes," you must attach the additional information described in the instructions.		x
4 Do you elect to postpone the part of the taxes attributable to a reversionary or remainder interest as described in section 6163?		x

Part 4.—General Information (Note: *Please attach the necessary supplemental documents. You must attach the death certificate.*)

Authorization to receive confidential tax information under Regulations section 601.504(b)(2)(i), to act as the estate's representative before the Internal Revenue Service, and to make written or oral presentations on behalf of the estate if return prepared by an attorney, accountant, or enrolled agent for the executor:

Name of representative (print or type) Arthur Andrew	State CA	Address (number, street, and room or suite no., city, state, and ZIP code) 123 Sandor Place, Sacramento, CA 95814

I declare that I am the ☒ attorney/ ☐ certified public accountant/ ☐ enrolled agent (you must check the applicable box) for the executor and prepared this return for the executor. I am not under suspension or disbarment from practice before the Internal Revenue Service and am qualified to practice in the state shown above.

Signature *Arthur Andrew*	CAF number 91234	Date	Telephone number (916) 447-0923

1 Death certificate number and issuing authority (attach a copy of the death certificate to this return).
  3400–123456 State Registrar's Office, Bureau of Vital Statistics

2 Decedent's business or occupation. If retired, check here ▶ ☐ and state decedent's former business or occupation.
  President, California Services Company, Sacramento, California

3 Marital status of the decedent at time of death:
  ☒ Married
  ☐ Widow or widower—Name, SSN, and date of death of deceased spouse ▶ ....

  ☐ Single
  ☐ Legally separated
  ☐ Divorced—Date divorce decree became final ▶

4a Surviving spouse's name Clarice Bell	4b Social security number 543 : 22 : 5454	4c Amount received (see instructions) $577,951.00

5 Individuals (other than the surviving spouse), trusts, or other estates who receive benefits from the estate (do not include charitable beneficiaries shown in Schedule O) (see instructions). For Privacy Act Notice (applicable to individual beneficiaries only), see the Instructions for Form 1040.

Name of individual, trust, or estate receiving $5,000 or more	Identifying number	Relationship to decedent	Amount (see instructions)
Kerry Bell	591-08-2343	Son	$22,000.00
Morton Bell	540-18-7272	Brother	9,000.00

All unascertainable beneficiaries and those who receive less than $5,000 . . . . ▶		
Total		**$31,000.00**

(Continued on next page)

Page 2

Form 706 (Rev. 8-93)

Part 4.—General Information (continued)

Please check the "Yes" or "No" box for each question.

		Yes	No
6	Does the gross estate contain any section 2044 property (qualified terminable interest property (QTIP) from a prior gift or estate) (see page 5 of the instructions)?		x
7a	Have Federal gift tax returns ever been filed?		x
	If "Yes," please attach copies of the returns, if available, and furnish the following information:		

7b Period(s) covered	7c Internal Revenue office(s) where filed

If you answer "Yes" to any of questions 8–16, you must attach additional information as described in the instructions.

		Yes	No
8a	Was there any insurance on the decedent's life that is not included on the return as part of the gross estate?		x
b	Did the decedent own any insurance on the life of another that is not included in the gross estate?		x
9	Did the decedent at the time of death own any property as a joint tenant with right of survivorship in which (a) one or more of the other joint tenants was someone other than the decedent's spouse, and (b) less than the full value of the property is included on the return as part of the gross estate? If "Yes," you must complete and attach Schedule E		x
10	Did the decedent, at the time of death, own any interest in a partnership or unincorporated business or any stock in an inactive or closely held corporation?		x
11	Did the decedent make any transfer described in section 2035, 2036, 2037, or 2038 (see the instructions for Schedule G)? If "Yes," you must complete and attach Schedule G		x
12	Were there in existence at the time of the decedent's death:		
a	Any trusts created by the decedent during his or her lifetime?		x
b	Any trusts not created by the decedent under which the decedent possessed any power, beneficial interest, or trusteeship?		x
13	Did the decedent ever possess, exercise, or release any general power of appointment? If "Yes," you must complete and attach Schedule H		x
14	Was the marital deduction computed under the transitional rule of Public Law 97-34, section 403(e)(3) (Economic Recovery Tax Act of 1981)?		x
	If "Yes," attach a separate computation of the marital deduction, enter the amount on item 18 of the Recapitulation, and note on item 18 "computation attached."		
15	Was the decedent, immediately before death, receiving an annuity described in the "General" paragraph of the instructions for Schedule I? If "Yes," you must complete and attach Schedule I		x
16	Did the decedent have a total "excess retirement accumulation" (as defined in section 4980A(d)) in qualified employer plans and individual retirement plans? If "Yes," you must complete and attach Schedule S		x

Part 5.—Recapitulation

Item number	Gross estate	Alternate value	Value at date of death
1	Schedule A—Real Estate		295,000 00
2	Schedule B—Stocks and Bonds		83,900 00
3	Schedule C—Mortgages, Notes, and Cash		184,301 00
4	Schedule D—Insurance on the Decedent's Life (attach Form(s) 712)		0
5	Schedule E—Jointly Owned Property (attach Form(s) 712 for life insurance) . . .		0
6	Schedule F—Other Miscellaneous Property (attach Form(s) 712 for life insurance) .		45,750 00
7	Schedule G—Transfers During Decedent's Life (attach Form(s) 712 for life insurance)		0
8	Schedule H—Powers of Appointment		0
9	Schedule I—Annuities		0
10	Total gross estate (add items 1 through 9). Enter here and on line 1 of the Tax Computation		608,951 00

Item number	Deductions	Amount
11	Schedule J—Funeral Expenses and Expenses Incurred in Administering Property Subject to Claims . . .	42,477 24
12	Schedule K—Debts of the Decedent	676 81
13	Schedule K—Mortgages and Liens	0
14	Total of items 11 through 13	43,154 05
15	Allowable amount of deductions from item 14 (see the instructions for item 15 of the Recapitulation) . . .	43,154 05
16	Schedule L—Net Losses During Administration	0
17	Schedule L—Expenses Incurred in Administering Property Not Subject to Claims	0
18	Schedule M—Bequests, etc., to Surviving Spouse	534,796 95
19	Schedule O—Charitable, Public, and Similar Gifts and Bequests	0
20	Total allowable deductions (add items 15 through 19). Enter here and on line 2 of the Tax Computation . .	577,951 00

Page 3

Form 706 (Rev. 8-93)

Estate of: KENNETH BELL, also known as KENNETH K. BELL

SCHEDULE A—Real Estate

(For jointly owned property that must be disclosed on Schedule E, see the instructions for Schedule E.)

(Real estate that is part of a sole proprietorship should be shown on Schedule F. Real estate that is included in the gross estate under section 2035, 2036, 2037, or 2038 should be shown on Schedule G. Real estate that is included in the gross estate under section 2041 should be shown on Schedule H.)

(If you elect section 2032A valuation, you must complete Schedule A and Schedule A-1.)

Item number	Description	Alternate valuation date	Alternate value	Value at date of death

1	Community property interest in personal residence located at 145 Perry Avenue, Sacramento, County of Sacramento, California, more particularly described as follows:
	
	Lot 9 on that map entitled "Plat of Deodora Ridge," as recorded in Book 6 of Maps at Page 8, Official Records of Sacramento County, California
	    Assessor's Parcel No. 0060290-0200
	    Value (based on referee's appraisal, copy of which is attached 1/2
				$ 145,000.00

2	Single family dwelling located at 9020 Boykin Way, Sacramento, described as the West 59.00 feet of the East 590.00 feet of Lot 248, as shown on the "Plat of Elvira," recorded in the office of the County Recorder, January 23, 1909, in Book 8 of Maps, Map No. 41.
	    Assessor's Parcel No. 006-175-0200
	    Value based on referee's appraisal, copy of which is attached
				150,000.00

Total from continuation schedule(s) (or additional sheet(s)) attached to this schedule .   .

TOTAL. (Also enter on Part 5, Recapitulation, page 3, at item 1.) .   .   .   . | $295,000.00

(If more space is needed, attach the continuation schedule from the end of this package or additional sheets of the same size.)

(See the instructions on the reverse side.)

Schedule A—Page 4

Form 706 (Rev. 8-93)

Instructions for Schedule A—Real Estate

If the total gross estate contains any real estate, you must complete Schedule A and file it with the return. On Schedule A list real estate the decedent owned or had contracted to purchase. Number each parcel in the left-hand column.

Describe the real estate in enough detail so that the IRS can easily locate it for inspection and valuation. For each parcel of real estate, report the area and, if the parcel is improved, describe the improvements. For city or town property, report the street and number, ward, subdivision, block and lot, etc. For rural property, report the township, range, landmarks, etc.

If any item of real estate is subject to a mortgage for which the decedent's estate is liable, that is, if the indebtedness may be charged against other property of the estate that is not subject to that mortgage, or if the decedent was personally liable for that mortgage, you must report the full value of the property in the value column.

Enter the amount of the mortgage under "Description" on this schedule. The unpaid amount of the mortgage may be deducted on Schedule K. If the decedent's estate is NOT liable for the amount of the mortgage, report only the value of the equity of redemption (or value of the property less the indebtedness) in the value column as part of the gross estate. Do not enter any amount less than zero. Do not deduct the amount of indebtedness on Schedule K.

Also list on Schedule A real property the decedent contracted to purchase. Report the full value of the property and not the equity in the value column. Deduct the unpaid part of the purchase price on Schedule K.

Report the value of real estate without reducing it for homestead or other exemption, or the value of dower, curtesy, or a statutory estate created instead of dower or curtesy.

Explain how the reported values were determined and attach copies of any appraisals.

Schedule A Examples

In this example, the alternate valuation is not adopted; the date of death is January 1, 1993.

Item number	Description	Alternate valuation date	Alternate value	Value at date of death
1	House and lot, 1921 William Street NW, Washington, DC (lot 6, square 481). Rent of $2,700 due at end of each quarter, February 1, May 1, August 1, and November 1. Value based on appraisal, copy of which is attached			108,000
	Rent due on item 1 for quarter ending November 1, 1992, but not collected at date of death			2,700
	Rent accrued on item 1 for November and December 1992			1,800
2	House and lot, 304 Jefferson Street, Alexandria, VA (lot 18, square 40). Rent of $600 payable monthly. Value based on appraisal, copy of which is attached			96,000
	Rent due on item 2 for December 1992, but not collected at date of death . . .			600

In this example, alternate valuation is adopted; the date of death is January 1, 1993.

Item number	Description	Alternate valuation date	Alternate value	Value at date of death
1	House and lot, 1921 William Street NW, Washington, DC (lot 6, square 481). Rent of $2,700 due at end of each quarter, February 1, May 1, August 1, and November 1. Value based on appraisal, copy of which is attached. Not disposed of within 6 months following death	7/1/93	90,000	108,000
	Rent due on item 1 for quarter ending November 1, 1992, but not collected until February 1, 1993	2/1/93	2,700	2,700
	Rent accrued on item 1 for November and December 1992, collected on February 1, 1993	2/1/93	1,800	1,800
2	House and lot, 304 Jefferson Street, Alexandria, VA (lot 18, square 40). Rent of $600 payable monthly. Value based on appraisal, copy of which is attached. Property exchanged for farm on May 1, 1993	5/1/93	90,000	96,000
	Rent due on item 2 for December 1992, but not collected until February 1, 1993 .	2/1/93	600	600

Schedule A—Page 5

Form 706 (Rev. 8-93)

Estate of: KENNETH BELL, also known as KENNETH K. BELL

SCHEDULE B—Stocks and Bonds

(For jointly owned property that must be disclosed on Schedule E, see the instructions for Schedule E.)

Item number	Description including face amount of bonds or number of shares and par value where needed for identification. Give CUSIP number if available.	Unit value	Alternate valuation date	Alternate value	Value at date of death
1	Community property interest in 5,000 shares AT&T preferred stock (CUSIP No. 030177) 1/2				$ 72,000.00
	Accrued but unpaid dividends 1/2				6,000.00
2	Community property interest in 1,000 shares Pacific Gas and Electric common stock, par $10 each (CUSIP 694308) 1/2				5,000.00
	Accrued but unpaid dividends 1/2				900.00
	Total from continuation schedule(s) (or additional sheet(s)) attached to this schedule . .				
	TOTAL. (Also enter on Part 5, Recapitulation, page 3, at item 2.)				$ 83,900.00

(If more space is needed, attach the continuation schedule from the end of this package or additional sheets of the same size.)

(The instructions to Schedule B are in the separate instructions.)   **Schedule B—Page 12**

Form 706 (Rev. 8-93)

Estate of: KENNETH BELL, also known as KENNETH K. BELL

SCHEDULE C—Mortgages, Notes, and Cash

(For jointly owned property that must be disclosed on Schedule E, see the instructions for Schedule E.)

Item number	Description	Alternate valuation date	Alternate value	Value at date of death
1	Cash found in possession of decedent 1/2			$ 258.25
2	Cash in Cash Management Account #2345 at Pacific Savings Bank, Main Street, Sacramento, California 1/2			90,000.00
3	Savings Account No. 2-022705-8, Atlantic Savings & Loan Association, Main Street, Sacramento, California, 1/2			85,000.00
4	2-1/2 Year T-Note Certificate #061-00571-4 12T, Better Future Savings and Loan Association, 700 L Street,Sacramento, California 1/2			9,042.75
	Total from continuation schedule(s) (or additional sheet(s)) attached to this schedule .			
	TOTAL. (Also enter on Part 5, Recapitulation, page 3, at item 3.).			184,301.00

(If more space is needed, attach the continuation schedule from the end of this package or additional sheets of the same size.)
(See the instructions on the reverse side.)

Schedule C—Page 13

Form 706 (Rev. 8-93)

Estate of: KENNETH BELL, also known as KENNETH K. BELL

SCHEDULE F—Other Miscellaneous Property Not Reportable Under Any Other Schedule

(For jointly owned property that must be disclosed on Schedule E, see the instructions for Schedule E.)
(If you elect section 2032A valuation, you must complete Schedule F and Schedule A-1.)

		Yes	No
1	Did the decedent at the time of death own any articles of artistic or collectible value in excess of $3,000 or any collections whose artistic or collectible value combined at date of death exceeded $10,000? . . . . If "Yes," submit full details on this schedule and attach appraisals.		X
2	Has the decedent's estate, spouse, or any other person, received (or will receive) any bonus or award as a result of the decedent's employment or death? . . . . If "Yes," submit full details on this schedule.		X
3	Did the decedent at the time of death have, or have access to, a safe deposit box? . . . . If "Yes," state location, and if held in joint names of decedent and another, state name and relationship of joint depositor.	X	

If any of the contents of the safe deposit box are omitted from the schedules in this return, explain fully why omitted.

Item number	Description For securities, give CUSIP number, if available.	Alternate valuation date	Alternate value	Value at date of death
1	Separate property of decedent: One yellow gold diamond ring DECEDENT'S COMMUNITY PROPERTY ONE-HALF INTEREST IN THE FOLLOWING:			$ 9,000.00
2	Two original oil paintings by Matt Bonnett 1/2			3,000.00
3	1985 Mercedes 450 SL Engine No. LSO57C807 1/2			22,000.00
4	1984 Lincoln Continental, Engine No. 7538042 1/2			10,000.00
5	Household furniture, furnishings and personal effects located at 145 Perry Avenue, Sacramento, California 1/2			1,750.00

Total from continuation schedule(s) (or additional sheet(s)) attached to this schedule. .		
TOTAL. (Also enter on Part 5, Recapitulation, page 3, at item 6.)		45,750.00

(If more space is needed, attach the continuation schedule from the end of this package or additional sheets of the same size.)
(See the instructions on the reverse side.)

Schedule F—Page 19

Form 706 (Rev. 8-93)

Estate of: KENNETH BELL, also known as KENNETH K. BELL

SCHEDULE J—Funeral Expenses and Expenses Incurred in Administering Property Subject to Claims

Note: *Do not list on this schedule expenses of administering property not subject to claims. For those expenses, see the instructions for Schedule L.*

If executors' commissions, attorney fees, etc., are claimed and allowed as a deduction for estate tax purposes, they are not allowable as a deduction in computing the taxable income of the estate for Federal income tax purposes. They are allowable as an income tax deduction on Form 1041 if a waiver is filed to waive the deduction on Form 706 (see the Form 1041 instructions).

Item number	Description	Expense amount	Total Amount
1	**A. Funeral expenses:**		
	Holy Cross Cemetery	665.00	
	Everland Funeral Home	1,469.72	
	Total funeral expenses		2,134.72
	B. Administration expenses:		
1	Executors' commissions—amount estimated/agreed upon/paid. (Strike out the words that do not apply.)		14,199.26
2	Attorney fees—amount estimated/agreed upon/paid. (Strike out the words that do not apply.) . . .		14,199.26
3	Accountant fees—amount estimated/agreed upon/paid. (Strike out the words that do not apply.) . .		....
4	Miscellaneous expenses:	Expense amount	
	(See attached schedule)		
	Total miscellaneous expenses from continuation schedule(s) (or additional sheet(s)) attached to this schedule . . .	11,944.00	
	Total miscellaneous expenses		42,477.24
	TOTAL. (Also enter on Part 5, Recapitulation, page 3, at item 11.) . . .		42,477.24

(If more space is needed, attach the continuation schedule from the end of this package or additional sheets of the same size.)
(See the instructions on the reverse side.)

Schedule J—Page 23

Estate of: KENNETH BELL, also known as KENNETH K. BELL

SCHEDULE J - Funeral Expenses and Expenses Incurred in Administering Property Subject to Claims - Continued - Page 24A

1. Probate referee, appraisal fee		$ 424.60
2. Filing fee, petition for probate of will		117.00
3. Publication costs		150.00
4. Fine Jewelry Co., jewelry appraisal		200.00
5. Jerrold Charles, preparation of fiduciary returns		150.00
6. R. Bates, notary fees		2.00
7. Miscellaneous automobile expenses:		
Battery	44.00	
License	50.00	
Storage	54.50	
Insurance, NAA	44.50	
		193.90
8. Home insurance		800.00
9. 3/2/85 Home repairs due to vandalism, paid to Barry Black		540.00
		$2,576.60

Expenses of sale of home from 1/7/89 to close of escrow, paid out of escrow:

Broker's fee, Ed Brown	6,000.00	
Reconveyance fee	25.40	
Forwarding fee	15.00	
Title policy fee	490.00	
Escrow fee	174.00	
Documentary transfer tax	134.75	
Recording charges, Order and Release and Reconveyance	11.85	
Title company's charge for delivery of payoff	5.00	
		6,856.00

Real property taxes, 1985-1986, 145 Perry Avenue, Sacramento, home	2,008.65	
Credit in escrow	502.75	
		2,511.40
Total miscellaneous administrative expenses		$11,944.00

Form 706 (Rev. 8-93)

Estate of: KENNETH BELL, also known as KENNETH K. BELL

SCHEDULE K—Debts of the Decedent, and Mortgages and Liens

Item number	Debts of the Decedent—Creditor and nature of claim, and allowable death taxes	Amount unpaid to date	Amount in contest	Amount claimed as a deduction
1	(See attached schedule)			
	Total from continuation schedule(s) (or additional sheet(s)) attached to this schedule			$ 676.81
	TOTAL. (Also enter on Part 5, Recapitulation, page 3, at item 12.)			$ 676.81

Item number	Mortgages and Liens—Description	Amount
1		
	Total from continuation schedule(s) (or additional sheet(s)) attached to this schedule	
	TOTAL. (Also enter on Part 5, Recapitulation, page 3, at item 13.)	

(If more space is needed, attach the continuation schedule from the end of this package or additional sheets of the same size.)
(The instructions to Schedule K are in the separate instructions.)

Schedule K —Page 25

SCHEDULE K - Debts of the Decedent, and Mortgages and Liens -
Page 25

Debts of decedent paid pursuant to Probate Code
section 929:

Pacific Gas & Electric Co. - residence utility, 145 Perry Avenue	$ 37.11
Ralph Anderson - January-March gardening, 145 Perry Avenue	60.00
Standard Oil - gasoline	9.36
Willie Wilde's Pharmacy, pharmacy expenses of decedent	62.39
Pacific Bell, residence utility	127.95
Daniel Medical Laboratory, laboratory fees of decedent	20.00
Hermione Baker, nursing services, January 1-9, 19__	360.00
	$ 676.81

Form 706 (Rev. 8-93)

Estate of: KENNETH BELL, also known as KENNETH K. BELL

SCHEDULE M—Bequests, etc., to Surviving Spouse

Election To Deduct Qualified Terminable Interest Property Under Section 2056(b)(7).—If a trust (or other property) meets the requirements of qualified terminable interest property under section 2056(b)(7), and

  a. The trust or other property is listed on Schedule M, and

  b. The value of the trust (or other property) is entered in whole or in part as a deduction on Schedule M,

then unless the executor specifically identifies the trust (all or a fractional portion or percentage) or other property to be excluded from the election the executor shall be deemed to have made an election to have such trust (or other property) treated as qualified terminable interest property under section 2056(b)(7).

If less than the entire value of the trust (or other property) that the executor has included in the gross estate is entered as a deduction on Schedule M, the executor shall be considered to have made an election only as to a fraction of the trust (or other property). The numerator of this fraction is equal to the amount of the trust (or other property) deducted on Schedule M. The denominator is equal to the total value of the trust (or other property).

Election To Deduct Qualified Domestic Trust Property Under Section 2056A.—If a trust meets the requirements of a qualified domestic trust under section 2056A(a) and this return is filed no later than 1 year after the time prescribed by law (including extensions) for filing the return, and

  a. The entire value of a trust or trust property is listed on Schedule M, and

  b. The entire value of the trust or trust property is entered as a deduction on Schedule M,

then unless the executor specifically identifies the trust to be excluded from the election, the executor shall be deemed to have made an election to have the entire trust treated as qualified domestic trust property.

		Yes	No
1	Did any property pass to the surviving spouse as a result of a qualified disclaimer?		x
	If "Yes," attach a copy of the written disclaimer required by section 2518(b).		
2a	In what country was the surviving spouse born? ___U.S.A.___		
b	What is the surviving spouse's date of birth? ___April 14, 1932___		
c	Is the surviving spouse a U.S. citizen?	x	
d	If the surviving spouse is a naturalized citizen, when did the surviving spouse acquire citizenship? ___N/A___		
e	If the surviving spouse is not a U.S. citizen, of what country is the surviving spouse a citizen? ___N/A___		
3	**Election out of QTIP Treatment of Annuities.**—Do you elect under section 2056(b)(7)(C)(ii) **not** to treat as qualified terminable interest property any joint and survivor annuities that are included in the gross estate and would otherwise be treated as qualified terminable interest property under section 2056(b)(7)(C)? (see instructions)		x

Item number	Description of property interests passing to surviving spouse	Amount
1	(See attached schedule)	
	Total from continuation schedule(s) (or additional sheet(s)) attached to this schedule	
4	**Total** amount of property interests listed on Schedule M **4**	534,796.95
5a	Federal estate taxes (including section 4980A taxes) payable out of property interests listed on Schedule M **5a**	
b	Other death taxes payable out of property interests listed on Schedule M **5b**	
c	Federal and state GST taxes payable out of property interests listed on Schedule M **5c**	
d	Add items a, b, and c **5d**	
6	Net amount of property interests listed on Schedule M (subtract 5d from 4). Also enter on Part 5, Recapitulation, page 3, at item 18 . . . . **6**	534,796.95

(If more space is needed, attach the continuation schedule from the end of this package or additional sheets of the same size.)

(See the instructions on the reverse side.)

Schedule M—Page 27

ESTATE OF KENNETH BELL,
also known as KENNETH K. BELL
Date of death: 1/7/19__

Supplement to Schedule M   Page 1

ITEM NO.	DESCRIPTION	VALUE
1	One-half the value of house and lot located at 145 Perry Avenue, Sacramento, County of Sacramento, California, more particularly described as follows: Lot 9 on that map entitled "Plat of Deodora Ridge," as recorded in Book 6 of Maps at Page 8, Official Records of Sacramento County, California ᴸᵃ Assessor's Parcel No. 0060390-0200 (Schedule A, Item 1)	$145,000.00
2	Single family dwelling located at 9020 Boykin Way, Sacramento, described as the West 59.00 feet of the East 590.00 feet of Lot 248, as shown on the "Plat of Elvira," recorded in the office of the County Recorder, A 23, 1909, in Book 8 of Maps, Map no. 41. Assessor's Parcel No. 006-175-0200 (Schedule A, Item 2)	150,000.00
3.	One-half the value of two original oil paintings by Matt Bonnett (Schedule F, Item 2)	3,000.00
4.	One-half the value of one 1984 Lincoln Continental, Engine No. 7538042 (Schedule F, Item 4)	10,000.00
5.	One-half the value of household furniture, furnishings and personal effects located at 145 Perry Avenue, Sacramento, California (Schedule F, Item 5)	1,750.00
6.	One-half the value 5,00 shares AT&T preferred stock (CUSIP No. 030177) One-half accrued but unpaid dividends	72,000.00 6,000.00
7.	One-half the value 1,000 shares Pacific Gas and Electric common stock, par $10 each (CUSIP 694308) One-half accrued but unpaid dividends	5,000.00 900.00
8.	All residue of estate to surviving spouse, paragraph Third of will	141,146.95
	TOTAL	$534,796.95

APPENDIX C

JUDICIAL COUNCIL PROBATE FORMS

The Judicial Council prepares a number of printed forms for use in various fields of law. The use of some is optional, but the use of others is mandatory. In the left-hand corner at the bottom of each form is printed the date with either "Adopted" (for mandatory use) or "Approved" (for optional use). The latter are listed in Rule 982 of the California Rules of Court. The legal forms approved by the Judicial Council for optional use will be accepted for filing by all courts.

A complete list of all Judicial Council forms used in decedents' estates as of January 1, 1995, follows. (The last date of revision of the form is given in parentheses.)

DE-305 (1989)	Affidavit re Real Property of Small Value ($10,000 or Less)
DE-174 (1988)	Allowance or Rejection of Creditor's Claim (for estates filed after June 30, 1988)
DE-122 (1977)	Citation (Probate) and Proof of Service
DE-170 (1985)	Creditor's Claim
DE-172 (1988)	Creditor's Claim (for estates filed after June 30, 1988)
DE-147 (1989)	Duties and Liabilities of Personal Representative (and Acknowledgment of Receipt)
DE-275 (1975)	Ex Parte Petition for Approval of Sale of Personal Property and order [same as GC-075*]
DE-270 (1975)	Ex Parte Petition for Authority to Sell Securities and Order [same as GC-070*]
DE-160 (1985)	Inventory and Appraisement [same as GC-040*]
DE-161 (1976)	Inventory and Appraisement (Attachment) [same as GC-041*]
DE-150 (1988)	Letters
DE-157 (1991)	Notice of Administration to Creditors
DE-120 (1989)	Notice of Hearing (Probate)
DE-121 (1989)	Notice of Petition to Administer Estate
DE-165 (1988)	Notice of Proposed Action (Objection-Consent)
DE-265 (1988)	Order Confirming Sale of Real Property (same as GC-065*]
DE-315 (1989)	Order Determining Succession to Real Property (Estates $60,000 or Less)
DE-140 (1988)	Order for Probate
DE-200 (1981)	Order Prescribing Notice [same as GC-022*]
DE-110 (1981)	Petition for Probate
DE-111 (1989)	Petition for Probate (for deaths after December 31, 1984)

DE-310 (1989)	Petition to Determine Succession to Real Property (Estates $60,000 or Less)
DE-135 (1985)	Proof of Holographic Instrument
DE-130 (1976)	Proof of Subscribing Witness
DE-131 (1985)	Proof of Subscribing Witness (for decedents after December 31, 1984)
DE-260 (1988)	Report of Sale and Petition for Order Confirming Sale of Real Property [same as GC-060*]
DE-154 (1989)	Request for Special Notice
DE-226 (1987)	Spousal Property Order
DE-221 (1987)	Spousal Property Petition
DE-125 (1989)	Summons (Probate)
DE-166 (1988)	Waiver of Notice of Proposed Action (and Revocation of Waiver)

*Forms bearing both DE and GC numbers may be used in decedents' estates, guardianships, or conservatorships.

GLOSSARY

abatement† The process of determining the distribution of the assets left by a deceased in his or her will when the assets are insufficient to satisfy all the bequests made in the will.

abstract of title A condensed summary of the history of the title to a particular piece of real property.

A-B trust A trust used mainly in California to equalize the holdings of married persons in order to take full advantage of the marital deduction.

accelerated depreciation Any method of depreciation that gives a larger deduction than the straight-line method in the earlier years of life of the asset.

accumulation distribution Distribution of the excess after deducting (1) any income required to be distributed currently, (2) amounts distributable at the discretion of the trustee, and (3) deductions for charitable contributions.

ademption A substantial testamentary gift that does not exist in the testator's estate at time of his or her death.

ad litem Someone acting, during the pendency of an action or proceeding, as a guardian ad litem appointed for a minor, or acting to bring an action.

adjusted basis For income tax purposes, the basis of property used to compute gains, which is cost minus depreciation plus capital improvements (and, possibly, plus recapture).

administration of estate† The management of a decedent's estate by an administrator or executor so that all the decedent's assets are collected, all debts, administration expenses, and taxes are paid, and all remaining assets are distributed to the persons entitled to receive them.

administrator† A person who is appointed by the court to manage the estate of a person either who died without a will or whose will failed to name an executor or named an executor who declined or was ineligible to serve.

administrator CTA (cum testamento annexo)† The court-appointed administrator of the estate of a decedent whose will failed to name an executor or whose named executor cannot or refuses to serve.

adverse party Any party having a substantial beneficial interest in a trust who would be adversely affected by the exercise or nonexercise of the power he or she possesses respecting the trust.

alternate valuation date† The date an estate administrator can choose as an alternative to the date of death for the valuation of a decedent's estate for federal estate tax purposes, which is six months after the date of death or the date the property is disposed of, whichever comes first.

amortization For income tax purposes, the systematic allocation of the cost or other basis of personal property over its estimated useful life; also used in speaking of a real estate loan, which is "amortized" over the life of the loan, as between principal and interest and balances.

ancillary administration A probate proceeding necessary in another jurisdiction when the decedent leaves assets in another state or county.

annual exclusion The sum of money that a donor may give each year, free of federal gift tax, to as many donees as desired (currently $10,000, or $20,000 for a couple by agreement), but a gift tax return must be filed.

annuity† A yearly payment of a fixed sum of money for life or for a stated number of years.

appraisal† Valuation; a determination of the worth or value of something.

ascertainable standard A reasonably definite external standard set forth in the trust instrument itself [IRC § 674(d)].

as is† A sale without an express or implied warranty in which the buyer takes a chance in making the purchase.

asset† Anything of value owned by a person or an organization. Assets include not only all real property and personal property, but intangible property such as bills, notes, stock, and accounts receivable.

attachment† The process by which a person's property is figuratively brought into court to ensure satisfaction of a judgment that may be rendered against that person.

bad faith† A devious or deceitful intent, motivated by self-interest, ill will, or a concealed purpose.

bailee's receipt† An acknowledgment in writing from the person to whom money or property is entrusted that such money or property has been received.

basis The basis of real property is the original cost or price.

beneficiary† A person who has inherited or is entitled to inherit under a will, a person for whom property is held in trust, or a person who is entitled to the proceeds of a life insurance policy when the insured dies.

bequest Personal property left by a decedent to a named person.

bond† An obligation to pay a sum of money upon the happening of a stated event.

book value The value of an asset as reflected by the books or by a company.

burden of proof† The duty of establishing the truth of a matter; the duty of proving a fact that is in dispute.

bypass trust A trust intended to save the "second tax," that is, the tax on the death of the second spouse to die.

California Law Revision Commission A commission created by the California legislature to make substantive changes in the California laws. Topics may be assigned by the legislature for study, or the commission may respond to suggestions from attorneys, judges, or others.

capital gains tax† Income tax upon financial gain resulting from the sale or exchange of capital assets.

carry-over basis A basis for tax computation for inherited property by which the gain is computed when the property is sold.

categorized account An account in which receipts are grouped together by category, not chronology.

causa mortis In contemplation of approaching death.

charitable deduction† A tax deduction from federal income tax to which a taxpayer is entitled, within the limitations imposed by the Internal Revenue Code, for contributions or gifts made to a tax-exempt charitable organization.

charitable remainder annuity trusts A trust where the donor receives a fixed percentage of the value of the trust as redetermined each year.

charitable trust† A trust established for a charitable purpose.

chattel An item of personal property other than real property.

chronological account An account that lists receipts in the order in which payments are made, not by category.

Clifford trust A temporary trust for not less than ten years at the expiration of which the donor receives back his or her property.

closely held business† A corporation in which all the stock is owned by a few persons or by another corporation and is not traded on a stock exchange; sometimes also referred to as a closely held corporation.

codicil† An addition or supplement to a will, which adds to or modifies the will without replacing or revoking it.

community property† A system of law under which the earnings of either spouse are the property of both the husband and the wife, and property acquired by either spouse during the marriage (other than by gift, under a will, or through inheritance) is the property of both.

complex trust Any trust other than a simple trust.

conflict of interest† The existence of a variance between the interests of the parties in a fiduciary relationship.

conservator† A person placed in charge of the property of an incompetent person by a court.

contemplation of death A concept that presumes that all gifts made by a decedent within three years of his or her death were made in the expectation of death, and which results in taxation of the gifts within his or her estate; also referred to as a "gift causa mortis."

contest A contest of a will by an interested party claiming that the decedent's will is not valid.

corporation† An artificial person, existing only in the eyes of the law, to whom a state or the federal government has granted a charter to become a legal entity, separate from its shareholders, with a name of its own, under which its shareholders can act and contract and sue and be sued.

corpus† A Latin term meaning "the body"; the subject matter or capital of a trust or estate, or the principal of a fund, as distinguished from the income or interest.

creditor's claim A document that creditors are required to file in an estate before they may be paid from the assets of the estate.

credits An amount subtracted directly from the amount of the tax computed to be paid, contrasted with a deduction that is subtracted from the income on which the tax is based.

Crummey trust Name given to a trust stemming from case of *Crummey v. Commissioner*, 397 F.2d 82.

curtesy An interest in a deceased wife's real property that passes on her death to her husband for his lifetime if they have had children who are able to inherit the property.

death certificate† The official proof of death issued by an appropriate public officer.

decedent† A legal term for a person who has died.

deed A writing signed by the owner of a property granting title of the property to another.

deemed transferor A person who is regarded as being the one who transferred the property.

depreciation Property is presumed to deteriorate or wear out through use, with the passage of time, and become obsolete; an allowance is made for this decrease in the value of property that produces income; the original cost is divided by its estimated useful life.

devise A gift of real property by will, although in California, after January 1, 1985, this term includes personal property as well.

devisee† The beneficiary of a devise.

direct skip A transfer subject to a tax imposed on an interest in property transferred to a skip person.

disclaimer† The refusal to accept, or the renunciation of, a right or of property.

discretionary trust† A trust in which broad discretion is vested in the trustee and is to be exercised by him or her in carrying out the purposes of the trust.

distributable net come (DNI) The amount of income on which the beneficiaries of an estate or trust are actually taxed, that is, their taxable income.

domicile One's permanent residence; the place where a person intends to live permanently, although he or she may reside at another place from time to time.

dower An interest in the part of a deceased husband's real property that is allowed to his widow for her lifetime.

earned income Income, as defined by tax law, from personal services, not from real property.

equity of redemption† The right of a mortgagor who has defaulted upon his mortgage payments to prevent foreclosure by paying the debt in full.

equivalent exemption The amount of property and lifetime transfers exempt from tax at death that equal the unified tax credit.

escheat† The right of the state to take title to property after the death of a person who has not disposed of the property by will and has left no heirs to inherit it.

escrow† A written instrument, money, or other property deposited by the grantor with a third party (the escrow holder) until the performance of a condition or the happening of a certain event, upon the occurrence of which the property is to be delivered to the grantee.

estate The property, real or personal, that a decedent owns or in which a decedent has a right or interest.

estate planning An attempt to obtain maximum benefits for the protection of family assets with legal tools by planning for possible contingencies.

estate tax A tax imposed on estates of certain value by the federal government.

executor† A person designated by a testator to carry out the directions and requests in the testator's will and to dispose of his or her property according to the provisions of his or her will.

extraordinary fees The fees that are allowed to be paid to the personal representative and attorney for services that are not of the regular, usual, or customary kind in the administration of an estate.

fair market value A standard for fixing the value of property defined as what a willing buyer would pay a seller if neither had to buy or sell.

family allowance The amount allowed by the probate court for the support of the surviving spouse and/or minor children.

family pot trust A trust set up after the death of the surviving spouse that keeps all the money together, rather than dividing it into shares.

fee simple An absolute ownership right in real property.

fiduciary† A person who is entrusted with handling money or property for another person, for example, an executor, a trustee, or a guardian.

fiscal year A period that may be chosen for an accounting, as in an estate or trust, other than a calendar year.

five-by-five power The power given to a trustee to take from the trust principal an amount not exceeding $5,000 or five percent of the principal, whichever is greater.

flower bonds Certain U.S. Treasury obligations that may be used to pay federal estate taxes, in which event they are redeemable at part.

Franchise Tax Board The state agency that collects and processes California income tax returns.

freehold An estate for life or in fee.

fresh start rule Relates to the carry-over basis of assets held by decedents, for decedents dying after 1979; assets were given a "fresh start" value as of December 3, 1976.

funded trust A living trust that holds property that has been transferred to it.

future interest† An estate or interest in land or personal property, including money, whether vested or contingent, that is to come into existence at a future date.

garnishment† A proceeding by a creditor to obtain satisfaction of a debt from money or property of the debtor which is in the possession of a third person or is owed by such a person to the debtor.

general power of appointment A power that is exercisable in favor of the decedent or the decedent's estate, creditors, or the creditors of his or her estate, with exceptions [IRC § 2014(b)]; generally speaking, a future interest in property.

generation-skipping An estate tax imposed when a decedent's interest in a trust passes to persons in a younger generation.

gift† A voluntary transfer of property by one person to another without any consideration or compensation.

gift causa mortis A gift of personal property, made in expectation of death, that will go to a donee upon the giver's death if the gift is not revoked before death.

good faith†   The absence of improper motive or of a negligent disregard of the rights of others; the honest and reasonable belief that one's conduct is proper.

goodwill†   The benefit a business acquires, beyond the mere value of its capital stock and tangible assets, as a result of having a good reputation and the respect of the public.

grantor   One who grants something, such as one who creates a trust; same as trustor or donor.

gross rent multiplier   A method used to determine the fair market value of property by dividing the sale price by annual rent.

gross-up rule   The rule that required the adding back into an estate of the gift tax paid on gifts made within three years of the date of death.

guardian ad litem †   A person appointed by the court to represent and protect the interests of a minor or an incompetent person during litigation.

heirs†   Persons who are entitled to inherit real or personal property of a decedent who dies intestate; persons receiving property by descent.

holographic will†   A will that is entirely written and signed by the testator in his or her own handwriting.

homestead property †   Real property that is free and clear of the claims of creditors, provided the owner occupies the property as his or her home; the place of residence of the family.

hypothecation†   A pledge in which the pledged property remains in the possession of the debtor.

Independent Administration of Estates Act   An act that gives the executor or administrator the option of administering the estate in a simplified manner and with a minimum of court supervision.

inheritance tax   A tax imposed under state law on property inherited from a decedent; a law abolished in California.

insolvent   Without funds; liabilities exceed assets.

installment sale   A sale in which the price is received by the seller in installments rather than all at once in cash, and which permits taxation of the gains received over the period specified rather than all at the time of sale.

interest in property†   A right, claim, share, or title in property.

inter vivos trust†   A trust that is effective during the lifetime of the creator of the trust; a living trust.

intestate†   Pertaining to a person, or to the property of a person, who dies without leaving a valid will.

inventory†   An itemized list or schedule of assets, property or other articles, sometimes with notations of their value.

IRA (dividend retirement account)†   Under the Internal Revenue Code, individuals who are not included in an employer-maintained retirement plan may deposit money (up to an annual maximum amount set by the Code) in an account for the purchase of retirement annuities.

irrevocable trust†   A trust in which the settlor permanently gives up control of the trust property.

issue   All persons who descend from an ancestor in a direct line: children, grandchildren, great-grandchildren, and lineal descendants.

joint tenancy†   An estate in land or in personal property held by two or more persons jointly, with equal rights to share in its enjoyment.

Keogh account†   The type of retirement plan that self-employed professionals and individuals or partners in an unincorporated business activity may set up under the Internal Revenue Code to obtain the tax advantages available to employees under a qualified pension plan.

kinship†   The circumstance of being related by blood; the fact of being kin.

leasehold   The right under a lease to hold real property for a fixed term.

legacy   Property left in a will; usually refers to cash.

legatee†   A person who receives personal property as a beneficiary under a will, although the word is often loosely used to mean a person who receives a testamentary gift of either personal property or real property.

lender's policy   A title insurance policy that insures the mortgage lender against losses from title risks and unrecorded matters but does not insure the owner's equity.

letters testamentary†   A document issued by the probate court appointing the executor of the estate of a decedent who died leaving a will.

lien†   A claim or charge on, or right against, personal property, or an encumbrance on real property, for the payment of a debt.

life estate   An ownership interest in property for one's lifetime.

life tenant   A person who receives the benefits of rent, income and possibly use of property during his lifetime only.

limited partnership   A partnership composed of one or more general partners who manage the partnership and assume liability, and one or more limited partners who have a limited liability.

lineal descendant†   A person in the direct line of descent such as one's child, grandchild, or great-grandchild.

liquid assets†   Assets that are easily convertible into cash.

living trust   A trust created in one's lifetime; same as an inter vivos trust.

lower generation beneficiary   A beneficiary of a generation that is younger than the donor such as children, nieces, and nephews, and their spouses, and grandchildren, grandnieces, and grandnephews.

malpractice†   The failure of a professional person to act with reasonable care; misconduct by a professional person in the course of engaging in his profession.

marital deduction   A deduction by the surviving spouse of one-half of the deceased spouse's estate or the unlimited marital deduction, whichever is greater.

marital deduction trust   A trust created for a spouse that will pay income for life to the surviving spouse.

metes and bounds†   A property description, commonly in a deed or mortgage, that is based upon the property's boundaries and the natural objects and other markers on the land.

minor   A person under legal age, in California, under age eighteen.

natural heirs†   Heirs of the body.

negligence†   The failure to do something that a reasonable person would do in the same circumstances, or the doing of something a reasonable person would not do.

no-contest clause   A clause in a will that attempts to disinherit anyone who contests the will's validity.

nonadverse party   Any party who is not an adverse party.

nonlineal descendant   A beneficiary who is not related but is assigned to a generation on the basis of his or her birthdate.

nonresident aliens†   A person who is neither a citizen nor a resident of the United States.

nonskip person   An individual who is of the same generation or one generation younger than the transferor.

notice of proposed action†   The formal notice that informs a person that an action will be taken if no objections to it are forthcoming.

notice to creditors   A notice to a decedent's creditors that the decedent has died and that they should file any claim they have in the estate; in California, notice is published.

nuncupative will†   A will declared orally by a testator during his or her last illness, before witnesses, and later reduced to writing by a person who was present during the declaration.

omnibus escheat proceedings   Proceedings in which the Attorney General presents a number of cases of unclaimed property that is ready to be permanently escheated to the state.

ordinary fees   The fees that are allowed to be paid to the personal representative and attorney for services that are customary or usual in the administration of an estate.

owner's policy   A title insurance policy that protects the property owner from loss of equity from title risks and any recorded matters.

paralegal (legal assistant)† A person who, although not at attorney, performs many of the functions of an attorney under an attorney's supervision.

partition A court proceeding to separate the interests of co-owners.

partnership† An undertaking of two or more persons to carry on, as co-owners, a business or other enterprise for profit; an agreement between or among two or more persons to put their money, labor, and skill into commerce or business, and to divide the profit in agreed-upon proportions.

patent† The exclusive right of manufacture, sale, or use granted by the federal government to a person who invents or discovers a device or process that is new and useful.

pendente lite Pending a lawsuit; the period of litigation or a proceeding.

pension† A retirement benefit in the form of a periodic payment, usually monthly, made to a retired employee from a fund created by the employer's contributions, or by the joint contributions of the employer and employee, over the period the employee worked for the employer.

per capita† A Latin phrase meaning "by the head," or by the individual; a method of dividing or distributing an estate in which all persons who are equally related to the decedent share equally in the estate.

permanent escheat The absolute vesting of title in the state to unclaimed property.

personal property† All property other than real property, including stock, bonds, or a mortgage.

personal representative† Ordinarily, the executor or administrator of a decedent's estate, although the term may also include others such as guardians, conservators, and trustees.

per stirpes Descendants of a decedent take per stirpes when they take by right of representation.

pickup tax A tax that would be paid to one branch of government but is picked up by another branch.

pipe dream trust An ideal trust that does not actually exist in which the donors could save taxes while helping their children and lineal descendants and still manage the property, decide when and how much the children would take, and have the assets for their own use should they need them.

P.O.D. payee† The recipient of funds from a P.O.D. (payable on death) account, which is an account payable to a person, upon request, during that person's lifetime and payable, after that person's death, to one or more named payees.

posthumous That which is done after one's death.

pour-over will A will in which property "pours over" from the will to an existing trust of the decedent.

power of appointment† The ability to act for another that includes an interest in the subject of the action.

prayer† Portion of a bill in equity or a petition that asks for equitable relief and specifies the relief sought.

predeceased A person who dies before another person dies is predeceased.

preliminary distribution A partial distribution of the property of an estate made before the final distribution that is made when the estate is ready to be closed.

present interest† An interest that is vested, as opposed to a future interest.

pretermitted A child or other issue unintentionally omitted from a will of a testator.

principal The corpus, the property, of a trust.

probate† The judicial act whereby a will is adjudicated to be valid; to prove a will to be valid in probate court.

property† The right of a person to possess, use, enjoy, and dispose of a thing without restriction, i.e., not the material object itself, but a person's rights with respect to the object.

proprietorship† A business owned by one person.

pro rata† Means "in proportion to"; proportionately according to the share, interest, or liability of each person.

protective election† An election that provides protection to the person making that choice.

qualified terminable interest property† An interest that is less than absolute in property that ends with the death of the person who holds the interest or upon the happening of some named event.

qualified terminable interest property (Q-Tip) trust A trust that permits the life estate of a surviving spouse in qualified terminable interest property to qualify for the marital deduction and that may pay income, and principal if needed, to a surviving spouse and also provide for an eventual gift to a charity.

quasi-community property Property of residents of a community property state acquired in another noncommunity property state.

real property† Land, including things located on it or attached to it directly or indirectly; real estate.

redemption† The recovery of pledged property by payment of what is due or by the performance of some other condition.

remainder† An estate in land to take effect immediately after the expiration of a prior estate (known as the particular estate), created at the same time and by the same instrument.

remainderman A person who takes the remainder.

res The principal, the property, comprising a trust.

residence A place where one currently lives or dwells, but not necessarily permanently.

residuary clause A clause of a will that makes provision for the distribution of any property remaining in an estate after distribution of the specific bequests.

residuary devisee† The beneficiary of a devise by a testator of the remainder of his or her real property.

residuary estate The estate remaining after payment of bequests, legacies, and debts and expenses.

reversion† A future interest in land to take effect in favor of the grantor of the land or his heirs after the termination of a prior estate he has granted; in other words, the returning of the property to the grantor or his heirs when the grant is over.

reversionary interest† A future interest, i.e., the right to the future enjoyment of a reversion.

revocable trust† A trust in which the settlor does not give up the right to revoke.

right of representation An inheritance is received by right of representation when heirs take whatever share a predeceased relative would have taken had they survived; see also per stirpes and per capita.

right of survivorship The surviving joint tenant automatically takes the other joint tenant's share.

rule against perpetuities A rule determining how long an interest in property can remain invested; perpetuities period varies from state to state.

salvage value In tax law, the estimated value that can be obtained through a sale of an asset at the end of its useful life.

self-proving will A will that includes an affidavit and incorporates an attestation clause as part of the will.

separate property† With respect to married persons, property acquired by either of them before marriage and held separately during marriage.

simple trust† A straightforward conveyance of property to one person for the use of another, without further specifications of directions.

skip person An individual who is at least two generations younger than the transferor.

special administrator† An administrator who administers some aspect of the estate of a decedent, as opposed to a general administrator, who administers the whole of the estate.

spendthrift clause A protective clause in a trust to prevent creditors from making claims on the beneficiary's interest and to prevent bankruptcy.

spousal attribution rule A rule for trusts that treats the grantor as holding a power or interest if the grantor's spouse is living with the grantor at the time of the creation of the power or interest.

sprinkling power A trustee's power to distribute income that is limited by an ascertainable standard, or a reasonably definite external standard that is set forth in the trust instrument.

sprinkling trust† A trust whose income the trustee may distribute among its beneficiaries as, when, and in the amounts he or she chooses.

statute of limitations† A federal or state statute prescribing the maximum period of time during which a civil action or criminal prosecution can be brought after the occurrence of the injury or the offense.

statutory fees The fees that are allowed to be paid to the personal representative and attorney by virtue of a statute.

stepped-up basis Where the value of property inherited is "stepped up" to its fair market value as of the date of death as set forth in the estate tax return.

straight life annuity† A yearly payment of a fixed sum of money until the death of the annuitant.

strict privity test A test based on privity, which connotes an identity of interest, a close relationship that exists between two parties having some legal right.

subscribing witness A person who either sees a document signed or hears the signer acknowledge his or her signature, and who signs his or her name to the document to attest to the validity of the document.

surety company† A company engaged in the business of acting as a surety, i.e., one who promises to pay the debt or to satisfy the obligation of another.

taxable distribution Any distribution from a trust to a skip person, other than a taxable termination or a direct skip.

taxable termination The termination, by death, lapse of time, release of power, or otherwise, of an interest in trust property unless, immediately after termination, a nonskip person has an interest in the property or, at no time after such termination, may a distribution (including a distribution or taxation) be made from a trust to a skip person.

tenant in common† A tenancy in which two or more persons own an undivided interest in an estate in land.

terminable interest† An interest in property that ends with the death of the person who holds the interest or upon the happening of some named event.

testamentary capacity The capacity to make a valid will; mental competency under the law.

testamentary trust† A trust created by will.

testate† Pertaining to a person, or to the property of a person, who dies leaving a valid will.

testator† A person who dies leaving a valid will.

throwback rule Under this rule, trust income in a complex or accumulation trust that is over and above the ordinary net income is carried back to the distribution year or taxed to the beneficiary as if it had been distributed to the beneficiary in the year accumulated.

Totten trust† A trust created by a bank deposit which a person makes with his money in his own name as trustee for another person.

transferor† A person who places property in the hands of another; passing property from the ownership or possession of one person to the ownership or possession of another, whether by the act of the parties or by operation of law.

trust† A fiduciary relationship involving a trustee who holds trust property for the benefit or use of a beneficiary.

trust equivalent Any arrangement that, although not a trust, has substantially the same effect as a trust, including life estates and remainder estates for years and insurance and annuity contracts.

trustor The person who creates a trust, the grantor.

unclaimed property All property that is abandoned, escheated, or distributed to the state.

uncontrolled discretion The trustee is not held to a standard of reasonableness, but only to one of good faith.

unfunded trust A trust without any property in it.

unified estate and gift tax The estate and gift tax schedule effective January 1, 1977, which combines lifetime gifts and estate to determine tax rate.

Uniform Gifts to Minors Act† A uniform law that allows gifts of money and securities to be made the subject of a transfer to a custodian for the benefit of a minor.

Uniform Probate Code An act adopted in a number of states that seeks to simplify the process of probate.

unitary transfer taxes Gift taxes on the transfer of funds to a Clifford trust based on a valuation of the right to receive the property over a ten-year period.

void† Null; without legal effect, although strictly speaking, a transaction that is void is a transaction that, in law, never happened.

voidable† Avoidable; subject to disaffirmance; defective but valid unless disaffirmed by the person entitled to disaffirm.

will† An instrument by which a person (the testator) makes a disposition of his or her property, to take effect after his or her death.

window minor's trust A trust for minors that contemplates distribution once the minor reaches age twenty-one but that provides for the donee to extend the trust beyond that time.

younger generation beneficiary A person in a generation younger (as defined) than the generation of the person who created the trust.

INDEX